Theater and Human Flourishing

THE HUMANITIES AND HUMAN FLOURISHING

Series editor: James O. Pawelski, *University of Pennsylvania*

Theater and Human Flourishing

Edited by

HARVEY YOUNG

OXFORD
UNIVERSITY PRESS

OXFORD
UNIVERSITY PRESS

Oxford University Press is a department of the University of Oxford. It furthers
the University's objective of excellence in research, scholarship, and education
by publishing worldwide. Oxford is a registered trade mark of Oxford University
Press in the UK and certain other countries.

Published in the United States of America by Oxford University Press
198 Madison Avenue, New York, NY 10016, United States of America.

Library of Congress Cataloging-in-Publication Data
Names: Young, Harvey, 1975– editor.
Title: Theater and human flourishing / edited by Harvey Young.
Description: New York : Oxford University Press, [2023] |
Includes bibliographical references and index.
Identifiers: LCCN 2022018866 (print) | LCCN 2022018867 (ebook) |
ISBN 9780197622278 (paperback) | ISBN 9780197622261 (hardback) |
ISBN 9780197622292 (epub)
Subjects: LCSH: Theater—Philosophy. | Well-being. | Positive psychology.
Classification: LCC PN2039 .T446 2023 (print) | LCC PN2039 (ebook) |
DDC 792.01—dc23/eng/20220711
LC record available at https://lccn.loc.gov/2022018866
LC ebook record available at https://lccn.loc.gov/2022018867

DOI: 10.1093/oso/9780197622261.001.0001

1 3 5 7 9 8 6 4 2

Paperback printed by Marquis, Canada
Hardback printed by Bridgeport National Bindery, Inc., United States of America

Acknowledgments

This project began in 2017, when James O. Pawelski emailed me to inquire whether I would be interested in joining him and his incredible team of researchers in thinking about the interconnections across theater and performance studies and psychology. It has been a wonderful, fulfilling, and rewarding adventure to explore these disciplinary overlaps with an eye toward human flourishing. Thanks to the efforts of James, who also serves as the book series editor, *Theater and Human Flourishing* exists.

For every email that I sent to or received from James, there were probably three or four more to/from Sarah Sidoti, assistant director of the Human Flourishing Project at the University of Pennsylvania. Sarah's fingerprints are all over this book (and also the larger series). Over the years, she wore many hats: logistics coordinator, early copyeditor, and more. In the world of theater, the person most central to the production process is the stage manager. Directors get the recognition, but stage managers actually make the show happen. Sarah was our stage manager.

I spent comparably less time with the researchers affiliated with UPenn's Human Flourishing Project, but that does not mean that they were not essential to the success of this book. They shared their recent writings and helped illuminate—for this book's contributors—the evolving thinking and scholarship in positive psychology. Although this book's contributors do not endorse a single approach to thinking about human flourishing, the writings of Louis Tay, Yerin Shim, Michael Ward, and, of course, James O. Pawelski provided a helpful through line and enabled conversations across distinct subject areas. I appreciated having the opportunity to consult with Talia Goldstein, whose twin expertise in theater and psychology provided helpful grounding during our authors' retreat. It was terrific to reconnect with Talia, whose undergraduate years as a theater major overlapped with my graduate studies in the same department over the same years at Cornell. Our quick stop at ShawneeCraft against a backdrop of live music with folks, in an adjacent room, throwing axes was a highlight.

I am grateful to the brilliant scholars who are contributors to this collection (in order of appearance in this book): Scott Magelssen, Laura Lodewyck,

John Fletcher, Kelly Howe, Stacy Wolf, Lisa Biggs, Erin Hurley, Gwyneth Shanks, Marcia Ferguson, and Stephanie Etheridge Woodson. I urge you to seek out their independent scholarly projects. They are not only must-reads but also must-haves on your bookshelf. This dynamic group agreed from the outset to participate in a rather lengthy process of consultations and meetings on human flourishing *before* writing their chapters. You can sense the impact of these conversations as well as the tremendous respect that we have for each other in the transcribed roundtable conversation that appears at the end of this book. I also appreciate the time and insights that Laura Taylor, assistant coordinator of the MA in Applied Positive Psychology, shared as part of our roundtable discussion. Our in-person retreat occurred at the Shawnee Inn and Golf Resort in the Poconos, which sits alongside the scenic Delaware River in Pennsylvania, where our work was aided by and benefited from the labor of the Shawnee staff—custodians, caterers, and housekeepers.

I greatly appreciate the financial support of Templeton Religion Trust, whose support of the Human Flourishing Project at UPenn provided the core funding for this project. I completed the bulk of the work on this book as a member of the Boston University faculty and utilized the resources (mostly online) of BU's Mugar Memorial Library.

The world literally changed between our October 2018 authors' retreat and the publication of this book. As a result of a deadly coronavirus, live entertainment venues were shuttered for eighteen months between March 2020 and September 2021. The absence of theater and performance (as well as live music) from our everyday lives helped people to appreciate anew the importance of sociality and live art to individual and collective well-being. As life slowed down (as travel was suspended and events were canceled), I gained a new appreciation for the simple joys of life: family dinners; walks with my wife, Heather; and conversations with Carla Della Gatta, Ken Lutchen, and Anthony Abeln, among others.

Over the past four years, it has been a joy to watch my children grow from kids to slightly older kids. Zeke, now thirteen, has moved from reading *Harry Potter* to pursuing a wide array of adventures both real (overnight summer camps, river canoeing) and fictional (Fortnite). Cora, now eight, has moved from picture books to *Zoey & Sassafrass* and Hip Hop dance. There's a version of human flourishing which consists mostly of witnessing one's own children acquire new tastes, develop new skills (like archery), and slowly maturing into ethical, moral, responsible individuals. This book is dedicated to Cora and Zeke.

Contents

List of Illustrations

Series Editor's Foreword

Imagine being invited to a weekend meeting to discuss connections between the humanities and human flourishing. You talk about ways in which the humanities can help us understand what human flourishing is—and is not. You explore how the humanities can help increase human flourishing. And you consider whether human flourishing is an absolute good, or whether it comes with certain limits and even potential dangers. How do you imagine the conversation playing out? What contributions might you make to the discussion?

The volumes in this series were borne out of just such a meeting. Or rather a series of such meetings, each gathering including some dozen scholars in a particular discipline in the humanities (understood to be inclusive of the arts). These disciplines include philosophy, history, literary studies, religious studies and theology, theater, cinema and media, music, and the visual arts. Participants were asked to consider how their work in their discipline intersects with well-being (taken to be roughly synonymous with human flourishing), along with a series of specific questions:

- How does your discipline conceptualize, understand, and define well-being?
- What does your discipline say about the cultivation of well-being? How does it encourage the implementation of well-being?
- In what ways does your discipline support flourishing? Do some approaches within your discipline advance human flourishing more effectively than others? Are there ways in which certain aspects of your discipline could more effectively promote well-being?
- Does your discipline contribute to well-being in any unique ways in which other endeavors do not?
- Are there ways in which your discipline can obstruct human flourishing?

As might be expected, the conversations in these meetings were rich and wide-ranging. Some of them headed in expected directions; others were more surprising. Each of them yielded opportunities to question assumptions and deepen perspectives. The conversations were rooted in disciplinary contexts and questions but yielded many generalizable insights on how to conceptualize human flourishing more clearly, how to cultivate it more effectively, and how to avoid negative consequences of understanding it in incomplete or overblown ways. I cannot properly describe or even summarize the richness of the discussions here, but I would like to point out a few of the highlights included in each of the resulting volumes.

Philosophy and Human Flourishing, edited by John J. Stuhr, addresses a number of fundamental questions. What is the value of discussing human flourishing in a world that in so many ways is decidedly not flourishing? In what ways is flourishing similar to and different from happiness? What is the role of morality in human flourishing? How does it relate to systemic privilege and oppression? To what degree is flourishing properly the concern of individuals, and to what degree is it a function of communities and societies? What are key factors in the fostering of flourishing? In addressing these questions, philosophers explore concepts such as mattering, homeostasis, pluralism, responsibility, and values, and consider the roles of individuals, educational institutions, and governments.

History and Human Flourishing, edited by Darrin M. McMahon, centers on the question, What is the value of history for life? This core question leads to a number of further inquiries. Is history only about the past, or does it have important implications for the present and the future? If the latter, then how can historical inquiry most effectively contribute to well-being? Does such inquiry currently focus in an imbalanced way on ill-being—on prejudices, class struggles, and wars? Such work is doubtless of great importance, not least by investigating how claims about happiness can serve as propaganda for continued oppression. But would hope for the future be more effectively kindled and concrete steps toward its realization more adeptly guided by increased attention to what has actually gone well in the past and what we can learn from it, or by more focus on how human beings have responded positively to adversity?

Literary Studies and Human Flourishing, edited by James F. English and Heather Love, focuses on the transformative power of literature. Scholars examine a range of topics, including the reparative possibilities of a literary encounter, the value of bibliotherapy and of therapeutic redescription, the genre of "uplift," and evolving methods for studying the activities and experiences of actual readers. A central question of this volume concerns the limits on transformations effected through literature. Several contributors worry that harnessing literary studies to the enterprise of human flourishing might lead readers merely to conform rather than to transform. To what extent might human flourishing serve as a palliative, enabling and encouraging readers to adapt to individual lives that lack moral depth and to social conditions that are rife with injustice, and thus obstruct the difficult and unsettling work of disruptive transformation needed for lasting individual and collective betterment?

Religious Studies, Theology, and Human Flourishing, edited by Justin Thomas McDaniel and Hector Kilgoe, explores ways in which individual and collective well-being can be increased through various religious perspectives and practices, including the Hindu concept of *sanmati* ("goodwill, wisdom, and noble-mindedness"), Buddhist meditation, and the cultivation of spiritual joy even while facing adversity. Scholars consider challenging questions concerning the proper contexts for learning *about* religion and for learning *from* religion, the right balance between the acknowledgment of suffering and the fostering of well-being, and the relationship between human flourishing and nonhuman worlds (including both natural and supernatural domains). A concern of some of these scholars is whether human flourishing entails a false universalism, one that seeks to reduce cultural diversities to one particular notion of what is desirable or even acceptable, and whether such a notion could be used to rate the value of different religions, or even ban religious practices (e.g., fasting, celibacy, or other ascetic austerities) that might be deemed misaligned with well-being.

Theater and Human Flourishing, edited by Harvey Young, considers the unique resources of theater and performance for imagining and enhancing well-being. Because theater involves both performers and audience members, it is inherently communal in ways many humanities disciplines and art forms are not. Theater allows groups of people—often strangers—to come together and experience the world in new ways. More than just an escape from ordinary life or a simple mirroring of reality, theater can provide opportunities for communal reimagining of the world, exploring new ways of thinking, feeling, and relating that can be experienced and then enacted to bring about a more flourishing future. Scholars examine connections between theater and human flourishing in more and less traditional spheres, looking at ways performance practices can be used to critique inadequate notions of human flourishing and to increase well-being in a wide variety of contexts, ranging from community theater to organizations serving soldiers with post-traumatic stress disorder (PTSD), and from oppressed groups to politically divided societies.

Cinema, Media, and Human Flourishing, edited by Timothy Corrigan, looks to film and a whole range of contemporary forms of digital media for what they can teach us about the nature of human flourishing and how it can be cultivated. These forms of communication have vast audiences and thus great power to support or subvert well-being. Contributors to this volume observe that human flourishing often seems to come piecemeal and as a hard-won result of conflict and struggle, and they explore ways in which well-being can be supported by collaborative practices for creating content, by the particular ways narratives are crafted, by certain genres, and by the various values that are embraced and transmitted. Contributors also consider how these popular forms can support individuals and groups on the margins of society by making more visible and sympathetic their struggles toward flourishing.

Music and Human Flourishing, edited by Anna Harwell Celenza, complements the commonly accepted and scientifically supported view that participating in music—as a listener, performer, or composer—can increase individual well-being. Instead of focusing on music as a performing art, this volume examines music as a humanities discipline, emphasizing the importance and value of music scholarship for fostering individual and collective human flourishing. How can music scholars (musicologists, ethnomusicologists, and music theorists) strengthen the effects of music on flourishing through a consideration of broader cultural, social, and political contexts? Contributors explore how processes of contemplation, critique, and communication within music scholarship can deepen the experience of music, resulting not just in the enhancement of individual well-being but in the more effective cultivation of wisdom and the greater realization of social justice.

Visual Arts and Human Flourishing, edited by Selma Holo, begins with the experience of artists themselves and the function of art in our society. If well-being is thought of as the happiness of self-satisfied complacency, then it would seem to be the antithesis of art, which is often disruptive, unnerving, and unsettling, asking viewers to question their assumptions and inviting them to see the world in new ways. But if well-being is understood more deeply as the flourishing that can arise from the full range of human experience, including the discomfort of contending forms of meaning and contested visions of reality, then it is difficult to think of it without art. Contributors to this volume consider the overwhelming personal necessity artists have to create, the role of well-being in art history, the increasing emphasis on human flourishing in architecture and public art, and salient questions of ethics, accessibility, and social justice in the context of art museums.

The Humanities and Human Flourishing, for which I serve as editor, is an interdisciplinary, capstone volume that contains contributions from the editors of the eight disciplinary volumes. After the disciplinary meetings were concluded, we gathered together to discuss what we had learned through the process. We considered both similarities and differences across the disciplinary discussions on human flourishing, identifying social justice and pedagogy as two common themes that emerged in the meetings. Like the other volumes in the series, this volume does not pretend to provide simple solutions or even unified answers to questions of how the humanities are or should be connected to the conceptualization and cultivation of human flourishing. Rather, it provides thoughtful questions and perspectives, distilled as it is from a deliberate process of extended engagement from diverse groups of scholars across eight different arts and humanities disciplines.

I would like to welcome you, the reader, to this book series. I hope you find it stimulating and even inspiring in its explorations into the complexities of the relationship between the humanities and human flourishing. And I hope you read across the volumes, as they are written in an accessible style that will yield valuable insights whether or not you have particular expertise in the discipline of the author whose work you are reading. To whatever degree you immerse yourself in this book series, though, I am sure of one thing: You will find it incomplete. As deep and as broad ranging as we tried to be in our explorations, none of the participants are under the illusion that the discussions and volumes brought it to a conclusion. We are keenly aware that a group of a dozen scholars, no matter how diverse, cannot speak for an entire discipline, and we realize that a focus on eight disciplines does not cover the entire domain of the humanities. Furthermore, our discussions and most of the writing were completed before the COVID-19 pandemic, which has made the nature and importance of flourishing all the more salient and has raised a host of new questions about well-being. Instead, we think of our work as an important beginning, and we would like to invite you to join the conversation. We hope a greater number and diversity of scholars, researchers, creators, practitioners, students, leaders in cultural organizations and creative industries, office holders in government, philanthropists, and members of the general public will bring their interests and expertise to the conversation, perhaps leading to new volumes in this series in the future. Investigations into human flourishing contribute to our knowledge and understanding of the human condition, and they have practical implications for the well-being of scholars, students, and societies. We hope our ongoing work together will enable the humanities to play a greater role in these investigations, effecting changes in scholarship, research, pedagogy, policy, and practice that will make them more supportive of human flourishing in academia and in the world at large.

Background and Rationale

For readers interested in more information on the background and rationale of this book series, I am happy to share further details on the perspectives, aims, and hopes that motivated it. A key catalyst for the development of this series was the dual observation that a growing number of individuals and organizations are focusing on human flourishing and that most of the headlines in this domain seem to be coming from the social sciences. Yale psychology professor Laurie Santos, for example, made the news when she developed a course on "Psychology and the Good Life"—and some 1200 students (nearly a quarter of Yale's undergraduate population) signed up for it.[1] As of this writing, her subsequent podcast, "The Happiness Lab," has reached 65 million downloads.[2] On an international scale, dozens of countries around the world have adopted psychological measures of subjective well-being as a complement to economic indicators, and a growing number of nations have embraced well-being, happiness, or flourishing as an explicit governmental goal.[3] The Organization for Economic Co-operation and Development (OECD), founded in 1961 to stimulate economic progress and world trade, has acknowledged the insufficiency of economic indicators

[1] David Shimer, "Yale's Most Popular Class Ever: Happiness." *The New York Times*, January 26, 2018. https://www.nytimes.com/2018/01/26/nyregion/at-yale-class-on-happiness-draws-huge-crowd-laurie-santos.html

[2] Lucy Hodgman, and Evan Gorelick, "Silliman Head of College Laurie Santos to Take One-Year Leave to Address Burnout." *Yale News*, February 8, 2022. https://yaledailynews.com/blog/2022/02/08/silliman-head-of-college-laurie-santos-to-take-one-year-leave-to-address-burnout/

[3] https://weall.org/; https://www.ons.gov.uk/peoplepopulationandcommunity/wellbeing/articles/measuresofnationalwellbeingdashboard/2018-04-25; https://www.gnhcentrebhutan.org/history-of-gnh/; https://www.worldbank.org/en/news/feature/2013/10/24/Bolivia-quiere-replicar-el-indice-de-felicidad-de-Butan; https://u.ae/en/about-the-uae/the-uae-government/government-of-future/happiness/;

alone for tracking progress. It launched its Better Life Initiative in 2011 to measure what drives the well-being of individuals and nations and to determine how countries can best support greater progress for all.[4] The United Nations publishes the World Happiness Report every year, releasing it on March 20, the UN International Day of Happiness.[5]

These are examples in the social sciences of what I have elsewhere called a "eudaimonic turn," an explicit commitment to human flourishing as a core theoretical and research interest and a desired practical outcome.[6] Over the last several decades, there has been a growing interest in human flourishing in economics, political science, psychology, and sociology, and in fields influenced by them, such as education, organizational studies, medicine, and public health. Perhaps the most well-known example of this eudaimonic turn in the social sciences occurred in psychology with the advent of positive psychology. Reflecting perspectives developed in humanistic psychology in the mid-twentieth century and building on increasing empirical work in self-efficacy, self-determination theory, subjective and psychological well-being, optimism, flow, passion, hope theory, positive emotions, and related areas, Martin Seligman and his colleagues launched the field of positive psychology. During a 1998 presidential address to the American Psychological Association, Seligman pointed out that mainstream psychology had become fixated on understanding and treating psychopathology. He argued that, although extremely important, healing mental illness is only part of psychology's mission. More broadly, he claimed, psychology should be about making the lives of all people better. He noted that this requires the careful empirical study of what makes life most worth living, including a deep understanding of flourishing individuals and thriving communities. Such study, he believed, would both increase well-being and decrease ill-being, since human strengths are both important in their own right and effective as buffers against mental illness. Known as "the scientific study of what enables individuals and societies to thrive,"[7] positive psychology has had a

---

[4] https://www.oecd.org/sdd/OECD-Better-Life-Initiative.pdf

[5] https://worldhappiness.report/

[6] James O. Pawelski, "What Is the Eudaimonic Turn?," in *The Eudaimonic Turn: Well-Being in Literary Studies*, ed. James O. Pawelski and D. J. Moores (Madison, NJ: Fairleigh Dickinson University Press, 2013), 3; and James O. Pawelski, "The Positive Humanities: Culture and Human Flourishing," in *The Oxford Handbook of the Positive Humanities*, ed. Louis Tay and James O. Pawelski (New York: Oxford University Press, 2022), 26.

[7] Constitution of the International Positive Psychology Association, Article 1, Section 2.

transformative effect on psychology and has deeply influenced many other fields of research and practice.

What role do the humanities play in all of this? What role could and should they play? How can the humanities help us conceptualize human flourishing more deeply, cultivate it more effectively, and critique it more insightfully? As a philosopher working in the field of positive psychology for more than twenty years, I have been concerned that there are not more voices from the humanities centrally involved in contemporary work in human flourishing. One of the core aims of this project and book series is to make a way for humanities scholars to play a larger role in this domain by inviting them to consider explicitly what contributions their work and their disciplines can make to the theory, research, and practice of human flourishing.

Historically, of course, human flourishing is at the root of the humanities.[8] The humanities were first defined and developed as a program of study by Renaissance scholars dissatisfied with scholasticism, which they perceived as leading to an overly technical university curriculum removed from the concerns of everyday life and unable to guide students toward human flourishing. They advocated, instead, a return to the Greek and Roman classics, reading them for insights and perspectives on how to live life well. Indeed, the Greeks and Romans had developed comprehensive programs of study (*paideia* and *artes liberales*, respectively) designed to teach students how to flourish individually and how to contribute to collective flourishing by participating effectively and wisely in civic life.

This emphasis on the understanding and cultivation of human flourishing that was so important to the Greeks and Romans was also of central concern to other philosophical and religious traditions that developed in the ancient world during what Karl Jaspers called the Axial Age.[9] Hinduism, Buddhism, Confucianism, Daoism, and Judaism, for example, along with the later Christianity and Islam, addressed the problem of human suffering and offered ways of promoting individual and collective flourishing. Although different in their cultural context and specific details, each of these traditions counseled against lives exclusively devoted to pleasure, wealth, power, or fame. They held that such lives only magnify suffering and that flourishing is actually fostered through a cultivation of virtue that allows

---

[8] Pawelski, "The Positive Humanities," 20–21; and Darrin M. McMahon, "The History of the Humanities and Human Flourishing," in *The Oxford Handbook of the Positive Humanities*, ed. Louis Tay and James O. Pawelski (New York: Oxford University Press, 2022), 45–50.

[9] Karl Jaspers, *The Origin and Goal of History* (Abingdon, UK: Routledge, 2011), 2.

for the transcendence of narrow, individual concerns in favor of a connection with the larger social world, the broader universe, or even the divine. Cultural forms such as literature, music, visual art, architecture, theater, history, and philosophical reflection were employed in the cultivation of virtue and the establishment of the broader and deeper connections valued for human flourishing.

Today, the humanities tend to be thought of less as a comprehensive program of study or means to cultivate virtue and more as a collection of academic disciplines. These disciplines are located largely within colleges and universities and are thus shaped by the values of these institutions. Much of higher education is driven more by the aim of creating knowledge than the goal of applying wisdom. To succeed in such an environment, scholars are required to become highly specialized professionals, spending most of their time publishing books and articles for other highly specialized professionals in their discipline. The courses they teach often focus more on the flourishing of their discipline than on the flourishing of their students, requiring students to learn *about* course content but not necessarily to learn *from* it. When human flourishing is addressed in the classroom, it is all too often done in a way that makes it difficult for students to apply it to their lives, and in many cases, it focuses more on obstacles to flourishing than on the nature and cultivation of well-being. It is important, of course, to understand and resist alienation, injustice, and malfeasance in the world and to expose corrosive ideologies that can permeate texts and other forms of culture. But it is also important to understand that flourishing is more than just the absence of languishing. And the argument has been made that "suspicious" approaches in the humanities need to be balanced by reparative approaches[10] and that critique needs to be complemented by a "positive aesthetics"[11] and a "hermeneutics of affirmation."[12] Meanwhile, students in the United States, at least, are reporting astonishingly high levels of anxiety, depression, and suicidality,[13] while at the same time coming under increasing economic

[10] Eve K. Sedgwick, "Paranoid Reading and Reparative Reading: Or, You're So Paranoid, You Probably Think This Introduction Is About You," in *Novel Gazing: Queer Readings in Fiction*, ed. Eve K. Sedgwick (Durham, NC: Duke University Press, 1997), 1–37.

[11] Rita Felski, *Uses of Literature* (Malden, MA: Blackwell, 2008), 22.

[12] D. J. Moores, "The Eudaimonic Turn in Literary Studies," in *The Eudaimonic Turn: Well-Being in Literary Studies*, ed. James O. Pawelski and D. J. Moores (Madison, NJ: Fairleigh Dickinson University Press, 2013), 27.

[13] Publications and Reports, National College Health Assessment, American College Health Association, accessed December 11, 2021, https://www.acha.org/NCHA/ACHA-NCHA_Data/Publi cations_and_Reports/NCHA/Data/Publications_and_Reports.aspx?hkey=d5fb767c-d15d-4efc-8c41-3546d92032c5

pressure to select courses of study that will directly help them find employment. Students who in the past might have followed their interests in the humanities are now more likely to major in STEM fields or to enroll in pre-professional tracks. Consequently, the number of students earning bachelor's degrees in the humanities is decreasing significantly.[14]

Would a eudaimonic turn in the humanities be helpful in addressing these obstacles of narrow professionalism, imbalanced focus, and student pressure? Would it help with what Louis Menand has called a "crisis of rationale" in the humanities, with scholars unable to agree on the fundamental nature and purpose of the humanities and thus unable to communicate their value clearly to students, parents, philanthropists, policymakers, and the general public?[15]Could the eudaimonic turn provide a unifying rationale in the humanities? Of course, there is a sense in which such a turn would actually be a eudaimonic *return*. This return would not be a nostalgic attempt to recover some imagined glorious past. The human flourishing historically supported by the humanities was significant, as mentioned above, but it was also very far from perfect, often embracing perspectives that supported unjust power structures that excluded many people—including laborers, women, and enslaved persons—from participating in flourishing and that enabled the exploitation of these individuals to the advantage of those in power. Tragically, our society suffers from some of these same injustices today. Instead of a glorification of a problematic past, which could well reinforce these injustices, a eudaimonic re/turn would invite us to focus our attention on perennial questions about human flourishing, building on wisdom from the past, but committing ourselves to a search for more inclusive answers that are fitting for our contemporary world.[16]

Not surprisingly, there is disagreement among scholars in these volumes, with some contributors endorsing the eudaimonic turn in the humanities and working to advance it and others putting forward a variety of concerns about the limitations and potential dangers of such an approach—and some even doing both. Scholars supporting a eudaimonic turn believe it could

[14] Jill Barshay, "PROOF POINTS: The Number of College Graduates in the Humanities Drops for the Eighth Consecutive Year," *The Hechinger Report*, November 22, 2021, https://hechingerreport. org/proof-points-the-number-of-college-graduates-in-the-humanities-drops-for-the-eighth-cons ecutive-year.

[15] Louis Menand, "The Marketplace of Ideas," American Council of Learned Societies Occasional Paper No. 49 (2001) http://archives.acls.org/op/49_Marketplace_of_Ideas.htm.

[16] Pawelski, "What Is the Eudaimonic Turn?" 17; Pawelski, "The Positive Humanities," 26; and McMahon, "The History of the Humanities and Human Flourishing," 45, 54.

revitalize the humanities by encouraging deeper investigations into the eudaimonic hopes that initially gave rise to their disciplines and the various ways in which contemporary work can support and develop these hopes. They believe these investigations could bring together scholars across the various humanities disciplines to create a common understanding and language for an examination of questions of human flourishing appropriate for our times. To be successful, such a project would not require complete agreement among scholars on the answers to these questions. On the contrary, diverse perspectives would enrich the inquiry, opening up new possibilities for human flourishing that are more equitable and widespread and that support the flourishing of the nonhuman world as well. Some contributors see significant potential in collaborating with the social sciences in their eudaimonic turn, a process that can be facilitated through the Positive Humanities, a new, interdisciplinary field of inquiry and practice focused on the relationship between culture and human flourishing.[17]

Scholars endorsing a eudaimonic turn in the humanities believe it could also inform, inspire, and support the work of museums, libraries, performing arts centers, and even creative industries (in music, movies, publishing, and other domains) to advance human flourishing more broadly in our society. They see a eudaimonic turn as also being of potential value to the millions of students who study the humanities each year. Without expecting humanities teachers and professors to take on therapeutic roles, they see considerable possible benefits in a pedagogical focus on how human flourishing can be understood and cultivated, with resulting courses intentionally designed to promote and preserve students' well-being and mitigate and prevent their ill-being.[18] Indeed, these scholars believe the volumes in this series might serve as useful texts for some of these courses.

Scholars with misgivings about a eudaimonic turn, on the other hand, raise a number of important concerns. Some contributors wonder whether human flourishing is a proper ideal in a world with so much suffering. Would such an ideal raise false hopes that would actually contribute to that suffering? Furthermore, are there more valuable things than human flourishing

---

[17] For more information on the Positive Humanities, see Louis Tay and James O. Pawelski, eds., *The Oxford Handbook of the Positive Humanities* (New York: Oxford University Press, 2022), especially the first three foundational chapters. Also, visit www.humanitiesandhumanflourishing.org.

[18] Furthermore, would students who perceive real life value in humanities courses be more likely to make room for them in their schedules, as suggested by the students who enrolled in Laurie Santos's course on "Psychology and the Good Life" in such large numbers? If so, could a side benefit of the eudaimonic turn be greater numbers of students signing up for courses in the humanities?

(e.g., ethics, the environment), and should flourishing be limited in favor of these greater goods? Is human flourishing inextricably linked to problematic ideological perspectives, perhaps ones that place too much emphasis on the individual and downplay or ignore issues of systemic injustice, or perhaps ones that serve the interests of a small number of persons in power and encourage everyone else to conform to the status quo? Is human flourishing a false universalism that might result in a failure to see and acknowledge deep cultural differences—or worse, that might see these differences as deviances that need to be suppressed and punished? Could an emphasis on well-being be employed to exploit individuals or groups of people, as notions of happiness have sometimes been used in the past? Are there other unexpected harms that might arise from a eudaimonic turn?

The unresolved tensions among the various chapters are part of what makes these volumes compelling reading. Are there ways to overcome concerns about the eudaimonic turn by clarifying its nature and aims, avoiding the dangers raised? Or will these concerns always persist alongside efforts to achieve individual and communal betterment through a theoretical and practical emphasis on flourishing? I welcome you, the reader, to join this discussion. What are your views on the perspectives expressed in these volumes? What points might you contribute to the ongoing conversation?

Process and People

I would like to conclude with a fuller account of the process by which the various volumes were created and an acknowledgment of the individuals and institutions who have made this book series possible. With the desire to give contributors ample time to reflect on how their work and their discipline relate to human flourishing, as well as to create opportunities to discuss these ideas with colleagues, we put into place an extended process for the creation of these volumes. After deciding on the eight disciplines in the arts and humanities we would be able to include in the project, we invited a leading scholar to chair the work in each of these disciplines and asked them to bring together a diverse group of some dozen noted scholars in their discipline.[19] For each group, we provided participants with some background

---

[19] For a full list of project participants, visit www.humanitiesandhumanflourishing.org.

reading[20] and asked them to prepare a draft essay on how their scholarly work informs the conceptualization and cultivation of human flourishing. Many participants chose to address the background reading—appreciatively, critically, or both—in their papers, although none were required to address it at all. We then circulated these drafts to the entire group in preparation for a three-day, face-to-face meeting, during which the disciplinary chair led a discussion and workshopping of the drafts. These disciplinary consultations, held in 2018 and 2019, were also joined by a junior scholar (usually a graduate student) in the field, one or two social scientists with work on relevant topics, and the Core Team.

Following these meetings, participants were asked to revise their drafts in light of our discussion, with the chairs serving as editors for the resulting disciplinary volumes. Given the nature of the project, I also read each of the contributions, providing comments along the way. From beginning to end, the process for creating and editing each of the volume manuscripts took well over a year and allowed for deep engagement with the subject matter and with other scholars. The disciplinary chairs and I were careful to emphasize that these discussions were intended to be robust and the writing authentic, with no foregone conclusions about the nature of human flourishing or the value of exploring it, and we were pleased by the range and depth of thinking undertaken by each group.

As mentioned above, after we held the eight disciplinary consultations, we held a ninth meeting where we invited the chairs of each of the disciplinary groups to present and discuss drafts of essays for a ninth, interdisciplinary volume sharing what they and their colleagues had learned through the process. We also invited a few humanities policy leaders, including past National Endowment for the Humanities Chairman William Adams, to join us and help think about the broader implications of this work.

---

[20] Martin E. P. Seligman and Mihaly Csikszentmihalyi, "Positive Psychology: An Introduction," *American Psychologist* 55 (1) (2000): 5–14; Darrin M. McMahon, "From the Paleolithic to the Present: Three Revolutions in the Global History of Happiness," in *e-Handbook of Subjective Well-being*, ed. Ed Diener, Shigehiro Oishi, and Louis Tay (Champaign, IL: DEF Publishers, 2018); James O. Pawelski, "Defining the 'Positive' in Positive Psychology: Part I. A Descriptive Analysis," *The Journal of Positive Psychology* 11 (4) (2016): 339–356; James O. Pawelski, "Defining the 'Positive' in Positive Psychology: Part II. A Normative Analysis," *The Journal of Positive Psychology* 11 (4) (2016): 357–365; James O. Pawelski, "Bringing Together the Humanities and the Science of Well-Being to Advance Human Flourishing," in *Well-Being and Higher Education: A Strategy for Change and the Realization of Education's Greater Purposes*, ed. Donald W. Harward (Washington, D.C.: Bringing Theory to Practice, 207–216); and Louis Tay, James O. Pawelski, and Melissa G. Keith, "The Role of the Arts and Humanities in Human Flourishing: A Conceptual Model," *The Journal of Positive Psychology* 13 (3) (2018): 215–225.

The compiling of the volumes was organized and overseen by the Humanities and Human Flourishing (HHF) Project at the University of Pennsylvania. HHF was founded in 2014 to support the interdisciplinary investigation and advancement of the relationship between the humanities and human flourishing. As the founding director of HHF, I am pleased that it has developed into a growing international and multidisciplinary network of more than 150 humanities scholars, scientific researchers, creative practitioners, college and university educators, wellness officers, policy experts, members of government, and leaders of cultural organizations. In addition to the disciplinary consultations described above and the resulting book series, we have published a number of conceptual papers and systematic reviews, developed conceptual models to guide empirical research, and created and validated a toolkit of measures. Designated a National Endowment for the Arts Research Lab, HHF has developed ongoing programs of research (including on art museums and human flourishing and on narrative technologies and well-being) to understand, assess, and advance the effects of engagement in the arts and humanities on human flourishing. We have published *The Oxford Handbook of the Positive Humanities* to help establish the Positive Humanities as a robust field of inquiry and practice at the intersection of culture, science, and human flourishing. For more information on HHF, including each of these endeavors as well as its current undertakings, please visit www.humanitiesandhumanflourishing.org.

I am deeply grateful to all the individuals and institutions whose collaboration has made this book series possible. I would like to begin by thanking Chris Stewart and Templeton Religion Trust for the generous grants that have underwritten this work. Thanks also go to the University of Pennsylvania for their robust institutional and financial support. (Of course, the views expressed in these volumes are those of the authors and do not necessarily reflect the views of Templeton Religion Trust or of the University of Pennsylvania.) I am grateful to the more than 80 contributors to these volumes for accepting our invitation to be a part of this work and bringing more depth and richness to it than I could have imagined. I am especially grateful to the chairs of each of the disciplinary groups for their belief in the importance of this work and their long-term dedication to making it a success. I also wish to express my appreciation for the hard work of the entire HHF Core Team, including Research Director Louis Tay, postdoctoral fellows Yerin Shim and Hoda Vaziri, Research Manager Michaela Ward, and especially Assistant Director Sarah Sidoti, who meticulously planned and oversaw each of the disciplinary consultations and used her expertise in academic publishing to help shape this book series in countless crucial ways. Most of the disciplinary consultations took place on the beautiful grounds of the Shawnee Inn & Golf Resort along the banks of the Delaware River. I am grateful to Charlie and Ginny Kirkwood, John Kirkwood, and all the folks at Shawnee for their gracious support and hospitality. Additionally, I am grateful to Jonathan Coopersmith and the Curtis Institute for donating space for the music group to meet, and to Bill Perthes and the Barnes Foundation for similarly donating space for the visual arts group. Thanks to the Penn Museum for a beautiful setting for the first day of our Chairs consultation and to Marty Seligman and Peter Schulman for donating further space at the Positive Psychology Center. Finally, I am grateful to Peter Ohlin and all the staff and reviewers at Oxford University Press for their partnership in publishing the volumes in this book series. I hope these volumes inspire further conversation, welcoming more people from a larger number of disciplines and a greater range of nationalities and cultural and ethnic backgrounds to inquire into what human flourishing is, how its potential harms can be avoided, and how its benefits can be more deeply experienced and more broadly extended.

James O. Pawelski
February 19, 2022

List of Contributors

Lisa L. Biggs is an assistant professor of Africana studies and theater arts at Brown University. Biggs is an actress, playwright, and performance scholar, originally from the Southside of Chicago. She is a former member of the Living Stage Theater Company, one of the preeminent theater for social change programs in the country. As an actress and teaching artist there, she offered improvisational theater workshops to participants ages 3 to 103. Her latest play, *After/Life*, tells the story of the '67 Detroit rebellion from the point of view of women and girls who witnessed it all. She is currently researching and writing about the impact of theater programs for women who are incarcerated in the United States. From 2013 to 2018 Biggs was a member of the faculty at Michigan State University.

Marcia Ferguson is a senior lecturer in the Theatre Arts Program at the University of Pennsylvania, which she directed from 2013 to 2016. She has published two books on theater, as well as essays and criticism in publications such as *The Christian Science Monitor*, *Theatre Journal*, *Western European Stages*, *Total Art*, and *Slavic and Eastern European Performance*. Equally passionate about acting, directing, teaching, and scholarship, she has co-created, performed in, and/or directed over thirty-four productions at Penn, the Edinburgh and Philadelphia Fringe Festivals, and elsewhere. She was nominated for a Barrymore Award for Best Supporting Actress (as Lady Anne in Edward Bond's *Restoration*) and has trained widely in a variety of acting techniques.

John Fletcher is the Billy J. Harbin Associate Professor of Theatre at Louisiana State University. He studies social change performance, evangelical Christianity, and community-based theater. His work appears in *Theatre Journal*, *Theatre Topics*, *Theatre Survey*, *Text and Performance Quarterly*, and *Performance Matters* as well as in the anthologies *Theatre, Performance, and Change*; *Performing the Secular: Religion, Representation, and Politics*; and *Theatre Historiography: Critical Interventions*. His monograph *Preaching to Convert: Evangelical Outreach and Performance Activism in a Secular Age* was published in 2013. His current research investigates the endpoints of activist performance.

Kelly Howe is an associate professor of theater at Loyola University Chicago. Howe coedited, with Julian Boal and José Soeiro, *The Routledge Companion to Theatre of the Oppressed* and coedited, with Julian Boal and Scot McElvany, *Theatre of the Oppressed in Actions: An Audio-Visual Introduction to Boal's Forum Theatre*. Her writing also appears in *Theatre Journal*, *Theatre Topics*, *Text and Performance*

Quarterly, *Comparative Drama*, and elsewhere. Howe served two terms as president of Pedagogy and Theatre of the Oppressed and remains on its board. She co-chaired and organized three of its international conferences and was the vice president for Conference 2016 for the Association for Theatre in Higher Education and chaired the Association's thirtieth-anniversary conference in Chicago.

Erin Hurley is a professor of drama and theater at McGill University. She is the author of two books: *National Performance: Representing Quebec from Expo 67 to Céline Dion* and *Theatre and Feeling*; editor of two books: *Theatres of Affect* and *Once More, with Feeling: Five Affecting Plays*; and author of numerous articles and essays. She is the recipient of multiple book awards for *National Performance*, including the Pierre Savard Award from the International Council for Canadian Studies and the Ann Saddlemyer Award from the Canadian Association for Theatre Research. In 2015, Hurley was inducted into the Royal Society of Canada.

Laura A. Lodewyck is an assistant professor of theater at North Central College in Naperville, Illinois, where she heads the Student Directed Series. Her research focuses on the transformative power of theater, particularly during times of war, and she is a scholar with the Latinx Theatre Commons' El Fuego initiative, whose mission is to produce and document new Latinx plays. A former American Association of University Women fellow, Lodewyck continues to advocate for increased representation of women onstage and in the theatrical canon through work such as the History Matters/Back to the Future initiative.

Scott Magelssen is a professor in the School of Drama at the University of Washington, where he also heads the BA academic program. His is the author of *Simming: Participatory Performance and the Making of Meaning*, which chronicles the ways tourism, businesses, and the military use live simulation and performance to create and reinforce meaning for participants, and *Performing Flight: Barnstormers, the Cold War, and Space Tourism*, which explores the way performance and human flight have shaped one another in public perception and consciousness. Magelssen edits the Theater in the Americas series and hosts the website Theater-historiography.org with Henry Bial.

Gwyneth Shanks is an assistant professor of performance studies and contemporary art at Colby College. Her research and teaching focus on performance studies, curatorial practice, museum studies, critical race studies, queer theory, and art history. She is a former Mellon Postdoctoral Fellow in Interdisciplinary Arts at the Walker Art Center in Minneapolis. In 2018–19, she was a Helena Rubinstein Curatorial Fellow in the Whitney Independent Study Program at the Whitney Museum of American Art. Her academic writing has appeared in journals and edited volumes, including *Third Text*, *Performance Matters*, and the *Journal of Dramatic Theory and Criticism*. Shanks is a choreographer and performer. As a performer she has worked with, among others, The Trisha Brown Dance Company, Marina Abramović, Jérôme Bel, Maria Hassabi, and Meredith Monk.

Stacy Wolf is a professor of theater, director of the Program in Music Theater, and director of the Princeton Arts Fellows at Princeton University. Wolf is the author of *Beyond Broadway: Musical Theatre across the U.S.*; *Changed for Good: A Feminist History of the Broadway Musical*; *A Problem Like Maria: Gender and Sexuality in the American Musical*; and the coeditor of *The Oxford Handbook of the American Musical* (with Raymond Knapp and Mitchell Morris). Before Princeton, Wolf taught in the Performance as Public Practice Program in the Department of Theatre & Dance at the University of Texas at Austin; in English and Theatre & Dance at the George Washington University; and in the School of Theatre at Florida State University. Recent honors include a Guggenheim fellowship, a Bogliasco Foundation fellowship, and the President's Distinguished Teaching Award at Princeton.

Stephani Etheridge Woodson is a professor of theater in the School of Film, Dance and Theatre at Arizona State University, where she specializes in community cultural development and community-engaged practices concerned with human thriving. Etheridge Woodson serves as director of the Herberger Institute's Design and Arts Corps, an initiative to partner all Herberger Institute students with community. Her research and creative interests focus on theater and performance with, by, and for children and youth; representational ethics; arts in wellness practices; and the group creation and performance of original work. She is a founding member of Cultural Engagements in Nutrition, Arts and Sciences, a transdisciplinary working group of scholars and artists who develop, implement, and evaluate innovative approaches to community and individual wellness, with arts practices at its center.

Harvey Young is professor of theater arts and English as well as dean of the College of Fine Arts at Boston University. He is the author of *Embodying Black Experience* and two other books and the editor of six books, most recently *Theatre after Empire* (with Megan Geigner). His work as an editor has been recognized with multiple awards for outstanding editing by the Association for Theatre in Higher Education and the American Society for Theatre Research. He is a past president of the Association for Theatre in Higher Education and a former editor of *Theatre Survey*. In 2021, Young was inducted into the College of Fellows of American Theatre and Drama.

Theatrical Flourishing

An Introduction

Harvey Young

A decade ago, a prominent theater scholar and I talked about the state of theater studies. My friend complained that the discipline is overly focused on "good" theater: the important and transformative potential of live performance. Exaggerating a bit, he declared, "Nobody writes about bad theater." These words have remained with me. Why is academic theater scholarship consistently and, seemingly, inherently positive when the domain of professional theater criticism has garnered a reputation for negativity? Why is it that scholars frequently reach the same conclusion: that theater—or, nearly, any live theatrical performance—is a social good?

The emphasis on "good" is notable since frequent theatergoers typically see more plays that they do not actively, passionately enjoy than those that they do. The preponderance of not good theater is evident in reviews by professional theater critics, people who see a lot of plays and allocate their highest ratings to only a handful of productions each year. The possibility that a critic might write a negative review is sufficiently high that critics themselves are the only people within the larger performance ecosphere who are looked upon with skepticism and often disdain. For some longtime critics, the joy of theater can dissipate over time to the extent that their disgruntlement becomes increasingly evident in their writing. Perhaps there is no better example in recent memory than John Simon, who died in 2019. The opening sentences to his various obituaries point to his complicated relationship—and notoriously decreasing satisfaction—with the performances that he witnessed. Robert D. McFadden, for the *New York Times*, writes, "John Simon, one of the nation's most erudite, vitriolic and vilified culture critics, who illuminated and savaged a remarkable range of plays, films, literature and art works and their creators for more than a half-century, died on Sunday in Valhalla, N.Y. He was 94." Harrison Smith chose remarkably similar words for the

Harvey Young, *Theatrical Flourishing* In: *Theater and Human Flourishing*. Edited by: Harvey Young, Oxford University Press. © Oxford University Press 2023. DOI: 10.1093/oso/9780197622261.003.0001

Washington Post: "John Simon, whose lively, erudite and ferociously acerbic columns on movies, music and theater made him one of America's most influential and reviled critics, died." In both, erudition, a deep knowledge informed by years of theatergoing, is closely associated with biting negativity.

Theater studies, in contrast to journalistic theater criticism, is decidedly more hopeful. Live performance is often framed as a positive element, a social good. If there are negative elements or associations, they are regularly dismissed as anomalies or exceptions which remain available for retrospective rehabilitation. For example, the literature on camp theater—which frequently centers plays and productions that were panned by professional critics who failed to recognize the subversive work of what Moe Meyer identifies as "a knowledge queer social agent"—often aims to be recuperative. The embrace of theater exists as an act of generosity recognizing the labor of creating a work that appeals to the sensibilities, imaginations, and aspirations of others. Theater scholar Sara Warner writes, Theater "is a site of yearning and fantasy, a liminal world where almost anything is possible" (6). The act of making theater—transforming an empty stage into a story world—is itself worthy of celebration. Even a structurally or mechanically "bad" play can exist as a place of wonder and serve as "both a respite and a resource for society's maligned and marginalized" (6). Therein lies the well-being potential of theater. It never relinquishes its status as a place for the imagination. Theater as a discipline (and as a set of methodologies) contrasts with psychology, which has tended to focus on the negative: problems and ailments. The two resonate differently. This distinction may explain why psychology has had little traction within theater studies. However, the development of a nascent branch, positive psychology, has the potential to bring the disciplines closer together.

Theater and Human Flourishing centers on theater studies informed by recent work in positive psychology with the aim of interrogating both the social good of theater and the personally restorative work of a range of live embodied performances. The contributors to this collection, all established or emerging performance scholars, build bridges toward psychology even as they center their investigations in theatrical and performance events: community theater productions, actor training, performance art, and more. Whereas a reader might imagine that a discipline already oriented toward the imagination and well-being would embrace the research of psychologists on human flourishing, the chapters reveal a pragmatic rather than a Pollyannaish perspective. The authors are quick to point out the problems within theater from psychologically unhealthy ways of taking on characters to the ways in which theater audiences can negatively police the behaviors of other attendees. Nevertheless, all agree that there is a social and personal good that emerges through live theater, ranging from the opportunity to pursue a passion as an amateur to radical movements toward social change as an activist.

On Being Positive

Psychologist Martin Seligman, in his 1998 presidential address to the American Psychological Association (APA), called for a shift in disciplinary orientation. He observed that "since World War II, psychology has become a science largely about healing." He continued:

> By my count, we now understand and can effectively treat at least 14 mental disorders that we could not treat 50 years ago. But these victories have come at a considerable cost. When we became solely a healing profession, we forgot our larger mission: that of making the lives of all people better. (559)

Seligman urged his association to "show the world what actions lead to well-being, to positive individuals, to flourishing communities, and to a just society" (559). Noting that researchers within the discipline "have scant knowledge of what makes life worth living," he encouraged them to strive toward being able to "articulate a vision of the good life that is empirically sound and, at the same time, understandable and attractive" (559). With this call and the enthusiastic response of APA's membership, positive psychology began to attract widespread attention.

Seligman's intervention, as Jeremy D. Clifton has observed, helped "[pull] scholars away from the exclusive focus on albeit very important topics like vice, weakness, illness, problems and despair and towards balancing that understanding with an emphasis on virtue, strengths, flourishing, potential and meaning" (123). Within the disciplinary subfield, researchers and investigators were inspired to look beyond extant applications of psychology to antecedents in earlier philosophical notions of well-being as well as in more contemporary humanistic disciplines. The aim has been to demonstrate that an embrace of humanistic disciplines which heretofore had placed an emphasis on human flourishing could benefit psychology and, perhaps, inspire growth beyond the management of medical ailments. James O. Pawelski writes, "Given the fact that human flourishing is at the root of the Humanities, there is a real sense in which this is a eudemonic *return*—not to some imagined golden age, but to the questions and concerns that gave rise to the Humanities in the first place and that have been at their core most of their history" (14).

Human flourishing is an old concept, anchoring itself in the Aristotelian idea of eudaimonia. In *Eudemian Ethics*, Aristotle matter-of-factly notes, "Happiness is at once the pleasantest and the fairest and best of all things whatever" (1214a). The philosopher further calls for an examination into well-being:

> [W]e must consider first what the good life consists in and how it is to be obtained—whether all of those who receive the designation "happy" acquire happiness by nature, as is the case with tallness and shortness of stature and differences of complexion, or by study, which would imply that there is a science of happiness, or by some form of training, for there are many human attributes that are not bestowed by nature nor acquired by study but gained by habituation—bad attributes by those trained in bad habits and good attributes by those trained in good ones. Or does happiness come in none of these ways, but either by a sort of elevation of mind inspired by some divine power, as in the case of persons possessed by a nymph or a god, or, alternatively, by fortune? for many people identify happiness with good fortune. (1214a)

Aristotle, acknowledging the importance of well-being, inquires whether it is an essential trait within select people or something that can be learned, cultivated, and repeatedly (through habituation) evoked. Seligman, in his address centuries later, cites this classical call to learn how to be happy.

Nineteen years before Seligman's presidential address, philosopher W. F. R. Hardie placed a spotlight on eudaimonia in "Aristotle on the Best Life for Man." Hardie reminds his reader that Aristotle in the *Nicomachean Ethics* offers not a blueprint for how to live a virtuous life but rather something more akin to "preliminary sketches made by an artist before he determinately creates the work of art to which the sketches point" (35). Hardie later adds, "Aristotle's manner and method in approaching his answer to his important question is exploratory and tentative" (36). Incomplete and more a hypothesis than an evidenced conclusion, Aristotle's suggestion is that contemplation of virtue and flourishing is important and implies that mindedness and mindfulness (not curtailed by politics or chosen for one's own material benefits) just might enable awareness of and access to eudaimonia. This introductory framework left much unanswered. How can the everyday person, who does not have the luxury of having a life dedicated to thinking and philosophizing, experience happiness and well-being?

Philosopher Kathleen Wilkes offers a plausible path forward that locates the potential of flourishing not only in philosophical contemplation but also in an array of other, more generally available activities. Wilkes asserts that "nothing can be an *arete* [virtue] unless it benefits its possessor—that there is no *genuine* 'doing well' that does not leave the doer better off, in some way, than before" (356). For Aristotle, who presumably spent his days philosophizing and teaching, contemplation was an obvious virtue that enabled flourishing. A free-diver might say that an awareness of breath and the ability to appreciate the needs and limits of the human body are the secret to well-being. A virtue needs to be accessible and, equally important, must appear within a person's larger perspective on the world. Valerie Tiberius, reflecting on the various strands and points of view on well-being within psychology, writes:

[M]any psychologists, regardless of which well-being ingredients they are concerned with, implicitly assume a subjective theory in the background. That is, they presume that the explanation for why the things they study (whether they are subjective feeling or objective modes of functioning) are good for people is ultimately that people want them, like them, or think they're important. (28)

These identified virtues are recognizable and, theoretically, available to the individual who chooses them as being desirable. Tiberius adds, "[T]his is background theory of well-being, and it is one that, historically, was very controversial. No one in the ancient world thought that what things are good for you would be determined by your own subjective attitudes" (29). It is for this reason that conceptions of how to attain well-being can vary dramatically across disciplinary perspectives. A psychologist might contend that the pathway toward flourishing relates to adopting a different perspective on life. A theater maker might say that it can be accessed through the arts, perhaps by attending theater or joining a team to put on a show. From the perspective of the contributors to this collection, both perspectives are valid. However,

Tiberius acknowledges that while scholars across disciplines might agree on the importance of human flourishing "there are times when we are actually trying to answer different questions" (21).

Theater Is Good

In her book *Utopia in Performance*, performance theorist and critic Jill Dolan writes, "[L]ive performance provides a place where people come together, embodied and passionate, to share experiences of meaning making and imagination that can describe or capture fleeting intimations of a better world" (2). This description summarizes the sense of magic that most people associate with live theater. Within a conventional arrangement, we enter a theater, take our seats, and wait for the lights to lower and for the show to begin. If all goes well, we are transported away from our everyday lives and sutured into the story world of the play. We travel back or forward in time. We journey to another city, either real or fictional. We enter households of strangers, tag along with characters, and witness the flow of their lives (and vicariously experience it alongside them). Both theater-making and theater-attending are activities that require sustained attention and the cognitive ability to consciously suspend disbelief in order to fully appreciate and realize the event taking place. In her chapter in this book, Marcia Ferguson identifies the "optimal involvement in a theatrical moment" as *theatrical flourishing*.

The complexity of theater anchors itself in its status as a discipline that freely and unapologetically borrows from other forms. Stephen Snow, Miranda D'Amico, and Denise Tanguay write, "Theater is the most integrative of all the arts: it can, and often does, include singing, dancing, painting, sculpture, storytelling, music, puppetry, poetry and, of course, the art of acting" (73). To participate in the making of a play (or even to attend as an audience member) is to engage in a process that involves multiple forms of expression. Within the theater, interpersonal relationships are relayed through word, song, gesture, and movement. For the theatrical observer, the scene of theater is the place where people can learn how to communicate. They also learn by listening about another's experience and perhaps feel with the characters. As Noel Carroll once observed, "Theater primarily makes us interested in watching people by responding to character emotionally" (436).

While it can (and often does) serve as a mirror to society, theater also exists as a site of experimentation and forecasting the future. Majority-minority theater communities can relay an experience of diversity and inclusion that differs from the everyday realities of cities which are not yet (but eventually will become) majority minority. Gender identities, beyond a simple binary, can be celebrated in theater even when their acceptance may not yet be mainstreamed elsewhere. Theater can help people appreciate what a spirit of inclusion feels like when communities succeed in overcoming persistent bias and discrimination. Dolan in *Utopia in Performance* offers, "I believe that theater and performance can articulate a common future, one that's more just and equitable, one in which we can all participate more equally, with more chances to live fully and contribute to the making of culture" (455). Performances can be a "rehearsal" for this future and, as such, help to inspire audiences to work toward the development of a utopic future in their everyday lives. Dolan adds, "I go to the theater and performance to hear stories that order, for a moment, my incoherent longings, that engage the complexity of personal and cultural relationships" (455).

This "ordering" effect is accomplished, in part, as a result of the ability of theater to offer a point of view on the world beyond the subject position of the audience member. In the theater, a place for viewing, and within the auditorium, a venue for hearing, we attend to the experiences of others. At times, the stage depicts how things should be, but more often it displays how things are. In so doing, it can offer a frank depiction of the everyday. Sitting and listening to the stories of others has the potential to introduce a range of perspectives which can help to expand our thinking and expand our sense of what is possible. Abstract desires can materialize into fictionalized scenarios within the theater that can inspire movements to make those imaginings a reality.

Theater galvanizes community. The copresence of performer and audience defines the uniqueness of theater, unlike the dynamics of other artistic forms, such as sculpture, painting, or even cinema, television, or radio, in which performers typically do not share the same space as their audience and often create (and complete) their artistry before the audience encounter. As Clayton Hamilton observed over a century ago, "A play is a story devised to be presented by actors on a stage before an audience" (3). It is its liveness, as witnessed event, that gives theater and performance a particular charge and special appeal. We gather together and silence our phones (in order not to distract ourselves or others) in order to share in the telling of a story. Although numerous scholars have debated whether live performance is truly a one-time-only event, there is widespread agreement that multiple performances of the same production are never exactly the same. It is this thrill of liveness as well as the possibility of variance that makes theater special. "Theater allows us to share a discovered story in the unique way that only live performance can, bringing the storytellers and audience together for the experience," writes Vincent Murphy (5).

Indeed, audiences play an outsize role in theater and performance studies. They make the event. Can you imagine a campaign rally without attendees? The performance of politics would fall flat. Or a comedy club with only two people, the comedian and an attendee? Audience presence is sufficiently significant that often-told anecdotes intended to underscore the dedication of actors are accounts of performances before a lightly populated audience. Such events are rarely enjoyable for the actor or the audience. Despite the passage of more than a decade, I still remember a performance that I attended at a Chicago storefront theater at which I was one of three people watching a five-person cast. The show went on. The performances were powerful and the story effectively told. That said, I was always conscious of my presence. I wanted to be less conspicuous. Did I have to laugh or applaud louder or longer to make up for the absence of others? The centrality of the audience in theater and performance has encouraged scholars to devote as much energy to addressing the impact of a performance on attendees as they do to studying the content (e.g., plot) of the performance itself. Susan Bennett, after referring to the influential work of Jill Dolan, notes, "One result in this expanded interest in the subjectivities and experiences of the theater audience has been that we are now rarely interested only in the performance but also in the cultural effects it produces in all the contexts involved in its production and reception" (225).

It is in and through theater that relative strangers gather to sit side by side in order to participate in a common, collective experience. Ideas of community are forged and practiced in the theater. Bennett writes, "I want to suggest that the theater audience is one particularly productive site where we might reexamine our practices and our interests, and do so in recognition that there is, at least for the moment, a broad sociocultural interest in our subject field" (228). In the pages that follow, the theater audience, as a key determinant in a theater and performance event, looms large. Again and again, contributors spotlight the position of the spectator not only to offer a vantage point on the performances addressed but also to make larger claims about how the experience of the theater impacts and affects the world beyond the stage. Not all of the chapters in this book place an emphasis on events that are immediately recognizable as theater in a conventional sense. There is not always a proscenium change with a clear demarcation separating actors and spectators. A play is not necessarily performed. Alongside chapters that address stagings of the musical *Guys & Dolls* or the play *Paradise Blue* are a range of other, equally theatrical performances occurring in art galleries, community political fora, and university arts initiative programs. When we recall the many performances of everyday life (*pace* sociologist Erving Goffman, anthropologist Victor Turner, and performance theorist Joseph Roach), it is easy to see each of these events as a form of theater and better appreciate the overlaps between performance and psychology.

Theater Flourishes

The contributors to this collection answer a common question: What (if any) is the relationship between theater and human flourishing? As you will see, they take different pathways which reveal the variability and multiple possibilities inherent within theater and performance studies. Some contributors explore events that would strike the average person as conventionally or traditionally theatrical, in which an actor performs onstage before an audience. Others place a spotlight on happenings and scenarios that did not (and were never intended) to occur onstage within a physical theater and involve participants who might bristle at being called "actors." Among the many links and overlaps across these pieces is a common awareness that performance works are meant for and strive to engage audience members who become a community through the experience of attending with others.

In addition, the contributors rally around the possibilities of theater. Perhaps one of the clear distinctions between theater studies and psychology is the former's embrace of indeterminacy. Theater is always changing. Subjectivities are never exactly alike. We generally embrace a level of uncertainty that might alarm a social scientist seeking to quantify and/or repeat results. Dolan writes:

> Thinking of utopia as processual, as an index to the possible, to the "what if" rather than a more restrictive, finite image of the "what should be" allows performance a hopeful cast, one that can experiment with the possibilities of the future in ways that shine back usefully on a present that's always, itself, in process. (*Utopia* 13)

The contributors write about the process that leads to (or prevents) flourishing. Within every chapter, there are moments when something truly spectacular happens and in which the meaning generated seems to exceed the reality of what is actually being witnessed onstage. Experiences of transcendence and transformation frequently occur within the theater, but the duration of those moments can vary dramatically across productions. They can be few and far between in a "bad play" or, sometimes, nonexistent. They are of extended duration in the productions and performance events we recommend to friends and family.

In "Actors as Surrogate Sufferers?," Scott Magelssen asks a question that many theater practitioners, especially teachers of acting, secretly have wondered: "Can we really say theater promotes human flourishing when it demands so much suffering from our actors?" After providing a brief, selective overview of "Western drama's foundational tenets concerning the high costs of healing the world's ills—costs involving the fetishization of pain, suffering, or ridicule to achieve happiness for select populations," he explores "the manner in which these paradigms are mapped onto actor training." It is not uncommon for actors to take extreme measures to connect with and inhabit a role. He writes:

> Psychologically immersive practices of building or embodying a character, particularly those grounded in modern Stanislavskian or Method acting, routinely expect and encourage actors to identify with negative and conflicted states of being in order either to be more affectively authentic or to accumulate a romantic gravitas that comes from sustained suffering over time.

He advises that, "as educators, fellow artists, and audience members, [people within the world of theater] ought to be more vigilant for situations when actors can be made vulnerable and exposed to intense or long-term traumatic situations that could damage their mental health." The chapter concludes with strategies employed by theater educator Catherine Madden to assist actors in alternative strategies to connect with their character rather than imaginatively or actively experiencing their characters' traumas.

Laura A. Lodewyck, in "The Potential of Pain: Conflict Dramaturgy and Transformation in the Theater," continues the discussion between theater and trauma with her study of *Telling* and *Theatre of War*, performance projects that seek to share the experiences of war and military life with the public. In the former, active members of the military are the performers who relay and indeed "tell" their individual stories. In the latter, professional actors present readings of classical texts, such as Sophocles's *Philoctetes*, before a military audience and, in so doing, link the experiences of the present with those recorded in the dramas of the ancient Romans and Greeks, whose lives were recognizably impacted by the threat and the experience of war. Lodewyck reveals the power—community-building and personal restoration—of the collective witnessing and sharing of these stories. She says "there is a slippage between the emotional experience of the individual and what this experience means for the collective." Furthermore, the performances "allow social barriers to be temporarily broken" to promote connection and mutual understanding. Even within "a hierarchical structure like the military," a talkback "allows for a subordinate to stand before an officer and speak their mind in a way rarely permitted within the military institution. The intensity of affect and hearing others speak before them also open up the audience's capacity to change."

It is not the capacity to change but rather the ability to understand another person's perspective on the world that exists as the central theme in John Fletcher's chapter, "Braver Angels: Performing Comity in a Polarized Era." Fletcher introduces Braver Angels, an initiative of David Blankenhorn's Institute for American Values, which aims to help people with opposing political beliefs—"red" or "blue"—to be able learn how to talk and listen to one another. This is not theater in the traditional sense. The audience, equally divided on the political spectrum, are the "actors" who talk about their experiences before silent witnesses and, in so doing, chip away at ill-fitting stereotypes. The aim is not to change minds but rather to help listeners appreciate the humanity of their political opponents and, perhaps, with this newfound common ground to feel equipped to engage in meaningful conversation and dialogue. Fletcher, who attended and participated in Braver Angels programming, describes the "takeaway" of the experience as "an untidy mix of exhaustion, reflection, and hope—a feeling not dissimilar to tragic catharsis or the afterglow of a well-played evening on stage. I have rarely felt more vividly human."

The potential for theater to bring about social change and not merely understanding is what drives Kelly Howe's chapter, "Beyond Survival: Theater of the Oppressed, Flourishing While Fighting, and Fighting to Flourish." Howe introduces Theater of the Oppressed techniques as designed by founder Augusto Boal and revised by numerous others, including herself and Boal's son Julian Boal. She asserts, "I propose that one of [Theater of the Oppressed]'s most significant contributions is precisely its inherent embodiment of the politically explosive notion that oppressed peoples deserve not only mere survival but flourishing: happiness, joy, pleasure, and sensuality." Although acknowledging some overlaps between Theater of the Oppressed techniques and flourishing, such as the importance of previsualization (Image Theater) to imagine the ideal that one seeks to create, Howe is skeptical of the flourishing concept if it does not prompt real social change and challenge the forces that oppress. Writing about (or reading about) human flourishing is not nearly as effective as taking to the streets and engaging in direct activism.

Stacy Wolf places a spotlight on amateur theater in "Community Musical Theater as a Human Flourishing Project." A blend of ethnography and performance theory, her chapter introduces a company of community theater artists who are in the process of putting on a show. Her study explores the meaning of theater to nonprofessionals (and, more to the point, people who try to feed their theatrical passions while maintaining a full-time job) and the power of *community* in community theater. These stagings do not enact the transformative change that Howe seeks. In fact, they feel quaint, almost folksy. However, this appearance is deceptive. Within the rehearsal room, there are compelling individual stories about race and gender in America as well as the operation of local politics. The nature of amateur theater (consisting entirely of volunteers) and the process of producing a show evidences four mechanisms or pathways of well-being as proposed by positive psychologists according to Louis Tay, James O. Pawelski, and Melissa G. Keith.

Lisa Biggs, in "Teaching Theater and Detroit History for Undergraduates to Flourish," reflects on a teaching experience at Michigan State in which she used the style of theater-making and the techniques of performance ethnography to build community within her classroom and then to assist her students in engaging both the larger community of Detroit and a historical incident of racial profiling and police aggression (the 1967 Detroit rebellion). Biggs champions the concept of *deep learning*, which requires that students learn through experience and not rapid "rote memorization." To facilitate this, she required her students to learn the history of Motown music by performing it, designing original choreography as they lip-synched to recordings. She instructed students to interview current and former Detroit residents about their memories of the incidents surrounding the 1967 rebellion with the aim of giving the students access to a subjective experience of history not always captured in books. She writes, "One of the biggest lessons students learned was how to step into the shoes of others with care, especially when playing a character whose race and background are different from theirs." She adds, "For human beings to flourish, I believe we need that kind of knowledge and connectivity."

Erin Hurley spotlights the importance of theater within a community to support (and create a sense of home for) minoritized subcultures. "In Changing States: English-Language Theater in Quebec," Hurley presents the history of English-language theater in greater Montreal, which became increasingly marginalized as the region (and the larger province) embraced francophone culture. She offers a unique case study: the minority art form on which she focuses is widely considered to be in the majority in the country (Canada) and the hemisphere (North America); however, her exploration reveals more traditional divides such as English existing as the common second language of non-French-speaking immigrants, which hints at a racialized nationalism that exists within the cultural preservation efforts to center francophone theater. Her various case studies grant insight into how English-language theater simultaneously offers access to a majority culture (outside of Quebec) and acts as "an assertion of an anglophone, multicultural minority" within the province. Concerning the latter's connection to human flourishing, Hurley explains that "linguistic or even existential precarity motivates express attention to community vitality."

The scene shifts from Montreal to Los Angeles in Gwyneth Shanks's "Refusing to Flourish: Jennifer Moon and Anat Shinar Perform Self-Help." Focusing on performance art, Shank centers a set of performances by Moon and Shinar that comment on and "challenge notions of human flourishing visible in self-help literature, revealing the unacknowledged structures of racial, gendered, and national exclusions that determine what it means to flourish." Similar to Howe, Shanks spotlights the skepticism that surrounds the self-help industries and the "potential for a radical refusal of flourishing." The resistance of the artists to embrace self-help and well-being narratives inserts a space of critique concerning industries whose alleged emphasis on well-being masks more spurious ambitions. The work of Moon and Shinar "reveal[s] the nationalistic, political, financial, and neoliberal structures that undergird the industry, and which it works to obscure through a rhetorical invocation of individual success, well-being, and flourishing."

In "On Laughter and the Bonds of Community," Harvey Young introduces two similar sets of experiences by acclaimed theater artists Dominique Morisseau and Lin-Manuel Miranda in which they separately recall being shushed in the theater by a fellow theatergoer who objected to their laughter. These stories serve as a prompt to consider both the merits of sincere, joyful laughter and the challenges to community-building that can exist within the theater. Laughter, as it turns out, is complex. It can delight and offend in equal measure. Young looks at how theaters and theater artists have begun to champion fewer restriction for audiences, with the aim of reaching new, younger, and more diverse audiences and enabling spectators to experience the positive experiential potential of live performance. He writes, "Many people have felt the thrill of laughing with others after hearing a joke and, in that moment, developed a profound sense of belonging."

In "Touching Theater: Practice, Criticism, and Aesthetics of Touch in the Flourishing Theatrical Moment," Marcia Ferguson places an emphasis on touch. Noting the criticism around bad touching—harassment and abuse in the theater—Ferguson contends that "it is just as important to theorize touch, to name it and use it in our practice, as it is to develop protocols to prevent its potential harm." She adds, "Just as we must collectively wake up to the reality of its misuse, we must cultivate a tandem awareness of its contributions to the well-being and flourishing of both spectator and practitioner." Although there have been extensive considerations of various aspects of theater production, it is touch—the physicality of actors in relation to their own and other bodies—which remains underanalyzed despite playing a major role in "nonlinguistic meaning" creation. Ferguson writes that touch contains "that ineffable essence of the performative moment beyond language, where perhaps the fullest expression of (theatrical) meaning paradoxically resides." She describes the narrative and emotional significance of physical acts—such as an actor tenderly brushing away a tear on the cheek of another actor—for an audience's ability to fully inhabit the moment and experience the emotional pull of a dramatic story.

In "Theater, Performance, and Community Cultural Development for Human Thriving," Stephani Etheridge Woodson outlines an ambitious new program in Arizona State University's Herberger Institute for Design and the Arts to involve all Herberger students (nearly six thousand) "across our more than 125 degree programs at all levels, freshmen to doctoral students." She shares the goals for the new program, Design and Arts Corps (DAC), which emphasizes community engagement and "utopic spaces in which all people thrive rather than just survive." Theater plays a central role as a result of its capacity to "build deep skills necessary to facilitate making processes that harvest creativity, negotiate conflict productively, and center human experiences and embodiment positively." The impact of DAC could be significant. Nearly 50 percent of Herberger students are students of color and the first in their family to attend college. They "have been taught by the K–12 system and [Arizona's] embrace of standardized testing to focus on their deficits, not their strengths." DAC offers a shift in perspective which could promote flourishing by emphasizing the importance of "[m]apping community abundance—as defined by the community" in its spotlight on "human thriving."

This book concludes with a roundtable conversation involving all eleven chapter contributors along with James O. Pawelski, Thalia Goldstein, and Laura Taylor. At an inn in the Poconos, the group read and discussed early, incomplete drafts of the chapters. The purpose of sharing in-progress work was to create opportunities for the authors to learn from one another before returning to revise, expand, and complete their chapters. As a result of these conversations, there were subtle shifts in the contributors' thinking and, more apparent to the reader, a desire to reference—to quote or otherwise engage—the insights of fellow authors. A theme that appears across chapters is how attending theater can serve as a rehearsal to bring about human flourishing and well-being in the real world. I hope this book helps people to see how meaningful change can begin with a play.[1]

Works Cited

Bennett, Susan. "Theatre Audiences, Redux." *Theatre Journal,* vol. 47, no. 2, 2006, pp. 225–30.

Carroll, Noël. "On the Necessity of Theatre." *Philosophy and Literature,* vol. 33, no. 2, 2009, pp. 435–41.

Clifton, Jeremy D. "The Eudaimonic Turn." *Journal of Psychology in Africa,* vol. 24, no. 1, 2014, 123–24.

Dolan, Jill. "Performance, Utopias, and the 'Utopian Performative.'" *Theatre Journal,* vol. 53, no. 3, 2001, pp. 455–79.

Dolan, Jill. *Utopia in Performance.* Ann Arbor: University of Michigan Press, 2005.

Hardie, W. F. R. "Aristotle on the Best Life for a Man." *Philosophy,* vol. 54, no. 207, January 1979, pp. 35–50.

---

[1] For more information about the Humanities and Human Flourishing project at the University of Pennsylvania, please visit www.humanitiesandhumanflourishing.org.

Hamilton, Clayton. *The Theory of the Theatre*. New York, Henry Holt, 1913.

Maxwell, Ian. "Why Theatre Matters." *About Performance*, no. 3, 1997, pp. 75–81.

McFadden, Robert D. "John Simon, Wide-Ranging Critic with a Cutting Pen, Dies at 94." *New York Times*, November 25, 2019.

Meyer, Moe. *The Politics and Poetics of Camp*. London, Routledge, 2005.

Murphy, Vincent. *Page to Stage: The Craft of Adaptation*. Ann Arbor: University of Michigan Press, 2013.

Pawelski, James O. "The Promise of Positive Psychology for the Assessment of Character." *Journal of College and Character*, vol. 4, no. 6, 2003.

Seligman, Martin E. P. "The President's Address." *American Psychologist*, vol. 53, 1999, pp. 559–62.

Smith, Harrison. "John Simon, Theater and Film Critic with an Artful and Vicious Pen, Dies at 94." *Washington Post*, November 25, 2019.

Snow, Stephen, Miranda D'Amico, and Denise Tanguay. "Therapeutic Theatre and Well-Being." *The Arts in Psychotherapy*, vol. 30, no. 2, 2003, pp. 73–82.

Tiberius, Valerie. "Recipes for a Good Life: Eudaimonism and the Contributions of Philosophy." *The Best within Us*, edited by Alan Waterman. New York, APA, 2013, pp. 19–39.

Warner, Sara. *Acts of Gaiety: LGBT Performance and the Politics of Pleasure*. Ann Arbor, University of Michigan Press, 2013.

Wilkes, Kathleen V. "The Good Man and the Good for Man in Aristotle's Ethics." *Mind*, vol. 87, no. 348, October 1978, pp. 553–71.

1

Actors as Surrogate Sufferers?

Toward a Model for Well-Being in Acting Training

Scott Magelssen

Theater people take it as a given that theater promotes human flourishing. But what if we're wrong? There is another claim that might just as easily be offered as a given: that we like our actors to *suffer*. We want them to cry so we can cry with them. We want them to feel the depths of their characters' abjection and pain, because if we think they're just pretending to feel these things it doesn't really *do it* for us. We award our highest honors in acting for stage and screen to those we imagine have gone through the most rigorous changes in mind and body, changes most of us couldn't imagine enduring ourselves without winding up in the hospital. And when our actors do wind up in the hospital—or in the obituaries—we shake our heads ruefully . . . but kind of admire their sacrifice.[1] And contemporary MFA acting programs and other conservatory-style training programs encourage students to empathetically experience pain and psychological precarity in roles and exercises as part of their regimens, to the extent that studies find it can take a toll on their physical and emotional health, even to the point of experiencing PTSD-like symptoms (Seton, "'Post-Dramatic' Stress"; Brandfonbrener). Can we really say theater promotes human flourishing when it demands so much suffering from our actors?

As a theater and performance scholar, I sincerely want to believe that theater is good for us—that it fosters eudaimonia, the "well-being" Aristotle described as humanity's greatest good, "the end at which all actions aim" (Pawelski, "Bringing Together" 207).[2] That theater can be good for humanity

---

[1] As Mark Seton observes, "The greatest accolade given to actors is often that of bravery and risk-taking rather than technical competency. We admire actors who appear to (or may claim to) 'lose themselves' in a role or who 'expose' themselves through their vulnerable portrayal" ("'Post-Dramatic' Stress").

[2] For Aristotle, well-being went beyond the sense of personal pleasure to comprise optimal living, "a life lived fully in its entirety," and an experience of happiness dedicated to and cultivated by virtue (McMahon, 5, citing *Nicomachean Ethics* I.vii.8).

Scott Magelssen, *Actors as Surrogate Sufferers?* In: *Theater and Human Flourishing.* Edited by: Harvey Young, Oxford University Press. © Oxford University Press 2023. DOI: 10.1093/oso/9780197622261.003.0002

is certainly not a new idea. Excepting some particular moments in history when it has been attacked or censured for immorality and corruption, theater has, for the most part, long been held to benefit human flourishing.[3] This regard for the positive effects of theater on humanity has been rooted, on the one hand, in theater's perceived restorative or remediating quality to redress social ills and, on the other, in its role as an art in fostering creativity, self-expression, and imaginative play, all viewed as important for developing a well-rounded person. Aristotle argued in the fourth century BCE that dramatic poetry, written and performed well, promoted *catharsis* (purgation/cleansing) of the negative elements of pity and fear.[4] Hamlet tells us that the purpose of playing "both at the first and now, was and is to hold, as 'twere, the mirror up to nature, to show virtue her own feature, scorn her own image, and the very age and body of the time his form and pressure" (*Hamlet*, III.ii). In the twentieth century, whether attributed to Vladimir Mayakovsky or Bertolt Brecht as its originator, the idea that theater is not only a mirror held up to nature but a "hammer with which to shape it" has become a foundational tenet for activist street theater and theater for social change: Augusto Boal's Teatro Oprimido, for instance, rehearses participants to enact progressive change in real life. ("That oppressed people deserve happiness and well-being—that they deserve something beyond mere survival," writes Kelly Howe in the opening of her essay in this volume, "was a central theme of Boal's practice.") In the 1960s and 1970s, Luis Valdez's Teatro Campesino equipped migrant farmworkers to fight for labor equity, self-actualization, and celebration of identity, and continues to serve underrepresented and underresourced communities. And Jane Taylor and William Kentridge's 1997 Handspring Puppet Company production of *Ubu and the Truth Commission* is an example par excellence of how theater can be a tool for processing a community's traumatic and violent past, in *Ubu*'s case apartheid South Africa. In our community and professional theaters and in our

---

[3] Episodes in Western history in which theater and drama have been the subject of attack include, in broad strokes, Plato's condemnation of drama as dangerously derivative of reality; the early Christian Church Fathers like Augustine and Tertullian's view of theatrical spectacle as idolatrous and dangerous to Christian morality; the fear of early modern English critics such as John Northbrook and Stephen Gosson that playhouses were sites of wickedness and vanity; William Prynne's damning and exhaustive antitheatrical treatise *Historio-Mastix*; Jeremy Collier's aggressive stance against English drama that promoted immorality and profaneness; Jean-Jacques Rousseau's belief that playhouses sapped masculinity and atrophied citizens' minds and morals; and U.S. legislators' accusations and court rulings that taxpayers ought not fund performance deemed to be pornographic. See, for instance, Barish; Freeman.

[4] Whether Aristotle viewed catharsis as taking place in the protagonist, in the spectators, or in the dramatic poem itself remains unclear.

training programs in higher education, we teach that theater is a space where the conflict and injustice of the world can be grappled with and resolved as a community. For practitioners, theater is an art and tradition that nurtures creativity and helps us explore and expose the profundity of the human condition, and drama and live performance are sacred spaces where audiences are transfixed and transformed for the better. Taken together, one might argue that theater and performance are some of the most powerful tools to effect eudaimonia and to combat human suffering.

As I suggested, however, while theater may ultimately offer its audiences the chance to heal, to learn, to vicariously experience conflict and resolution, the performers' own well-being, like that of the tragic protagonist, may often be sacrificed for the good of others. Recent studies suggest that the performers we as a society value may actually be put in harm's way as they take on the emotional labor of both their characters and their audiences, and traditional training practices to achieve these ends in performance may have deleterious effects on performers' mental health and emotional safety. Stories of actors' reckless behavior, mental illness, and suicide are in wide circulation in popular culture, but we don't really know precisely how and to what extent emotional and physiological labor and identification with trauma in actor training and craft can take its toll on our actors' bodies. It can be especially perilous for actors from groups that have experienced disproportionately high levels of trauma and suffering because of their identity, particularly for Black, Indigenous, POC, LGBTQ, and other minoritized actors who are tasked with psychologically experiencing trauma associated with those identities onstage or in class exercises. Theater and drama can and ought to be a resource by which to effect human flourishing. This essay argues that by teasing out some of Western drama's foundational tenets concerning the high costs of healing the world's ills—costs involving the fetishization of pain, suffering, or ridicule to achieve happiness for select populations—and the manner in which these paradigms are mapped onto actor training, we might more responsibly engage in healthful and positive custodianship of our actors that promotes well-being.

From their origins, the traditional genres of tragedy and comedy have conceived of the world as always in a state of risk and in a perpetual cycle of turmoil and remediation, and the burden of making the world better by the end of the play falls on the shoulders of the characters—who are never guaranteed to make it to the end unscathed. Western dramatic plots typically work from a point of chaos and disorder toward a point of health. That is to say, the inciting incident, whether it happens within the time-space of the text or at some point beforehand, has effected an "out-of-jointness" with the world, which must be "set right" (*Hamlet*, I.v.90–91). For·example, in Sophocles's fifth-century BCE tragedy *Oedipus*, the inciting incident is that Oedipus, in spite of Laius's, Jocasta's, and his own efforts, has actualized the prophecy concerning him: he has killed his father and has had children with his own mother. The consequences of his accidental misdeeds have thrown the cosmos into chaos (the crops and livestock are dying, women and their babies are dying in childbirth, plague and disease wrack the city) (Sophocles, ll. 31–38). Only by discerning the killer of Laius, and consequently his true identity, is Oedipus able to become the tragedy's scapegoat, blinding himself and casting himself out of Thebes in order to restore cosmic order.[5] Likewise, in Shakespeare's seventeenth-century tragedy *Hamlet,* the unlawful murder of Old Hamlet and the murderer Claudius's usurpation of the crown have thrown Denmark, as Marcellus states, into a state of "rottenness" (I.iv.90). A ghost haunts the battlements as a result of the foul and most unnatural murder, and the prince has gone mad. Only by Hamlet's hatching a plot to "catch the conscious of a King" and ousting Claudius from his illegitimate occupation of the throne (and the attendant deaths of nearly every one of the stakeholders in the process, including Hamlet himself) is Denmark able to be restored to order. In tragedies, the time is always already out of joint, and by "cursed spite" protagonists are "born to set it right," that is, charged with the goal to achieve happiness of the cosmos by identifying and eliminating obstacles in the way, including other human beings (antagonists) and often the self (the tragic hero). The resolution (read "happy ending") for serious dramas means the world is put back in order and rottenness eliminated, but only at great cost. In comedy, the stakes are lower in the enterprise of setting things right—often it is a matter of getting each of the young lovers matched with the correct mate—but very often the out-of-joint antagonists (Knemon, Malvolio, Titania, Caliban, Tartuffe) still must be routed or receive their comeuppance in order to achieve a happy ending.

We as audience members are moved by the suffering we watch the actors go through. Though the rest of us don't suffer as much as our surrogate victims, we are supposed to feel at least a little distress in the witnessing of it,

---

[5] Sometimes the suffering in the next few centuries of theater's development was much more than simply representational. The first century CE Roman poet Martial wrote accounts of the passions of Prometheus and Orpheus wherein the performers representing the protagonists were actually killed as part of the spectacle (torn apart by bears and what have you).

especially to remind us of the stakes. Jody Enders writes in *Medieval Theatre of Cruelty* that ever since ancient Greece, we've gotten the idea that learning doesn't stick unless it hurts going in.[6] This is one explanation for why the lessons of tragedy need to be painful, why parochial school teachers rap your knuckles with rulers, and why acting programs are notorious for intense exercises that cause students to weep in despair and emptiness (more on that in a moment). We incorporate pain and discomfort into learning because it's supposedly good for us. But as Tracy C. Davis argues in *Theatricality and Civil Society*, *not* feeling the pain of the protagonist is what makes theater *theatrical*. While we may sympathetically suffer with someone in pain if we know them personally, the act of spectatorship by necessity involves an element of judgment and disinterest: "it is the act of withholding sympathy that makes us become spectators to ourselves and others" (quoted in Ridout 35).

The idea, here, of what Jeremy Bentham would call "the greatest good for the greatest number" is paramount (Thebes and Denmark are restored to order), but the principal characters in serious drama must be the sacrificial surrogates that effect the happiness of the culture, and even then, only for the small elite class they represent (McMahon 7, citing Bentham). Actors, then, have been the surrogate sufferers for their audiences since the actor was invented two and a half millennia ago. But the actor's suffering as an important criterion of good and authentic art came into its own in performance theory relatively recently in the long nineteenth century, with the development of Romanticism and suffering and alienation (Weltschmerz) as noble and poetic qualities starting at the beginning of that period, and the emergence of psychological realism at the end of it. This is also when the modern acting training program was invented. In the current state of theater, it would seem, the reperformance of out-of-jointness needs to be perpetually embodied and affectively experienced by our actors in their training, rehearsals, and performances. Psychologically immersive practices of building or embodying a character, particularly those grounded in modern Stanislavskian or Method acting, routinely expect and encourage actors to identify with negative and conflicted states of being in order either to be

---

[6] In *Medieval Theatre of Cruelty: Rhetoric, Memory, Violence,* Enders identifies the link between trauma and learning as originating with the ancients. Aristotle, for instance, teaches us that truth can most properly be effected for tragic audiences through representations of pity and fear, and Cicero and his contemporaries believed that confession spoken under torture was probably more *true* because physical pain gives the speaker the "force of necessity" (2, 1).

more affectively authentic or to accumulate a romantic gravitas that comes from sustained suffering over time.[7]

To be sure, the basic human act of temporarily suspending one's own assumptions, stereotypes, and convictions to identify with someone else's point of view in nontheatrical situations is difficult emotional labor. As John Fletcher points out in this volume in his essay on Braver Angels workshops, it is hard *not* to have a nonneutral response to the beliefs of someone with whom we politically disagree. Fletcher's and his fellow participants' suppression of verbal and nonverbal response was "surprisingly hard" in the workshops, and he described participants experiencing strain and anxiety when asked to temporarily role-play as someone on the opposite end of the political divide. ("It is one thing to pretend to talk to argues-at-family-get-togethers Uncle Steve; it is another thing altogether to *become* Uncle Steve without criticism or caricature," writes Fletcher.) To understand what's going on emotionally with this difficult emotional process, Fletcher invokes Arlie Russell Hochschild's work on the emotional labor of workers like flight attendants and bill collectors, who often need to maintain a physical comportment and demeanor at odds with the emotions they may be managing to elicit such outward appearance. For Braver Angels workshop participants, it's hard enough to maintain Hochschild's "surface acting," what Fletcher describes as "putting on a false affective front at odds with actual feeling." How much more difficult, then, writes Fletcher, are the emotional demands of those in Hochschild's study who must engage in "deep acting," strategies, "altering one's inner self to produce required affects" (Fletcher, citing Hochschild). This might be closer to the territory in which theater actors are asked to repeatedly immerse themselves, altering their inner self to appear truthful to their audience.

Theater scholars in higher education know from their own students (and perhaps their own memory) about the emotional labor involved in acting

---

[7] Most contemporary acting teachers do not teach a strictly Stanislavskian method (it's difficult to pin down exactly what that would be), and those who draw upon the Stanislavskian tradition of psychological immersion do so using decades of interpretation. Some of the stereotypically intense immersion techniques associated with Method acting, argue some historians and acting teachers, are a dangerous corruption of Stanislavski's principles, though they continue to bear his imprimatur. McFarren argues that the Affective Memory exercises of Lee Strasberg, which demand that actors recall painful memories of their past to achieve truthfulness on stage, "has been erroneously endowed with Stanislavski's authority, and has generally held a privileged but somewhat illegitimate place in teaching American actors the System. The fact that many other significant acting teachers, Bobby Lewis and Uta Hagen among them, have felt compelled to address misconceptions about working with one's personal emotion as a component of their teaching further substantiates the paradoxical utility of the phenomenon and the controversy of the exercise" (192).

training. Generally speaking, we may agree that as long as the student is balancing the emotional labor of performing with fulfilling the requirements of their curriculum and healthy patterns of eating, sleeping, and exercising, we can assume that they are okay. Further, we may assume that a regimen of performing demanding roles will naturally result in fostering in the student confidence, resilience, and well-developed creative and intellectual skills. These assumptions, however, have also perpetuated invisible trauma. Alice Brandfonbrener's research, for instance, finds that performers' repeated and long-term exposure to heightened states of vulnerability and enacting degrading stereotypes amounts to nothing less than "psychological hazards" (101). Lanon Prigge finds that even if acting students sense that they are experiencing a downturn in their emotional health as a result of their training and performances, or perceive that they are repeatedly put into unhealthy or contentious situations, they will "tend to avoid questioning or labeling" them as such, "owing to academic and workplace related pressures to succeed 'above all else'" (13, citing Cohen, McDaniels, and Qualters). Further, the student will often justify inappropriate behavior on the part of colleagues or instructors because such behavior is perceived as in keeping with the industry culture in which they are seeking to establish themselves (Prigge 13). Prigge finds that when students do express ethical discomfort in courses related to their discipline, their concerns are downplayed in the name of "keeping it in the family." Faculty members "often avoid the situation, direct students to ethical experts . . . or respond from personal ethical orientations" rather than report to their supervisors or the appropriate campus officers who have procedures in place for dealing with possible misconduct (13, citing Cohen et al.). Such tendencies enforce the practices of avoidance and naysaying within a continuum of formation and habituation (Prigge 14).

Prigge cites a growing body of research attesting to the problem, and to the fact that we've known about the problem for at least six decades.[8] The very first article in *Theatre Topics*, a journal published by the Association for Theatre in Higher Education starting in 1991, included director Suzanne Burgoyne Dieckman's essay about her Creighton University production of *The Crucible*, Arthur Miller's "psycho-social investigation into the root

---

[8] Prigge's sources include Kaplan; Rule; Bloch; Dieckman; Seton, "Forming (In)Vulnerable Bodies"; Seton, "'Post-Dramatic' Stress"; Seton, "Culture or Cult"; Seton, "Churchill Report"; Seton "The Ethics of Embodiment"; Shalin.

causes of human evil," in which Dieckman, drawing on the work of Jerzy Grotowski and Peter Brook, encouraged her student actors to delve into their own psyches to confront the "dark side of human nature" (1, 4). While audiences and reviewers found the production's depth of character surprisingly powerful for a student production, Dieckman wasn't prepared for the "psychological fallout" of her actors' approaches to the play, which resulted in students experiencing feelings of terror onstage, lashing out and blaming their fellow actors for their own perceived failures (mirroring the group hysteria and scapegoating in the play), despairing views on marriage and relationships, and recurring nightmares (6). The traumas experienced by her cast led her to call for an open discussion of the dangers of psychologically immersive work with actors and a code of ethics governing the responsibilities of directors and theater educators.

The academy in general is already a pretty perilous place, and this is especially true for graduate students. In 2014 the graduate student government at University of California–Berkeley, as a follow-up to a groundbreaking 2006 Berkeley study on mental health in higher education, found that 64 percent of graduate students in the arts and humanities reported high levels of depression, and 10 percent of all graduate students had contemplated suicide at some point during their program of study. And these numbers are higher for more at-risk populations like students of color, international students, and LGBTQ students (The Graduate Assembly; Jaschik). Rigorous study, high-intensity crunch times in the academic calendar, the atmosphere of constant critique, poor quality of sleep and nutrition, and perceived stigma attached to failure or asking for help are some of the reasons for these numbers.[9] Add to this the demanding psychological regimen of building roles by identifying with characters going through trauma and suffering and the additional high-stress times of the production season, and our graduate actors may be exceptionally at risk for deteriorating mental health.

Prigge's observations on the complicity of faculty in perpetuating behavior running counter to students' human flourishing are supported by Mark Seton's research in acting programs in higher education. Seton adds that there is a tendency for teachers to fall back on the idea that "it's always been this way" or that they may have experienced similar ethical dilemmas or emotional trauma and surviving it was the means to their own success. "If

---

[9] See Magelssen, "Our Academic Discipline"; Alison E. Robb and Clemence Due, "Exploring Psychological Wellbeing in Acting Training."

it was good enough for me," Seton quotes one of his informants telling him, "it's good enough for them" ("Culture or Cult" 2). Another phenomenon that contributes to perpetuating negative environments in acting programs is the refrain that if a student is ever feeling they cannot "hack it" (a negative or distressing emotional situation), they shouldn't be in the business, because, after all, it only gets far more intense in the move from training to the profession (3).[10] Seton is particularly concerned with pedagogical practices that deliberately intend to put students into highly charged situations that will increase their emotional vulnerability and force them to submit themselves to psychological states of precarity or abjection "for their own good" (1).

When a performer is playing a role in a realistic dramatic production, they are often encouraged to psychologically attach their character's success or failure in achieving their goals to very high stakes. Jonathan Chambers's aptly titled essay "Or I'll Die" describes the mandate of contemporary approaches to acting that you must get what your character desires by the end of the play or you will suffer the worst consequences imaginable. Such stakes, writes Chambers, are sought in hopes of giving the actor the kind of emotional charge required for a successful performance. Grounded in the philosophy of Sigmund Freud and his fellow humanists, and prescribed by Konstantin Stanislavski, is the "assertion that the actor must in the course of performing a role 'fight . . . for [their] very existence" (Chambers 165, citing Waxberg 47–50, in turn citing Stanislavski). Argues Chambers:

> When student actors are first introduced to the protocols of contemporary, realistic acting, they are frequently encouraged to weigh the effectiveness and value of their choices against the bold hypothetical, "I must achieve my goal or I'll die." That is, the pursuit of the chosen objective and super-objective is configured so that the stakes become a matter of life and death . . . [given] the notion that death is categorically terrible and that any reasonable person will undertake most any action in order to evade it unconditionally. (162)

[10] "When I have expressed concern about such examples to other acting teachers," writes Seton, "many defended their peers' actions with cautious 'support.' These teachers assured me that what their peers were trying to do was to inculcate beneficial behaviours. It was claimed that this could only be achieved by 'breaking through' the resistance of students who desire to learn. Resistance by students was variously interpreted as hesitation through fear of failure, or fear of change, or just laziness" ("Culture or Cult" 2).

Actors are also often encouraged to draw upon their own emotional memory of trauma in order to better portray their characters and achieve a representation of the life-or-death stakes described by Chambers. This means frequently dredging up negative affective and emotional states from the past in order to experience them again so that the actors may organically display the consequences of experiencing these negative emotions on their face and body.

In some cases, actors can even take on PTSD-like symptoms ("increased physiological arousal or hypervigilance, intrusive thoughts [flashbacks], and dissociation [numbing]") after experiencing an invented, fictional trauma in a production (McFarren 157). Not only is it risky to lean heavily on affective memory techniques recalling actors' own traumatic experiences, writes Seton, but "the enactment and witnessing of trauma in the context of rehearsal and subsequent performance can also leave its imprint on the actors' lives, even if they had never experienced the trauma prior to performing the role" ("'Post-Dramatic' Stress" 2). Still, the idea persists that it is ultimately good for actors in training to regularly experience genuine pain and suffering for the benefit of their craft and their mastery of representing these emotions for audiences and their fellow actors, the argument being that the willful exposure to and immersion into these painful states will build the resilience and muscles to do so again with more facility and command. Modern acting training is tantamount to homeopathy. Exposure to the toxins of trauma and suffering builds strength and resistance in this pedagogical model—if it doesn't kill you first.

Another problem with the high level of emotional labor and risk-taking on the part of our student actors is that we and our colleagues who are charged with their training and care are likely not trained in the psychological or cognitive behavioral fields that can best attend to and process the pain of their real traumatic experiences, or in helping them move on from an emotionally charged role once they are done with the play. "While acting schools are effective in shaping actors in 'taking on' a role," observes Seton, "there is far less guidance, if any, about 'removing' a role or debriefing after a season of performances" ("'Post-Dramatic' Stress" 1). Cheryl McFarren observes that acting teachers may be very skilled in helping students take on a role requiring hyperarousal and traumatic recall, but when actors do not have strong support networks or professional guidance to help shed that role, they may actually prolong the addictive, codependent, or destructive behaviors of their characters long after the play has ended (184, 201). Even if they recognize they are engaging in unhealthy behavior, the actors may avoid seeking help for fear of being judged incompetent or weird for being so overtaken by their work (Seton " 'Post-Dramatic' Stress" 1, citing Burgoyne, Poulin, and Rearden). On top of this, Seton observes that actors experience concomitant risk factors associated with the theater lifestyle, including sleep deprivation, poor dietary habits, excessive use of caffeine, tobacco, and alcohol, and "a higher use of street drugs than [Seton has] encountered either in musicians or in dancers" (" 'Post-Dramatic' Stress" 3).

MFA acting programs and other conservatory-style training programs encourage the experience of suffering as a way to build character in their actors, putting them through the embodied emotional and affective suffering of their characters both to achieve resolution for their characters and to accumulate gravitas and resilience over time. But growing evidence suggests that actors-in-training often sustain lasting damage or trauma from their experiences in these programs. Perhaps emotionally abusive situations can be so entrenched in acting training programs because the perpetrators of the abuse are the selfsame charismatic mentors who help actors achieve the heights of emotional resonance with their characters and the audiences who reward them. Furthermore, these mentors are otherwise one of the actors' few sources of nurturing and support in the high-stress and competitive profession, in which they can often find themselves far from home and/or other support networks. Acting students, reports Seton, often find that pursuing redressive action against a colleague or faculty member they feel is causing them emotional distress would mean removing a figure who at the same time is providing emotional and professional support in the rest of their curriculum. For actors, removing these supports on which they depend can be devastating and leave them with "nothing" ("Culture or Cult" 3).

Here, then, is one of the most difficult nuts to crack: early in my research for this essay I wondered whether the solution to high levels of emotional turmoil and distress in acting programs could be alleviated by more fully incorporating acting approaches less reliant upon psychological immersion or "inside-out" approaches to character development. Brechtian distance comes quickly to mind, as do physical or outside-in techniques for building character like those of François Delsarte, Tadashi Suzuki, Rudolf Laban, or Anne Bogart and Tina Landau. But even if we were to drop rigorous psychological immersion techniques from the curriculum entirely, the power dynamics supported by the structures of acting programs often involve acting teachers functioning as charismatic gurus whose job is not just to teach content and technique but also to emotionally train their actor-disciples with psychologically forceful pedagogy. Because of the rigors and expectations of contemporary acting training, these processes can involve high levels of emotional entanglement, regimens of doling out and withholding praise, total emotional and physical buy-in resulting in isolation from previous social groups, initiation cycles of psychological breaking down and building up to purge students of habits, encouragement to overcome learned personal barriers to emotional and sexual intimacy, and trial-by-fire situations in which students are stripped of comfort and emotional security in order to achieve states of altered consciousness and emotional breakthroughs required for the job. In other areas of life, these could be labeled cult-like or codependent situations. Seton, in "Culture or Cult: When Does the Disciplining of the Actor Become Abuse?," draws comparisons between acting training and the cycles of indoctrination Marc Galanter describes in his research on "charismatic groups." (Galanter avoids the word "cult" because of its popular culture associations.) Similarities include pushing students to (and past) their breaking point to cure them of perceived laziness or fear, breaking down and stripping them of comfort and confidence in order to build them back up with a new identity, and the grooming of initiates into intense cohesive affiliations based on shared beliefs that take advantage of already perceived marginal or counterculture status. In both types of groups, the participants' success involves investing trust and devotion in the individuals causing them the most harm. Or, as Seton puts it, "[i]n such cases, leaders inflicting distress on the dependent person are also perceived as those who will provide eventual relief" (5). Seton has witnessed situations "on a regular basis" in which the acting teacher would "set up many students for initial failure and discomfort, in acting tasks, until the moment they 'got it'—then there would be applause and a sense of euphoria/relief that another student has 'passed' through this early stage of initiation" (6). It's a racket, in other words, in which the actor is convinced to invest their commitment and energy into a solution proffered by the instructor, but the instructor is also the one that has invented the problem to be solved. Drawing on Michel Foucault, Seton argues that the necessity of submitting to the system of discipline to be successful requires these disciples to internalize the systems of coercion, resulting in the overall order of things in which actors' voluntary submission to situations that jeopardize their safety and well-being is perceived as okay and even healthy—as opposed to more explicit abuse required "by obvious coercion from the institution" (5).

I want to pause and mark this idea of coercion as particularly relevant to issues of human flourishing. Proponents of positive psychology like Martin Seligman assert that well-being is fostered when free individuals can pursue goals and experiences by free choice for their own sake, rather than be forced into behaviors and situations "by other people or by negative circumstances." "Well-being" in this model, writes James O. Pawelski, "is basically a theory of uncoerced choice" ("Defining the 'Positive'" 360). Whether or not we can agree that acting training exercises and role development that rely on the actor's psychological immersion into negative or traumatic states are irresponsible pedagogy, we may at least acknowledge that to make an actor enter these states against their better judgment and self-preservation, or to employ social conditioning and techniques meant to exhaust and overcome resistance to these barriers, is precarious, if not insidious. It's not that charismatic acting teachers are sadistic or even mindful that they can cause long-term harm. This is the way they themselves learned to act; they want to share with their students the sublime highs of emotional breakthroughs and of nailing the depths of a character's despair, and they would in fact feel irresponsible releasing their wards from training without toughening them against precarities of the real-world profession.

We are all, to put it baldly, complicit in a coercive system of actor suffering. We cherish our actors as surrogates for our trauma. The more we as audiences see the actor experiencing real precarity, the more we value their performance, even if we perceive they are being overtaken emotionally by their character. We celebrate the idea that pain builds character. We idealize the figure of the romantic (and starving) artist and beatify those we've lost to mental illness—who've made the greatest sacrifice to give us the art we value. We're unaware of or slow to change the institutionalized structures putting our acting students at risk. We must, though, seek ways to better enable our actors and their allies to intervene in situations where they may be harmed in an acting exercise, in a performance, or in situations where accumulated emotional labor and distress over time are overwhelming.

Where do we go from here? It would be naïve to think that changing the pedagogical models or training methodologies in acting training programs would make for healthier acting students with greater well-being, since the power relations and intense social rituals endemic to these programs would likely remain. I'm not saying that plays should be free of characters that endure rigor, suffering, and hardship, or that plays should not be about the world out of joint and protagonists born to set it right. Theater, in order to be taken seriously and in order to serve as a tool for addressing injustice and other kinds of rottenness, should have, as Aristotle and others have argued, a certain magnitude. I'm not even saying that actors should be discouraged from psychologically identifying with their characters' painful or traumatic emotions. As Laura Lodewyck reminds us in her chapter in this volume:

> The fullness of human experience includes both joyful and grievous events, and theater as an art takes them both seriously. . . . Part of the continued contradiction of theater, as with other forms of artistic expression, is the bittersweet evocation of emotion from what is not strictly "enjoyable" content. That is, great moments of self-realization and deep connection occur when experiencing incredibly negative stories.

It is probably good for us to experience together a healthy fluctuation of feelings of joy, calm, pleasure, challenge (eustress), and distress to keep our brains functioning well and at optimal balance. Moreover, I do believe that theater and performance can be a terrific means for airing and grappling with the world's problems and injustice; for enabling individuals to build confidence, stick-to-itiveness, poise, and social persuasion; and for granting occasional access to the sublime.

But as educators, fellow artists, and audience members, we ought to be more vigilant for situations when actors can be made vulnerable and exposed to intense or long-term traumatic situations that could damage their mental health. Catherine Madden, a colleague in the University of Washington's School of Drama, teaches acting in our Professional Actors Training Program (PATP), a three-year conservatory-style MFA degree program that includes training in Stanislavski-derived practices as well as Suzuki Method, Viewpoints, Alexander Technique, Linklater, Archetypes, voice, singing, clown, and stage combat. When I spoke with her about this chapter Madden acknowledged that she has worked with performers who have been harmed by what she describes as irresponsible and "poor" acting instruction. The idea that persists in these cases, as Madden describes it, is that "sacrificing the health of the actor is art." It's important, she says, to allow the actors to enter and explore darker and deeper artistic spaces, but a good instructor will help equip actors with tools for how to come back out again so they're not continuing to carry the elements out of those spaces into their daily lives. "Actors need to know how to get in and out," she says. "The goal is to leave the room *challenged* but not *damaged*."[11]

Madden, who teaches Integrative Alexander Technique in addition to publishing widely and lecturing and leading workshops internationally, works closely with actors both within her classes and who are working on UW School of Drama productions. At the time she spoke with me about actor training and mental health, for instance, our PATP students were preparing for two emotionally rigorous productions in the near future. *The Women of Lockerbie*, Deborah Brevoort's historically based 2003 drama composed in the manner of a formal Greek tragedy, tells the story of several characters who have been dealing for seven years with the devastating losses of loved ones in the bombing of Pan Am Flight 103 in 1988. Principal among the characters is Madeline Livingston, a New Jersey woman whose college-age son died in the flight on his way home from London for the holidays. Madeline spends much of the play in a state of raw grief, scouring the hills around Lockerbie, Scotland, for any remains of her son, which have never been recovered. *Frozen*, Bryony Lavery's 1998 drama, gives us the character of Nancy Shirley, whose ten-year-old daughter was kidnapped and murdered by a serial child molester and killer. Over the course of the play, Nancy undergoes a journey that involves overcoming emotional paralysis and even finding it possible to forgive. Both plays require "hefty" emotional work for the actors, and Madden serves as a resource for dealing with the material in a safe way.

Part of how Madden achieves this is through habitually incorporating best practices into the rehearsal and training studio process. Every class session she teaches in the PATP students' three-year curriculum, for instance, includes formal three-component warm-up and cool-down rituals designed to prepare them for emotionally difficult work and to transition them back out of it at the end of the session. Madden has adapted these techniques from acting and movement teacher Richard Alan Nichols, who himself drew upon the work of acting teacher Eric Morris, whose theory of acting draws on the methods of Lee Strasberg and Martin Landau.[12] Students in the first component take a moment to assess how they feel and to acknowledge without

[11] Catherine Madden, personal interview, January 8, 2019. The following quotes from Madden, unless indicated otherwise, are from this same interview.

[12] Madden describes the warm-up and cool-down exercises in *Integrative Alexander Technique Practice for Performing Artists* (315–18). The exercises draw on the warm-ups outlined by Morris and Hotchkis.

judgment what's going on in themselves. (This is ideally done out loud, but it's not necessary, says Madden.) Next is what Madden calls an "omnisensory sweep," which involves the actors moving through the space and choosing to respond to the sensory stimuli around them, not pausing to dwell or fixate on any one thing. Finally, the third step is a set of "I like _____" statements, with the actors filling in the blank and moving in response to the imagined stimuli. By undergoing these components at the beginning of the session, the students (1) acknowledge with the "I feel _____" statements where they are emotionally so that they can leave outside the rehearsal/performance space anything that might interfere with the work at hand; (2) respond to the current moment and present circumstances with the omnisensory sweep; and (3) get into a constructive frame of mind with the "I like _____" statements.

The cool-down process after the scene work or acting exercise, explained Madden, allows actors to say, "I took myself somewhere. I'm acknowledging how I feel about that—how I've responded to that. I'm using my senses to take in the world I'm currently in." And the "I like _____" statement "is about [you]. It gets you to think constructively [about being back in your own reality]." Repeating these warm-ups and cool-downs in every class session is key to maintaining a boundary between the "sacred space of art and what we do there" and the space of real life, as well as the actors' own meta-awareness of the techniques their body can use to mediate between them. "It's telling the system," as Madden puts it, "I'm using this tool to change how I'm feeling." There are times, she observed, when a routine warm-up and cool-down aren't enough to get an actor out of a particularly dark space after a session— "Sometimes," she says, "you're still in the world"—and these situations can be addressed with "auxiliary backups," as simple as reciting the alphabet (or a nursery rhyme or sonnet) backward, to reset, in a manner of speaking, the emotional and cognitive state. But these are generally useful only if the actors have gone through the initial warm-up and cool-down practices already.

Madden hasn't always incorporated these transitional techniques into her teaching. There was a crucial moment in her own performance work, however, when she was a graduate student at Washington University in St. Louis, that convinced her of its necessity. It was when she was playing Linda Loman in Arthur Miller's *Death of a Salesman* and found, upon reflecting with her colleague playing Happy that neither character ever got what they wanted, resulting in night after night feeling like failures after rehearsal. The accumulated psychological weight of perpetually deferred psychological need and the toll it was taking on their well-being led to Madden's commitment to helping herself and her actors maintain a healthy separation between self and character.

Madden doesn't agree, however, that the root problem of actors getting stuck in the negative states in which they are psychologically immersed should be blamed on the methodologies themselves. Maintaining a safe exit back out of emotionally rigorous states is a foundational part of many acting techniques, she explained, such as Michael Chekhov's notion of crossing over the threshold and back. In fact the idea that actors need to suffer and punish themselves to reach the necessary emotional heights and depths, an idea that some actors (Madden guesses this is more the case with undergraduate actors) bring with them into their training programs, is a fundamental misunderstanding of acting as a whole. While actors necessarily draw on their own experiences and behaviors to create roles and tell stories, that doesn't mean that actors should become mired in trying to re-create an event or an emotion from their lives. (That would indeed be poor, self-indulgent acting, she says.) Madden notes that "most of the material of 'ourselves,' our biopsychosocial history," is readily available to fuel creativity, and actors can inventory for themselves a repertoire of stimuli they know causes an action response in them. From an Alexander-informed approach, which begins with attention to a healthy, flexible relationship between the head and spine in movement, Madden continued, any time an actor tries to incorporate a tool that is not usable for them, they'll "tighten" overall, which kills imagination. (This might include trying to use an emotional event from an actor's past that they may still be working through, which in this case can actually hinder success.) That tightening can cue the actor, Madden says, to search for an alternate tool for evoking stimuli that can still externally manifest the character's necessary behaviors for the audience. Sometimes this alternative idea can even come from what seem to be low-stakes stimuli. If Madden needs to express disgust with another character on stage, for instance, she can think of pickles, which she intensely dislikes. She once directed an actor who needed to behave as if he were being chased by an army to instead behave as if he were being chased by people with buckets of ice water. (He hated being cold.) These lower-stakes stimuli were able to create the necessary behavior for the scene. "Behave as you need to behave," Madden says. "You need to make choices that help you be in the reality of the play." Actors who have the tools to move into and out of the sacred space of performance are able to make strong choices that derive from their experiences to fuel the work they are doing. And this can indeed be strong material that is revealing of self—spontaneous, edgy, challenging, exhilarating. "If I use warm-ups and cool-downs pristinely as a teacher or director," says Madden, "my actors are willing to explore [the artistic space] more deeply, because they know I am going to . . . provide both entrance and exit." They can trust, in other words, that Madden is not expecting "a dredge out of their own life" but rather "a dredge *into* the world the play is asking them to be in."

Taken together, the kinds of approaches Madden uses with her students and actors—warm-ups and cool-downs, an explicit focus on maintaining a boundary between the actors' own lives and those of their characters, and techniques for emotional identification and empathy that avoid emotional memory drawing on their own painful or intense experiences—can help foster an environment in which actors are not expected to endure suffering that can actually result in long-term harm. These techniques, paired with a safe and trusting learning environment in which actors know they won't be brought to dark or threatening emotional spaces and "left there" by their mentor, promise to responsibly train actors to evoke empathy and emotion in their audience without taking the brunt of the suffering in the exchange.

Actors should be allowed to take risks that push their limits and work their emotional levels. They should be allowed and, yes, encouraged to take on challenges that foster learning, growth, and aesthetic precision. We must, however, be more mindful of structures of coercion that force actors to take risks that will harm them, even if they are convinced this harm is in their best interest. Furthermore, directors and theater educators can look to best practices like those Madden incorporates into her work, that equip actors with the tools they need to prepare for and come back from psychologically heavy or disturbing "artistic spaces" in ways that maintain health and wholeness. In this way, we can more responsibly work toward theater and performance practices that foster well-being for all of us, actors included.

Works Cited

Barish, Jonas. *The Anti-Theatrical Prejudice.* Los Angeles, University of California Press, 1981.

Bentham, Jeremy. *An Introduction to the Principles of Morals and Legislation*, edited by J. H. Burns and H. L. A. Hart. Oxford, Clarendon Press, 1996.

Bloch, S., et al. "Effector Patterns of Basic Emotions: A Psychophysiological Method for Training Actors." *Journal of Social and Biological Structures,* vol. 10, 1973, pp. 1–19.

Brandfonbrener, Alice. "The Forgotten Patients." *Medical Problems of Performing Artists Journal*, vol. 7, no. 4, 1992, pp. 101–02.

Burgoyne, Suzanne, and Karen Poulin with Ashley Rearden. "The Impact of Acting on Student Actors: Boundary Blurring, Growth, and Emotional Distress." *Theatre Topics,* vol. 9, no. 2, 1999, pp. 157–79.

Chambers, Jonathan. "'Or I'll Die': Death and Dying on Page and Stage." *Theatre Historiography: Critical Interventions,* edited by Henry Bial and Scott Magelssen. Ann Arbor, University of Michigan Press, 2010, pp. 162–74.

Cohen, P., M. McDaniels, and D. Qualters. "Air Model: A Teaching Tool for Cultivating Reflective Ethical Enquiry." *College Teaching,* vol. 53, no. 3, 2005, pp. 121–22.

Dieckman, S. 1991. "A Crucible for Actors: Questions of Directorial Ethics." *Theatre Topics,* vol. 1, no. 1, 1991, pp. 1–12.

Enders, Jody. *Medieval Theatre of Cruelty: Rhetoric, Memory, Violence.* Ithaca, NY, Cornell University Press, 2002.

Freeman, Lisa. *Antitheatricality and the Body Public.* Philadelphia, University of Pennsylvania Press, 2017.

The Graduate Assembly. "Summary of Findings." Graduate Student Happiness & Well-Being Report, University of California, Berkeley, 2014. http://ga.berkeley.edu/wp-cont ent/uploads/2015/04/wellbeingreport_2014.pdf.

Hochschild, Arlie Russell. *The Managed Heart: Commercialization of Human Feeling.* 1979. Berkeley, University of California Press, 2012.

Jaschik, Scott. "The Other Mental Health Crisis." *Inside Higher Ed,* April 22, 2015. www. insidehighered.com/news/2015/04/22/berkeley-study-finds-high-levels-depression-among-graduatestudents.

Kaplan, D. "On Stage Fright." *The Drama Review,* vol. 14, no. 1, 1969, pp. 60–83.

Madden, Catherine. *Integrative Alexander Technique Practice for Performing Artists: Onstage Synergy.* Bristol, UK, Intellect, 2014.

Magelssen, Scott. "Our Academic Discipline Is Making Us Sicker." *Theatre Survey,* vol. 57, no. 3, September 2016, pp. 389–94.

McFarren, Cheryl Kennedy. "Acknowledging Trauma/Rethinking Affective Memory: Background, Method, and Challenge for Contemporary Acting Training." PhD Dissertation, University of Colorado, 2003.

McMahon, Darrin M. "From the Paleolithic to the Present: Three Revolutions in the Global History of Happiness." *Handbook of Well-Being,* edited by Ed Diener, Shigehiro Oishi, and Louis Tay. Salt Lake City, UT, DEF Publishers, 2018.

Morris, Eric, and Joan Hotchkis. "Get Ready to Get Ready." *No Acting Please: A Revolutionary Approach to Acting and Living.* Los Angeles, Ermor Enterprises, 2005, pp. 31–77.

Pawelski, James O. "Bringing Together the Humanities and the Science of Well-Being to Advance Human Flourishing." *Well-Being and Higher Education,* edited by Donald W. Harward. Washington, DC, Association of American Colleges and Universities, 2016, pp. 207–16.

Pawelski, James O. "Defining the 'Positive' in Positive Psychology: Part II. A Normative Analysis." *The Journal of Positive Psychology,* vol. 11, no. 4, January 2016, pp. 357–65.

Prigge, Lanon Carl. "Serious Play: Exploring the Ethical Tensions of License and Limits in Drama, Theatre, and Performance Education." PhD Dissertation, University of Stellenbosch, 2015.

Ridout, Nicholas. *Theatre and Ethics.* Houndmills, UK, Palgrave, 2007.

Robb, Alison E., and Clemence Due. "Exploring Psychological Wellbeing in Acting Training: An Australian Interview Study." *Theatre, Dance and Performance Training,* vol. 8, no. 3, 2017, pp. 297–316.

Rule, J. "The Actor's Identity Crises (Post Analytic Reflections of an Actress)." *International Journal of Psychoanalytic Psychotherapy,* vol. 2, no. 1, 1973, pp. 51–76.

Seton, Mark. "Churchill Report: Actor's Healthcare UK." Gilbert Spottiswood Churchill Fellowship Report, 2009. https://www.academia.edu/1185733/ChurchillReport_Actors_HealthcareUK.

Seton, Mark. "Culture or Cult: When Does the Disciplining of the Actor Become Abuse?" Academia, 2007. https://www.academia.edu/244484/Culture_or_Cult_When_does_the_disciplining_of_the_actor_become_abuse.

Seton, Mark. "The Ethics of Embodiment: Actor Training and Habitual Vulnerability." *Performing Ethos,* vol. 1, no. 1, 2010, pp. 5–20.

Seton, Mark. "Forming (In)Vulnerable Bodies: Intercorporeal Experiences in Sites of Actor Training in Australia." PhD dissertation, University of Sydney, 2004.

Seton, Mark. "'Post-Dramatic' Stress: Negotiating Vulnerability for Performance." *Conference Papers of Australasian Drama Studies Association,* 2006. http://ses.library.usyd.edu.au/handle/2123/2518.

Shalin, D. "Signing in the Flesh: Notes on Pragmatist Hermeneutics." *Sociological Theory,* vol. 25, no. 3, 2007, pp. 193–224.

Sophocles. *Oedipus.* Translated by Robert Fagles. *Wadsworth Anthology of Drama,* edited by W. B. Worthen. Boston, Cengage Learning, 2006, pp 71–88.

Waxberg, Charles. *The Actor's Script: Script Analysis for Performers.* Portsmouth, NH, Heinemann, 1998.

2

The Potential of Pain

Conflict Dramaturgy and Transformation in the Theater

Laura A. Lodewyck

In the closing performance of *Telling: Austin, TX*, Steve, a colonel in the army and a former commander of the Texas Army National Guard Field Artillery Battalion, moved downstage of the intimate black box stage to deliver his final monologue. It is scripted to begin, "I just made DA board for Full-bird Colonel. I've been in for 23 years. I think everyone should go into military for at least 1 or 2 years." As an experienced leader and natural performer, the role of Steve was written to head into the closing moments of the play with a brief statement touching on the value of military experience and what this service continues to mean for his family, including his promise to his wife that he would leave the Guard if he were notified of upcoming deployment again, and the fact that "she wouldn't discourage our daughter but she doesn't want it to happen" (*Telling: Austin*). Instead, he stopped and stood in silence for a long moment.

Breaking off after his first few lines, he suddenly veered off script into extemporaneous testimonial. Turning to his cast members, he addressed each of them in turn with a personal message, in an emotional flood of words, as if afraid he'd be stopped. With most of the cast now in tears, it was uncertain how the play might continue. Steve pivoted again to the playwrights and director: "So, damn you, [because] damn you means thank you in officer speak when we don't want to get too emotional." He quickly laughed and jumped back to the script, gesturing to Laura, whose closing monologue came next: "Blah, blah, blah, I'm not sure my wife would agree that everyone should be in the military, but if my daughter wanted to do it, I think she'd let her. And Laura! You go now [and start your monologue]." After a few moments, laughing and still wiping away tears, the next actress, a daughter of a Vietnam veteran, gave a huge sigh and began her final monologue: "I love going to see my dad now. He's always home." Laura later told me that

Laura A. Lodewyck, *The Potential of Pain* In: *Theater and Human Flourishing*. Edited by: Harvey Young, Oxford University Press. © Oxford University Press 2023. DOI: 10.1093/oso/9780197622261.003.0003 she "loved" the spontaneity of Steve's addition. "It was fitting," she says, "that he in the end, the natural leader, the corporal of the show, looks at me and says 'I'm sorry.'" She laughs. "And I'm sitting there bawling my eyes out!" She adds, "It was good. I liked it."

The Telling Project, a series of original plays based on the stories of veterans and military family members and performed by the individuals themselves, aims to make these kinds of emotional connections for the purpose of community building. Jonathan Wei, *Telling*'s founder, initially created the project to leverage theater's social networks and its immediately affective content, in order to connect military and civilian community members and to educate the larger community about experiences unique to military members and their families. Wei began the project at the University of Oregon when he was coordinator of nontraditional student programs. He had been seeking ways to expand campus panel discussions beyond those already informed about military and veteran issues. In looking for effective methods to tap into groups beyond the immediate veteran community, Wei thought to recruit existing theater audiences and apply the method of performance.

Beyond distributing information to civilians, Wei sought to generate a meaningful experience for the audience members, particularly nonmilitary ones who were likely receiving highly "mediated" information from particular sources, such as specific national news outlets. Wei believed that understanding another's perspective could help bridge what is often termed the military-civilian divide, or the idea that most civilians have little understanding of the realities of military service and are generally not called on to face the daily sacrifices of a country at war. Wei said he wanted to bring in theater audiences to "create a situation where these folks could actually have the opportunity to see something that was broader perspective. Even more than that, just to see people—and not even see, you know, *feel*."

Empathy is a simple concept with a fraught history. Research psychologists have generated at least eight discrete definitions and applications of empathy, such as imagining how another might feel versus "feeling distress" at another's situation (Batson 7–8). A basic and applicable description, however, is delineated simply as "matching the emotional state of another" (Goldstein and Winner 20). As a psychological concept, empathy could be considered a uniformly useful phenomenon and something that brings about change for the better. Matching another's emotional state, after all, could be the first step to insight into another's situation, inciting action to improve, relieve, or share in the experience in some way. Lindsay Cummings, however, describes how scholars such as Susan Leigh Foster and Amit S. Rai tracked the related concept of sympathy as a tool of colonialism, in that it has been used to unify shared white European culture and implemented as a means to reduce the other to something knowable within one's own experience, and thus an object able to be appropriated (14–15). Cummings points out the similar implications of empathy "in this age of late-late capitalism and neo-liberalism," where "empathy tends to focus our attention to a single person, and on our own responses to that person, potentially obscuring social, historical, and cultural contexts in the process" (15). Likewise, movements in the popular imagination, such as Paul Bloom's *New York Post* Best Book of 2016, *Against Empathy*, argue that empathy can have unintended—and even harmful—material consequences because of the human inability to empathize with masses of individuals rather than a single person. Bloom argues, in part, that empathetic decisions are not necessarily congruent with moral ones.

James Pawelski addresses similar tensions in the question of prudential values versus moral values in the pursuit of well-being. In other words, something that is "good for a person" and something that is "right for a person" may not always share the same value (352). Flourishing may occur on an individual or a larger communal level, and these frames of prudential and moral values may emphasize these differing aspects of scope. Pawelski points out that when writing of flourishing in an individual, psychologists may be referring to subjective states, something in the realm of prudential values. However, when looking at the well-being of communities and the role of a good person in a just society, psychologists are likely citing moral values (352–53). Empathetic experience, though key to an emotionally powerful theatrical event, is by these metrics not necessarily creating positive change and promoting flourishing on a larger societal scale. What, then, is flourishing in the theater? Can performance reconcile the tension between the prudential and the moral? What makes powerful emotional experiences in the theater a tool for transformation for good, and can this exist on both an individual and a communal scale?

As far back as Aristotle's championing of catharsis, it has been believed that theater has the capacity to transform. Change on an individual level is supported by theories of embodied cognition, in that we make meaning through the body, even to the extent that the movement of one's body in space directly influences one's feelings or behavior.[1] Research also indicates

---

[1] See foundational work from Barsalou; Niedenthal; Niedenthal et al.; as well as recent distinctions of terminology and meaning from Da Rold and the application of principles of embodiment in real-world practice, such as religious ritual (Seligman).

evidence of neural overlap between seeing and doing.[2] The difficulty in evidencing change through the necessarily communal event of theater (as an audience requires plurality in order to share intersubjectivity across others) is that compelling emotional evidence exists primarily at the level of the individual. It is the individual bodies that cry, gasp, and laugh within the crowd. Psychologists have found individual benefits to theatrical participation, from improved cognitive function in aging populations[3] to advantages in the social and cognitive development of youths, such as increases in measures of what is termed theory of mind, or "understanding others' mental states" (Goldstein and Winner 20, 33). There also exists substantial data on the importance of social connectedness and relationships, but measured by their effect on subjective belongingness and individual health outcomes.[4] In its affective frame, flourishing is often an individual, psychological concept.

This is not to say that individual change cannot carry over to the social or political collective and accomplish material transformation in the world through people's actions. This is, obviously, one of the aims of theater for social change. As Kelly Howe observes in this collection, one of theater's radical aims in the tradition of Augusto Boal is that oppressed people have a right to flourish and to claim happiness. The opposite extreme of this potentiality, however, is that the individual psychological frame may be used as a tool of social control. Boal famously theorized "Aristotle's coercive system of tragedy" and how the catharsis model of tragedy purges the spectators' desire to go against the established social order (37–41). Brecht likewise wrote about the dangers of "culinary theatre," where the audience derives empty pleasure from the theatrical experience and dismisses the will to act following the emotional release of a play (35). Beyond the form of theater, contemporary analyses of neoliberal systems, such as the pop culture text *McMindfulness*, critique the corporate emphasis on self-care models of wellness and emotional regulation through stress relief, which shifts the onus of responsibility to the individual and distracts from systemic problems.

[2] For the debate on the extent to which mirror neurons (a concept based in research on neurons in macaque monkeys that "fire" when both seeing and doing an action) can be presumed to be the basis for what researchers term "action understanding," see the rebuttal by Hickok.

[3] For an overview of existing findings, see Noice and Noice.

[4] See Cohen; Lee and Robbins; Cacciopo and Hawkley.

Individuals are, of course, intimately connected to social networks and practices. Emotional contagion, or the common automatic practice of "synchronizing" with others' behaviors and mimicking their emotional states, largely without conscious awareness (Hatfield, Cacioppo, and Rapson 96), has been demonstrated across widely disparate contexts. Evidence of "mood ripples" within managerial settings (Barsade 668) and of "transfer" of emotions, even absent physical and nonverbal interaction in the forum of social media (Kramer, Guillory, and Hancock 8788), illustrates the potential power that individuals' emotions may have in shaping others' feelings.

In performance-specific contexts, the interplay between feeling and community reveals the tension between the individual and the collective. In "Performing Emotions: How to Conceptualize Emotional Contagion in Performance," Erika Fischer-Lichte writes on historical theatrical conditions that created the possibility for change within spectators through repeated encounters with liminality. She argues that both the cleansing of catharsis and the infectious intent of contagion represent contact with the liminal, in that they "imply a process of somatic transformation" (28). Using Christoph Schlingensief's 2004 *Kunst und Gemüse: Theater ALS Krankheit* (translated as *Art and Vegetables: Theatre A(L)S Disease*), Fischer-Lichte relays how performance can affect audiences in "reassessing underlying value systems" through reconsidering one's lived emotional reactions in the context of a social and aesthetic event (35). She suggests audiences could come to reappraise feelings like shame and fear, as well as social notions like equating health with purity, by reevaluating their discomforts along with others' visible reactions in a theatrical situation that "enabled an encounter and communication between 'healthy' people, a sick person and a group of disabled people" (34). In a recent Australian study on audiences in orchestral performances, researchers found experimental evidence to bolster what many observe anecdotally: that encountering a live performance as part of an audience enhanced individual emotional engagement (Garrido and Macritchie 165). The sense of "social bonding"—or the extent to which audience members felt connected to each other, to the musicians, or to society at large—influenced the degree to which being among others enhanced their emotional experience (160). In a study on "communal consumption" in symphony audiences (intended to inform arts marketing), researchers identified a complex interplay between the individual and the collective in terms of subjective awareness (O'Sullivan 209). Audiences identified the importance of the social ritual, along with a multilayered relationship to the presence of others. For instance, many were distracted by small audiences or audience diversity, and thus felt anxiety about the future of the art as they were simultaneously enjoying it (219).

Despite acknowledging the significance of the event as a collective ritual and a social event, audiences in this symphony study felt that their personal emotional reactions were individually dependent (O'Sullivan 216). However, research about emotional contagion tells us that beyond individual awareness of emotional experience, the echoing of others' feelings could be nonconsciously activated. Emotional change takes place within bodies, but also across bodies. Ultimately, both subjective emotional response and a sense of belonging clearly mediate what accounts for meaningful experience in the theater.

Theater scholar Jill Dolan famously termed felt moments of potential for a better world in performance "utopian performatives,"[5] drawing on cultural anthropologist Victor Turner, who spoke of the power of "communitas,"[6] or cohesion in the shared experience of an event within a community. Performance generates a particular kind of relationship that links performers to audiences, and performers to their fellow cast members, in a presumably shared moment of feeling. More than individual episodes of reading a novel, viewing artwork, or listening to music, theater's power and paradox is in the communal, lived presence of the shaping of a story that is both deeply visceral and necessarily ephemeral. Theater is built on the felt encounter with other individuals. These individuals exist as both imagined characters and corporeal realities. It is an exchange that engages emotion, risk, and the phenomenon of creating the experience of an event together. As Stacy Wolf observes in this volume, the practice of theater's collaborative storytelling is a distinctive event that transcends shared communal activities that may be practiced in parallel together (such as yoga practice) and runs deliberately in opposition to mediated activities of social technologies in its "intimate liveness." Marcia Ferguson likewise speaks in this volume to the various potentials of touch onstage to uniquely communicate as both a semiotic vehicle of storytelling and a physical indicator of living bodies in space. The shared somatic

---

[5] In *Utopia in Performance*, Dolan describes "small but profound moments in which performance calls the attention of the audience in a way that lifts everyone slightly above the present, into a hopeful feeling of what the world might be like if every moment of our lives were as emotionally voluminous, generous, aesthetically striking and intersubjectively intense" (5).

[6] Turner asks, "Is there any of us who has not known this moment when compatible people—friends, congeners—obtain a flash of lucid mutual understanding on the existential level, when they feel that all problems, not just their problems, could be resolved, whether emotional or cognitive, if only the group which is felt (in the first person) as 'essentially us' could sustain its intersubjective illumination" (48).

experience within mutual contexts of time, space, and story builds meaning across these experiences in ways that are unique to theater.

The content of a performance event does not, of course, need to be positive to bond individuals within the event; Dolan writes of the audience's shared engagement in the terrible tragedy of *Medea*, moved by Fiona Shaw's blood-drenched performance. As Dolan states, "these performances allow audiences to deepen their connection to their political and social lives by rehearsing a depth of feeling that can demonstrate effective and *affective* civic engagement" (162). Here, Dolan is ostensibly speaking of individuals collectively—the felt encounter takes place within a person, and the civic engagement follows in the actions of the individuals made collective. In even the most compelling examples, there is a slippage between the emotional experience of the individual and what this experience means for the collective.

The past decade has seen a "cognitive turn" in theater and performance studies, where some scholars (though not the field as a whole) have turned to cognitive psychology to understand and explain the mechanisms behind involvement in performance. Scholars have looked at concepts ranging from theory of mind and empathy to linguistic systems and distributed cognition to explain how performance accomplishes individual understanding or interpersonal connection at what is ultimately a biological level.[7] These investigations help to situate the social and cultural meaning of performance, validating that something "real"—that is, a function that is physically, neurally evident—occurring during the powerful anecdotal experiences that people describe. Because theater is multisensory, and because it engages emotions and interpersonal interaction, cognitive research would indicate that performance has the power to cultivate significantly positive (and, by the same account, possibly negative) effects. From this perspective, it may even be an activity uniquely qualified to do so. Neural activation, however, does not wholly identify what is exciting and fulfilling about theater.

A productive model of human flourishing emphasizes the eudaimonic, or a concern for the "good life" or "a life lived fully," rather than a hedonistic turn based on moments of pleasure (Pawelski and Moores 3; McMahon 4). The fullness of human experience expands well beyond the pursuit of pleasure; further, "both the positive and the negative seem to be crucial for cultivating

---

[7] See Kemp and McConachie for a diverse overview of the various interventions using cognitive theories.

the good life" (Pawelski 350). The context here is primarily the idea of re-silience. That is, since life contains negative events and emotions, the flour-ishing individual must learn to "cop[e] with them as effectively as possible" (349–50). This is demonstrably true. However, past the need to learn how to productively confront bad experiences, flourishing in the theater rests on a surprising focus on a kind of negativity.

Certainly, not all conflict is negative in the sense that it is harmful. In con-flict is the potential for change. Conflict is, in essence, the heightened rec-ognition of a problem. It points to the possible upheaval of the normative order. The reckoning of conflict can lead to restorative action, as powerfully demonstrated across national protests that affect legislative change. From a theatrical perspective, conflict is useful not only because it drives a story for-ward but because it is inherently liminal. In order to reach change, a char-acter must move through conflict. Put another way: What is drama without conflict? One of the primary principles of traditional script analysis is that a play is action, and action is nothing without conflict. As Michael Chemers highlights in the foundational dramaturgical text *Ghost Light*, drama moves through distinct "lines of conflict": psychic, individual, personal, social, natural, supernatural, or supertextual (80–82). As a Eurocentric theatrical concept dating back to Aristotle's *Poetics*, a dramaturgy of conflict is not the singular model. Still, a primary impulse in American theater is to seek con-flict as the guts of drama (and, it should be said, the core of comedy). Conflict is the key to narratives that audiences typically find engaging. We are drawn to find it, and to tell it.

This may seem antithetical to the concept of eudaimonia. However, here I explore conflict through performance using two contemporary American theatrical initiatives that differ structurally in preparation and execution, and I investigate how each draws on the form of tragedy or the content of conflict in realizing human flourishing. *The Telling Project* and *Theater of War* accomplish similar aims through distinct genres (a verbatim theater tra-dition versus a staged reading), dramatic content (original stories versus new translations of ancient Greek tragedy), and performance participants (com-munity volunteers versus professional actors). One conventional under-standing of theater is the spectacular Broadway-style musical, a commercial form with its own positive outcomes. However, I will focus on the conscious manipulation of the theatrical form and the ways in which it allows individ-uals and communities to realize a fuller potential of human experience in leveraging emotionally negative experiences.

I want to be clear that I am not suggesting that trauma or posttraumatic stress is desirable in any way or should be featured as an object of entertainment. In fact, the form of theatrical representation greatly matters. For instance, though negative emotional content may lead to connectedness and positive emotional experiences, the genre of psychological realism may be problematic in its potential to reinscribe trauma by reproducing it or by displaying a kind of pornography of suffering. On the other hand, the raw emotional confrontation of performance may temporarily disrupt normative social boundaries and allow for exploration and change. Though it is certainly not desirable, suffering and trauma are part of the continual history of war. The United States has been in military conflict continuously throughout the twenty-first century (the longest ongoing conflict being the war in Afghanistan; more recently, the current Operation Inherent Resolve in Syria and Iraq), and an astonishingly low percentage of Americans currently serve.[8] Trauma and suffering is a significant component of many participants' stories in these projects, and theatrical performance can allow individuals the agency to flourish through the conflict and tragedy and to choose how they will use performance as a tool for public knowledge and personal fulfillment. Just as there exists a prudential and a moral good, we cannot presume to decide what is "good" for those who wish to tell their story or see it represented onstage. In its focus on conflict, theater lends itself to this task.

Nonfictional content of this kind could, of course, be told through publication, visual art, or documentary form. (In fact, depending on the cast, it is not uncommon for those who volunteer their stories for *Telling* to also be pursuing other artistic endeavors, independent of the play.) Certainly, there have been well-received films chronicling military experience, with actors fictionalizing these historical accounts. There exists powerful artwork, fiction, and poetry that communicate the sharp loss and reverberations of war. Documentaries such as Tom Donahue's *Thank You for Your Service* showcase interviews with veterans and family members in their own words for the sake of critiquing the civilian understanding of veterans' experiences. However, in a project like *Telling*, Wei felt strongly that a live, embodied encounter in a shared space was critical: "[T]his isn't about stories. This is about these

---

[8] The most recent Pew Research Center publication states that active military comprised 0.5 percent of the U.S. population in 2009, falling to 0.4 percent in 2015, plus an additional roughly 800,000 National Guard and Reserves called on to deploy to conflict (Parker, Cilluffo, and Stepler).

people. That's why we can't use other people [playing their parts]. You have to see them interacting with those stories. That's the important part of these performances. You're registering a *person*" (*Telling*). While there are a multitude of ways in which participants could share stories and reach audiences, theater is the only form that demands one do so in real time, in an embodied exchange.

Telling's tagline, "It's time to speak. It's time to listen," illustrates the central vision of the theatrical piece: veterans, active military members, and family members from a given community come together on stage to enact what military service has meant to them—in all its honor, humor, fulfillment, trauma, and pain—and what they want audiences to know. This model leads to noncoercive ways that individuals can realize agency to leverage sometimes highly negative emotion and experiences. For instance, *Telling: Austin* actors revised their performances in practice in order to reveal or control particular aspects of their story, and thus the audience's emotional experience.

Significantly, *Telling* uses professional playwrights to give a strong dramatic structure to the content of individuals' stories, based on their interviews with the cast members. *Telling* is therefore in the vein of Jan Cohen-Cruz's description of community-based theater, as "being with the whole person" rather than focused on solely aesthetic concerns (365). But *Telling* is also a deliberately aesthetic project. In practice, *Telling's* unspoken assertion is that in order for it to be a truly emotionally informative experience for a civilian audience, it must be good theater. As a project in the tradition of verbatim theater, it is not wholly testimonial. However, as theatrical performance, it capitalizes on what Fintan Walsh characterizes as a quality of theatrical storytelling, and the form of the theatrical monologue in particular. That is, the form of the monologue "resembles the therapeutic encounter" but is not equivalent to it (62).

Alongside the artistic goals, the deliberate formation of a script as the basis of *Telling's* format allowed individuals the security of prepared statements. *Telling* emerged from the panel discussions that Wei organized at the University of Oregon, where he feared that the panelists

> were a little vulnerable in that situation.... [Y]ou're responding to questions as they come. The questions can be really, you know, in good faith, and the answers are in good faith; but because it's extemporized, you can end up forgetting things that you wanted, that you might later have wanted to say;

or even worse, saying things that you ultimately ended up uncomfortable as having as public knowledge. (*Telling*)

A written script allowed performers to relax within the boundaries of the play text.

After many iterations of these performances and rehearsals, however, the performers knew what they wanted to say. Such modifications were often significant to the cast. During one *Telling: Austin* performer's story about her relationship at the time, Jen recounts, "I just said, you know, 'and everybody thought I was divorced, and I was still married.' That was it. And this past weekend, I was like, 'No *really* . . . absolutely everybody on base thought that I was divorced!' I really wanted the crowd to understand." Jen elaborated on the need to explain the significance of the omission: "[R]eally, in the civilian world, if you don't want to be married to somebody anymore and you're still married, then you're separated, and it's fine for you to date. It's not a big deal; who cares. But in the military, you go to freaking—you know, *brig* for that." She laughs. "You go put on an orange jumpsuit and march around base for that." In recounting her improvised elaboration of the dialogue onstage, Jen explains that at one point she actually considered quitting the play because it was very important that her story not be misunderstood. In deciding what she wanted to reveal, the actor's process became the public product in the moment of its making.

The concept of embodied exchange may seem vague in the abstract. Aren't all experiences necessarily "embodied"? Aren't observers always in a dialectical exchange of sorts with something like an exceptional piece of art, in that what they bring to the encounter is reflected back to them in some way? The ways embodied exchange functions in a live performance are salient and specific, however. One of the most arresting testimonies of *Telling: Austin* is that of Regina, a survivor of military sexual assault. A marine filled with the pride and accomplishment of her military role, Regina detailed her disturbing story of being drugged and raped by two fellow marines. In hearing each aspect of that violent night from her first-person perspective, the audience experienced each new realization along with Regina. The culmination of this revelation occurs when she pauses, suddenly, to realize she wasn't feeling well after a beer given to her from a fellow marine. She shifts to explain how she immediately tried to report her assault to a superior and was warned that if she did so, she would get in trouble for underage drinking. Infuriated, she insisted on filing a report anyway, relenting only after hearing a haunting line that she recalls exactly: "There are plenty of tree lines to hide your body. . . . [Y]ou heard me, Marine, there are plenty of tree lines" (*Telling*). Regina had come forward publicly prior to the production, founding a nonprofit foundation and art installation called *Fatigues Clothesline*,[9] which allows survivors to reveal their accounts of sexual assault by writing on military uniform shirts that are turned inside out.

Regina was already vocal about her military experiences, but explaining this particular story was far more complicated in the medium of performance. In interviews with Regina and the cast, everyone spoke of her challenges with the performance process. Initially, it was impossible for her to get through that particular monologue, occasionally stopping rehearsals, leaving the room, or getting lost in the speech or being unable to continue. Understandably, performing her story in direct address to others was an incredible challenge. By the time she reached the public *Telling* performances, however, she was ready: in multiple iterations, Regina evolved the monologue into a carefully self-controlled performance, knowing when to pause, when to check in with the audience, and how to allow reactions from the crowd—the audible gasps and vocalizations—to fully land before she continued. The exchange between performer and spectator allowed Regina to use the audience, in the moment, to shape her delivery.

From the actor's perspective, the immediacy of performance endowed Regina with power. In her account of the performances, she named the reclamation of dominance and control: "[K]nowing that I'm able to reach out to the audience, make them my prisoner, and have them experience *somewhat* what I've gone through. It's very powerful. And it has helped me come out of my shell even more. And watching the reaction *from* the audience—like I said, that's my justice, right there." In this small black box theater, the front row mere feet from the performers, the lived exchange of audience and performer was palpable to all. Bodies shifted uncomfortably, heads shook or nodded along, and mouths gasped or froze in horror, most within view of the performer. No recorded or written testimony would have accomplished the same ends.

---

[9] In *Fatigues Clothesline*, Regina describes how difficult it is to report military sexual trauma, categorizing it as "incest" because of the deep betrayal of the military family, and speaks to the need for her and others to reclaim pride in their service. Besides survivor advocacy, the organization's purpose is to urge legislation to change governmental policy and improve the process of response to reports of military sexual trauma.

This testimony applies the techniques of performance and is shaped by the methods of theater on every level. *Telling* does not rely on human spontaneity alone, but on the craft of dramatic literature and the performance conventions of theater. Regina's words are carefully constructed into a dramatic arc. Each piece of information builds the rhythm and uncertainty of the story into an even more devastating peak of theatrical tension, with the recognition of a horrifying reversal of fortune, allowing audiences to imagine how the night unfolded for Regina. Reclaiming the shape of this narrative is significant, in both its realization onstage and its theoretical basis. One of the reported hallmarks of trauma is the way that it may fracture an experience into sensory fragments. By shaping the narrative, the playwrights imagined Regina's shattered trauma whole again. This created linear sense for an audience, carrying them on the narrative journey, and allowed Regina to—quite literally—rewrite her story. Regina reveled in this agency and the dominion she felt over the audience's embodied experience. Confined by the mutual agreement of audience and performer, they were to remain for as long as she wished to hold them, forced to encounter her emotions and confront their own. This is perhaps a variation on the utopian performative that Dolan describes, but one full in its violence of confrontation. Instead of bringing together like-minded individuals, it connects disparate experiences through the imaginative frame of a play.

Each *Telling* performance, though specific to the group of individuals from that community, generally follows a conventional Aristotelian narrative arc. In the tradition of verbatim theater, the playwrights write from intensive interviews with potential cast members, using the interviewee/performer's own words to shape the story. However true to life the words are, the play's story is artificially constructed from selected events in order to build the narrative's rise and fall. There is an opening exposition chronicling each individual's introduction to the military; rising action with an inciting incident, often bringing the cast together to humorously reenact boot camp scenarios; a high point of dramatic tension, when each individual speaks to a meaningful, sometimes traumatic experience; and after this climax, a denouement that settles to a conclusion. This is also the familiar Western construction of the genre of psychological realism (as opposed to, for instance, traditions of avant-garde or contemporary postmodern plays). This does not limit the way the action plays out: some scenes take place in dialogue, some in monologue, and some in physical movement. This performative freedom allows the play to access the perceived truth of the experiences without reenacting the events strictly as they occurred.

A strict application of psychological realism can be incredibly problematic in representing violence. That is, plays that show violence in a believably realistic way must balance the need for emotional resonance with the exploitation of the act itself. Violence is, of course, a part of human life. The fullness of human experience includes both joyful and grievous events, and theater as an art takes them both seriously. In the *Poetics*, a foundational treatise on theater, Aristotle wrote that the pleasure audiences receive from viewing plays is derived from the playwright's skillful evocation of pity and fear. Greek tragedy, the subject of this reflection, is traditionally considered to be a paragon of theatrical work. Part of the continued contradiction of theater, as with other forms of artistic expression, is the bittersweet evocation of emotion from what is not strictly "enjoyable" content. That is, great moments of self-realization and deep connection occur when experiencing incredibly negative stories. But despite Greek tragedy's obvious violence, the act of violation is rarely seen onstage in these ancient plays. Though there were also likely historical, practical reasons not to stage something like the gouging out of Oedipus's eyes for an audience, Aristotle writes that it is in fact preferable to tell the audience of this horrific act rather than act it out before them.

This does not always hold true for contemporary drama, which may revel in the believable confrontation of acts of violence. While audiences may marvel at the realistic depictions and the skillful acting that create the scene, they are also necessarily taking pleasure in the act of violence itself. This not only reproduces the violence but also replicates and reinforces the victim-perpetrator relationship. Sometimes, too, the lines between the illusion and the experience of violence become blurred. Marlon Brando, along with director Bernardo Bertolucci, infamously collaborated to film the rape of Maria Schneider's character in *Last Tango in Paris* without informing her of certain details, to make her "reaction" seem more real. When Schneider expressed her fury following the scene, Brando reportedly told her, "Maria, don't worry, it's just a movie" (Malkin). Chicago's Profiles Theatre, frequently praised for its gritty and authentic productions, was exposed for subjecting its performers to actual physical and psychological abuse. One actress recounts that she nightly covered her body in ice packs after performing their critically acclaimed production of *Killer Joe* and would sit outside her dressing room following performances unable to stop crying (Levitt). Viewing realistic violence onstage may accomplish something powerful and affective for audiences, but comes at a cost.

Scholars such as Vivian Patraka have written persuasively about the limits of the genre of realism in staging violence. In the case of *Telling: Austin*, though the play follows the conventional dramatic arc of realism, Regina's story of sexual assault interrupts the reenactment of events with a direct, first-person address. *Telling* productions are not simply a series of monologues, though these scenes comprise an important part of the piece. Cast members physically perform their conversations and interactions with others or depict events such as boot camp exercises. All the violence experienced in the play, however, is designated as monologue description. Whereas a war film such as *Saving Private Ryan* intends to shock audiences with copious naturalistic images of battle and is pursuing its own aesthetic purposes in doing so, *Telling* uses person-to-person contact to establish a human connection and an empathetic understanding between strangers. Representing the violence against Regina would of course be wholly disrespectful and exploitative—and entirely beside the point. If *Telling* aims to connect civilian audiences with military members in showing how they are connected and how they are alike, enacted violence can serve to fetishize and differentiate. Monologues from a first-person point of view, on the other hand, prove essential in helping the audience take the actor's perspective. *Telling*'s success lies not only in its meaningful content but in the intentional theatrical form each production takes.

A parallel American theater project, Bryan Doerries and Phyllis Kaufman's *Theater of War*, takes a different approach to theatrical connection and in reclaiming traumatic experiences. The project began with a reading from *Philoctetes*, the Greek tragedy about an ancient wounded warrior, for medical students at Cornell University's Weill Medical College. The play was reimagined as set in a VA hospital. A year later, *Theater of War* performed their first staged reading of "The Philoctetes Project" for a military audience at the U.S. Marine Combat/Operational Stress Conference. Though intended as a two-hour event composed of a reading followed by a post-discussion talkback, military members and spouses lined up to talk for hours. A classicist and director by trade, Doerries had been inspired by a formative tragic event in his own life, the death of his girlfriend from cystic fibrosis, to explore how Greek tragedy illuminated truths about loss and life. He felt it was deeply resonant and affirming to those who had endured great tragedy themselves. Others have established a detailed connection of Greek heroic literature with modern military practice, such as Jonathan Shay in his book *Achilles in Vietnam*. However, *Theater of War* advances the idea that it is essential to hear the stories performed.

Theater of War does not stage this work in a traditional, fully staged production. Many of the performances take place in conference centers or auditoriums. None makes any effort toward theatrical illusion. As a staged reading, a *Theater of War* performance typically takes place with actors in street clothes seated behind a table. The actors have microphones and a script before them. There is no set, no costumes, and no lights or sound—the traditional mise-en-scène of a theatrical performance is entirely absent. The actors are largely unrehearsed, and intentionally so. If a reading does take place in a theater, the house lights are left on, leaving audience and actors in full view of one another. The performance employs professional actors, who are usually recognizable television actors or celebrities. Each performance is followed by a talkback, led by a panel of experts, such as chaplains or mental health professionals. Instead of immersing audiences in a full-length play, *Theater of War* may use selections of the drama and is intentional about attending to the language, with the moderator encouraging audience and panel members to write down quotes to discuss following the reading. Doerries also uses his own translations, which include modern phrasing such as "thousand-yard stare." *Theater of War* has expanded to address a variety of topics through dramatic performance, such as police violence, domestic violence, and addiction, performing for both military and civilian audiences. Though one critique of the work is that it relies on a neoliberal normalization of violence, common across this work is the belief that the staged reading format accomplishes something specific and productive for audiences in opening a temporary space to feel and to speak.

Theater of War performs for both military and general audiences, but never pursues a sleek, spectacular theater. Instead, it evokes visceral emotion through the actors' performative investment. Doerries's tale of an initial reading for a military base recounts how the intensity of the actors' performance "activated" the audience by disorienting and disturbing them, and how he witnessed both actors and audience members slightly shaking with what he termed a "baseline tremor" (personal interview). To evoke this effect, Doerries instructs his actors to be loud, fast, and raw. The performance itself is aggressive and disturbing, with a script such as *Philoctetes* demanding the actor vocalize the protagonist's repeated cries of pain and abandonment. The actors howl, shake, spit, and scream. Doerries claims that this sensory "assault" is necessary to get military audience's attention and to evoke a capacity to disturb and reflect in nonmilitary citizens. The focus on this level of activation may be why the piece demands professional actors for its success; though the reading is deliberately unrehearsed, these expert performers are capable of working heightened emotion through the language and embodying high levels of feeling in externalized ways that command the audience.

Theater of War is built on the presumption that performers' modeling of emotion and evocation of the audience's feelings allow social barriers to be temporarily broken. In a hierarchical structure like the military, the highly charged staged reading, followed immediately by a talkback, allows for a subordinate to stand before an officer and speak their mind in a way rarely permitted within the military institution. The intensity of affect and hearing others speak before them also open up the audience's capacity to change. In one example, a civilian physician tearfully approached the microphone during the talkback to confess that she had been intentionally ignoring what she recognized as posttraumatic stress in her veteran patients because she didn't want to be complicit in the war. Afterward, veterans told Doerries that the truth of her comment, and her promise to change, was far more meaningful than any superficial cliché about gratitude: "[T]here's nothing politically they can say we haven't heard. That woman took as big a risk in baring her soul and telling what was ugly about herself to the audience as the guy who talked about the war crime he felt complicit in" (Doerries). These mixed civilian-military performances ostensibly serve a different purpose than the readings exclusive to the military, but they both draw on the jarring emotion of the performance and the visceral attendance to bodies performing, and necessarily experiencing, anguish. Like viewing a violent act onstage, the screams of despair of Philoctetes's solitary suffering or Tecmessa's loss of her husband to suicide are fundamentally real in the actors' bodies. With no effort toward theatrical illusion, the voices and bodies represent the character, but also serve as a physical spectacle of human suffering. The audience witnesses the actors' sharp breaths, their reddened faces and clenched jaws, their voices torn and raw. As a performance, it is not necessarily aesthetically—or emotionally—pleasant to witness. However, a performance like this may access a deep common humanity necessary to reach the fullness of eudaimonia.

The human experience flourishes when it allows for a physically manifested ·personal connection. Theater, at its core, employs the risk of emotion and the intimacy of physical presence, extended by the presence of a group and the possible emotional contagion. For the duration of the theatrical event, a community is formed. Though not all audience members will approach the experience from a set of shared values, social and cognitive processes allow an individual to see—and, more important, feel—the point of view of another. Whether this leads to social change or an individual shift in perspective depends on many larger contextual elements, but the form of performance is flexible to allow for differing applications, drawing on the established conventions of theater and drama.

Theatrical projects like these fulfill an urgent societal need and address the complexity of human experience, including tragedy and suffering. As theater and the tradition of tragic drama represent, the full richness of life is appreciated only in the relationship to loss. It also makes audiences sit up and attend. It can enable normative social structures to temporarily dissolve long enough to allow otherwise silenced voices to be heard. It blends the individual with the collective in the process of change. Further, the emotional activation of suffering endures. We see it in the very structure of drama. It is perhaps why, after the Greek warrior protagonist of the ancient tragedy *Ajax* dies, the play continues for hundreds of lines. The tragedy is, of course, Ajax's suicide, but more than that, it is about suffering, including the suffering that preceded his death and the suffering that his death furthers. In the aftermath of his suffering, audiences find pain, but also meaning.

Works Cited

Barsade, Sigal G. "The Ripple Effect: Emotional Contagion and Its Influence on Group Behavior." *Administrative Science Quarterly,* vol. 47, no. 4, 2002, pp. 644–75.

Barsalou, Lawrence W. "Grounded Cognition." *Annual Review of Psychology,* vol. 59, 2008, pp. 617–45.

Batson, Daniel. "These Things Called Empathy: Eight Related but Distinct Phenomena." *The Social Neuroscience of Empathy,* edited by Jean Decety and William Ickes, pp. 3–16.

Bloom, Paul. *Against Empathy: The Case for Rational Compassion.* New York, Ecco, 2016.

Boal, Augusto. *Theatre of the Oppressed.* Los Angeles, Theatre Communications Group, 1993.

Brecht, Bertolt. *Brecht on Theatre: The Development of an Aesthetic.* Edited and translated by John Willett. New York, Hill and Wang, 1957.

Cacciopo, John T., and Louise C. Hawkley. "Social Isolation and Health, with an Emphasis on Underlying Mechanisms." *Perspectives in Biology and Medicine,* vol. 46, no. 3, 2003, pp. S39–S52.

Cohen, Sheldon. "Social Relationships and Health." *American Psychologist,* vol. 59, no. 8, 2004, pp. 676–84.

Cohen-Cruz, Jan. "A Hyphenated Field: Community-Based Theatre in the USA." *New Theatre Quarterly,* vol. 16, no. 4, 2000, pp. 364–78.

Cummings, Lindsay. *Empathy as Dialogue in Theatre and Performance.* London, Palgrave Macmillan, 2016.

Da Rold, Federico. "Defining Embodied Cognition: The Problem of Situatedness." *New Ideas in Psychology,* vol. 51, 2018, pp. 9–14.

Doerries, Bryan, interview by author, Beverly Hills, June 9, 2012.

Dolan, Jill. *Utopia in Performance: Finding Hope at the Theater.* Ann Arbor, University of Michigan Press, 2005.

Fischer-Lichte, Erika. "Performing Emotions: How to Conceptualize Emotional Contagion in Performance." *Habitus in Habitat I: Emotion and Motion,* edited by Sabine Flach, Daniel Margulies, and Jan Söffner. Bern, Peter Lang AG, International Academic Publishers, 2010.

Foster, Susan Leigh. *Choreographing Empathy: Kinesthesia in Performance.* London and New York, Routledge, 2011.

Garrido, Sandra, and Jennifer Macritchie. "Audience Engagement with Community Music Performances: Emotional Contagion in Audiences of a 'Pro-Am' Orchestra in Suburban Sydney." *Musicae Scientiae,* vol. 24, no. 2, 2020, pp. 155–67.

Goldstein, Thalia, and Ellen Winner. "Enhancing Empathy and Theory of Mind." *Journal of Cognition and Development,* vol. 13, no. 1, 2012, pp. 19–37.

Gullick, Charlotte, Christine Leche, Schandra Madha, and Jonathan Wei. *Telling: Austin, TX.* 2013. Theatrical script.

Hatfield, Elaine, John T. Cacioppo, and Richard L. Rapson. "Emotional Contagion." *Current Directions in Psychological Science,* vol. 2, no. 3, 1993, pp. 96–99.

Hickok, Gregory. "Eight Problems for the Mirror Neuron Theory of Action Understanding in Monkeys and Humans." *Journal of Cognitive Neuroscience,* vol. 21, no. 7, 2009, pp. 1229–43.

Kemp, Rick, and Bruce McConachie. *The Routledge Companion to Theatre, Performance, and Cognitive Science.* London, Routledge, 2018.

Kramer, Adam D. I., Jamie E. Guillory, and Jeffrey T. Hancock. "Experimental Evidence of Massive-Scale Emotional Contagion through Social Networks." *Proceedings in the National Academy of Sciences,* vol. 111, no. 24, 2014, pp. 8788–90.

Lee, Richard M., and Steven B. Robbins. "Measuring Belongingness: The Social Connectedness and the Social Assurance Scales." *Journal of Counseling Psychology,* vol. 42, no. 2, 1995, pp. 232–41.

Levitt, Aimee. "At Profiles Theatre the Drama—and Abuse—Is Real." *Chicago Reader,* June 8, 2016.

Malkin, Bonnie. "Last Tango in Paris Director Suggests Maria Schneider 'Butter Rape' Scene Not Consensual." *The Guardian,* December 3, 2016.

McMahon, Darrin M. "From the Paleolithic to the Present: Three Revolutions in the Global History of Happiness." *Handbook of Well-Being,* edited by Ed Diener, Shigehiro Oishi, and Louis Tay. Salt Lake City, UT, DEF Publishers, 2018. https://www.nobascho lar.com/chapters/8/download.pdf

Niedenthal, Paula M. "Embodying Emotion." *Science,* vol. 316, 2007, pp. 1002–5.

Niedenthal, Paula M., Lawrence W. Barsalou, Piotr Winkielman, Silvia Krauth-Gruber, and François Ric. "Embodiment in Attitudes, Social Perception, and Emotion." *Personality and Social Psychology Review,* vol. 9, no. 3, 2005, pp. 184–211.

Noice, Tony, and Helga Noice. "Participatory Arts for Older Adults: A Review of Benefits and Challenges." *Gerontologist,* vol. 54, no. 5, 2014, pp. 741–53.

O'Sullivan, Terry. "All Together Now: A Symphony Orchestra Audience as a Consuming Community." *Markets and Culture,* vol. 12, no. 3, 2009, pp. 209–23.

Parker, Kim, Anthony Cilluffo, and Renee Stepler. "6 Facts about the US Military and Its Changing Demographics." Pew Research Center. April 13, 2017. https://www.pewr esearch.org/fact-tank/2017/04/13/6-facts-about-the-u-s-military-and-its-changing-demographics/

Patraka, Vivian. *Spectacular Suffering: Theatre, Fascism, and the Holocaust.* Bloomington, Indiana University Press, 1999.

Pawelski, James. "Defining the Positive in Positive Psychology." *The Journal of Positive Psychology,* vol. 11, no. 4, 2016, pp. 339–56.

Pawelski, James, and D. J. Moores. "Introduction: What Is the Eudaimonic Turn? *And* The Eudaimonic Turn in Literary Studies." *The Eudaimonic Turn: Well-Being in Literary Studies,* edited by James O. Pawelski and D. J. Moores. Lanham, MD, Fairleigh Dickinson University Press and Rowman & Littlefield, 2014, pp. 1–64.

Purser, Ronald E. *McMindfulness: How Mindfulness Became the New Capitalist Spirituality.* London, Repeater Books, 2019.

Rai, Amit S. *Rule of Sympathy: Sentiment, Race, and Power 1750–1850.* New York, Palgrave 2002.

Rizzolatti, Giacomo, Leonardo Fogassi, and Vittorio Gallese. "Neurophysiological Mechanisms Underlying the Understanding and Imitation of Action." *Nature Reviews Neuroscience,* vol. 2, no. 9, 2001, pp. 661–70.

Seligman, Rebecca. "Mind, Body, Brain, and the Conditions of Meaning." *Ethos,* vol. 46, no. 3, 2018, pp. 397–417.

Shay, Jonathan. *Achilles in Vietnam: Combat Trauma and the Undoing of Character.* New York, Scribner, 1994.

Telling: Austin, TX. By Charlotte Gullick, Christine Leche, Schandra Madha, and Jonathan Wei, directed by Stacey Shade Ware, performance by Laura Hammons, Jennifer Hassin, Leila Levinson, Steve Metze, Anisa Moyo, Malachi Muncy, Laura Muncy, and Regina John Vasquez. The Telling Project, May 4, 2013, Emma S. Barrientos Mexican American Cultural Center, Austin, TX.

Turner, Victor. *From Ritual to Theatre: The Human Seriousness of Play.* New York, Performing Arts Journal Publications, 1982.

Walsh, Fintan. *Theatre and Therapy.* London, Palgrave Macmillan, 2013.

3

Braver Angels

Performing Comity in a Polarized Era

John Fletcher

Gettysburg, Pennsylvania, September 2018.[1] I watch people shuffle into a small meeting room at the public library on an early Saturday morning. Drawn from the cluster of surrounding towns, they stop at a check-in table, collect and affix color-coded nametags, grab a bagel, and sip coffee. Some make awkward small talk. Others sit quietly. Everyone here has set aside eight hours to talk with a group of mostly strangers about their deepest political beliefs, longings, and fears. Few if any know what to expect beyond one fact: at least half of their conversation partners stand on the opposite side of an ideological divide. Everyone, me included, wears nametags that indicate our position on a political binary: red for right/conservative/Republican, blue for left/progressive/Democrat. The room has roughly equal numbers of reds and blues. We all seem to be thinking the same thing behind our politeness: *That person voted for/against President Trump*. It is awkward. This is a meeting of rivals, people who might normally avoid each other in life or unfriend each other online.

I am here as an observer, specifically as a researcher who studies activist performances, expressive acts that manifest and play out political beliefs and disagreements.[2] Viewing the gathering through my scholarly lens, I recognize that, thanks to our color-coded nametags and the adversarial circumstances

---

[1] My thanks to various Braver Angels volunteers in Gettysburg, Pennsylvania, and Houston and Austin, Texas, for their help in the research phase of this project: Kira Hamman, Reena Bernard, Tom Smerling, Currie Thompson, Steve Saltwick, and David Throop. I am also deeply grateful to Harvey Young for his invitation to participate in the Humanities and Human Flourishing project and to Harvey, James Pawelski, Sarah Sidoti, and my colleagues in the Theater and Human Flourishing retreat for their inspiration and helpful feedback.

[2] By "performances" I mean not only conventional stage productions but also protests, marches, rallies, debates, and facilitated encounters that employ theatrical conventions such as scripting, staging, display, and spectacle. I call "activist" those performances produced to further some political cause in society, usually by inspiring some change in their audiences.

John Fletcher, *Braver Angels* In: *Theater and Human Flourishing*. Edited by: Harvey Young, Oxford University Press.
© Oxford University Press 2023. DOI: 10.1093/oso/9780197622261.003.0004

of this encounter, we are not merely noting but enacting political identities. Costumed with ideological markers we usually avoid displaying in public, we have cast ourselves as *reds* and *blues*, players in a script predicated on our inevitable conflict and redolent with patriotic import. I note that attendees' body language bespeaks forced relaxation, as if they are open to experiment but poised to bolt if attacked. I note a similar tension in myself, a combination of combativeness and vulnerability that I recognize from my stage experience. I feel like I'm about to play a high-stakes (and underrehearsed) dramatic scene before a live audience. It is not an altogether pleasant sensation.

But then, as Scott Magelssen reminds us elsewhere in this volume, performance is not always an altogether pleasant experience. "We like our actors to *suffer*," he writes. Even watching theater involves something other than simple entertainment. According to Aristotle, Western theater runs on a fuel of deplorable mistakes, terrible revelations, and tragic reversals. He argues that drama works as a spiritual syrup of ipecac, forcefully expunging the pity and fear it summons. I warn my students about theater's dubious blessing at the start of every semester of Script Analysis class. *We have relatively few plays about happy people getting along merrily*, I explain. *Expect to read some distressing stuff.* Theater is drawn to the negative. It needs conflict, struggle, tension, and instability to work. It solicits the discomfort of performer and spectator alike, unhousing us from ourselves and pushing us to live in another's story for a time. I regard such acts of empathic reach as generally beneficial for us as individuals and as a society. I want to believe theater contributes in this way to human flourishing, even if the process requires tolerating a bit more pity, fear, and purgation than the positive word "flourishing" usually connotes.

Similar observations might be made about democracy. It is (we trust) good for us, but it is not always enjoyable. As political theorist Chantal Mouffe argues, any liberal democratic society worthy of the name is agonistic; it operates via struggles (agons) between opposing visions for governing (103).[3] And while contests on stage may make for a stimulating night out, real-life political agons often qualify as agonizing, ordeals we hope to get through as soon as possible. Democracy, like drama, implies conflict. But real-life democratic conflicts seem at least as likely to foster pathology as they do flourishing. I do not suggest anyone in the Gettysburg workshop suffered

---

[3] For simplicity's sake, I use the words "democracy" and "democratic" to refer to what Mouffe specifies as "liberal democracy," the conflictual coarticulation of the liberal tradition of human rights and the democratic tradition of popular sovereignty (2–4).

the kind of trauma Magelssen discusses. Nonetheless, the event underlines for me the risky, hard work that both theater and democratic politics demand from their participants. To do theater and to do democracy, we must suffer in the sense of *enduring*. We suffer each other. Aristotle and Mouffe argue that human flourishing can emerge from enduring the tension of agonism. The workshop promised to test that premise.

In my research, I have focused lately on a bad feeling particular to democratic politics and activist drama: *enmity*, the ill will directed toward those who espouse opposing views. As I detail later, although tension defines democratic politics, current bad feelings between political opponents have reached levels unseen for decades in the United States and elsewhere, prompting widespread concern about polarization's threat to democratic society. In this chapter, I study Braver Angels, the national organization sponsoring the workshop I relate above. One of several grassroots "depolarization" initiatives that emerged in response to the 2016 U.S. presidential elections, Braver Angels operates mainly through small workshops and group activities. Participants from opposing political worldviews ("red" and "blue" teams) encounter each other through facilitated exercises designed to inspire self-reflection, deep listening, and informed understandings of the other side. I argue that the comity that Braver Angels aims for manifests in and as performance, specifically the emotional labor of open, nonreactive interchange; their workshops facilitate surface acting that consciously suppresses the enmity signals that often define political engagements. After giving an overview of the current hyperpolarized climate, I introduce Braver Angels, analyzing its primary workshop exercises as they unfolded in events in Gettysburg and elsewhere. How, I ask, do these exercises and the emotional labor they require enact comity in an age of enmity?

Polarization and Enmity

Political animosity per se is nothing new. Seldom do political opponents love each other. Polarized enmity, however, describes a different phenomenon.

Political scientist Lilliana Mason describes an ongoing debate among experts about the fine distinctions between political *polarization* (distance between stances of groups/parties) and *sorting* (homogeneity of stances within a group/party).[4] I follow Mason's lead in bracketing this debate,

---

[4] I presented portions of the following paragraphs on polarization at the 2018 Association for Theatre in Higher Education conference as part of the roundtable "Ends of Activism."

focusing instead on *social* or *affective polarization* (18). Mason argues that the salient dynamic between groups like liberal/conservative, rural/urban, Republican/Democrat, or white/POC emerges not from policy differences but from the sense of identity that groups provide their members. If I identify as conservative (for instance), and especially if I view my conservativeness as a core feature of who I am, I will likely feel animus toward those I perceive as liberal *simply because they're on the opposing team*. The primary drivers of polarization, in other words, are symbolic, identity-oriented rather than issue-specific (21–22). Enmity trumps policy.

Synthesizing a range of scholarship in social psychology and political science, Mason identifies three features of social polarization. First, in a zero-sum competition such as a campaign for office where only one side can win, polarized groups will exhibit *outgroup prejudice* toward each other. This prejudice exceeds mere dislike, rendering me vulnerable to an array of cognitive biases. I am apt to impute bad faith intentions to my foes while carefully contextualizing my own side's actions. I'm primed to interpret evidence about my opponents through a filter that casts them in a bad light. I'm liable to homogenize, radicalize, and demonize the other side while nuancing, justifying, and making exceptions for my own side. Crucially, these biases operate unconsciously, even if I'm wary of the danger of bias.[5] The second element of social polarization Mason notes involves *activism*, the increased tendency to act on behalf of my group, especially in contest with my opponents. I like to imagine that my political actions originate in noble ideals deeply held and filtered through well-reasoned strategies. Often, however, my speech, my politicking, and my protests draw energy from an unrefined, reptile-brain desire to beat the other team. Finally, Mason notes that social polarization fosters *emotional reactivity*: I feel happy when my group wins; I feel angry or threatened when my group loses, even if I personally am not directly affected by the win/loss in question (23). These three features, then—outgroup prejudice, activism, and reactivity—comprise the social polarization of identities.[6]

Polarization is not by itself negative. Tactical polarization can be valuable for social movements, summoning participation and emotional investment within activist groups and activating onlookers against a group's rivals

---

[5] See Beck for a good overview of social cognition findings.

[6] What Mason describes as social identity polarization matches what other scholars talk about as *tribalism*, the ingroup-versus-outgroup dynamics that both found and threaten democratic politics. See also Greene. I avoid using the term "tribalism" to label this phenomenon, preferring synonyms such as "team" or "ingroup/outgroup."

(Alinksy 130–36; Abujbara et al. 76, 116). Today's digital media-fueled social polarization, however, exceeds tactical utility. Scholars have long noted that the internet operates according to an "attention economy," competing for users' pageviews, clicks, and retweets to garner ad or subscription revenue (Goldhaber). Such commercialization installs into online platforms a perverse incentive to traffic in stories and images that shock, outrage, or frighten, often by appealing to and strengthening ingroup/outgroup tensions. On sites like Facebook and Google, proprietary algorithms "learn" my political identity and feed me search results, headlines, opinion pieces, and reactions tailored to flatter and sharpen that identity. Such algorithms simultaneously filter out news that casts my political ingroup in a bad light or that highlights positive features of my group's opponents (Harris).[7] As a result, these platforms cultivate online communities bound by (consuming, discussing, sharing) a similar outlook on the world, an outlook whose defining feature isn't accuracy but conformity. Behavioral science research suggests that epistemological enclaves such as these tend to both homogenize and radicalize group members' beliefs. Exposed primarily to discourse circulated by and for people who agree with my worldview, I will drift toward more extreme versions of that worldview (Sunstein 68–75). Supercharged by such biased and biasing filters, then, my views of myself, my opponents, and the world in general grow ever more alienated from and opposed to those of "the other side." My working definition of "human flourishing" calcifies into something like *making sure the other side is defeated*.

This polarized enmity threatens liberal democratic function. Democratic politics require antagonism and competition. But these impulses must operate under two metaconditions: trust in the legitimacy of democratic politics and affirmation of my opponents' right to participate in those politics. I may disagree vehemently with my rivals on some issues, but on others I must see opponents as people I can work with. Civic enmity, as political philosophers Scott Aikin and Robert B. Talisse phrase it, occurs when "one acknowledges that one's political rivals *have* an equal say, but can no longer understand why they are *entitled* to it." With enmity, I don't merely disagree with my rivals; I view them as terminally misguided or even dangerous. In a 2016 Pew Research Center study of partisan antipathy, around half of

---

[7] Exacerbating this trend are agents such as the Russia-based Internet Research Agency, which exploit algorithmic quirks and pump divisive content into online discourse with the aim of deepening social polarization. See Kahan.

surveyed Democrats and Republicans indicated that they were "afraid" of the other side (1). Such enmity, adds philosopher Kevin Vallier, manifests a breakdown of both *social trust* that strangers will abide by the same basic norms as I do and the *political trust* that I place in my government to work for me (4, 17). The result is what political scientist Lee Drutman terms the "doom loop" of democratic politics. Compromise becomes anathema. Opponents become mortal enemies. Legislative processes deadlock. Government loses the minimal legitimacy required to sustain it, and participants begin entertaining more desperate, militant alternatives.

Enter Braver Angels

The Gettysburg gathering represents people reaching for alternatives to those alternatives. The two moderators, a man and a woman seated at the head of the table, begin the meeting by introducing themselves. Together, they review the workshop's goals, which are helpfully provided on handouts: (1) "More understanding of the experiences, feelings, and beliefs of those who differ with us," (2) "Discovering any areas of commonality in addition to differences," and (3) "Learning something that might be helpful to others in our community and the nation." They emphasize that the focus is curiosity, not changing minds. "Eighty percent of the work," advises one moderator, "is listening."[8] They ask participants' consent in affirming these goals as well as in empowering moderators to gently course-correct discussions in light of these goals. Everyone is asked to "bring their best selves" to the workshop. Ten to twenty observers (including me) sit in a larger circle surrounding the main table and its participants. We slightly outnumber the main group. The moderators briefly welcome us, explaining how Braver Angels values observers, many of whom are either spreading news about Braver Angels or are

---

[8] Here and throughout, quotes and descriptions are from my notes observing and participating in a range of Braver Angels activities, especially the Gettysburg Red-Blue Workshop (September 8, 2018), the Austin Red-Blue Workshop (September 28, 2018), and the Houston Skills Workshop (September 22, 2018). I attended the Second Annual Braver Angels Convention in the summer of 2019, and I have since become a certified moderator, leading multiple workshops in person and online throughout 2020 and 2021. At the behest of Braver Angels, I anonymize the identity of any participant I describe or quote. Additional notes come from online moderator training videos (including archived workshop videos) and manuals, which are made available to moderators and moderators-in-training whose applications have been screened and approved by Braver Angels.

training to be moderators. Observers, however, are enjoined not to participate in the workshop, either verbally or nonverbally.[9]

Moderators then ask participants to state their name, where they live, their political affiliation ("red" or "blue"), and their reasons for coming. By design, the group has seven reds and seven blues, each seated in alternating blue-red order around a table. The observers mirror this half-and-half split. In contrast to everyone else, the moderators keep their political persuasions private for the duration of the workshop. Participants and observers range from their twenties to their seventies. Most are white. As the participants introduce themselves, many identify as ministers or Bible teachers. Several are leaders in local political parties. All of them cite a deep concern with polarization and the danger it poses. "My family is so divided," laments one participant. They "won't consider anything I say." Others tell similar stories of silencing themselves at home or work, culling Facebook friends, or clashing unproductively with neighbors. *Something must be done*, they insist.

Braver Angels formed as the brainchild of writer, activist, and founder-president of the Institute for American Values, David Blankenhorn. In the early 2000s, Blankenhorn gained notoriety as an opponent of same-sex marriage, serving as a star witness for the defense in 2010's *Perry v. Schwarzenegger*, where he argued for upholding California's anti-gay-marriage Proposition 8. Blankenhorn sounded a moderating tone at odds with those of many other conservative gay marriage opponents of the era. He grounded his objections in secular convictions about civil society rather than in Christian fundamentalism, and he affirmed the equal dignity of love between same-sex couples.[10] Throughout this period, he frequently clashed with same-sex marriage proponent Jonathan Rauch (see Blankenhorn and Rauch, "Arriving"). Over time, these encounters grew into a mutual respect between the two, culminating in a jointly authored *New York Times* op-ed proposing a compromise (Blankenhorn and Rauch, "A Reconciliation"). In 2012, Blankenhorn publicly announced a change of heart, arguing in favor of full legal recognition of same-sex marriages (Blankenhorn, "How My View").

The acrimony of that debate and the camaraderie he developed with Rauch moved Blankenhorn to seek ways to detoxify other cultural contentions.

[9] Observers are allowed and encouraged to interact with others (participants and observers alike) during the workshop's frequent breaks for refreshments and lunch.

[10] For an explanation of Blankenhorn's beliefs about civil society, see Institute for American Values. For background on Blankenhorn, see Schulzke.

Capitalizing on the moderate, see-things-from-both-sides bona fides he had earned in the marriage debates, Blankenhorn soon gathered an impressive group of intellectuals, activists, politicians, and academics (including Rauch) to form a 501(c)(3) nonprofit originally called Better Angels.[11] The name referenced Abraham Lincoln's first inaugural address, where, contemplating the looming Civil War, Lincoln appealed to "the better angels of our nature."[12] As discourse surrounding the 2016 presidential election grew ever more divisive, the group formally launched, rebranding itself as Braver Angels in early 2020.[13]

The group's core principles mirror those outlined in the Gettysburg workshop: understanding opponents and their views, searching for areas of common ground, and working for unitary rather than divisive principles. Such goals sound familiar enough, but Braver Angels distinguishes itself from other activist and bridge-building organizations in several ways. It does not aim to change people's political orientations; participants consent to refrain from conversion attempts for the space of the workshop. Nor does Braver Angels attempt to adjudicate between competing factual or ethical-philosophical claims of reds and blues. Most significant, Braver Angels does not seek to chart or claim some neutral middle ground between sides. "It's not trying to end partisanship," explains reporter David Graham, pointing out that the red-blue setup itself presupposes meaningful, durable polarities. "Its premise," he writes, "is not that everyone needs to agree, but simply that they need to be able to talk to one another, and that such a skill has been lost." The goal isn't enlightened centrism but what Blankenhorn calls "accurate disagreement" (see Blankenhorn, "Blue Said"). Differences of values and

[11] Technically, Braver Angels operates as part of Blankenhorn's Institute for American Values (IAV). An earlier version of the group's website explained, "IAV is currently doing business as (DBA) Better Angels, which means that people and organizations can make checks out and issue payments to Better Angels if they wish and we can pay people as Better Angels. . . . Although the entire corpus of IAV work dating back to 1987 is preserved on the IAV website, the only activity IAV is engaged in now is Better Angels" (Better Angels, "Legal and Financial Information"). This explanation is no longer on the website; I reference the Internet Archive version in my works cited. The group's profile on Guidestar, which the current website links to, confirms that this relationship is still in place as of this writing (Guidestar).

[12] Lincoln's full quote: "I am loath to close. We are not enemies, but friends. We must not be enemies. Though passion may have strained, it must not break our bonds of affection. The mystic chords of memory, stretching from every battle-field, and patriot grave, to every living heart and hearthstone, all over this broad land, will yet swell the chorus of the Union, when again touched, as surely they will be, by the better angels of our nature" (Lincoln).

[13] In fall 2019, an older nonprofit, The Better Angels Society, sued Better Angels for copyright infringement. A court ruling found that the two groups were similar enough in purpose that some brand confusion might occur (Grzincic). Better Angels thus renamed itself Braver Angels. In this essay, I have honored this change, updating my sources where possible.

opinions matter, in other words, but hyperpolarization warps real differences into distorted and damaging caricatures. Healthy antagonism mutates into political enmity. Braver Angels seeks to disrupt that enmity while preserving the reality of difference.

With a small professional staff advised by a board of directors, Braver Angels does much of its logistical work online. (During the COVID-19 pandemic in 2020–21, Braver Angels transitioned all of its workshops and meetings to online Zoom formats.) Anyone may join for twelve dollars, which connects them to email news updates, members-only online resources, and monthly group chats with Blankenhorn and other staff on Zoom. Regional organizers and trained workshop moderators connect through similar teleconferencing meetings. The group follows "the Braver Angels rule," meaning that every level of the organization (staff, boards, local leadership, and workshops) consists of a nearly equal number of red and blue members, with a maximum sixty-forty split allowed. The organization publishes regular articles, podcasts, and YouTube interviews. Red and blue members are encouraged to co-write op-eds for their local newspapers and websites decrying polarization and touting Braver Angels principles. The website also hosts videos of sample workshops as well as training materials for prospective moderators. As of this writing, Braver Angels boasts over six thousand paying members and hundreds of volunteer leaders, moderators, and organizers (Braver Angels, "Press Release").

Blankenhorn's first forays into depolarization consisted of long retreats with groups of "red" and "blue" participants meeting face-to-face. Those experiences led him to tap William "Bill" Doherty, a Minnesota-based family therapist specializing in counseling for couples contemplating divorce. Over dozens of workshops, Doherty and Blankenhorn honed the format into a shorter, smaller, and more intensively moderated workshop. Their experiments garnered positive media attention and mostly glowing testimonials. The spectacle of apparent political enemies simply listening and interacting respectfully has proven prime fodder for hopeful stories by major networks and magazines across the nation (see Ferguson; Sisk).

Today, Braver Angels offers a growing number of several workshop models. In addition to the Red-Blue workshop (in three-hour and day-long versions), the group sponsors Skills for Bridging the Divide workshops, designed to hone cross-partisan conversational techniques; Depolarizing Within workshops, about tempering polarizing tendencies within oneself and one's political group; Families and Politics workshops, tailored to help navigate contentious family gatherings where relatives disagree politically; Debates that resemble more facilitated discussions than us-versus-them sparring matches; and structured one-to-one conversations with people on "the other side." The signature activity of Braver Angels, however, remains the original, day-long Red-Blue workshop I've been describing. In this chapter, I focus mainly on the Red-Blue format, with some reference to the Skills, Depolarizing Within, and Debate models.

Workshopping Accurate Disagreement

Doherty's long-form Red-Blue workshop model travels through three main exercises: stereotypes, fishbowl, and questions of curiosity. The trajectory traces an arc from critical self-reflection to careful listening to respectful interaction. Moderators are vetted and trained in intensive workshops (which can now be accessed online). They use a detailed guide from Braver Angels, complete with a schedule breakdown, scripts for exercise instructions, transition dialogue, sample phrases for intervention and redirection, and troubleshooting tips (Braver Angels, "Red-Blue Workshops Moderator Guide").

In the first exercise, moderators split the group into reds and blues, each color retreating to a separate space accompanied by one moderator. (I followed the reds in the workshops I observed.) The moderator directs the group to brainstorm some stereotypes they believe the other side has of them, recording the terms on a large poster-size sheet. She instructs the group to boil the list down to five main stereotypes.[14] The moderator then processes each stereotype one by one. Participants first explain why that stereotype is unfair or false. Then they must suggest a "kernel of truth" to the stereotype; perhaps, for example, the stereotype was true only historically, or it is currently exhibited by a small but noisy segment of the side. "If it doesn't make you wince," advises the moderator, "it's probably not a kernel." The moderator writes down both the refutations and the kernels on more poster sheets. Now and then the moderator probes for clarity or gently pushes the group to make sure that the kernels produce the requisite winces. Reds and blues then rejoin each other, taping their session's sheets to the walls for all to

[14] According to the Red-Blue Workshops Moderator Guide, the most common stereotypes reds list are *racist, uncaring (for people in need), anti-woman, anti-immigrant,* and *anti-science bible thumpers.* Blues most often list *arrogant/elitist, dependent on Big Government, baby-killers, fiscally irresponsible,* and *unpatriotic* (Braver Angels, "Red-Blue Workshops" 32).

see. A representative from each group walks everyone through their group's findings. Moderators then ask participants to share what they learned about the other side from these reports and whether they discern areas of common ground.

The "fishbowl" exercise follows. One side's members form a small circle of chairs in the center of the room. In a larger circle surrounding them, the other side's members sit. For the next twenty minutes, one side listens as the inner circle discusses two questions: "Why do you think your side's values and policies are good for the country?" and "What are your reservations about your side?" As in the first exercise, the conversation sticks to one side's reflection about itself; moderators gently interrupt any diatribes about the other side. The sides then swap places, and the new inner circle discusses the same questions (with admonition from the moderator that the answers are not to address or refute what the other side said on the previous turn). This too is followed by a debriefing period where participants report back things that struck them, with moderators steering comments away from criticism of the other side.

The final major exercise of the workshop once more splits up reds and blues. This time, moderators ask each breakout group to generate four "questions of curiosity" to pose to the other side. These questions, they stress, may not be "gotcha" questions (*How could you claim to be antiracist and vote for a bigot like Trump?*), nor can they assume beliefs, facts, or framings the other side might not share (*Are you fine weakening the family through no-fault divorce?*). Instead, questions must emerge from genuine curiosity about the other side's beliefs and policies. In the breakout sessions, moderators take a strong hand in guiding these questions, identifying covert attack questions and modeling alternative phrasings more likely to elicit quality responses. Groups then split and recombine to make two mixed subgroups, each with three or four reds and three or four blues. The reds and blues then take turns posing their questions, answering them, and—with careful moderation—following up for more information.

After one last report-back session, participants brainstorm next steps, places in their own lives and communities they might use the discoveries and connections they made over the course of the day. Moderators introduce participants to the idea of Braver Angels Alliances: long-term, locally organized coalitions of reds and blues who commit to remaining in contact and working together on issues of common interest (see Braver Angels, "Alliances"). Everyone checks in one last time with takeaway thoughts and impressions, takes a group photo (with those who wish to participate), and departs. The day is over.

Braver Angels' other workshops echo the listening-sharing practices the Red-Blue workshop realizes. The Skills for Bridging the Divide and Depolarizing Within workshops each rely on a lecture-with-exercises format where a single moderator shares tips and tricks and leads participants through brief exercises. Detailed handouts and slides reinforce step-by-step points in the moderator's lectures.[15] Most of the points stress analyzing and interrupting cycles of polarization. The Skills workshop about talking to political opponents, for example, introduces the failure modes that often occur when we try to talk with "the other side": ignoring, escalating, and trying to convert. Confronted with someone standing on the other side of a political divide, we might duck out or change the subject. We might fall into a defense/attack mode, replicating the us/them dynamics of online culture and ending in a shouting match. Or we might seek to overwhelm opponents with evidence. (After all, if only they understood things as we do, they'd see the folly of their ways and convert to our side, right?) The workshop then pivots to introducing and trying out conversational strategies to sidestep such pitfalls. Example scripts provide models for signaling invitation to conversation, reflecting what the other says, and asking open "questions of understanding." Role-play exercises allow participants to test and refine their own approach to embodying these scripts. Crucial to the enterprise is the relinquishment of any attempt to convert or defeat those on the other side. As in the Red-Blue workshop, "accurate disagreement," not victory, is the goal.

The Depolarizing Within workshop focuses on conversational interventions into one's own and one's group's tendencies to stereotype, dismiss, ridicule, or otherwise express contempt for the other side. The workshop begins with introspective challenges designed to make participants aware of their own degree of affective polarization. How often, asks one question, do you find yourself referring to "those people" on the other side dismissively and unreflectively while insisting on nuanced representations of your own side? After reviewing these polarizing tendencies, the workshop offers a four-step counterstrategy for talking with polarized members of one's

---

[15] Throughout this section, I refer to both my notes from workshops and debates I have observed as well as the scripts, instructions, and videos in the training section of the Braver Angels website, especially the "Skills Workshop Comprehensive Presenter's Guide," the "Depolarizing Within Moderator Guide," and the "Debate Chair Training Manual." These materials are updated constantly, so my citations refer to the guides as of specific dates.

own group: Listening (*I hear how concerned you are about X*), Affirming (*I'm worried about X, too*), Pivoting (*Lately I've talked one-on-one to some people who support X, and it's made me rethink some things*), and Perspective (*I find that the X supporters I see on the news aren't representative of what many X supporters actually think*). As with the Skills workshop, small role-playing exercises push participants to try out their own versions of conversational steps. Much of what the workshop does is slow down and spell out conversational moments that might otherwise get skipped over. Instead of jumping right to the point one wants to make, the workshop insists, a depolarizing conversationalist makes the effort to explicitly signal—one might say *perform*—discrete acts of listening, affirmation, pivoting, and challenge. Such signaling can feel artificial. It lacks the high drama of "owning" one's enemy through a clever talking point. But the structure's artifice and the deliberate tempo serve a purpose: disrupting the emotionally reactive feedback loops that drive polarization.

A similarly productive artificiality characterizes the Braver Angels Debates, a form developed more recently by Braver Angels staff member April Lawson. Patterned after Oxford Union chamber debates. Lawson's model resembles a formalized community discussion more than a traditional, us-versus-them debate. Moderated by a chair, Debates feature a single resolution (say, *Public school teachers should be allowed to train in and carry firearms to work*). Unlike the case in other Braver Angels activities, Debate participants do not mark their red/blue affiliations. After giving a brief introduction to the Debate rules, the chair invites speeches for and against the resolution alternative. Questions from the gathered participants follow each speech. All proceedings operate through a quaint set of parliamentary conventions. Participants must address the moderator as Madam (or Mr.) Chair. The chair wields a gavel, pounding it to recognize speakers or gently correct breaches of protocol. The primary rule is that those who wish to question a speaker must direct their inquiries through the chair. Thus, questioners ask not "How can you support a standard that guarantees increased gun accidents?" but "Madam Chair, I wonder how the speaker might account for the increased risk of gun injuries that his proposal invites?" Having participated in several Debates, I can attest that this aspect of the exercise feels faintly silly, like an adult game of Mother May I.

Yet that silliness (which chairs regularly acknowledge) forms part of the Debate's mechanism. The old-fashioned conventions—"Madame Chair," the gavel, being recognized—grant a quasi-*Verfremdungseffekt* sense of theatricality in which participants have permission to take risks. It tempers a potentially acrimonious debate with a sense of theatrical playfulness. Routing disagreements through the chair proves integral. The difference between a direct attack and a third-party question seems trivial in theory; in practice, however, the chair provides a beneficial triangulation that diffuses the impassioned dyadic energy of partisan disagreement.[16] Addressing the chair adds a roadblock between emotion and action, requiring that speakers detour around polarizing pitfalls such as ad hominem responses or intimidation tactics. The format makes criticizing and being criticized seem more manageable, less threatening to one's social identity, than a person-to-person confrontation. As with all Braver Angels exercises, the Debate uses some degree of facilitated role play to help participants practice deliberative rather than reactive encounters.

Ordinary, Hard Work

Despite the considerable press Braver Angels gets for its "groundbreaking," "important" efforts, most of the organization's insights are nothing new. Variations on the exercises espoused by Skills and Depolarizing Within workshops echo those common to practically any field that does team building, group therapy, or conflict transformation (including theater).[17] I led and participated in variations on most of these in classrooms and conferences for years before encountering them again in Braver Angels. The workshops' goals are equally modest. *Try listening without trying to win or convert. Suspend attacks and defenses. Look for commonalities.* Nor are Braver Angels' depolarizing mechanisms especially mysterious. Face-to-face with their rivals, investing attention and care into hearing and respectfully engaging the other person, participants dampen the us/them dynamics reinforced on social media. Starting first with self-criticism in the safe enclave of their own side, participants venture outside of media echo chambers, opening themselves to hearing "what the other side thinks" from the other side itself. Participants articulate and appreciate nuance, seeing at least the possibility of alternative frames for values, issues, or problems. Braver Angels activities basically un-internet red-blue relations.[18]

---

[16] I owe this insight to Liz Fletcher, LCSW.
[17] For studies of theatrical facilitation techniques, see Peterson; Kuftinec.
[18] Even the online versions of these workshops depend upon Zoom's face-to-face affordances.

Modest as such means and goals are, though, the workshops demand immense effort. I was shocked at how exhausting it can be simply to observe
Red-Blue sessions. The "bring your best self" instruction that underlies the
workshop's ground rules translates to affect management. The moderators
remind (and re-remind) participants that authentic listening involves nonverbal as well as verbal signals. Eye-rolling, sighing, and similar body language communicate judgment rather than curiosity. The moderators enjoin
observers (those not directly participating) to suppress all verbal and nonverbal participation for the duration of the workshop (breaks and lunch
excepted). Participants also mimic this blank-slate listening during the fishbowl exercise. Such suppression proves surprisingly hard. Reflecting afterward, several observers and participants alike noted the odd strain exacted
by *not rolling your eyes*.

Other workshops only intensify these constraints. Faced with a (pretend)
opponent, we not only have to not react with hostility; we must perform active curiosity and positive feedback. We muffle shock, outrage, impatience,
and annoyance at alarming views in the rhetorical cotton: *I hear you saying
that . . .* ; *It probably won't surprise you to hear that I see things differently . . .* ;
Madam Chair, I would ask the speaker . . . Some workshops' role-play exercises
impose the added strain of occupying the (scripted) views of opponents. It is
one thing to pretend to talk to argues-at-family-get-togethers Uncle Steve; it
is another thing altogether to *become* Uncle Steve without criticism or caricature. Even the playfulness of the Debate format cannot completely dispel an
electric tension—not merely at confronting in-person, face-to-face disagreement but also at making the effort to perform "your best self" fully open to
listening to an opponent's perspective.

Such efforts (and the relief once they cease) recall Arlie Russell Hochschild's
writing on emotional work, "the management of feeling to create a publicly observable facial and bodily display," sustaining that countenance by
inducing or suppressing feeling (7). Hochschild focuses especially on commercial institutions imposing emotional requirements on workers. Airline
flight attendants must be unflappable and cheerful; bill collectors must be
by turns understanding and unyielding. Drawing on Erving Goffman and
Konstantin Stanislavski, Hochschild further distinguishes between "surface
acting," putting on a false affective front at odds with actual feeling, and "deep
acting," altering one's inner self to produce required affects (35–37). Other
writers extend the idea of emotional work beyond commercial settings. As
James C. Scott points out, in social contexts of oppression or unequal power,

the privileged often mark themselves by the amount of acting they do not have to do to get along (28–29). In Braver Angels workshops, however, all participants commit to surface acting work. That is, they agree (at least) to *not react*, suppressing the expressions that reinforce their alignment with "us" against "them." In so doing, they defuse the emotional reactivity and activism elements of social polarization. Such affective work subtends, perhaps even enables, the critical work of setting aside the biases of outgroup prejudice to make room for curiosity and change.

Braver Angels imposes a performed ethos, a for-the-nonce habitus, of mutual good faith. To be sure, the ethos relies on intense emotional work and rigidly facilitated structures. Braver Angels workshops do not present themselves as a replacement for normal politics. They are instead a proof-of-concept run at comity, a demonstration that agonism without agony is possible. The Red-Blue workshop resembles an antiprotest, creating rather than breaking civility.

The Trouble with Civility

At that term, however, various left-progressive alarms go off. *Civility* has a tarnished reputation in many social justice communities. The seemingly anodyne concept all too often functions as a way of minimizing activist anger through appeals to tone (*Maybe you'd get more support if you were a little calmer?*). Civility tends to reflect and preserve the communicative conventions of a society's (often white, male) powerholders. A panoply of ready-made cultural stereotypes—the angry Black man, the killjoy/hysterical feminist, the uncultured poor person—all mobilize civility appeals to dismiss minority expressions of political discontent with extant power structures. Sometimes civility needs disrupting. In this light, a Red-Blue workshop might prove a hard sell to people who are already obliged to do tons of emotional work just to live their lives, such as people of color in white space, queer and trans* folk in cis-het space, women in patriarchal space.[19] It is no casual thing to ask structurally disenfranchised identities to be vulnerable and nonreactive with people who may be incredulous toward the very idea of systemic oppressions—or, worse, people who may openly support

---

[19] For an explanation of white space (a model I am adapting to account for sexual and gendered axes of identity), see Anderson.

cis-het-centric, racist, or patriarchal systems. Such unpaid labor sounds aw-fully close to the emotional, activist, and educational work minorities are already too often formally and informally tasked with doing: teaching the privileged classes lessons in Privilege 101 while *not acting too upset about it*. I can't say that my experience so far with Braver Angels completely dispels my reservations on this score.

That said, no one obligates anyone to join a Braver Angels workshop, and most workshops underline the need to be selective about when and with whom to attempt depolarizing overtures. Nationally, the organization boasts the support of plenty of people who live singly or multiply marginalized lives. The privileged, after all, aren't the only people with an interest in ac-curate disagreement. A government and culture deadlocked in doom-loop enmity does little to advance the cause of redressing structural oppressions. Affectively polarized systems, Braver Angels points out, don't work for anyone, including and especially those on the margins of society. The participants of color in the workshops I observed (all of which took place in majority-white settings) were among the most active, eager attendees. They seemed to have little difficulty sharing their anger or pain. Selection bias plays a role in this observation; I did not observe or interview people who chose not to come. Yet for those who did participate, the workshops' strict moderation was designed to make sure their opponents were at least open to hearing them. Certainly, it would be obnoxious to pressure those already unjustly tasked with emotional work to do still more of it. But it would also be troubling to assume that depolarization can or should be solely an affair of the privileged.

As it turns out, the hardest sell Braver Angels faces involves attracting red-leaning people. In accordance with Braver Angels principles, a Red-Blue workshop cannot happen if organizers (who must also be red-blue pairs) fail to recruit equal numbers of red and blue participants. Yet, across the nation, organizers report that finding red members to participate represents, in one moderator's words, "the bottleneck." By a factor of three to one, he told me, blue workshop volunteers outnumber red ones, even in majority-red areas. Logistic and geographic factors may explain some of the discrepancy. But for many reds I spoke to, their reticence stems from apprehension: they're afraid to participate. One red participant said he came braced to flee the minute blues started attacking him, *as he assumed they would*. Another red I spoke to (an observer) feared that, as a realtor in a deep blue neighborhood, coming out as conservative could kill his business. Several reds reported feeling like they had to keep silent about their beliefs or face personal or professional blowback.

Cognizant of such sentiments among reds, Braver Angels has begun devoting considerable efforts to the red-recruitment problem. In January 2019, they disseminated a document for organizers and moderators titled "Getting and Keeping Reds in Better Angels" and written by red-identified volunteer Paul Norris. Norris affirms and explains reds' reticence, writing that "the predominance of blues in entertainment, academia and the news media leave many or most reds feeling that their values are being assaulted on a daily basis." Because of this, he continues, "reds will show up to Better Angels events fearing or expecting to be ambushed, face conversion attempts or endure personal attacks driven by anger and judgment" (5). Norris makes several suggestions for combating this problem, chief among them getting blues to recognize the reality of red fears in this matter. Norris reinforces similar arguments by Braver Angels founders. Blankenhorn regularly urges people (especially blues) to recognize the extent to which they converse in an ideological dialect that can alienate those not already in the in-group (Blankenhorn, "Blue Said"). Terms that seem positive or neutral to one side (such as "diversity" for blues or "traditional values" for reds) can read as exclusionary code words to the other. In moderator training materials, Doherty and Blankenhorn acknowledge that even the language of facilitation itself comes with a blue tinge. Having "native speakers" of red dialects in all aspects of planning and implementation, Braver Angels stresses, is vital to combatting reds' sense of apprehension (Braver Angels, "3 Workshop").

I realize some readers (especially left-leaning ones) may greet these red concerns with incredulity. To be clear, I do not equate the *material* risks informing a red's nervousness about attending a workshop with the precarity of (say) a left-leaning queer Black woman navigating everyday life. But the *felt* risks of cross-partisan encounters matter, too. Recall that, within many red media echo chambers, the only picture of blue-leaning people many reds know is of media stars and millionaires broadcasting contempt for conservatives. Conversely, within many blue media echo chambers, Trump and his most extreme MAGA hat–wearing supporters monopolize the image of what it means to lean right. Are such impressions inaccurate? Tendentious? Surely. But the effects they have in perpetuating polarization remain. Neuroscientist Jonah Kaplan describes research he and his colleagues have done in scanning the brains of people as they are asked to consider counterarguments strongly opposed to their beliefs. "The response in the brain that we see," he says, "is very similar to what would happen if, say, you were walking through the forest and came across a bear." Our body shifts into a fight-or-flight response (quoted in McRaney). We experience deep political difference as somatic as well as mental stress. Artificial and protected as a Red-Blue workshop may be, the subjective experience of meeting an enemy is intense. Comity is not for the faint-hearted.

The Risks and Rewards of Emotional Labor

For the participants I observed, right and left, the stress of participating paid off in simple but meaningful discoveries that their fears of the other side were ill-founded. One red reflected how surprising it was to hear that her blue neighbors supported the U.S. Constitution. A blue found it shocking how damaging the red list of stereotypes was. Blue stereotypes like "fuzzy thinker" or "tree-hugger" may sting, but red stereotypes like "racist" or "anti-woman" bespeak deeply stigmatizing moral judgments. "No wonder they distrust us," she concluded.[20] One red in Austin seized on the blues' statement that they value "speech and actions that honor others' experiences." That description, he explained, helped him see that blues' concerns about "PC" language was more about honoring people being described than it was about tut-tutting him personally. Blues confessed surprise at how nuanced and thoughtful reds were regarding issues like immigration as well as how conflicted reds generally were about having Trump as a representative of their beliefs.

The standout moment for me, though, came in the final phases of the Gettysburg Red-Blue workshop, when reds and blues posed "questions of curiosity" to each other. In the discussion around a question about political correctness, one red (a white woman) turned to the gathered blues (most of whom were people of color), took a breath, and ventured an admission. "I keep hearing about 'white privilege,'" she said, awkward and flustered. "It's always made me angry. But, really, I just don't know what it means. What is 'white privilege'?" I cringed (inwardly, doing my best to maintain a neutral exterior). This scenario—*Please, person of color, explain to me, a white*

[20] In their training materials, Blankenhorn and Doherty note that such moral asymmetry of red and blue stereotypes is common in Red-Blue workshops. Red stereotypes that emerge from the stereotypes exercise are in general much graver and more stigmatizing than blue stereotypes. Norris elaborates that, rightly or wrongly, "reds tend to see blues as the more aggressive party and the side more likely to indulge in name calling and personal attacks" (5).

person, my own structural privilege—encapsulates the paradigmatic, eye-roll-inducing nightmare of white-centric social activism. Every apprehension I had about Braver Angels being an exercise in assuaging privileged people's feelings came flooding back. Yet the blues responded with generosity. "I don't know that you can understand it," said one blue. "My white husband doesn't. My daughter even doesn't. You don't know what it's like to enter a room and lead with your race." She then related a story of being accosted verbally in a local grocery store by a man who told her to learn English or go back to her own country. Jaws dropped around the table. This blue had been an active participant throughout the day—funny, self-deprecating, charmingly honest. She chuckled a bit here at the memory: "I'm from Connecticut!" The red who asked the question shook her head in disbelief, sat back, deeply affected by what she had heard.

Are such moments of acting and honesty, of risk and generosity, human flourishing in action? I do not know. I do know the takeaway for me and other participants of the Gettysburg workshop and other Braver Angels activities I have seen involves an untidy mix of exhaustion, reflection, and hope—a feeling not dissimilar to tragic catharsis or the afterglow of a well-played evening on stage. I have rarely felt more vividly human. Like any intense bodily experience—pain or vomiting—the extended effort of comity shocks me into myself. It leaves me haunted, thinking and rethinking. Seeing others, including my political enemies, similarly stunned multiplies the impact. This, I think, is how accurate, honest disagreement with other humans feels: not so much good or bad as powerful—sacred, even.

Such felt authenticity causes me to reflect on all that surface acting—suffering (in the sense of *tolerating*) the tension of agonism—that Braver Angels asks of participants. Hochschild, we should recall, distrusts emotional work. She worries that, by performing an emotional state at odds with our actual one for some institutional end, we risk alienating "a source of self that we honor as deep and integral to our individuality" (7). Much work has been done to protect and reclaim the sources of self that only rage can access. The blue zones of the U.S. cultural and political spectrum are currently witnessing a necessary corrective to centuries of marginalized people (women especially) having been obliged to suppress their anger at injustice for the sake of others' comfort (see Traister; Cooper; Chemaly; Ahmed). In this light, as someone multiply privileged, I acknowledge how complicated it is to endorse the emotional effort of suppressing the passions of political enmity, especially for the sake of interacting with those whose positions cause that anger. But *complicated* doesn't mean *wrong*. In the workshops I saw, being able to suspend an angry retort enabled a deeper—not warm-and-fuzzy, not even necessarily pleasant, but deeper—appreciation of the other person. Not reacting helped me to get to a place that absorbing the daily outrages of my standard newsfeeds rarely does. Anger, fed-upness, and righteous indignation can move us to action, but they can also render us vulnerable to manipulation and narrow-mindedness. "Calls for greater civility can be manipulative and disingenuous ways to get people to shut up," acknowledges philosopher Amy Olberding. "But demonstrations of incivility can also be a manipulative and disingenuous way to get people to shut up—i.e., incivility can also be a social dominance strategy." At its best, I would venture, Braver Angels' comity exercises build up a degree of ideological inoculation, creating resistances not to strong passions but to thoughtlessness and solipsism. The imposed openness means that anger gets not so much replaced by as complemented with curiosity.

Still, like theater with a wrenching catharsis, Braver Angels is not for everyone. Those who volunteer for a depolarization workshop are likely already more open to depolarization, a self-selected group of people able and willing to take on the strain of interaction and assume the burden of comity's emotional work. Braver Angels moderators are trained to emphasize that the techniques they teach require special conditions (safety, mutual respect, consent of those involved) to work. Neither they nor I recommend depolarizing overtures as the perfect, one-size-fits-all activist approach. Some moments call for anger, decisive action, and boundary setting. In such cases the slow work of nuanced inquiry and becalmed exchange risks smothering cries for justice and equality beneath a veneer of politeness.

The group's depolarizing techniques also depend upon the good faith of participants. Especially since the 2020 election and its aftermath, I worry that Braver Angels' "bring your best self" approach may be at a disadvantage in reacting to bad faith mis- and disinformation agents that increasingly warp political discourse. As media scholars Whitney Phillips and Ryan Milner note, manipulators, propagandists, and "conspiracy entrepreneurs" flood channels of democratic communication with damaging half-truths or falsehoods about opponents while undermining the legitimacy of electoral systems and news media. Such bad actors exploit norms civic interchange, often circulating under the cover of innocent discussion (*Lots of people are saying . . . I'm just asking questions . . .*) while actually fomenting civic enmity and political distrust. *He's not really a U.S. citizen. She's a secret child abuser.*

The only way "they" can win is if they cheat; if they win, you know they cheated.
These messages are polluting, Phillips and Milner argue, in that their damaging effects spread even via attempts to fact-check or discredit their content (140–45). Affective polarization calcifies into what Russell Muirhead and Nancy L. Rosenblum term "epistemic polarization," an us/them divergence over the basic components of a shared reality. Whereas affective polarization makes democracy difficult, epistemic polarization renders collective political action impossible (129). I harbor deep concerns about Braver Angels' ethos of open listening vulnerability to and effectiveness against epistemic pollution. The racist messaging and partisan lies that led to the January 6, 2021, insurrection attempt in which the U.S. Capitol was stormed, for example, may require sharper interventions than generous "questions of understanding." Some ideas and expressions ought not be suffered.

That said, labeling certain beliefs as polluting still leaves me facing the reality of the believers themselves. I may be certain about the wrongness of their views, yet those who disagree with me persist. They do not evaporate when my side wins elections. They do not vanish from my neighborhood, institutions, or nation because I block them on social media. No degree of fury, incredulity, pity, or fear from me magically converts them to my side. If we are not to destroy each other in civil war or doom-loop stagnation, then, we must suffer each other. Such enforced comity between us need not always play out with inside voices or soft-touch language. I have begun to think of activist strategies in terms of gears on a manual transmission car. Braver Angels–style depolarization is one gear among many. It doesn't work for every kind of road or every kind of load. You'll burn out the engine if you stay in it forever. But it's a useful gear to be able to shift into when necessary. It can get us out of ruts and navigate impasses that antagonism alone cannot. It's a mode to use when the end isn't "victory" but a better, less agonizing contest over what human flourishing can and should mean.

Works Cited

Abujbara, Juman, Andrew Boyd, Dave Mitchell, and Marcel Taminato, editors. *Beautiful Rising: Creative Resistance from the Global South*. New York, OR Books, 2017.

Ahmed, Sara. *Living a Feminist Life*. Durham, NC, Duke University Press, 2017.

Aikin, Scott F., and Robert B. Talisse. "Civic Enmity." *3 Quarks Daily*, October 8, 2018. www.3quarksdaily.com/3quarksdaily/2018/10/civic-enmity.html. Accessed March 1, 2019.

Alinsky, Saul. *Rules for Radicals: A Practical Primer for Realistic Radicals.* New York, Vintage, 1989.

Anderson, Elijah. "The White Space." *Sociology of Race and Ethnicity*, vol. 1, no. 1, 2015, pp. 10–21. doi:10.1177/2332649214561306.

Beck, Julie. "This Article Won't Change Your Mind: The Facts on Why Facts Alone Can't Fight False Beliefs." *The Atlantic*, March 13, 2017. www.theatlantic.com/science/arch ive/2017/03/this-article-wont-change-your-mind/519093/. Accessed March 1, 2019.

Blankenhorn, David. "Blue Said, Red Said." *The American Interest*, vol. 13, no. 5, March 7, 2018. https://www.the-american-interest.com/2018/03/07/blue-said-red-said/. Accessed March 3, 2019.

Blankenhorn, David. "How My View on Gay Marriage Changed." *New York Times*, June 23, 2012. www.nytimes.com/2012/06/23/opinion/how-my-view-on-gay-marriage-changed.html. Accessed 1 Mar 2019.

Blankenhorn, David, and Jonathan Rauch. "Arriving at a Compromise on Gay Marriage." Interview by Neal Conan. *Talk of the Nation*, NPR, March 2, 2009. www.npr.org/templa tes/transcript/transcript.php?storyId=101349852.

Blankenhorn, David, and Jonathan Rauch. "A Reconciliation on Gay Marriage." *New York Times*, February 22, 2009. www.nytimes.com/2009/02/22/opinion/22rauch.html. Accessed March 1, 2019.

Braver Angels. "Alliances." 2020. https://braverangels.org/what-we-do/alliances/. Accessed May 15, 2020.

Braver Angels. "Debate Chair Training Manual." Updated March 3, 2020. Braver Angels Google Drive. Accessed May 17, 2020.

Braver Angels. "Legal and Financial Information." December 27, 2017. web.archive.org/ web/20180213153054/https://better-angels.org/legal-and-financial-information. Accessed March 1, 2019.

Braver Angels. "Press Release." January 24, 2019. https://braverangels.org/better-angels-announces-state-of-the-union-address-on-january-31st/. Accessed May 15, 2020.

Braver Angels. "Red-Blue Workshops Moderator Guide." Updated March 12, 2020. Braver Angels Google Drive. Accessed May 15, 2020.

Braver Angels. "Skills Workshop Comprehensive Presenter's Guide." Updated March 15, 2020. Better Angels Google Drive. Accessed May 17, 2020.

Braver Angels. "3 Workshop Design Assumptions." YouTube, May 17, 2019. youtu.be/ 7tMmu60XgBM. Accessed May 15, 2020.

Braver Angels. "What We Do." 2020. https://braverangels.org/what-we-do/. Accessed May 15, 2020.

Chemaly, Soraya. *Rage Becomes Her: The Power of Women's Anger.* New York, Atria Books, 2018.

Cooper, Brittney. *Eloquent Rage: A Black Feminist Discovers Her Superpower.* New York, St. Martin's Press, 2018.

Drutman, Lee. "We Need Political Parties. But Their Hyperpartisanship Could Destroy American Democracy." *Vox*, September 5, 2017. www.vox.com/the-big-idea/2017/9/ 5/16227700/hyperpartisanship-identity-american-democracy-problems-solutions-doom-loop. Accessed March 1, 2019.

Ferguson, Andrew. "Can Marriage Counseling Save America?" *The Atlantic*, December 2019. https://www.theatlantic.com/magazine/archive/2019/12/better-angels-can-this-union-be-saved/600775/?mc_cid=f45340583e&mc_eid=0b1de896f9.

Goldhaber, Michael H. "The Attention Economy and the Net." *First Monday*, vol. 2, no. 4, April 7, 1997. firstmonday.org/article/view/519/440. Accessed March 1, 2019.

Graham, David A. "The Bipartisan Group That's Not Afraid of Partisanship." *The Atlantic*, December 29, 2018. https://www.theatlantic.com/politics/archive/2018/12/better-ang els-affective-polarization-political-divide/578539/. Accessed March 1, 2019.

Greene, Joshua. *Moral Tribes: Emotion, Reason, and the Gap between Us and Them.* New York, Penguin, 2018.

Grzincic, Barbara. "In Brief: Ken Burns' Nonprofit Wins Trademark War of 'Better Angels,' Judge Rules." *Westlaw News*, November 18, 2019. https://www.reuters.com/arti cle/better-angels-lawsuit/in-brief-ken-burns-nonprofit-wins-trademark-war-of-bet ter-angels-judge-rules-idUSL2N27Z023. Accessed May 13, 2020.

Guidestar. "Institute for American Values." 2019. www.guidestar.org/profile/13-3400377. Accessed May 15, 2020.

Harris, Tristan. Interview by Ezra Klein. "How Technology Is Designed to Bring Out the Worst in Us." *Vox*, February 19, 2018. www.vox.com/technology/2018/2/19/17020310/ tristan-harris-facebook-twitter-humane-tech-time. Accessed March 1, 2019.

Hochschild, Arlie Russell. *The Managed Heart: Commercialization of Human Feeling.* 1979. Berkeley, University of California Press, 2012.

Institute for American Values. "To Study and Strengthen Civil Society." October 2011. americanvalues.org/catalog/pdfs/2011-10.pdf. Accessed March 1, 2019.

Kahan, Dan. "What's Worse? Macedonian 'Fake News' or Russian Distortions of Social Proof?" *Cultural Cognition Blog*, Yale Law School, March 5, 2018. www.culturalcognit ion.net/blog/2018/3/5/whats-worse-macedonian-fake-news-or-russian-distortions-of-s.html. Accessed March 1, 2019.

Kuftinec, Sonja Arsham. *Theatre, Facilitation, and Nation Formation in the Balkans and Middle East.* New York, Palgrave Macmillan, 2009.

Lincoln, Abraham. "First Inaugural Address." March 4, 1861. *Abraham Lincoln Online*, 2018. www.abrahamlincolnonline.org/lincoln/speeches/1inaug.htm. Accessed March 1, 2019.

Mason, Lilliana. *Uncivil Agreement: How Politics Became Our Identity.* Chicago, University of Chicago Press, 2018.

McRaney, David, host. "The Neuroscience of Changing Your Mind." *You Are Not So Smart*, episode 093, January 13, 2017. https://youarenotsosmart.com/2017/01/13/ yanss-093-the-neuroscience-of-changing-your-mind/. Accessed March 3, 2018.

Mouffe, Chantal. *The Democratic Paradox.* New York, Verso, 2000.

Muirhead, Russell, and Nancy L. Rosenblum. *A Lot of People Are Saying: The New Conspiracism and the Assault on Democracy.* Princeton, NJ, Princeton University Press, 2019.

Norris, Paul. "Getting and Keeping Reds in Better Angels." Braver Angels, January 21, 2019. Braver Angels Google Drive. Accessed March 2, 2019.

Olberding, Amy. "Twenty Theses Regarding Civility." *Daily Nous* (blog), August 30, 2019. http://dailynous.com/2019/08/30/20-theses-regarding-civility-guest-post-amy-olberding/. Accessed May 17, 2020.

Peterson, Sheila, editor. *Applied Theatre: Facilitation: Pedagogies, Practices, Resilience.* New York, Bloomsbury, 2016.

Pew Research Center. "Partisanship and Political Animosity in 2016." June 2016. www. people-press.org/wp-content/uploads/sites/4/2016/06/06-22-16-Partisanship-and-animosity-release.pdf. Accessed March 1, 2019.

Phillips, Whitney, and Ryan M. Milner. *You Are Here: A Field Guide for Navigating Polarized Speech, Conspiracy Theories, and Our Polluted Media Landscape.* Cambridge, MA, MIT Press, 2021.

Schulzke, Eric. "Liberal Thinker Champions Family Values." *Deseret News* (Salt Lake City, UT), August 29, 2012. www.deseretnews.com/article/765600372/David-Blankenhorn-Cultivating-the-roots-of-American-culture.html?pg=all. Accessed March 1, 2019.

Scott, James C. *Domination and the Arts of Resistance: Hidden Transcripts.* New Haven, CT, Yale University Press, 1990.

Sisk, Chris. "Group Uses Marriage Counseling Methods to Help Bridge Political Divide." *Weekend Edition Saturday*, NPR, December 2, 2017. www.npr.org/2017/12/02/567336148/group-uses-marriage-counseling-methods-to-help-bridge-political-divide. Accessed March 1, 2019.

Sunstein, Cass. *#republic: Divided Democracy in the Age of Social Media.* Princeton, NJ, Princeton University Press, 2017.

Traister, Rebecca. *Good and Mad: The Revolutionary Power of Women's Anger.* New York, Simon and Schuster, 2018.

Vallier, Kevin. "Social and Political Trust: Concepts, Causes, and Consequences." John S. and James L. Knight Foundation, April 5, 2018. kf-site-production.s3.amazonaws.com/media_elements/files/000/000/184/original/Topos_KF_White-Paper_Vallier_V4_ado.pdf. Accessed March 1, 2019.

4

Beyond Survival

Theater of the Oppressed, Flourishing While Fighting, and Fighting to Flourish

Kelly Howe

> But that's why we are alive, to go after utopias, to go after dreams, not
> to reach them but go after them all over and over again.
>
> —Augusto Boal

Augusto Boal, the late Brazilian theater theorist and practitioner who initially developed the body of techniques and theory known as Theater of the
Oppressed (TO), is arguably famous partly because of his ability to write
with a joy that leaps off the page—an energy that was similarly infectious in
person, as many of us who learned from him at some point attest.[1] When I
read several of Boal's books as an undergraduate student, I was struck by the
audacity of writing about the often cynicism-inducing world with so many
hopeful exclamation points. Speaking of audacious, here is perhaps Boal's
most famous sentence: "Maybe the theater in itself is not revolutionary, but
these theatrical forms are without a doubt a *rehearsal of revolution*" (*Theatre
of the Oppressed* 141). His books and practice constitute a political sensibility aimed at analyzing oppression *for the purposes of dismantling it*. That
oppressed people deserve happiness and well-being—that they deserve
something beyond mere survival—was a central theme of Boal's practice.
When, after decades as a theater practitioner, Boal successfully ran for the
post of *vereador* (city councilperson) in Rio de Janeiro in the 1990s, his

---

[1] The epigraph quotes Augusto Boal's comments as part of the Legislative Theatre opening session
of the 2008 Pedagogy and Theatre of the Oppressed Conference in Omaha, Nebraska. It was Boal's
last appearance at that gathering, in which he participated annually; he died on May 2, 2009, a few
weeks before he was to appear at the next conference.

Kelly Howe, *Beyond Survival* In: *Theater and Human Flourishing*. Edited by: Harvey Young, Oxford University Press.
© Oxford University Press 2023. DOI: 10.1093/oso/9780197622261.003.0005

campaign slogan was "Have the courage to be happy" (*Coragem de ser Feliz* in Portuguese) (Boal, *Legislative* 13–14; Heritage). TO is concerned with the right of humans to flourish; that it has spread across the world so impressively is partly a reflection of the reality of widespread human suffering but also a reflection of the recognition that most forms of suffering are not inevitable.[2]

In this essay, I first—for those who may be unfamiliar with TO—offer a brief overview of the core branches of its oft-referenced tree. Then I offer a few examples of groups using TO toward the causes of health and well-being. I hope those examples together will constitute a concrete point of departure for what becomes a theoretical examination of some key moments in which happiness, well-being, and pleasure are addressed within the foundational texts of TO, in this case meaning texts by Boal himself. In the course of that examination, I ask: What might TO as a practice and political sensibility have to offer toward the cultivation of well-being? I propose that one of TO's most significant contributions is precisely its inherent embodiment of the politically explosive notion that oppressed peoples deserve not only mere survival but flourishing: happiness, joy, pleasure, and sensuality. Because TO pairs the category of oppression with a life beyond survival, it not only suggests that human suffering is not natural or inevitable, but it also suggests that oppressed people have a right to something beyond "getting by," something *beyond* the mitigation of hardship and pain. TO constructs a formalized aesthetic space that can (but does not always) interrupt neoliberal logics that sustain and intensify human suffering. As such, it could be in many ways well-positioned to navigate neoliberalism's threats to well-being. At the same time, as I will note, some aspects of TO do not need much shape-shifting to be deployed in support of exactly the systems that TO hopes to dismantle. Ultimately, in these pages, I will also suggest a few of the reasons why some aspects of the discourses of human flourishing and positive psychology would spark fierce debate among TO practitioners and scholars—and likely be considered by some to run counter to the core impulses of TO itself.

---

[2] At the same time as the Theater and Performance Studies working group of the Humanities and Human Flourishing Project was meeting and preparing drafts, I was in the process of finishing work as co-editor (with Julian Boal and José Soeiro) of *The Routledge Companion to Theatre of the Oppressed* (2019). Given the fact that such a large project was a primary scholarly focus for well more than four years, my most recent ideas about Theater of the Oppressed—as well as my sense of the "TO world" in general—have, as this essay reflects, been indelibly shaped by my co-editors especially, but also by all of the many contributors to that project, even those not directly quoted in these pages. I am grateful to each and every one of them.

Since the 1970s, TO has been used around the world in a range of social struggles and other settings. With its attention to power shaped by, among other contexts, the immensely turbulent and violent state repression of the Brazilian military dictatorship that began in 1964, TO descends from a range of Latin American political, artistic, and pedagogical genealogies—as well as European and North American theater practices, among others. TO reached beyond its initial places of evolution long ago. That reality is partly a result of Boal's exile from his home country in 1971, an exile that began after he endured months of imprisonment and torture by the dictatorship. Boal's trajectory of exile forced him and his family from Brazil to Argentina, then to Portugal and to France. He would later return to Brazil. He shared his techniques not only in the places he lived but also in many regions to which he was invited as a guest, and other "multipliers" (his term) took them up. TO is astonishingly popular, its books widely translated and its techniques practiced virtually all over.

The tree—as Boal called it—of TO includes a vast array of theater techniques aimed at analyzing power relationships for the purposes of dismantling oppression. TO "games" constitute part of the trunk of the tree. Usually they are sequentially the first techniques used in a group's work to defamiliarize and dehabituate the body's routines and explore possible ways of moving in the theatrical space and life beyond it. With another body of techniques constituting a branch of the tree, Newspaper Theater (in terms of historical chronology, the first branch), participants stage news and other written texts for the purposes of analyzing how oppressive systems shape the information that we receive. Image Theater, in contrast, decentralizes logocentric epistemologies, enacting primarily nonverbal exploration and analysis, gradually working up to complex embodied conversations about specific oppressions. In Forum Theater (the most famous set of TO techniques), a play depicting an oppression is staged at least twice at the same performance. The second time, a facilitator (known as the "joker," calling on the term's association with the notion of a wildcard) invites audience members to intervene in place of a character and rehearse new ways to struggle against the oppressions staged. Rainbow of Desire techniques, developed during Boal's time in Europe, analyze internalized oppressions and, in this respect, possess what many (Boal included) have characterized as particularly therapeutic dimensions. Legislative Theater applies Forum Theater and other techniques to processes of generating and proposing policy and law; Boal first enacted it as a candidate then *vereador* in Rio de Janeiro. Aesthetics of the Oppressed explore additional ways to incorporate other art forms into TO practice. The final "branch" of TO, Direct Actions, does not necessarily involve theater per se. Boal believed that insights garnered through TO should always be applied beyond the theatrical space. He knew that, for all its potential in the process of struggling for a better world, theater alone is not enough. It is one weapon among many.

Though these subsets of TO are in some ways distinct, they share many core premises, including but not limited to the following: (1) theater belongs to all people (not only those who have been marked through division of labor and division of theatrical space as "artists"); (2) the spectator can become what Boal calls the "spect-actor," hopefully toppling presumed boundaries between stage and audience; (3) oppressed people are experts in their own lives and should, can, and will be the architects of their own emancipatory struggles; (4) our bodies have been estranged from us by systems of oppression—especially by labor—and to re-meet them can be a deep (if contradictory) pleasure as well as a vital component of struggle; (5) the oppressed must have spaces for thinking in the subjunctive mood, for exploring not only what *is* but was *is possible*. Per Boal, "In the Theatre of the Oppressed, reality is conjugated in the Subjunctive Mood, in two tenses, the *Past Imperfect*—'what if I were doing that?'—or the *Future*—'what if I were to do this?'" (*Aesthetics* 39). TO focuses on using theater for the analysis of the gap between what is and would could be. Though several branches of TO can feature public performances as part of that analysis, TO also tends to be process-based—at least to the extent that those generating the theater are/should be those doing the investigation because they themselves are the ones who actually struggle with the oppression in question. TO often happens in workshops set aside for the purpose of analysis and exploration or in public spaces where the audiences are invited to transform into participants rather than receivers of a product. In this way, TO is an embodied epistemology more than (or, certainly, as much as) a tool of public expression. Boal imagined TO as a form in which people raise questions about their oppressions that they sincerely do not know how to answer—and then probe those questions collectively within the corporeal grammar of theatrical forms.

In one way or another, the majority of people who enact TO do so with at least expressed intentions that would align with the subject of this collection of essays: the enhancement of well-being and human flourishing, both of which are core aims of the field of positive psychology. Also characterized by some as a movement, positive psychology emerged partly "as a complement to the deficit orientation of mainstream psychology" (Pawelski, "Defining" 361). In other words, positive psychology sprang from a concern that psychological discourses and methods had largely been focused on addressing diagnosed conditions and problems or forms of suffering that can accompany them. James O. Pawelski calls these approaches "indirect" methods for cultivating human flourishing and points out that positive psychology seeks to balance indirect and direct pursuits of well-being. He writes, "[T]he position of positive psychology is that the indirectly positive goals of mainstream psychology are not sufficient for human flourishing. By the same token, however, it is also important to acknowledge that insofar as the goals of positive psychology are merely directly positive, they, too, are insufficient for human flourishing" ("Defining" 358). Pawelski elaborates, "In addition to merely sustaining life, however, we are also deeply concerned with its quality, and for that reason we seek to thrive physically, mentally, and socially" ("Bringing" 207). Positive psychology asks how psychology as a field can serve the cause of humans doing more than surviving. How can all people, even those who would not be constructed as "sick" or already "unwell," be as well as possible?

Though the emphases, discourses, and concrete practices of positive psychology are different from TO in many ways, there are some overlaps. TO gathers people together to rehearse how they can dismantle obstacles to flourishing. It has been used in a staggering array of contexts. Some of the oppressive systems that TO has been used to fight (or, depending on the situation, *explore*) include but are by no means limited to the following: capitalism, inhumane working conditions, racism, xenophobia, colonialism, imperialism, patriarchy, heterosexism, cisgender normativity, ableism, environmental destruction, hunger and food insecurity, privatization, homelessness and other forms of housing precarity, lack of access or limited access to education, schooling itself, debt, ageism, the prison industrial complex, policing, bullying, insufficient or complete lack of healthcare, nationalism and its attendant abuses of migrants and refugees, governmental bureaucracy, censorship, fascism, authoritarianism, militarization, and other forms of violence (physical, psychic, legislative, cultural, etc.). Whatever the form of oppression, it is very likely that someone has used TO to struggle against it or at least ask questions about it. The interlocking systems preventing well-being can feel so overwhelming, connected, and mutually constitutive that they can almost seem amorphous, and yet at the same time they are concrete, materially real, and all too tangible for the bodies they script and inhibit.

Though all these forms of oppression relate to the possibility or impossibility of human flourishing, some uses of TO explore barriers to health and well-being more explicitly than others. TO has, for instance, frequently been used in what has come to be known as the medical humanities and the health humanities. The former often focuses primarily on a variety of oppressive systems informing doctor-nurse-patient relationships and the education and training of medical professionals, and the latter is often associated with a broader scope of inquiry that also encompasses other groups and explorations of well-being in general. The Centre for Community Dialogue and Change in Bengaluru, India, for example, frequently works with medical students and faculty using TO, as does the Cleveland Clinic's Lerner College of Medicine and its Center for Ethics, Humanities and Spiritual Care.[3]

Beyond the use of TO in the medical and health humanities, many plays, projects, and ongoing struggles offer examples of the use of TO toward health and well-being. Jana Sanskriti—the collective based in Badu, a village in West Bengal, a group that eventually grew into a TO movement thousands of people strong—has been in existence since the 1980s. The group has used TO (Forum Theater especially) to analyze and struggle against oppressions related to health and healthcare (particularly maternal and child health), domestic violence, child trafficking, child abuse, and a host of other topics, all of them with deep and wide implications for health and well-being.[4] Headlines Theater (also known as Theater for Living) of Vancouver frequently tackled health and well-being in its Forum Theater productions, addressing questions of mental health, addiction, death, the relationship between chronic poverty and cuts to welfare and social services, and more.[5] With their Forum Theater play *Maria 28*, the group Peles Negras, Máscaras Negras (Black Skins, Black Masks) examines oppressions faced by Black women working in domestic spaces in Portugal. *Maria 28* highlights, for example, the significant health problems that such laborers face, among them the very common development of tendinitis in the domestic workplace, a condition that often gets them fired from the very work that *caused* it.[6] In the United States, the Workers' Theater Collective/Workers Resistance Theater of the Chicago Workers' Collaborative uses Forum Theater as a form

---

[3] For more information, see the website of Centre for Community Dialogue and Change, http://www.ccdc.in/; Lerner College's curriculum, at https://portals.clevelandclinic.org/lcm2/Academics/Curriculum/Humanities.

[4] See Ganguly; Jana Sanskriti website, http://www.janasanskriti.org/.

[5] See Theatre for Living, "Project Legacy 1981–2018," http://theatreforliving.com/legacy.htm.

[6] See chullage and raquel.

of organizing, as African American and Latinx temporary workers struggle in unity for better working conditions in factories and other businesses in the Chicagoland area, many of which try to pit the two groups against each other in the service of capital and its violence.[7] The collective's plays themselves depict a range of horrifying workplace conditions that threaten even a modicum of well-being: low wages that reinforce other forms of precarity, sexual violence and harassment, retribution for attempts to organize, arbitrary dismissal, lack of observance of workplace law and regulations, and pressure to perform at dangerous paces and without adequate breaks for restroom use or anything else. The stories staged by the collective arise from the lived experiences of workers who perform in the plays. They use TO to—among other things—build strength and unity among themselves; advocate for better conditions; construct alliances with other organizations, groups, and individuals; and call attention to the reprehensive business practices that threaten worker health, dignity, and well-being at every turn.

At the risk of stating the obvious—but doing so to consider the relationship between TO and the study of human flourishing—TO begins with an oppression (in terms of its content). In this respect, TO engages in the sort of logics that positive psychology *challenged* within the broader field of psychology. TO's very title starts from the vantage point of addressing *problems*—oppression, social ills, injustice—as opposed to starting from a focus on flourishing. Boal specifically mentions that he could have given TO a name that would have centered happiness and well-being—as those are among its concerns—but to have done so would not have fully invoked the connotations he desired:

> When I pronounced *Teatro do Oprimido* for the first time, it sounded strange. Still today, for some, it sounds like *Deprimido* (Depressed), although it is about uprising, about what you consider worth struggling for, about being happy. Imagine if I had called it Theatre of Happiness, Theatre of Revolution, Theatre of the Invented Future!—pretentious. It stayed as it is, and now I like it: *Theatre of the Oppressed*. (*Hamlet* 311)

At the same time, the subjunctive grammar of TO converges with the subjunctive grammar of positive psychology. In an introduction to an issue of *American Psychologist* on positive psychology co-authored with Martin E. P.

---

[7] See Chicago Workers Collaborative website, http://www.chicagoworkerscollaborative.org/.

Seligman, Mihaly Csikszentmihalyi writes, "I have struggled to reconcile the twin imperatives that a science of human beings should include: to understand what *is* and what *could be*" (Seligman and Csikszentmihalyi 7, emphasis in original). TO and positive psychology *share* an interest in not only responding to what is but imagining would could be.

Theoretically, TO configures happiness as a particular absence. "What is happiness? Without doubt—it is the absence of oppression," Boal writes in *Games for Actors and Non-Actors*, one of the foundational texts of TO (189). In fact, though TO centers oppression, some of its techniques actually focus specifically on thinking about what the exact opposite or absence of oppression would be like, imagining—as does positive psychology—genuine flourishing. For example, with some Image Theater techniques, a group makes "ideal" images before heading backward to stage images of transition that could build toward the conditions for the flourishing depicted. Put another way, TO can stage images of thriving and imagine how a group might get there through collective organizing.

In TO, Boal conjoins theater, happiness, and access to learning: "Theatre should be happiness; it should help us learn about ourselves and our times. We should know the world we live in, the better to change it" (*Games* 16). What are for many people constituent aspects of happiness—particularly pleasure and fun—are often described as central aspects of TO in the moment of its doing, both in Boal's theory and in the reflections of practitioners/scholars in many contexts, myself included. Boal attributes the pleasure and fun of TO specifically to the fact that it asserts that the analysis of lived experience should be undertaken by the entire body that is *doing* the living in the first place. See, for example, this section from *Games for Actors and Non-Actors*:

> As the most important element of theatre is the human body, this book is concerned with physical movements and the relations between people and people, and people and things, playing with such factors as distance, weight and volume. None of the exercises should be done with violence, nor should any cause pain; all should be done with pleasure and understanding. Nothing should ever be done in a competitive manner—we try to be better than ourselves, not better than others. (15–16)

Boal underscores later that a particular exercise "should be done gently, without violence, with pleasure, almost sensually" (*Games* 88–89). He adds,

"As I have said before, the exercises must be fun to do, the experience should include pleasure, not pain" (108). Furthermore, he offers, "[W]e have, before all else, a body—before we have a name, we inhabit a body! And we rarely think of our body as the fundamental source of all pleasures and all pains, of all knowledge and all research, everything!" (124). In particular, as I have written elsewhere,

> [w]ith this focus on sensory knowing, Boal frequently aims to recuperate lost (or stolen) forms of sensuality. . . . TO hopes, among other things, to reclaim joy and pleasure, to make a world where we are free to experience both. In TO, we know not only by looking and listening and talking; we know by moving and feeling and sensing. (82)

In *Games for Actors and Non-Actors*, Boal asserts that TO is fundamentally about happiness *over* mere survival. TO shares that goal with positive psychology. TO believes that the world can be "a place to live *and* be happy" (emphasis mine), not merely the former:

> Let us hope that one day—please, not too far in the future—we'll be able to convince or force our governments, our leaders, to do the same: to ask their audiences—*us*—what they should do, so as to make this world a place to live and be happy in—yes, it is possible—rather than just a vast market in which we all sell our goods and our souls.
> Let's hope.
> Let's work for it! (276)

Here Boal both insists that all humans deserve something beyond survival and implies that a primary dynamic thwarting the ability to survive and thrive is (of course) capitalism.

Why would I say, as I did at the beginning of this writing, that it is politically explosive to suggest that oppressed people have a right to happiness? Some might say that asserting the right to something more than survival is not exactly a radical proposition, but in the context of neoliberal capitalism it is. TO's insistence that the oppressed specifically have a right not only to "get by" but to flourish is no doubt part of what has led to TO's perhaps paradoxical global popularity in neoliberal times. Take, for example, the United States, where hypercapitalism and neoliberal discourses have successfully chipped away at any notion of the right to joy, pleasure, fun, and so on. Neoliberal discourse configures joy as privilege and is ultimately fine with however the distribution of joy shakes out. Perhaps the most obvious cultural example of this notion lies in the persistent critique of struggling people receiving state income who also purchase items that could be construed as leading to more than survival. This pernicious (deadly, I would argue) notion surfaces again and again, morphing in its specific dialogue: "She says she's struggling, but I see she got her nails done." "If those people are so poor and so in need of social assistance, why do they have a satellite dish?" "You shouldn't be able to use state food assistance to buy fancy steak." The subtext (or actually just plain old text) is that bare-bones survival is all anyone on the losing end of capitalism has a right to ask for. And we see all around us that neoliberalism's rapaciousness does not accept even survival with bare-bones food and shelter as a right: "If you want healthcare, get a job. Or start a GoFundMe." "I wonder what he did to end up on the streets." "We shouldn't be giving these people handouts." Under such logics, to the extent that you are "free," you are "free" to die. As Boal says in *Legislative Theatre,* "Knowledge and health are power, so economic elites try to conceal knowledge and destroy health. An ignorant and debilitated people is more easily dominated" (41).

In such a context, one dimension of TO's appeal as a mode of struggle becomes especially legible. Even just to say that oppressed people specifically *deserve* joy, pleasure, sensuality (let alone to carve out aesthetic spaces for joy, pleasure, and sensual relationship to the body *as praxis*) becomes a novel, politically charged act. First, the insistence on the term "oppressed" orients the attention toward structural factors that limit or determine prospects of survival and well-being. Second, such a stance interrupts the assumption of happiness as something that must be earned or even "worked for" by positing happiness instead as a right, a reasonable thing to have the capacity to experience regardless of employment status or other statuses in relation to systems of oppression. In this sense, TO also implicitly interrupts the hegemonic assumption that the world should necessarily be organized around work—and that work *earns* the right to joy and pleasure, dispensed by market norms. You should have more than just the right to *pursue* happiness, suggests TO. Its various techniques can cultivate spaces that are prefigurative, at least as that term has been described by TO practitioners from the Argentinean social movement La Dignidad's (not currently operating) Escuela de Teatro Político (School of Political Theater): prefigurative spaces, the authors from La Dignidad write, are "spaces that reflect the social modes of organization we hope will become true in a broader way in the future" (Escuela 317). TO techniques allow for pleasure and joy as part and parcel of struggles against oppression. As Jill Dolan suggests in her explication of what she calls "utopian performatives," theater can stage sensations of the world we want, and those felt experiences can help us to consider how to build that world (5). Ideally, TO experiences themselves at least partially prefigure aspects of their goals.

TO's assumption of oppressed peoples' capacity for humor, laughter, fun, and joy also unsettles power-laden assumptions of many cultural workers who think they are engaged in theater for social change. As just one example from my own practice years ago, here I rewind briefly to the first day of an experience working with adolescents in a community center. As part of our time together over the weeks that would follow, the participants and I were going to create a performance that we would then share at the end of the program. When I talked about that plan and asked if they had any questions, one student immediately asked something along the lines of "Can our plays be funny? Can our plays have jokes?" I responded that of course they could, but I must have also looked a little perplexed. I imagine my expression that way because the same student then quickly added that the previous teacher who had come to make theater with the students had "wanted us to focus on our problems." The students lived in a neighborhood that many people viewed reductively as a space of violence and oppression. Though it is hard to know precisely what had happened in the previous theater experience at the community center, youth participants were chafing against certain assumptions of negative experiences where they lived. As is commonly acknowledged in some TO circles (though I would say not enough of them), many practitioners of theater for social change fetishize oppressions and condescendingly construct reductive notions about the everyday lives and, more specifically, the capacity for humor and pleasure of oppressed peoples. The problems with this disposition are many, of course; for reasons of space, I will not linger on all of them here. Stephani Etheridge Woodson gestures toward similarly condescending dynamics in her own chapter in this volume when she notes her "deep suspicion about 'needs'-based rhetoric" deploying categories like "at-risk" to describe children and youth. Suffice it to say that obviously people struggling against oppressions are complex, multidimensional beings with the capacity for a full tapestry of joy, fun, pleasure, humor, and nuance alongside other experiences. This is a core assumption of TO, and to suggest that they are not capable of such feelings is part of the dehumanization constructed by systems of oppression.

It is also true, however, that TO acknowledges that people struggling against oppressions often do not have enough *time* for pleasure and for fun, and as a result TO tries to pair the typically arduous work of political struggle with opportunities for play. On a practical level, TO fashions an aesthetic-political space that also has the potential to make political struggle more *bearable* (or even something far more than bearable), less of a mental and physical drain, and thereby more accessible. TO practitioner, sociologist, and member of the Left Bloc of the Portuguese Parliament José Soeiro speaks to this dynamic:

> This brings another problem with which I personally have been confronted. In the context of political struggles (and of a political mandate, too), theatre competes with many other repertoires of action, some whose immediate effectiveness seems more evident. Why, still, insisting on theatre? I have no answer for that. But I can say that political activism must not be a frustrating annoyance. Theatre, with all its properties, sometimes allows us to look in another way for what we had already seen. It creates, sometimes, that form of joy that results from being together, understanding the world together, and laughing along while fighting oppression. And that's no small thing. (194)

Katy Rubin, founding and former executive director of Theatre of the Oppressed–NYC, echoes aspects of Soeiro's sentiments:

> TONYC is not simply a place in New York City where people practice and train in Theatre of the Oppressed (TO); in fact, at its core, it's hardly that. Much more, it is a resource for New York City's change-makers (in neighborhoods, government, and nonprofits) to bring radical fun, creativity, and the experiences of those most impacted by oppressive systems into existing movements for social justice—and into legislative chambers, in order to advance those movements. (414)

To strive for the survival of life on this planet, the lessening of suffering, and the possibility for equitable opportunities for human happiness, we need to make the necessary struggles for social change doable, bearable, livable, even enjoyable. TO aims to make even the experience of struggle more than mere survival itself.

Pleasure, fun, and joy often make struggle and movement organizing themselves more appealing; they also often *enhance the quality* of analysis and learning. As Argentinean practitioner and researcher Cora Fairstein puts it, "I do not separate fun and reflection. Fun, laughter, and humor are very powerful weapons that I always try to have on my side. I do not think that you cannot reflect while someone is having fun; rather, I think the opposite. Fun clears, reassures, and generates space for deeper analysis" ("Games" 148). The notion of fun strengthening or deepening analysis is central to TO. Similarly, when discussing one of Boal's Forum Theater and Rainbow of Desire rehearsal techniques, U.S. scholar-practitioner Mady Schutzman explains that the exercise "becomes a tool that manages to extract a great deal of joy, comradery, and awareness from what had been a seemingly irreversible vortex of worry and paralysis" ("Therapy" 340). In both of these examples, these practitioners draw a line connecting knowledge creation and joyful, fun aesthetic spaces. That connection is often underscored by the field of positive psychology. For example, in her foundational essay exploring positive emotions, psychology researcher Barbara L. Fredrickson considers how "positive emotions broaden the scope of attention, thinking, and action" (312). As a field, positive psychology offers language for describing how the kind of happiness and joy often cultivated by TO can sharpen and expand one's analysis of the available range of possibilities.

TO, like many other efforts toward human flourishing, also becomes a laboratory for questioning what constitutes human happiness in the first place, from both individual and social vantage points. Boal's exercise "Multiple Images of Happiness," for example, is part of both the Image Theater and Rainbow of Desire sequences. The exercise poses these embodied research questions: "[W]hat does happiness look like? Is one person's idea of happiness compatible with someone else's? Does one person's happiness depend on another's happiness. . . ?" (*Rainbow* 114). In both practice and theory, the possibility of and right to human happiness are central features of TO. But TO's potential for working for well-being also stems from its interest in the pleasure of analysis itself, the pleasure of learning, the pleasure of inhabiting a space where one's lived experiences are considered worthy of staging and collective consideration. Boal argues, "[I]t is a pleasure to relive on stage vivid scenes from real life, and by reliving them, to understand them" (*Legislative* 67). In her contribution to this book, Lisa Biggs evokes a literally priceless value of representing one's story. "For human beings to flourish," she writes, "we need that kind of knowledge and connectivity." Throughout his writings and talks, Sanjoy Ganguly, founder of Jana Sanskriti, insists time and again that one of the primary appeals for the villagers who join their work is TO's provision of "intellectual space" for "the active engagement of intellect and senses" (132). He adds, "The globalization of capital wants to robotize the human being to make people blind followers of the system, whereas Theatre of the Oppressed can open a democratic space where people by and large can grow intellectually, rationally" (152).

But to what end does TO engage the intellect and senses? Much debate persists about whether, when, and the extent to which TO practices invite analysis of systems and possible collective strategies as opposed to emphasizing the ability or responsibility of the individual to "solve" that which they are struggling against, through either heroic actions or merely "changing their mindset." Julian Boal, a practitioner and scholar based in Rio de Janeiro who is Augusto Boal's son and was one of his primary facilitation collaborators, has written extensively about how TO might fit all too cozily within neoliberal narratives of individualized achievement, heroism, optimized performance, and evaluation/testing. "Since [within neoliberalism] the quality of our individual calculating capacity is our greatest guarantee of access to a certain level of well-being, Forum Theatre," he laments, "can become a suitable stage where we can exhibit it in a non-offensive and playful transposition of the much more aggressively competitive behaviors of our routine" (299). In this respect, he argues, "TO is nowadays often used not as a tool for struggle, but rather as a lesser auxiliary factor of our domination" (298). Indeed, many TO practitioners worry about the possibility of TO tilting toward individual "solutions" for what would be better (and likely only) fought collectively.

Moreover, focusing on individuals overcoming oppressions through positive traits, characteristics, or practices can stoke grab-your-bootstraps-why-don't-you sentiments. After all, why not optimize your performance? Welsh TO practitioner Iwan Brioc speaks to some aspects of this dynamic:

> What I struggle with most in doing TO these last few years is how what
> would previously have been seen as external oppression is attributed to a
> cop in the head [Boal's term for internalized oppression, developed as part
> of his Rainbow of Desire techniques]. This indicates to me that neoliber
> alism has become so embedded in our psyche so as to appear as a given
> rather than as an ideology—a reality rather than a pernicious narrative.

What some years ago workshop participants would have expressed as external oppressions are now considered personality deficiencies. Working long hours in poorly paid, meaningless jobs translates to: "Why am I too tired to pursue my dreams and too fearful to leave my crap job?" ("Therapy" 342–43)

Brioc describes moments when, at least in his experience, what he would call discourses of "well-being" appear to short-circuit systemic analysis and collective organizing: "I have countless examples of workshop participants being treated poorly at work looking for internal reservoirs of resilience in preference to organizing a union or finding solidarity with individuals (even in the same workshop) to campaign for change" (343).

On this score it is important to note that when scholars of human flourishing tilt toward discussion of virtues, optimal traits, good citizenship, and so on—and as they sort out what some of those virtues and traits might be—they sometimes tread into what would be controversial territory in the TO world. Depending on the context, some of the traits associated with human flourishing by positive psychology make many TO practitioners nervous, occasionally even angry: coping, civility, moderation, responsibility, work ethic, self-regulation. In positive psychology, things like "the ability to cope in stressful situations," "greater tolerance for risk," and "increased performance on job interviews" are sometimes viewed as "character development skills so important in life" (Pawelski, "Bringing" 215). But one could argue that—while many people who want to enhance those skills in others and themselves do so with sincerely good intentions and often even to profoundly beneficial results for the people in question—some of those abilities are more specifically important to capitalism itself, not necessarily inherently important to life. These abilities sometimes make one's life empirically better or happier in various ways. Many positive psychologists want people to have these traits or skills precisely because they do not want people to suffer. But these traits can also help one *adjust* to existing power relationships *rather than disrupt them*. Even originality and creativity, depending on who demands them, have the potential to emphasize individuals serving or working within systems, including those systems that were not designed to support their well-being at all. As Julian Boal worries regarding TO specifically, "what seems . . . disturbing for us to investigate is why so many games, exercises, and forms of TO have been so easily recruited by countless human resources services

worldwide. Such research would undoubtedly reveal unwanted affinities between this method of critical theatre and the present state of our subjugation" (294). Indeed, theater can reinforce our subjugation rather than help us
undo it.

That said, as many scholars and practitioners have affirmed, psychological flourishing is inextricably related to collective justice and collective
well-being. As Schutzman phrases it, "While 'therapeutic' discourses and
practices may have conventionally been associated with individuals, we
know full well that (given that individuals constitute families, communities,
governing bodies, resistance movements—that is, culture) there is no way
in which we can advocate for separation between the two" ("Therapy" 345).
Fellow U.S. TO practitioner and scholar Brent Blair echoes Schutzman: "We
cannot possibly explore collective socio-political transformation without
investigating the psychological and spiritual health of our communities, and vice versa" ("Therapy" 344). But as a result of its central tenet of
foregrounding the needs and perspectives of those struggling against oppression, TO also invites us to ask: When are traits, skills, and experiences
associated with human flourishing regarded as such partly because they
help some people succeed in systems that quietly depend on swallowing
others whole? How do we continue to advance the cause of human flourishing while dismantling the systems that have naturalized logics of scarcity,
competition, and necessary inequality? Often the agents of such systems
justify current arrangements of power by pointing to examples of "exceptional"—or lucky—people who have been able to thrive or imagine more
than fleeting happiness on the horizon. An approach to studying human
flourishing that is compatible with the political spirit of TO would need to
value above all TO's capacities for galvanizing collective action, with a recognition that TO—at least at its roots—was never intended to prepare individual people for a capitalist workforce or to help them sharpen the self for
competition. Rather, it was intended to help oppressed people fight together
against precisely the systems that deceptively frame suffering as individual
in nature, systems that defer change to the individuals who supposedly must
"optimize" to perform their routines.

But how do we know what TO accomplishes? Efficacy has often been a
key focus of the study of the humanities and human flourishing, and TO
presents many complex challenges on this score. In a form of theater focused on change, how do you *know* anything *happened*? It is important to

ask concretely what is happening in spaces of TO and whether or not they are contributing to the dismantling of oppression. We must be attentive to the extent to which TO can easily tilt into the commodification of feelings that do not necessarily improve lives concretely or make social systems more just. Often those reputed to be "good" facilitators have been received as such because they facilitate a feeling of possibility. But when is TO merely vending good feeling? This question—and many other rigorous critical questions—must be asked. At the same time, I suggest that there can be no generalized study about "outcomes" of TO as a set of theories and practices *itself*, relative to the question of human flourishing or anything else. The practice of TO is necessarily context-specific such that any real claims about efficacy can be pondered only within each context. More important, however, the issue with any study of outcomes in TO is that, ideally, TO should be so deeply embedded within a larger movement for social change that it should be difficult to determine when "outcomes" can be attributed to TO itself. It should also be difficult to find a moment (or moments) at which to measure TO's impact, given that its work is never done. Emancipation, as Julian Boal and José Soeiro insist, is "a slow and impatient collective work" (102). Indeed, Augusto Boal writes, "In truth, a session of Theatre of the Oppressed has no end, because everything which happens in it must extend into life. Theatre shall never end! Theatre of the Oppressed is located precisely on the frontier between fiction and reality—and this border must be crossed" (*Games* 275–76).

People can discuss and document what happens in TO work—as well as its meanings for participants. They can analyze its implications rigorously. But it would be antithetical to TO to measure a session against specific, predetermined outcomes.

> All the methods that I have discussed are methods of a rehearsal-theater, and not a spectacle-theater. One knows how these experiments will begin but not how they will end, because the spectator is freed from his chains, finally acts, and becomes a protagonist. Because they respond to the real needs of a popular audience they are practiced with success and joy. (Boal, *Theatre* 141)

Almost everything about TO as Augusto Boal articulated it runs counter to the demands of efficacy measurement, specifically that of the sort often required by grant writing and funders. When projects are funded, granting organizations frequently pressure practitioners to project and "assess" outcomes. But "proof" of "outcomes" that have been pre-identified is of course not necessarily anything like proof of an anti-oppressive social movement. TO's emancipatory potential cannot even begin to manifest unless the specific work sincerely asks a question for which an answer has not already been scripted.

The material contradictions of grants and other funding mechanisms threaten to (and often do) turn TO into the scripted false dialogues Boal hoped to help dismantle in the first place. A study of human flourishing and TO would need to proceed with such an awareness. In *Theatre of Good Intentions: Challenges and Hopes for Theatre and Social Change*, Dani Snyder-Young cautions:

> Artists must set benchmarks for their own work that are useful to them. . . . [I]t often feels like there is a world of difference between artists and community participants asking the questions: "What are our goals? How will we know we've achieved them?" and funding bodies and institutional authorities asking the same questions. As a result, *efficacy* and *assessment* can feel like positivist tools of authorities that are, if not actively antagonistic, more often than not external to the process of using theatre to make change in community settings. . . . Institutional agendas have a great deal of impact on the work artists are able to do. When artists cannot explain their work to those institutional authorities, there is the danger of losing the resources required to make the work. (5, emphasis in original)

Relatedly, British practitioner Adrian Jackson writes "that the trick is to try to devise one's own measures: measures which resist, or at least augment, the numerical and instrumental outcomes which many funders require": "I am fond of citing the methodologies of a radical health practice in South East London in the 1930s, the Peckham Pioneers, who measured 'the spring in people's step,' 'the gleam in people's eye.'" He adds, "Theatre . . . is a slow burn, and its effects are not always obvious for some time' (182). Sometimes even the feelings that people have when doing TO are the outcomes that matter most in and of themselves; sometimes they are not.

In any event, TO can construct prefigurative spaces for living aspects or moments of well-being *as* people work for the possibility for all to flourish now and in the future. After all, as Augusto Boal asserts in the epigraph to this chapter, to "go after" utopias is part of well-being, and we should never discount the effects of opportunities to do that, regardless of what is reached as a result of the pursuit. In this way, TO does not defer well-being until later or convert it into a product, even as it chases it. For those reasons especially, we should share and analyze our specific TO experiences as often as possible. My ambivalence about efficacy and measurement does not lead me to suggest that we cannot push ourselves to articulate what TO can and does do. In fact, for example, in Porto, Portugal, in 2015, at the impressive gathering on TO and activism known as Óprima, I witnessed some of the most rigorous analysis of theater's political implications that I have ever experienced, in what were essentially face-to-face plenary discussions/critiques on the Forum Theater plays staged at the conference. The entire gathering was in the room for these critiques. Some of the most intensive scholarly analyses published on political theater that I have read could not touch the depth of critical engagement and kind of interrogation I heard there. What made the critique sessions so impressive was that participants never took for granted that it is universally better to do TO than not to do TO (many do), yet they were not focusing on "proving" anything but instead on sharpening the questions asked by the dramaturgical structure of each play, thereby deepening the political and affective engagement of each piece. The emphasis was on sincere, well-constructed questions, not on the outcome.

We should never conflate goals and achievements, and we can continue to evolve (as many practitioners have) in how we make the case for the value of TO for flourishing and well-being, when used in certain ways, under X or Y conditions. At this point in my own experience with TO, I believe, however, that the vast majority of that analysis must be qualitative, though others will disagree. I have also come to feel strongly that there are many moments when scholarly publication and formal study are not the most appropriate or just forms of engagement. I believe that chapters like this one can be useful to share information about approaches across discourses, fields, and movements, as long as they are written in a way that does not compromise ongoing movement struggles. But in other moments, depending on the situation, if one has time to produce scholarly output in that way, sometimes one should instead put all that time and energy into the struggle at hand instead. The point of TO is not scholarly publication, though obviously scholarship and documentation can amplify and serve the struggle, even helping it amass crucial material resources by offering vocabulary to use when applying for funding. For those who are trying to gather such concrete resources, analysis of the ways that TO can enhance human flourishing and well-being can provide useful content. That said, if someone suggests that they can isolate TO as a lone or even a determining factor in a particular change or achievement, that should also beg analysis about the degree to which that TO work is embedded within mass struggles, their messy contradictions, their alliances, and the combined tools they engage—of which TO must always be only one of many.

Having juxtaposed TO and positive psychology in this chapter, I find myself returning to larger questions about what can be at stake in doing so, other than the very real value of translating across disciplines and illuminating shared and contrasting assumptions. I probably think about this question with even more heat underneath it given that I have revised the final version of this chapter in the context of a global pandemic that has rendered precarious people even more precarious. Those who were already hurting are hurting more, and many of those who were not hurting before are hurting now. The global implications for mental and physical health are of such a scale that they can often feel very hard to fathom. Risk and suffering are nightmarishly unevenly distributed, as usual. Understandably in these days, survival has been prioritized above all, but even within the framework of public health actions widely accepted, there has been a tacit assumption that it is inevitable that some people's survival will just have to be more feasible than others'. Some work is "essential" regardless of the risk. Some risk is "essential." Never mind how disproportionately that risk falls to already oppressed people. "That's the way it goes," each day whispers to some people and screams to others. In a world rife with suffering, it can feel hard for many to imagine anything beyond securing the conditions to survive. Without offering any pat conclusions for the sake of a chapter, I simply close by hovering inside the space where TO and positive psychology overlap most dynamically, however different they are in many ways: the insistence on reaching for something more than getting by. And as I do, I'm reminded that, in the days to come, mere survival will probably feel to some like more of a win than ever. For many, it has always been contingent and hard won. Thriving will realistically continue to seem to many like a mirage, if visible on the horizon at all. But that stark likelihood also speaks to the value of all practices, techniques, methods, fields, and movements—TO and positive psychology among them—that could potentially help humans insist on their right to flourish. I hope people engaging in either TO or positive psychology will do so as concretely as possible, in ways that center above all the realities, the needs, and the rights of the most precarious among us.

Works Cited

Boal, Augusto. *Aesthetics of the Oppressed*. Translated by Adrian Jackson. London, Routledge, 2006.

Boal, Augusto. *Games for Actors and Non-Actors*. 2nd ed. Translated by Adrian Jackson. London, Routledge, 2003.

Boal, Augusto. *Hamlet and the Baker's Son: My Life in Theatre and Politics*. Translated by Augusto Boal and Candida Blaker. London, Routledge, 2001.

Boal, Augusto. *Legislative Theatre*. Translated by Adrian Jackson. London, Routledge, 1998.

Boal, Augusto. *Theatre of the Oppressed*. Translated by Charles A. McBride and Maria-Odilia Leal McBride. New York, TCG, 1985.

Boal, Augusto. *The Rainbow of Desire: The Boal Method of Theatre and Therapy*. Translated by Adrian Jackson. London, Routledge, 1995.

Boal, Julian. "Theatre of the Oppressed in Neoliberal Times: From Che Guevara to the Uber Driver." *The Routledge Companion to Theatre of the Oppressed*, edited by Kelly Howe, Julian Boal, and José Soeiro. London, Routledge, 2019, pp. 289–302.

Boal, Julian, and José Soeiro. "Identities, Otherness, and Emancipation in Theatre of the Oppressed." *The Routledge Companion to Theatre of the Oppressed*, edited by Kelly Howe, Julian Boal, and José Soeiro. London, Routledge, 2019, pp. 94–103.

chullage and raquel. "Peles Negras, Máscaras Negras (Black Skins, Black Masks): *Maria 28*, Racism, and Domestic Work." *The Routledge Companion to Theatre of the Oppressed*, edited by Kelly Howe, Julian Boal, and José Soeiro. London, Routledge, 2019, pp. 381–87.

Dolan, Jill. *Utopia in Performance: Finding Hope at the Theater*. Ann Arbor, University of Michigan Press, 2005.

Escuela de Teatro Político del Movimiento Popular la Dignidad. "Political Organizations: La Dignidad—Theatre and Politics in Movement." Translated by Mirta Zimmerman. *The Routledge Companion to Theatre of the Oppressed*, edited by Kelly Howe, Julian Boal, and José Soeiro. London, Routledge, 2019, pp. 316–21.

Fredrickson, Barbara L. "What Good Are Positive Emotions?" *Review of General Psychology*, vol. 2, no. 3, 1998, pp. 300–319.

"Games: Demechanization and Serious Fun. An Interview with Cora Fairstein, Birgit Fritz, and Roberto Mazzini." *The Routledge Companion to Theatre of the Oppressed*, edited by Kelly Howe, Julian Boal, and José Soeiro. London, Routledge, 2019, pp. 143–49.

Ganguly, Sanjoy. *Jana Sanskriti: Forum Theatre and Democracy in India*. London, Routledge, 2010.

Heritage, Paul. "The Courage to Be Happy: Augusto Boal, Legislative Theatre, and the 7th International Festival of the Theatre of the Oppressed." *TDR (1988–)*, vol. 38, no. 3, 1994, pp. 25–34. www.jstor.org/stable/1146376.

Howe, Kelly. "Constraints and Possibilities in the Flesh: The Body in Theatre of the Oppressed." *The Routledge Companion to Theatre of the Oppressed*, edited by Kelly Howe, Julian Boal, and José Soeiro. London, Routledge, 2019, pp. 76–85.

Howe, Kelly, Julian Boal, and José Soeiro. *The Routledge Companion to Theatre of the Oppressed*. London, Routledge, 2019.

Jackson, Adrian. "The Rainbow of Desire: Boal and Doubt." *The Routledge Companion to Theatre of the Oppressed*, edited by Kelly Howe, Julian Boal, and José Soeiro. London, Routledge, 2019, pp. 180–86.

Pawelski, James O. "Bringing Together the Humanities and the Science of Well-Being to Advance Human Flourishing." *Well-Being and Higher Education: A Strategy for Change and the Realization of Education's Greater Purposes*, edited by Donald W. Harward. Washington, DC, Association of American Colleges and Universities, 2016, pp. 207–16.

Pawelski, James O. "Defining the 'Positive' in Positive Psychology: Part II. A Normative Analysis." *The Journal Positive Psychology*, vol. 11, no. 4, 2016, pp. 357–65.

Rubin, Katy. "Theatre of the Oppressed NYC: Radical Partnerships on the Ground in New York City." *The Routledge Companion to Theatre of the Oppressed*, edited by Kelly Howe, Julian Boal, and José Soeiro. London, Routledge, 2019, pp. 414–19.

Seligmann, Martin, and Mihaly Csikszentmihalyi. "Positive Psychology: An Introduction." *American Psychologist*, vol. 55, no. 1, 2000, pp. 5–14.

Snyder-Young, Dani. *Theatre of Good Intentions: Challenges and Hopes for Theatre and Social Change*. New York, Palgrave Macmillan, 2013.

Soeiro, José. "Legislative Theatre: Can Theatre Reinvent Politics?" *The Routledge Companion to Theatre of the Oppressed*, edited by Kelly Howe, Julian Boal, and José Soeiro. London, Routledge, 2019, pp. 187–94.

"Therapy: Theatre of the Oppressed and/as Therapeutic Praxis—An Interview with Brent Blair, Iwan Brioc, and Mady Schutzman." *The Routledge Companion to Theatre of the Oppressed*, edited by Kelly Howe, Julian Boal, and José Soeiro. London, Routledge, 2019, pp. 336–47.

5

Community Musical Theater as
a Human Flourishing Project

Stacy Wolf

On a Monday night in mid-April 2018, less than a week before *Guys & Dolls'*
opening night, sixty people were scattered around the Third Avenue Players'
two-hundred-seat theater.[1] Four teenage techies on ladders focused the
lights, a few more people put the finishing touches on the set with hammers
or paintbrushes, and a few more backstage organized the body mics. The
eight-piece orchestra, assembled in a "pit" on the floor in front of the stage,
tuned their instruments, and the musical director reviewed the opening
measures of the score. The audible and emotional buzz, the constant movement of bodies, the proliferation of headsets, and the plunking piano were
just like any other rehearsal at any other theater less than a week before
opening. The only difference: everyone here has a job or goes to school in the
daytime, and no one is being paid. This is a place of human flourishing. This
is community theater.

Across the United States each year, more than 1.5 million people participate in over forty-six thousand productions at more than eight thousand
community theaters. At least 86 million family members, friends, neighbors,
and fellow thespians attend these productions, most of which are shows in
the Broadway musical repertoire such as *The Sound of Music, Into the Woods,*
Beauty and the Beast, and the show I'll focus on here, Frank Loesser's *Guys*
& Dolls.

[1] Thanks to Wendy Belcher, Deborah Paredez, Jill Dolan, Leslie Rowley, Laura Taylor, Claudia
Voyles, Tamsen Wolff, the 2019 Musical Theatre Forum (Ray Ace, Joanna Dee Das, Liza Gennaro,
Raymond Knapp, Nathan Lamp, Jeff Magee, Doug Reside, Curtis Russell, David Savran, Dominic
Symonds, Jessica Sternfeld, Jason Witt, Elizabeth Wollman), and the Theatre & Performance Studies
H & HFP participants for reading drafts of the essay. My thanks to Harvey Young and James Pawelski
for their vision, leadership, and editorial advice, and to Marissa Michaels for editing assistance.

The theater makers of the Third Avenue Players are composites based on fieldnotes and
interviews from numerous community musical theaters across the United States that I visited between 2012 and 2019 (see Wolf, *Beyond*).

Stacy Wolf, *Community Musical Theater as a Human Flourishing Project* In: *Theater and Human*
Flourishing. Edited by: Harvey Young, Oxford University Press. © Oxford University Press 2023.
DOI: 10.1093/oso/9780197622261.003.0006

At first glance, community musical theater might not seem like a performance form worthy of study, and professional theater artists, critics, and academics typically dismiss community musical theater out of hand.[2] Reasons for disparagement are clear and, for some detractors, commonsensical. Professional artists joke about community theater's mediocre production values and self-important "artists" (like the desperately earnest and egocentric crew in *Waiting for Guffman*). Activist political theater makers disregard musical theater as a genre, assuming that the entertainment-oriented, profit-seeking repertoire of the Broadway musical can't possibly lead to anything good.

The Broadway musical theater repertoire at first seems light and entertaining, and its social and political commentary liberal at best. Many shows are misogynist, heterosexist, classist, and racist, and many theaters (including professional as well as high school and community theaters) produce musicals without attending to their pervasive and demeaning stereotypes, merely reproducing them.[3] As well, musical theater's licensing and distribution mechanisms are corporate and profit-seeking; that is, the proliferation of middlebrow culture supports a global capitalist network of licensors.

More locally, only those whose jobs allow them sufficient leisure time have the privilege of participating in a "hobby" like community musical theater. At base, the time required excludes many people, so class is a barrier. Also, some leaders of community musical theaters are strong-willed and temperamental divas (men as well as women) who wield their power unfairly. And the aesthetic quality of community musicals is sometimes unpolished.

In addition, as much pleasure as the Broadway musical theater canon provides, it's also a source of frustration and disappointment. Many more women than men participate in amateur school, summer camp, and community musical theater, but there are not enough roles for them. Broadway musical theater's relentless heterosexism (and aggressively watchful licensors) discourages cross-gender casting in shows. (*Beauty and the Beast*, *Into the Woods*, and *Grease* were the most frequently produced high school musicals in the 2010s [Nadworny]). Further, many of the younger female roles are stereotypical ingénues, and the older parts, evil shrews. In spite of the pleasure

---

[2] See Sherman.

[3] See Liu, for example, about a protest against Asian stereotypes in a production of *Anything Goes* at Princeton High School in Princeton, New Jersey, in 2019.

of performing, of singing and dancing, many women find themselves perpetuating negative images of women. In talking to hundreds of women and
girls over the seven years of my fieldwork, I found a wide range of awareness of the politics of representation, with high school and college-age young
women as the sharpest critics and most dissatisfied theater artists. In short,
the Broadway musical theater repertoire can be the cause of distress rather
than well-being.

But, as I hope to demonstrate in this chapter, musical theater making—
despite its very real shortcomings—also enables self-efficacy, social inte-
gration, and a positive life outlook; that is, local community musical theater
supports key aspects of human flourishing. To a certain degree, the positive
effects of involvement in community musical theater are self-evident in that
people volunteer to participate during their leisure time outside of work and
school and homemaking; that is, they're intrinsically motivated. But research
in positive psychology—a subfield of psychology that focuses on what makes
individuals and communities thrive instead of focusing on the diagnosis and
treatment of psychopathology—offers a more specific framework to analyze what community musical theater does and how it leads to or obstructs
human well-being (Seligman and Csikszentmihalyi).

Community Musical Theater in the United States

From 2012 to 2019, I spent hundreds of hours at a number of community
musical theaters across the United States, observing auditions and rehearsals
at every stage of production, from first read-through to tech and dress;
attending performances; and helping the cast and crew strike the set. I sat
in on board meetings and listened to casting and design conversations. At
one theater when the timing was right, I even got invited and went to a cast
party. As an indigenous, empathetic ethnographer of amateur community
musical theater productions—that is, someone with considerable inside
knowledge of how musical theater is made and the goal of telling people's
stories in an empathetic, critically generous way—I'm convinced that participation in musical theater benefits people across gender, sexuality, race,
ethnicity, class, region, age, and ability.[4] I've witnessed the satisfaction of a
group of performers executing difficult choreography in unison, hitting the

---

[4] On critical generosity, see Dolan (who cites David Román).

right notes in harmony, or delivering their lines correctly and with feeling. I've noted stagehands moving a piece of furniture with speed and precision, and a lighting designer calling the light cue (because there is seldom enough time for the stage manager to learn how to call the show) so that the actors are illuminated when the scene begins. I've seen people laughing and crying, frustrated and confused, proud and joyful. Though not without its offstage drama, conflicts, power struggles, shifting alliances, and friendships and romances gained and lost, the overall experience for those who dedicate hours of their non-work life to making local, community musical theater is enormously fulfilling and positive. Most of those who participate in community musical theater as directors, musical directors, choreographers, stage managers, musicians, designers, techies, prop masters, set builders, and actors, and who see shows in their local communities, find immense satisfaction in the activity. People simply love doing it.

In 1917, playwright, director, and activist Louise Burleigh coined the term "community theater" to describe local, amateur theatrical activities that aimed to engage citizens in their towns, promote patriotism, and instill civic pride through performance. Burleigh and other advocates saw community theater as a unique opportunity for the masses to be civically engaged through active participation in art (Burleigh xxxii). Fellow proselytizer Percy MacKaye described community theater as a "civic festival," a "ritual of democratic religion," compelled by people's "aspiring, playful, creative, child-like, religious instinct" (7).

As Broadway musicals' visibility grew in mid-twentieth century U.S. culture through the production and sales of cast albums and performers' regular appearances on television, like the *Ed Sullivan Show*, licensing companies began to offer Broadway musical librettos and scores, and more community theaters added musicals to their seasons. By the twenty-first century, musicals dominated community theaters' seasons, and some that produce non-musicals struggle to attract audiences to those plays. As Nina, a veteran community theater producer, told me, "We haven't been able to sell plays, you know. People want big musicals, they do. Musicals let people say, 'I'm gonna sit back and I'm gonna listen to the music and relax.'"

Musical theater—specifically the mainstream, commercial Broadway repertoire—offers particular pleasures of melody-humming, toe-tapping engagement for creators and audiences alike. Most theater artists, scholars, and students are well aware of the attraction and benefits of community musical theater, whether we once participated in homegrown, amateur shows or now teach students who performed in or worked on their local community theater shows.

Further, musical theater scholars, including Raymond Knapp, Carol Oja, David Savran, Elizabeth Wollman, and others (myself included), have demonstrated musical theater's serious engagement with U.S. politics and culture, arguing that the mainstream, commercial musical is always in conversation with the issues of the day.[5] Moreover, as musicologist Rose Rosengard Subotnik argues, Tin Pan Alley songs (which formed the repertoire of musicals of the 1930s and 1940s, many conventions of which persist today), long disdained by musicologists, are a uniquely American "hybrid genre" that "did not demand faithfulness in performance to their written form" and so "could be performed at any moment in any place by anyone amateur or professional" (213). This "performers' music" "would get stuck in the soundtrack of people's minds," she writes, "to be triggered forever in situations expected and unexpected" (215). In addition, ordinary people could sing these well-crafted songs and gain a sense of mastery and confidence. Subotnik concludes, "Thus, far from stifling an individual's power to stake out a meaningful life in a depersonalized society, such songs, in my judgment, offered an important source of empowerment to ordinary people" (215).

In addition to its accessibility, musical theater is a deeply and distinctively collaborative, communal enterprise. It brings people—theater makers and spectators—together in the same room at the same time, often across generations, to experience a story told through song and dance, once and only once. It differs from visual arts, creative writing, and other art forms and from exercise, gardening, yoga, and other hobbies which can be done communally but are not collaborative. A chorus, an orchestra, and nonmusical theater are the closest cousins to musical theater, though they lack the same conjunction of music and theater and dance. Musicals are, as Dominic Symonds writes, made of "corporeal gestures of vocality and physicality that engage bodies in acts of expressive commitment" (Symonds and Taylor 2). Musical theater's intimate liveness even counters the technological mediation and anticommunitarian trends of contemporary culture. As Laura Lodewyck writes elsewhere in this volume, "Theater is built on the felt encounter with other individuals."

The "community theater" designation adds another defining element to musical theater, underlining the local, the volunteer, and the amateur—labels

---

[5] See, for example, Knapp; Oja; Savran; Wolf, *Changed*; Wollman.

that call up admiration, condescension, or horror, depending on one's perspective.[6] Theater commentator and arts advocate Howard Sherman defends community theaters, arguing that they provide a creative outlet for adults—those who did theater in high school but did not pursue it professionally—and that many community theater productions feature large cast plays that professional theaters can't afford to do. "By slagging community theatre," he writes, "we're undercutting our own best interests and evidencing our own cultural elitism."

Though participants and audiences of community theater productions feel, experience, and attest to its value, scholarship that makes connections between community musical theater and psychological well-being is lacking, and neither theater studies nor psychology has sufficiently explored its positive effects. The field of positive psychology offers a framework and a series of useful concepts ("mechanisms") through which to examine how community musical theater fosters human flourishing.

Positive Psychology's "Mechanisms" of Human Flourishing and Community Musical Theater

In "The Role of the Arts and Humanities in Human Flourishing: A Conceptual Model," Louis Tay, James O. Pawelski, and Melissa G. Keith observe that "the arts and humanities occupy a remarkable place in human life," from childhood stories through adult "cultural pursuits." They note with chagrin that public perception and public policy disregard the importance of the arts and humanities in favor of STEM fields, and they call for more scientific, psychological research "to investigate empirically whether or not the arts and humanities have a significant impact on individual and collective well-being, particularly beyond merely economic outcomes" (215). Studies demonstrate, for example, the correlation between musical study and cognitive control, between art training and cognition, between musical participation and a "positive outlook on life," and between engagement with the arts as a reader, spectator, or audience member and increased positive affect (216).

---

[6] Bill Ivey explains how, in the early twentieth century, the concept of "participation" in the arts shifted to appreciation for the arts, thereby diminishing the public significance and relevance (and funding of) amateur arts practices (Tepper and Ivey 5).

Their article outlines a "conceptual model" and calls for more research "to establish an integrative understanding of the effect of the arts and humanities on well-being" (215).

This chapter aims to contribute to that research with an ethnographic study of community musical theater. The examples here are taken from fieldnotes and interviews from a number of community theaters in various parts of the United States that I visited between 2012 and 2019. I use the architecture of the psychological model to examine what kinds of human flourishing are enabled by participation in community musical theater production. Positive psychology can help us specify how people benefit from participation in community musical theater.

According to Tay, Pawelski, and Keith, the potential well-being effects of engagement in the arts and humanities can be defined broadly in terms of "immediate positive neurological, physiological, and affective changes," "psychological competencies" like "adaptivity, creativity, and self-efficacy," and "general well-being effects"—that is, more "positive emotions" and feelings of "autonomy, environmental mastery, personal growth, positive relations, purpose in life, and self-acceptance" (220). They also include positive normative outcomes, such as character, values, ethical behavior, and civic engagement.

Everyone who works on a show potentially experiences these well-being effects, and Tay, Pawelski, and Keith posit four "mechanisms," or pathways, that may facilitate these types of positive effects: immersion, embeddedness, socialization, and reflectiveness. Importantly, each stage of production and rehearsal, from first sing-through to choreographing a musical number to stumble-through to tech/dress—and everything in between—provides the circumstances in which such human flourishing can happen.

Immersion

Four months before the final dress rehearsal that opened this chapter, rehearsals began for *Guys & Dolls*. The multiracial cast of twenty, ranging in age from fifteen to sixty-five, included students, teachers, a lawyer, a stay-at-home dad, an administrative assistant, and a doctor, among others. They sat in rows of seats in the theater, divided by voice parts. They chatted and laughed, bragged about recent shows they'd performed in or saw at other local community theaters or at the Broadway touring house downtown.

Rose, *Guys & Dolls*' music director, had spent hours and hours over the past weeks preparing for this first music rehearsal, guiltily shortchanging her lesson plans for the fifth grade math classes she taught at the elementary school. The original 1950 cast album of *Guys & Dolls* was on a nonstop repeating loop on her phone, and she also listened to other revivals and the movie with Frank Sinatra. She'd already decided that they would first learn the ensemble number "Sit Down You're Rockin' the Boat," the big, raucous, gospel-inflected, 11 o'clock showstopper.[7] The song was fun, the harmonies were complex but not impossible, and she could count on Charles—who was playing Nicely-Nicely, the gambler who leads the song—a Third Avenue Players' regular, to be an enthusiastic and encouraging partner in the rehearsal. She loved that the song demanded, formed, and then celebrated the formation of a community, which she and Lacey, the *Guys & Dolls*' director, aimed for in every production they did.

To prepare for rehearsal, Rose had pored over the score and divided the cast into eight voice parts, hoping that some of the more experienced singers would be able to carry their line alone. She played the chords on the piano—which wasn't the easiest task because the clarinet was her instrument, not the piano, and she stuck Post-its on measures that might be tougher for the singers to learn. Rose was an experienced music director, but like Lacey, her good friend and frequent collaborator, *Guys & Dolls* would be her first big, classic musical.

"Hi everybody! Let's turn to page fifty-five," Rose said, getting their attention over the clatter of phones being put away, water bottles being closed, backpacks zipped, and pencils removed from their cases. "I know this isn't the first song in the show, but it's a great number and will help us to get attuned to each other's voices." She told everyone their voice part. "Jay will play it once," she said, nodding toward the accompanist, who was musical-directing the orchestra, a group of twelve players whom the actors would meet at the sitzprobe during the last week of rehearsal in five months' time. "Those of you who can sight-read, do, and the rest of you, do your best, but don't worry, we'll go over all of it. It's a lot of harmony!" She raised her arms and they were off.

This music-learning rehearsal exemplifies "immersion." As Rose taught the large group the song, every person was thoroughly absorbed in the activity, focused and concentrated, listening and following along in the music.

---

[7] For a short and well-observed reading of the song, see Harris.

Immersion is linked to what Tay, Keith, and Pawelski call "immediacy," to flow, to deep engagement; they write, "One's attention is captured, resulting in the experiencing of various levels of sensory and emotional states and first-order cognitions" (217).[8] This sense of being "carried away," in their words, describes what frequently happens at this early stage of rehearsal, when the performers are learning new material and are 100 percent attentive. This kind of immersion is rare in our culture, which is dominated by scattered attention and distractions, especially smartphones.

The music-learning activity, singing Loesser's catchy, rousing, and harmonic score, is similar to participating in a chorus. Over time and focused on the task at hand, the singers form a group characterized by what social psychologists call "high entitativity."[9] Measure by measure, Jay played and Rose sang and each voice section learned their part. When Rose asked the company to sing together, harmonies rang out in the auditorium, and everyone clapped and stomped, temporarily transforming the stark rehearsal room into the musical's packed-with-gamblers Mission. Everyone was concentrating, listening to their own voice, the voices of those around them, and the music created by many voices harmonizing.

As powerful as this moment was, though, not everyone experienced immersion at the time. Trey, whose rich bass filled out the sound, was in the ensemble, but he only half-listened, preoccupied because he was jealous of Charles, who landed the part he wanted. "There are so few good roles for Black men around here," he later told me. "I was disappointed not to get this part, and I was honestly very frustrated for the first few rehearsals and even debated quitting." Still, Trey enjoyed himself at this rehearsal and decided to stay in the show, which he was glad about in the end. "Looking back," he said, "I guess I would say that working on that song got me here," putting his hand on his heart, "and that was it."

---

[8] Tay, Pawelski, and Keith's examples in this section of the article pertain more to engagement in reception as spectators, audience members, or readers. But I would suggest that participants experience the same emotions as spectators as well as other processes through the embodiment and envoicement of performance.

[9] See Savage and Symonds.

Embeddedness

One month and twelve rehearsals later, Destiny and Ron, who played Sarah Brown and Sky Masterson, rehearsed the last scene in Act 1. Lacey, the director, sat on the back of a seat in the third row, her marked-up script at her side. The actors were mostly off book, but when they forgot what line was next, they looked toward the stage manager, who sat in the front row, following closely and ready to feed it to them. No one else was called for rehearsal that night, as Lacey's goal was to clarify the relationship between the two characters and to make this scene hum with the desire born from the romantic leads' initial animosity that characterizes most musicals in the Broadway canon.

"Let's just review where we've been and where we are," said Lacey. They talked about how Act 1, Scene 10 takes place outside of the Mission. Sarah and Sky have just returned from an evening in Havana, where Sky took Sarah to win a bet, and an unknowing Sarah got drunk and kissed Sky. It's 4:00 a.m., they're back in New York and sober, and they enter the scene. Sarah, according to the stage directions, "is in a very pensive mood." Sky, following, is "also in a very thoughtful mood" (Loesser et al. 70). "What do you think happened between the end of the previous scene and now?" Lacey asked, and they all discussed it. The actor playing Adelaide, to whom Nathan has finally proposed, walks by the other two actors, back in character, and they have a short conversation with her and watch her leave. "Miss Adelaide certainly seems happy," says Sky. "She's in love," replies Sarah. Seven lines follow, then Sky sings the ballad "My Time of Day," which leads into "I've Never Been in Love Before," their romantic duet. In this short scene, the audience must see the characters fall in love.

"Start with Sky's line as both of you watch Adelaide exit, and let's just try it," instructed Lacey. Destiny and Ron stood center stage and said the lines. "Good. Fine. Try it again," prompted Lacey, "but this time, take a breath and a pause between each line." They did it again, and it seemed more like they were actually listening to each other. "Good, better. This time, forget the blocking and stand with your backs to each other. Try to send the meaning of the words through your back." Ron giggled and Destiny raised her eyebrows, but they did it, and the air was thicker still. Destiny and Ron looked at each other, pleased, and at Lacey, and they all knew the actors had discovered something. For the next fifteen minutes, they repeated this tiny section of the scene, each time with a new instruction from Lacey. The three talked about each line, too, trying to decipher the subtext and the shifting emotions line by line. (Standard time calculations for rehearsals are one hour of rehearsal for one minute of stage time.) the last time they said their lines, Lacey said, "Yes! You nailed it."

The satisfaction of improvement, which happens throughout the rehearsal period, but especially in the early, decision-making days, is a sign of "embeddedness,"[10] or the "socio-cognitive psychological processes that underlie the development of particular perspectives, habits, or skills," including "self-efficacy," "self-regulation," "emotional regulation," "integrative complexity," and "feelings of autonomy, relatedness, and competence" (Tay, Pawelski, and Keith 217). These types of processes, which lead to this broad range of enduring effects, happen throughout the theater-making experience, but especially during these intense, back-and-forth, start-and-stop early to mid-stage rehearsals. The sense of improvement or "positive outcomes" is constant and steady at this stage.

Socialization

One morning six months earlier, while Destiny, a cardiologist, was on general rounds at the hospital, her phone pinged. As she waited for the nurse to collect the patient's vitals, she glanced down and read the text: next year's Third Avenue Players season was announced! They were doing *Guys & Dolls*! She felt herself gasp and then pulled her attention back to her patient. Through the rest of the day, she found herself humming the songs. She'd never been in *Guys & Dolls*, but they'd done it at her high school when she was a student. She loved the show and knew it well and wanted to get cast.

Way across town, Abby's phone also pinged as she was operating the forklift on a construction site for new townhouses. She didn't know what *Guys & Dolls* was, but it didn't sound good to her. She'd heard rumors that they might do *Rent*, which she knew was financially risky for the theater, whose audiences tended to be older and more conservative, but she had been a "Renthead" in her younger days and knew she'd have a good shot at the role of Joanne. Now she wasn't sure if she would even audition. Or maybe she would volunteer to build the set. Did *Guys & Dolls* have a complicated set that would be fun to build? she wondered. That seemed like a fine idea, and

---

[10] In subsequent articles, Tay, Pawelski, and Keith replaced "embeddedness" with "acquisition."

she felt resolved by the end of the day. For this show, she would not audition at all but would work on the set.

Lacey also heard the ping, and she was relieved that the audition notice finally went out and she could believe that it was real and that she was getting to direct this big, romantic, clever, classic musical. For the past seven years that she'd been involved with the Players—since she moved to the area—even though she was a theater major and the president of the student theater group in college, the board always wanted her to direct something small. Lacey had done *The Fantasticks*, *Falsettos* , and *The Last Five Years*, and she loved directing each of them, but she'd been lobbying for a bigger project for a while. She'd watched the male directors simply announce what they were doing—even the ones who started directing after she joined the Players—but she always had to sell her idea and prove her worth. Lacey wasn't overly sensitive or paranoid; she only had to look around to see that the male directors and designers were more respected, got free rein with productions (whether or not they could keep costs under budget), and were treated as "artistes." She wondered if it was because there was such a dearth of male actors that all men were treated better than the women. She already felt bad about the hundred excellent women who would audition that she wouldn't be able to cast.

Lacey imagined whose phone pinged—that is, who signed up for alerts from the Players—and who she should send the audition notice to and who she should email or text directly to ask them to audition. She was determined to cast a racially diverse group of performers, even as she knew that white women would outnumber any other demographic ten to one. (She remembered with a grimace a July 7, 2018, tweet by a writer, Lucy Huber, which she immediately related to: "High school girls in musicals: Ive being [sic] going to theater camp since 1st grade and taking professional voice lessons since I was 10, so excited to be townsperson #3 this spring! HS boys in musicals: The drama teacher cornered me after Alegbra 2 [sic] and said I had to be Shrek.") Because Lacey had worked with the Players and other community theaters in the area for a few years, she'd built a solid network of people to contact. Lacey sent a text to her music director, choreographer, and designers to remind them to let their friends know about auditions. The extra time and energy would be well worth it.

At a community theater, the audition announcement launches the process as a reality for the creative team of director, music director, and choreographer and triggers reactions among potential performers. "Socialization" begins, too. In positive psychology, socialization refers, in part, to people taking on different roles in their lives, which enhances well-being. The season announcement enables potential participants to anticipate the new roles they might take (or take on) (Tay, Pawelski, and Keith 218).[11] Destiny was excited, already imagining herself playing Adelaide or maybe even Sarah. Abby was disappointed, wavering between auditioning and participating backstage. Lacey was eager to hold auditions, cast the show, and get started. She wanted to be in the role of director, to set the tone for rehearsals, to make creative choices, to manage a big group of people, and, of course, to get the best work out of her actors that she could.

Two months later, well into the rehearsal process, Lacey, Destiny, Abby, and fifty more people involved with *Guys & Dolls* experienced the multiple role-playing of socialization in different ways. First, at a minimum, they each played a role at home, another role at work, and another at the theater. Because the people who participate in community musical theater are amateurs, because they come to rehearsal after a day in an office, in a classroom, in a lab, in a store, or at home caring for children or elders, the role that they take on at the community theater is different from their role in other settings. In addition, within her role as director—and she was entirely aware of this fact—Lacey fulfilled many different roles: artist, counselor, and coach, to name a few. When Lacey decided to cast her twelve-year-old, musical theater–obsessed daughter in the show, she had to block out her "mother role" when directing the girl.[12]

Destiny perceived that she occupied several roles in addition to her away-from-the-theater identities. Being cast in the show as one of the leads made her feel her responsibility as an actor and a leader of the company. "I knew the rest of the cast, especially the younger members in the company, looked to me, and no matter how I felt when I got to rehearsal every night—sometimes I was tired or in a bad mood—I smiled and was nice to everyone and did whatever Lacey asked of us." In this way, then, Destiny inhabited the role of an actor. Then within that container, she played Sarah, crafting the character through external and internal choices. Because the music was difficult, Destiny could never lose herself completely in Sarah; she had to stay aware of

---

[11] Tay, Pawelski, and Keith write, "Socialization reflects the degree to which individuals take on various roles and identities within communities and cultures" (218).

[12] Families and multiple generations frequently participate in community musical theater. Stories abound of parents who got involved because they drove their kids to rehearsal week after week, and kids who caught the theater bug from being at the theater with their parents. Community musical theater may be one of the few settings (church would be another) in which people of all ages do an activity together.

her breathing and her diaphragm, supporting the sound, so she also played the role of a singer.

Abby decided not to audition for the show but volunteered to be the props master and to help build the set. As much as when she'd performed in a Players show, she took her responsibility seriously, making sure that each item was what Lacey wanted and that the champagne bottle, the deck of cards, the thick, heavy book for cold-suffering, unmarried Adelaide's self-diagnosis in "Adelaide's Lament," and all of the other props for the show were in their proper places for each scene. After the first few rehearsals, Abby was glad that she hadn't auditioned because it seemed to her that "aside from the fun roles of Adelaide and Sarah, the women in the show were just strippers and sex objects." She added, "I don't think I would have wanted to do that," though she admitted that the group of six in the female chorus seemed to be having fun and laughing a lot. "We're family!" one of the six told me.

As Lacey hoped, she persuaded a handful of newcomers to audition for *Guys & Dolls*, including David, who auditioned because, he said, "it was always my dream to play Nathan Detroit, but most directors won't cast a skinny Korean guy as the 'New Yawk' tough guy gambler!" Lacey knew David because their kids went to the same school, and she once overheard him talking about doing musical theater when he was in college. He hadn't performed for a while, but it wasn't hard to persuade him to audition because he loved the show. Lacey was thrilled that an Asian American man decided to try out, and when he sang "Sue Me" at his audition, she was sold.

Once rehearsals started, David found the schedule challenging, but he remembered, he told me, "how great it is to be directed by someone as talented" as Lacey. At his job as an IT director, he managed a team of thirty people and often felt stressed and overwhelmed, but at the theater he just followed her directions and tried his best. He worked hard to learn his music and lines and blocking, but he "loved" being just one cast member without feeling responsible for the whole production, with "someone else taking the long view." He felt the process as a "creative release." Musical theater rehearsal is where people feel themselves differently than at work.

"Socialization can occur when individuals learn various ways of relating within a community; it can also occur when individuals learn new ways of relating across different cultural environments," write Tay, Pawelski, and Keith (218). This process of socialization happens every time a new group assembles to rehearse and create a new production. Each production process initiates a new cultural environment—in this case, *Guys & Dolls*—which is comprised of the cast and crew, the producing institution or theater, and the show itself. David didn't think he would do another show with the Players unless they selected another of his favorite shows. The Players' regulars teased that he was a "butterfly"—someone who does one show and then flies away— as opposed to Destiny, Abby, Rose, and Lacey, who were worker "bees," returning year after year to keep the theater going. The regulars, or "bees," as sociologist Robert Bellah writes, "define the pattern of loyalty and obligation that keep the community alive"; they enact what he calls "the practices of commitment" (quoted in Kemmis 81).

Positive psychology, as articulated by Tay, Pawelski, and Keith, values the "accumulation and diversification of social roles" and asserts that "multiple identities can enhance resiliency" (218), which is precisely what community musical theater fosters. Unlike, say, a community chorus in which everyone does the same activity—singing—musical theater production requires many different tasks. Unlike the professional theater, in which most artists hone one skill throughout their entire career, community theater allows people to take on different roles according to their desires, skills, and willingness to work. Abby, as noted above, both performed in shows and also worked backstage. Lacey was a stage manager before she started directing. Ron choreographed as often as he acted in a show. Each new role promotes well-being in community musical theater participants.

Reflectiveness

For David, every minute of rehearsal as well as his "homework"—listening to his songs on the mps3 files that Rose made for him in the car on his way to work; working on his lines in the evening, after he put the kids to bed; practicing his choreography as he waited for the coffee to brew—aimed to make Nathan Detroit into himself and himself into Nathan Detroit. As a mechanism of positive psychology, David's process is "reflectiveness": "an intentional, cognitive-emotional process for developing, reinforcing, or discarding one's habits, character, values, or worldview" (Tay, Pawelski, and Keith 218). David said that he thought a lot about Nathan's character, about why he loves gambling ("He does not see himself as an addictive gambler, though I think he probably is") and why he won't marry Adelaide ("He's a stereotypical Nineteen-fifties guy who wants to stay free and a bachelor. He sees marriage as getting tied down and trapped, even though he does love her").[13] As linguistic anthropologist Shirley Brice Heath writes, "[A]dults who take part in theater attest [to how] enactment extends their capacity for assessing how the thinking processes of others operate" (Brice Heath and Gilbert 403). "[S]ociodramatic play," she continues, offers "ample opportunities . . . in figuring out how others think and what is in the mind of another character" (403).

To develop their characters—a distinctly reflective activity—most of the Players' actors combine Method-based, motivation- and objective-oriented acting techniques with an imitative bricolage enabled by the vast number of YouTube clips available. For *Guys & Dolls*, Kelly, who played Adelaide, started by comparing the character to herself. Then, as is her practice, she wrote a character biography and thought about Adelaide's objectives for the whole show ("to get Nathan to marry her!") and for each scene. She also looked at productions on YouTube, she admitted with a little embarrassment; in general, actors born before around 1980 reluctantly admit if they seek out and watch YouTube clips. "I want to create my character on my own without any preconceived ideas," said Kelly, "but I couldn't resist seeing what was out there." In contrast, younger actors are entirely upfront about the value of imitation. "Yes, of course I looked online!" said Destiny, seemingly baffled by my question. "After I watched twenty different versions of every song, I could decide exactly how I wanted to sing it," she explained.

The extended rehearsal period that is typical for community musical theater also promotes reflectiveness. Third Avenue Players' rehearsal schedule of two nights a week plus one afternoon each weekend for around four months (and then every night the week before opening for tech and dress rehearsals) is standard for community theaters. In contrast, professional theaters rehearse during regular business hours for three to four weeks. Community theater's long rehearsal cycle is a logistical necessity because people must juggle their commitment to the production with their professional and personal responsibilities, but the actors also benefit from an extended period for reflection.

[13] The musical is based on Damon Runyon's short stories that take place in the 1930s, but *Guys & Dolls* opened in 1950 and features post–World War II gendered character types.

By the week of dress rehearsal, all four leading actors—Destiny, Ron, Kelly, and David—agreed that *Guys & Dolls* is a "very silly show." "It's fun. It's escapism," Ron said. "It's classic musical comedy entertainment." But they also said that the show made them think about romance and how people fall in love, and about the stereotypical assumptions that men avoid marriage and women want to get married and try to trap the men. "The ending is ridiculous because Adelaide and I sing 'Marry the Man Today,' and then suddenly, we're all getting married, and it's like, how did that happen? But that's musical theater," said Destiny. "Does the show or the ending make you think about your own relationships?" I asked. "Well, I'm sure not trapping any man to marry me!" answered Destiny. "And I'm trying not to be a jerk," David added. For these actors performing in the show enabled "reflectiveness [that] can promote critical thinking and perspective taking . . . resulting in an evolution of the self and enhanced meaning and purpose" (Tay, Pawelski, and Keith 218).

These actors, focused entirely on *Guys & Dolls* for months, were not aware of how the Third Avenue Players' board, made up of eight volunteers who ran the theatrical organization day to day, practiced reflectiveness on a grander scale during the grueling and sometime fraught season selection process. Not-for-profit community theater aims to perpetuate itself; its key goal is to keep doing shows. Success means that a production earns enough through ticket sales that the organization can finance the next show. When the board chooses the season's musicals, they must consider, for example, title recognition and appeal to audiences, licensing costs, production costs for set and costumes, and cast-ability.

Third Avenue Players' board—though not all community theater boards—also thinks about the organization's role and identity in the community beyond providing entertainment. "Yes, we think about what shows we're doing," longtime board member and frequent director Carlos told me. "Some people don't care—they just want us to do something like *Annie* with a hundred little girls, or *The Sound of Music*, which will always sell out. But some board members, including myself, care a lot about which shows we choose." During my research, I witnessed numerous discussions among predominantly white board members about the season, race, and inclusivity, which often began with the question "Can we cast the show [e.g., *In the Heights*, *Miss Saigon*, *Ain't Misbehavin'*]? Will BIPOC actors come out for it?," demonstrating the board's awareness of their theater's dominant whiteness. If a theater organization is reflective about the politics of representation, it can improve its practices and make itself more welcoming and inclusive and alter the cliquish, clubby (and often white) reputation attached to some community theaters.[14]

Once the season is chosen, other opportunities for reflectiveness emerge, such as race-conscious casting. Carlos explained, "We don't interfere at all once we've hired a director. It's up to them to decide how they want to cast the show, with color-blind casting or not." Carlos was reflective about his own casting and directing practices, though. "But for me, yeah, I want to see everyone on stage, all races and everyone," he said. After the show is cast, during the months of rehearsal, every person working on the show—director, musical director, choreographer, designers, actors, and producers—makes numerous interpretive choices, all of which add up to a unique production in a unique place at a unique moment.

Community musical theater often engages people for many years, and over that time their aesthetic and political perspectives, intentions, and goals can and often do change. Community theater artists can reflect on their projects and choices. For example, Carlos told me how his views on casting have changed: "[A]bout ten years ago, I directed a production of *Once on This Island,* which is meant to be an all-Black cast, and cast it with actors of a wide range of ethnic backgrounds, including several white actors. At the time, I thought this was a good and reasonable approach. I look back now and cringe; that particular show ought not to be performed in that way, and I'm embarrassed I did it!" He added, "We're all trying to get better, but we're still finding our way."[15]

Expansiveness and Transformation

At different stages of the rehearsal process, community musical theater artists experience the mechanisms of immersion, embeddedness, socialization, and reflection. Taking into account the wide range of potential well-being outcomes these mechanisms can facilitate, I believe community musical theater produces (at least) two overarching positive outcomes: expansiveness and transformation.

[14] Creating a truly diverse and inclusive theater became more pressing in 2020 during the COVID pandemic and the United States' racial reckoning and activism following the murder of George Floyd. Though I completed my research in 2019, theater makers at all of the venues I visited and studied told me that they are prioritizing racial equity, diversity, and inclusion going forward.

[15] The 2018 Tony Award–winning revival of *Once on This Island* featured a racially diverse BIPOC cast of Black, Latinx, Asian American, and biracial performers.

When opening night finally arrived, the cast and crew were excited and nervous and more than ready for an audience. The tech rehearsal two nights before had been predictably long and nerves were fraying by 11:00 p.m., the mandated end of the evening. Lacey stayed upbeat and encouraging that night, but she was worried about the lighting cues, which sometimes happened a beat or two too late, and about David/Nathan, who sometimes inexplicably (because he worked hard and was always well-prepared) went blank and forgot a line. Lacey decided not to mention the off timing or the missed lines because she didn't want to make anyone more nervous. As director, she had to navigate what Gwyneth Shanks identifies elsewhere in this volume as "the pleasurable and painful contradictions between the self and the collective." All in all, though, the final dress rehearsal went fairly smoothly, but everyone seemed tired and no one could remember what was fun or funny about the show. After five months of rehearsing, they needed an audience. And tonight they had one.

At 7:45 on opening night, the theater was loud, filled with family and friends who'd been hearing about the show for months and were eager to support their loved ones, their arms full of bouquets of flowers. Other people involved with the Players were there, too, curious to see how this big ambitious show turned out, including some who weren't cast, silently hoping that it would flop.

As Destiny applied her makeup and quietly warmed up her voice, she was excited to show her friends what she could do in the role of Sarah. She knew it had been risky for Lacey to cast her; hardly the ingénue type, she was tall with a strong voice and a commanding presence. Kelly, whom Lacey cast as Adelaide, was a more typical ingénue, and the director intentionally pushed against those well-worn, conventional, and what all three women considered antifeminist musical theater types. Throughout the rehearsal process, Destiny loved learning and singing Sarah's soprano ballads and pretending she was drunk and falling in love with Sky in the scene outside the bar in Havana. In past Players' shows, she was always cast as the comic sidekick or the bitchy friend. This was the first time she got to play the romantic lead. She relished the final duet with Adelaide, "Marry the Man Today," as they sang their determination to remake their men to their own liking . . . after they married them.

Ron loved playing Sky Masterson. Though he was accustomed to being cast as the romantic lead in Players' musicals, his day job as a Safeway grocery store manager required him to be calm, efficient, and in control. Being in the musical allowed him to sing and dance, to inhabit his body in a way that was affirming and delightful but, he was aware, not typically encouraged in men. Ron enjoyed putting on stage makeup, slicking his hair back, and donning a silky striped suit and tie and Oxford shoes.

As actors and as people, both Destiny and Ron said they felt more expansive in themselves and transformed by the experience of rehearsing for and performing in *Guys & Dolls*. For one, they absorbed some of the qualities of their characters, which were different from their own personalities. Ron found himself using a softer voice in the store to try to get his way; Sky taught him how to ply his charms. Destiny found herself thinking about Sarah's religious morals at the start of the musical and how alcohol and a handsome man softened her resolve. She wasn't sure if Sarah made the right decision to marry Sky (though Destiny acted like Sarah chose well in the play), and she wondered what it means to be true to yourself. Their characters allowed—no, required—the actors to imagine choices that they might have repressed and to inhabit roles that they weren't normally allowed to perform. This expansiveness contributes to overall personal transformation. As Erin Hurley writes elsewhere in this volume, "[T]he arts are a public good in part for their contributions to a people's growth through self-expression."

After the show was over, and the cast and crew struck the set and went home to their families, Destiny and Ron felt both sad and relieved. They'd done so many shows over the years, they knew how to mete out the necessary time and energy to commit to this production two nights and one weekend afternoon a week for five months. But their families missed them. They were tearful to leave the cast and crew to whom they'd become so close over the months, including and especially each other. Though they had known each other in passing before *Guys & Dolls*, they became friends, saw each other on good days and bad days, often bolstering each other to get through rehearsal. They felt their lives had expanded with new social relations and deeper bonds.

The entire cast, creative team, and crew of *Guys & Dolls* were expanded and transformed by the experience, in fact. Some became close over the months. Some became better friends, and some hoped never to work on a show together again. But all of them grew as people and as artists. The performers' skills grew—they were all stronger singers, dancers, and actors than they had been five months earlier. And their cultural capital grew, too, as they now all intimately knew a classic show of the Broadway canon.

After *Guys & Dolls* closed and during the lull before auditions for the next show, Lacey, Rose, and Carlos talked about what went well with the performance and what they might improve in future Third Avenue Players shows to make each one a better, more expansive and transformative experience for everyone involved. The three felt confident in the Players' level of artistry, but they wanted to expand participation, to establish best practices for their group, to move toward what Marcia Ferguson, in an essay in this volume, calls "optimal involvement." Unlike some community theaters, whose leaders just want to pay the bills and hope there is enough in the coffers to do another show, the three had higher aspirations for human well-being. They talked about outreach to new and more diverse communities, about taking performances to different venues around the city, and about expressly inviting newcomers to participate. They talked about articulating a set of values and drafting a "contract" for rehearsal protocols, including intimacy awareness and unconscious bias training. They knew that some longtime members would scoff at these actions ("Just do the show and do it well," they'd say), but they wanted to push the theater to a higher level of ethical and fair theatrical practices.

The trio knew that human flourishing was possible because of community musical theater's unique conjunction of form and context. First, musicals are exuberant, embodied, expressive, and pleasurable. Music draws people together. Acting calls on the imagination. Dance necessitates proprioceptive awareness and physical coordination. Musical theater production requires cooperation and coordination, attention to detail, and persistence. All in all, people are drawn to the challenges and seductive appeal of the quirky, embodied, hybrid form of musical theater. Second, the local, volunteer aspect of "community" connects the artistic practice with place. As community theater advocate Virgil Baker wrote in 1952, "The motivating force that keeps a community theatre alive and functioning is the desire of the individuals who compose it for a fuller, richer, life experience" (230).

Works Cited

Baker, Virgil. "The Community Theatre as a Force in Adult Education." *Educational Theatre Journal*, vol. 4, no. 3, 1952, pp. 227–30.

Brice Heath, Shirley, and Lisa Gilbert. "Creativity and the Work of Art and Science: A Cognitive Neuroscience Perspective." *Routledge Handbook of the Arts and Education*, edited by Mike Fleming et al. New York, Routledge, 2014, pp. 398–409.

Burleigh, Louise. *Community Theatre in Theory and Practice*. Boston, Little, Brown, 1917.

Dolan, Jill. "Critical Generosity." *Linked Fate and Futures*, vol, 1, nos. 1–2, 2012, accessed June 6, 2020, https://public.imaginingamerica.org/blog/article/critical-generosity-2/.

Harris, Kathryn. "'Sit Down, You're Rockin' the Boat": An Unusual 11 O'clock Number." MTI, March 24, 2010, accessed May 13, 2019, https://www.mtishows.com/news/sit-down-youre-rockin-the-boat-an-unusual-11-oclock-number.

Kemmis, Daniel. *Community and the Politics of Place*. Oklahoma City, University of Oklahoma Press, 1990.

Knapp, Raymond. *The American Musical and the Performance of National Identity*. Princeton, NJ, Princeton University Press, 2005.

Liu, Siyang. "Anything Goes? No, Not Really." *The Daily Princetonian*, April 4, 2019, https://www.dailyprincetonian.com/article/2019/04/anything-goes-no-not-really.

Loesser, Frank, et al. *Guys and Dolls: A Musical Fable of Broadway*. New York, MTI, 1950.

MacKaye, Percy. *Community Drama: Its Motive and Method for Neighborliness*. Boston, Houghton Mifflin, 1917.

Nadworny, Elissa. "The Most Popular High School Plays and Musicals." *Morning Edition*, NPR, July 30, 2020. https://www.npr.org/sections/ed/2019/07/31/427138970/the-most-popular-high-school-plays-and-musicals.

Oja, Carol J. *Bernstein Meets Broadway: Collaborative Art in a Time of War*. New York, Oxford University Press, 2014.

Savage, Karen, and Dominic Symonds. *Economies of Collaboration in Performance: More Than the Sum of Its Parts*. Cham, Switzerland, Palgrave Macmillan, 2018.

Savran, David. *A Queer Sort of Materialism: Recontextualizing American Theater*. Ann Arbor, University of Michigan Press, 1998.

Seligman, Martin E. P., and Mihaly Csikszentmihalyi. "Positive Psychology: An Introduction." *American Psychologist*, vol. 55, no. 1, 2000, pp. 5–14.

Sherman, Howard. "Theater the Theater Community Disdains." *Huffington Post*, February 21, 2012. https://www.huffpost.com/entry/theatre-the-theatre-commu_b_1914300. http://www.hesherman.com/2012/02/21/theatre-the-theatre-community-disdains/.

Subotnik, Rose Rosengard. "Shoddy Equipment for Living? Deconstructing the Tin Pan Alley Song." *Musicological Identities: Essays in Honor of Susan McClary*, edited by Steven Baur et al. Burlington, Vermont, Ashgate, 2008, pp. 205–18.

Symonds, Dominic, and Millie Taylor. "Singing the Dance, Dancing the Song." *Gestures of Music Theater: The Performativity of Song and Dance*, edited by Dominic Symonds and Millie Taylor, New York, Oxford University Press, 2014, pp. 1–8.

Tay, Louis, James O. Pawelski, and Melissa G. Keith. "The Role of the Arts and Humanities in Human Flourishing: A Conceptual Model." *The Journal of Positive Psychology*, vol. 13, no. 3, May 2018, pp. 215–25. doi:10.1080/17439760.2017.1279207.

Tepper, Steven J., and Bill Ivey, eds. *Engaging Art: The Next Transformation of America's Cultural Life*. New York, Routledge, 2008.

Wolf, Stacy. *Beyond Broadway: The Pleasure and Promise of Musical Theatre across America*. New York, Oxford University Press, 2020.

Wolf, Stacy. *Changed for Good: A Feminist History of the Broadway Musical*. New York, Oxford University Press, 2011.

Wollman, Elizabeth L. *The Theatre Will Rock: A History of the Rock Musical from* Hair *to* Hedwig. Ann Arbor, University of Michigan Press, 2006.

6

Teaching Theater and Detroit History
for Undergraduates to Flourish

Lisa L. Biggs

I moved to Michigan in 2013 to teach theater and performance studies at Michigan State University (MSU) in the Residential College in the Arts and Humanities (RCAH). I grew up in Chicago, just about two hundred miles from campus, but knew little about the state. As I unpacked, I began teaching myself Michigan history. I was struck early on by the 1967 Detroit rebellion,[1] the fiftieth anniversary of which loomed on the horizon. As I got acquainted with my MSU colleagues, I engaged them in conversations about Detroit and slowly realized that many Michiganders were reluctant to discuss the unrest for varying reasons. Many white people who lived in and around East Lansing, the state's capital, about eighty miles from Detroit and home to MSU, believed that Black Detroiters had been responsible for the 1967 "riot" and that they were to blame for the city's failure to recover. They attributed Detroit's ongoing decline to the presence of uncaring, immoral, and simply criminally minded "Blacks" who they believed had "burned the city down for no [good] reason" and continued to make life there unbearable. African American, Latinx, and Native/Indigenous people, in contrast, generally cited decades of systemic racism and capitalist economic exploitation as the root causes of the "rebellion." Detroit, they argued, had not recovered due to the economic and political decisions taken by local corporate leaders and politicians. While battered, they believed, it was still a vibrant, culturally rich, if somewhat sketchy place to live and work.[2]

---

[1] I use the term "rebellion" to signal an organized, conscious effort to contest and overthrow the existing government and the status quo, as articulated by many Black Detroiters when describing the events of July 1967. I use the terms "civil unrest" and "civil disturbance" interchangeably because they articulate an attempt to register discontent with and to disrupt the status quo, if not to fully overthrow the government. I use the term "riot" sparingly and only to signal the beliefs of those who characterized the actions of people on the street as spontaneous, violent, uncontrolled, criminal acts.

[2] Many, many thanks to my MSU colleagues Austin Jackson, Tama Hamilton-Wray, Dylan Miner, J. Estrella Torrez, Kevin Brooks, and Jeff Wray, and to Kristin Horton, Billicia Hines, Kemati Porter,

Lisa L. Biggs, *Teaching Theater and Detroit History for Undergraduates to Flourish* In: *Theater and Human Flourishing*. Edited by: Harvey Young, Oxford University Press. © Oxford University Press 2023.
DOI: 10.1093/oso/9780197622261.003.0007

Since the Detroit rebellion/riot/disturbance/civil unrest began in the early morning hours of Sunday, July 23, 1967, the city has become emblematic of a certain narrative about American urban decline. Dance and performance studies scholar Judith Hamera, herself a former Detroiter, finds that the city stands as an exemplar of popular declensionist narratives that attribute the loss of people, jobs, homes, schools, and other vital infrastructure to ill-conceived African American civil rights organizing (2). The most popular myth asserts that a group of *angry militant Negroes* burned the city down for no reason and that Detroit has been a mess ever since. Like other urbicidal narratives, it attributes decades of high un- and underemployment, poor housing, struggling schools, crime, ineffective governance, crumbling infra-structure, inadequate healthcare systems, and myriad other social problems to the presence of low-income African Americans and other people of color (McKittrick 251). The city that birthed the American automotive industry, armed the nation to fight World War II, and gave life to Motown is now fundamentally unsafe and in need of stringent antipoor, anti-immigrant, anti-Black public polices backed by aggressive policing. I spoke with many Michiganders, including many African Americans, for whom, some fifty years later, the '67 Detroit unrest still evoked deep feelings of outrage, confu-sion, and shame.

Though often overlooked in discourses about human flourishing, the arts and humanities, theater and performance studies in particular, have a significant role to play in promoting and sustaining wellness. Plays are fundamentally about human life and relationships, and the best theater engages us in discourses about well-being. Theater and performance studies classrooms can offer students invaluable learning tools to help them make critical decisions that can enhance their prospects of living well and of con-tributing to human flourishing on a larger scale. Louis Tay, James Pawelski, and Melissa Keith suggest the performing arts can encourage the develop-ment of several key determinants of human well-being, including by creating opportunities to forge supportive social bonds, teaching/learning history, grounding participants in repertoires of local expressive cultural practices, and providing direct feedback and strong encouragement to participants to strengthen their growing capabilities. As the social bonds between and among students grow, their understanding of core concepts and their

Kevin Quashie, Dotun Ayobade, Tricia Rose, and Elmo Terry-Morgan for insights gained through our conversations.

competencies also grow, as does their sense of accomplishment. Over time they have a clearer sense of who they are as individuals and as members of their communities. With time, practice, and the support of their peers and professors, they recognize themselves as the inheritors of a rich cultural legacy and as people capable of impacting current and future social practices.

In this chapter, I embrace an autoethnographic approach to scholarship to reflect upon aspects of my own pedagogy to encourage human flourishing through performance in a series of interdisciplinary cultural history/performance studies classes I taught at MSU from 2015 to 2017 about the '67 Detroit rebellion. The performance-based, *deep learning* exercises I developed for the primarily first- and second-year undergraduates in the RCAH taught Detroit (and by extension state and U.S.) history. The Motown lip sync contest, oral history interviews, and culminating devised performance project allowed students to demonstrate their knowledge and understanding of Detroit history. But most important, students forged supportive social bonds through the coursework, the kind that researchers have found are integral to human flourishing because they refuse dispossession and segregation and encourage investigation, experimentation, and innovation. Inhabiting the archive in this way, the stories and our experiences working together became a part of our own experiences, embedded, if you will, in our hearts and our minds. Lesson plans intended to teach students Detroit history prepared them to also interrogate, and ultimately interrupt, the declensionist narratives about Detroit so they might encourage greater connection and, through it, greater human flourishing in Michigan.

A Short History of the '67 Detroit Rebellion

In the wee morning hours of Sunday, July 23, 1967, the Detroit Police Department (DPD) broke up a party in an unlicensed afterhours club in the Economy Printing building at the corner of Twelfth Street and Clairmount. Twelfth Street was then a pulsing African American residential and commercial center. During the day, the street brimmed with people shopping for everything from groceries to beauty supplies and family photos. With the fall of night, it transformed into "the Strip," a red-light district with sex workers lining the sidewalk. Though publicly maligned by city elites as a Black ghetto slum, Twelfth Street was the product of decades of state-mandated discriminatory racial, spatial, and economic programs that prevented African

Americans from living and working elsewhere (Boyd; Fine; Sugrue). The combination of legal and underground street economies reflected the limited choices that African Americans faced living in Detroit, where corporate industries and private employers aggressively limited when, how, and where they worked and how much they could earn.

William "Bill" Scott Jr., an automotive industry laborer and part-time civil rights organizer, leased the second-floor apartment in the Economy Printing building as a political organizing office by day. In the off-hours when the United Community League for Civic Action was not pressing voter registration drives or building support for Black political candidates, Scott used the space as a "blind pig," an unlicensed afterhours club where working-class African Americans could drink, dance, flirt, maybe gamble a bit, joke around, talk, and generally socialize (McGraw). DPD routinely raided places like Scott's where African Americans engaged in leisurely pursuits in their free time. About 3:30 a.m. the morning of July 23, they sent one of the city's few African American cops to infiltrate the party. Because the regular security/doorman (Scott's nineteen-year-old son, Bill Scott III) was off that night, the cop was able to squeeze in on the coattails of a group of "fine ass" women from out of town. Police stormed the building about fifteen minutes later and were surprised to see a crowd of about eighty people celebrating the return of two African American service men from the war in Vietnam, a crowd much larger than the more manageable thirty or so they had anticipated. Undeterred, the police rousted the revelers and forced them down the stairs into the hot night air to await transport to the city jail in the one paddy wagon on duty that night.

The partygoers, now standing around on the street, complained about the raid and the rough treatment. Their protest drew people up and down the block. Folks who lived and worked on the Strip gathered at their windows and in doorways to watch. Already dissatisfied with the poor quality of city services and with decades of unrelenting police violence and harassment, they started catcalling the cops, criticizing them for busting the party and not solving any real crimes, such as the recent murder of Vivian Williams, a local Black woman who had been shot to death on the Strip ("Woman Standing"). When the onlookers caught word the police had injured at least one woman by pushing her down the stairs and had possibly sexually assaulted another, their long-pent-up anger and frustration exploded.

The first brick carried a hundred years of history as it broke open a squad car window. A hail of other bricks and bottles soon followed as people took to the streets to stop the raid, liberate the captives, and unload their anger. Outnumbered, the cops soon vacated the area. Folks then turned their rage on nearby white-owned businesses that had a history of discriminating against African Americans, like the Commercial Shoe Store, which prohibited Black customers from trying on their merchandise and had an exceptionally strict (no) return policy. By 8:00 a.m., they had broken into several Twelfth Street storefronts, and the city was starting to burn. Throughout the day residents continued to direct their anger primarily at the police and at businesses that symbolized and upheld the white establishment, leaving most but not all Black-owned businesses untouched, along with the public "libraries, schools and civic buildings" (Darden and Thomas 83). Arsonists working at the behest of local land- and business-owners exacerbated conditions by setting fires so these proprietors could collect the insurance money. The fire department, always slow to respond to emergencies in Black neighborhoods, was quickly overwhelmed and drove away, leaving more property at risk.[3] African American family homes and mom-and-pop businesses that were initially protected by word-of-mouth and strategically placed "Soul Brother" signs in their windows were also breached, looted, and burned. The fires soon raged out of control.

Mayor Jerome Cavanaugh asked for immediate assistance from the state police as the unrest spread to other parts of the city, and Governor George W. Romney soon called up the Michigan National Guard. Comprising poorly trained white men from across the state, most of whom had never lived in an urban area and had little regard for African Americans, the Guard began to patrol the city streets at nightfall, their weapons loaded and with orders to shoot to kill looters. Over the next several days, they shot dozens of young men and boys, most on suspicion of looting and in an overreaction to rumors of rooftop snipers. The shootings escalated the already heightened tension between city residents, law enforcers, and elected officials. Calm was restored only after President Lyndon Johnson sent in federal troops. The 181st Airborne division of the U.S. Army parachuted into Detroit on Tuesday, July 25. These servicemen, many of them African Americans who had served in Vietnam, knew how to talk to people with respect and authority and were able to de-escalate the conflict. Forty-eight hours after they arrived, calm was officially restored on Thursday, July 27.[4]

---

[3] The crisis was exasperated when residents unleashed their frustrations on the fire trucks, driving them out of the area.

[4] The *Detroit Free Press* timeline of the rebellion is "Detroit '67."

In five short days, some fourteen hundred homes and businesses were damaged or destroyed. Detroit police arrested nearly eight thousand people, including nine hundred women and nearly one hundred girls, and countless people were injured. Most distressing, forty-three people died—thirty-three Black, ten white—the majority beaten, bayoneted, or shot to death by the state's own National Guard for allegedly looting local businesses ("Detroit '67"; Boyd; Fine; Sugrue).

In the days and weeks after calm was officially restored, the majority (86 percent) of African Americans living near Twelfth and Clairmount identified "socioeconomic deprivation or racial discrimination" as the catalysts of the unrest and called for "programs to end discrimination, especially in employment," and to abate "ghetto conditions" to prevent future rioting (Darden and Thomas 83). Local community leaders, including Rev. Dan Aldrige, Rev. Lonnie Peek, and Rosa Parks, staged a People's Tribunal in late August 1967 to address the inequalities built into the state's justice system. While it was no substitute for a criminal legal trial, the Tribunal created a space for Detroiters to again nonviolently voice their fervent opposition to the status quo. For many who suffered devastating losses, including the mothers of the three teenage boys killed by Detroit police at the Algiers Hotel, the Tribunal's symbolic guilty verdicts would be the only justice they would ever receive (McGuire).

White Michiganders took almost the polar-opposite stance. They largely rejected Black Detroiters' assessments, believing instead that "outside agitators," "criminals," and "black extremists" caused the "riot," according to surveys conducted in the days and weeks immediately following the unrest (Darden and Thomas 83). White reporters and commentators regularly attributed the causes of the unrest to "official timidity" in response to what they read as large-scale disrespect for law and order. A typical article in the *Detroit Free Press* was headlined "Detroit's Disaster Traced to Leniency" and charged prominent local civil rights organizers with voicing "inflammatory preachments" that ignited the flames (Lahey). As frightened and aggrieved white Detroiters accelerated their flight to the suburbs, they demanded greater protection for themselves through tougher laws, fewer social services, more aggressive policing, and greater punishment for Detroit's remaining residents.

By 2013, deindustrialization and the subsequent declines in employment, housing, and population that had hit Detroit hard beginning with the end of World War II and which accelerated after 1967 through the

1990s war on drugs were being felt throughout the entire state. Michigan had become a central station in the corridor of white grievance with high rates of un- and underemployment, addiction, and incarceration. White grievance politics, fueled by racial resentment and a perceived loss of white privilege, undermined opportunities for constituencies with shared socioeconomic and political concerns to collaborate.[5] Instead, the deep divides and soul-crushing dismay about the loss of work, lack of affordable decent housing, poorly appointed schools, contaminated water, and inadequate access to healthcare were readily apparent almost everywhere you turned.

The deeper I dove into the archives, and the more experiences I had speaking with Detroiters and visiting the city, the more the erasure of women and girls grated on me. I kept returning to one image by photographer Lee Balterman of a Black woman in a sleeveless sundress walking with a boy about ten or twelve years old and pushing a baby in a stroller toward a National Guardsman on a bright, sunny day immediately following the worst of the unrest. The Guardsman seems fairly relaxed, wearing sunglasses and smoking a cigarette as he leans against what might be a parking meter. Across the street, however, several firemen are hosing down the smoking embers of two burned-out storefronts. The baby in the stroller, less than a year old and wearing a loose T-shirt, looks directly at the camera, while the boy walks next to the woman, holding a fresh popsicle in one hand. The woman's face is obscured by the boy's head, but the sharp angle of her back and bend of her elbow trailing behind them evoke a sense of urgency and effort. She is moving them all through this mess. It was the popsicle in the boy's hand that caught me, a symbol of lazy summer childhood days that seemed so out of place because it was so normal. It invited me to think more about how hard women worked, mothers in particular, to provide a sense of normalcy and safety for their children and for others around them. How little do we know of that story? From the archives, we know women and girls were on the streets and that they worked to restore a new kind of peace in Detroit. They too had a stake in the city's past and its future. The published histories, however, have ignored their actions and their analyses of the context that ignited the rebellion.

---

[5] For a detailed analysis of white grievance politics, see Hooker; Metzl.

My work in the archives revealed similarities with men's perspectives in many ways, but also moments of divergence and of contradiction. Women and girls rebelled because they had legitimate grievances against the government and against local institutions for racial and gender-based discrimination. African American women were fed up with the patriarchal demands of American society and its racism, which worked in tandem to erase their agency, dismiss their complaints, and exclude them from public, political life. The *angry militant Negro* was not only a racist script; it was a patriarchal and a classist one that negated low-income, African American, working women's intellectual labor, their experiences, and their agency. It was especially harmful to cash-poor, vulnerable women like those who scratched out a living through sex work on Twelfth Street because the narrative it circulated and the behaviors it invited produced and justified their repression.

Speakers I encountered who used the *angry militant Negro* script seemed to want to do more than just communicate their analysis. I often felt that they hoped to sway my thinking, my research and teaching, and my future engagements with Detroit(ers). One elderly Black man I encountered at a Detroit community center squarely placed the blame for the riot on the shoulders of local Black criminals who, he said, had destroyed not only his family home but his entire block and had laid waste to "the entire community." He was adamant in his dismissal of my questions about systemic factors, as was another senior, a Black woman I met at a fiftieth-anniversary planning meeting in the city. She pursed her lips when I asked her questions about how police brutality, income inequality, and poor housing had set the stage for the unrest. Leaning over to me at the end of the event as she gathered up her bags, the dark brown curls of her wig gracefully falling over one eye, she told me pointedly, "They wasn't worryin about none of that. It was a bunch of [hoodlums] and they just burnt it all up. They didn't care about nobody." Closer to campus, at a predominantly white church in East Lansing, casual chitchat over cookies with a longtime parishioner suddenly turned dark when I mentioned I wanted to teach rebellion history at MSU. Carl, a tall white man in his early seventies, cut me off with a curt "The rioters burned the city down for no reason, for no reason at all." In fact, the script was so pervasive, and these kinds of interactions were so common, I stopped counting them. Under these circumstances, I felt that in order to set the stage for undergraduate *deep learning* about Detroit, I had to organize my MSU courses to address it, and to direct our time toward recovering knowledge of some of the city's most marginalized women and girls.

Undergraduate Teaching for Deep Learning

Almost fifty years later and ninety miles away from Detroit, undergraduates at MSU were undergoing tremendous intellectual, social, and emotional growth. The majority eighteen- to twenty-four-year-old students were learning to live more independently and encountering ideas and experiences in and outside the classroom that, as educator Susan Ambrose wrote, "challenge[d] their existing values and assumptions" (Ambrose et al. 158–59). George Zimmerman's acquittal for the 2012 murder of seventeen-year-old Trayvon Martin had helped ignite the national #BlackLivesMatter movement. The subsequent deaths in 2013 of Renisha McBride, a young woman summarily executed on the front steps of a white Detroit suburban home when she sought help after a minor traffic accident, and of Eric Gardner and Michael Brown, both in 2014 at the hands of police, put police power and white vigilante violence at the forefront of public discourses. Regular debates with their professors and with their peers and opportunities to engage in on- and off-campus protests profoundly shaped RCAH students' sense of who they were, their purpose in life, and their moral values. Required academic coursework, in comparison, could feel arbitrary and tedious, especially when instructors did not compel them to engage in *deep learning*, what Ambrose characterizes as learning that moves beyond rote memorization and the pressure to pass a single exam.

Deep learning encourages students' development as whole people and, as such, has to occur in stages to be effective and long-lasting. Teaching and learning specialist Kathy Takayama emphasizes that the structure of the brain requires that students first absorb, then sort, file, and in the end "personally make meaning" of new information and experiences. Having a chance to it-erate and apply what they have learned accelerates the deep learning process and leads to long-lasting knowledge acquisition.[6] However, deep learning is not effective, and can actually be sidetracked, when misconceptions embedded in students' preexisting knowledge frameworks go unaddressed. Before any deep learning can occur, students must first access their most deeply held beliefs. Most RCAH students were young white women from Michigan who had not grown up in or near Detroit. At the beginning of my first course on Detroit history in fall 2015, The Presence of the Past, I asked them what they knew about the city. Almost to a person, they said they had

[6] For additional information on human learning, see Bransford et al.

been to the city but knew little about the '67 rebellion except perhaps the myth of the *angry militant Negro*. So to encourage deep learning, I had to confront that malignant fiction early on.

I began by lecturing (something I rarely do) about the conditions that led up to the rebellion, walking students through what felt like a mountain of published histories; articles published in the *Detroit Free Press, Michigan Chronicle, Illustrated News*, and the anarchist *Fifth Estate*; documentary films; and investigative reports issued by the U.S. Senate and other state entities (Darden and Thomas; Fine; Georgakas and Surkin; Lachman; Maraniss; Smith; Sugrue; Thompson; Wolcott). I wanted them to understand how historical racial, spatial, economic, and political discrimination enacted throughout the twentieth century had limited work, housing, educational, and political opportunities for African Americans in Detroit, but that Black folks were not without agency. We discussed how the Great Black Migration, spurred by African Americans' urgent need to escape the Jim Crow South and respond to the automotive industry's call for labor, transformed the city's landscape between 1910 and 1950. Students learned how discriminatory housing polices and forced removal programs throughout the twentieth century produced the overcrowded, slum conditions on Twelfth Street by the 1960s, and how African Americans' nonviolent efforts to redress unequal treatment, hold public officials and local white business leaders accountable, and improve local housing, work, policing, and public education systems had been aggressively opposed and undermined by the white political establishment for decades.

Once they had a handle on the basic facts and timeline leading up to the '67 rebellion, I addressed the question of why the violence occurred, and specifically worked to complicate the myth of the *angry militant Negro*. Building on the historical context we all now shared, I presented the *angry militant Negro* myth as something akin to Nigerian writer Chinua Achebe's definition of a *malignant fiction*, a false belief or "superstition" rooted in no "proven facts" (148). *Malignant fictions* are harmful not only because they circulate untruthful information but because they shut down opportunities for self-discovery, for collaboration, and for innovation in favor of indifference, prejudice, and bigotry (151). By labeling the *angry militant Negro* a malignant fiction, I knew I was walking on potentially shaky ground; students might misinterpret my intention and assume I was calling them or anyone they knew racists or bigots. To prevent that, I emphasized the importance of considering how the myth functioned in public discourses and how it invited racist behavior in everyday life in much the same way that a play script invites, but does not fully dictate, how an actor performs a role (Bernstein 12).

To deepen students' social bonds in preparation for this kind of deep learning, and to teach them more of Michigan's rich heritage of expressive cultural practices, the next logical step for me was a Motown lip sync contest.

Motown/Music/Knowledge

In the late 1960s, Motown, the Detroit-based recording company founded by Berry Gordy to develop, promote, and sell "Afro-American music, without apology," was lauded for its ability to "produce a sound and an image that both glorified 'Negro' talent and appealed to white sensibilities," writes Suzanne Smith (140). But even as the company promoted itself as an entertainment enterprise dedicated to producing danceable songs about the ups and downs of teenage romance, Motown executives, producers, and artists could not ignore the turbulence of the times. Urgent calls for Black liberation through peaceful civil disobedience had shifted to more strident demands for Black nationalism, economic independence, and armed self-defense following the 1965 assassination of Malcolm X. Motown execs stridently worked to "avoid controversy," but Smith finds that "the music, as with all forms of cultural expression, had a life of its own" (140). To Motown's diverse audiences, its songs could articulate anything from "the life of the party to a call for revolution" (140).

People who came of age in the 1960s, especially in Detroit, know Motown. That music was the soundtrack of their lives. It spoke to their hopes, dreams, and aspirations as they grew into young adulthood. So deeply was Motown woven into the fabric of everyday life, Motown superstars Martha and the Vandellas' popular party song "Dancing in the Street" became a spontaneous anthem for many who hit the streets in 1967. Its captivating opening lyric, "Calling out around the world, are you ready for a brand new beat?," rang with the urgency of the moment, communicating that some kind of change was a-coming regardless of whether people wanted it to or not. Singers may or may not have considered themselves part of the vanguard of the movement for Black equality, but they appropriated the Vandellas' "party song" for explicitly political action. *The party song* as an invitation to join in a fun, sexually charged, Black cultural, leisure activity (e.g., the party) marked by music and dancing now pressed upon the notion of *the party song* as a summons to join in political organizing to upend the current political structure and usher in a new, more inclusive society.[7] Partyers during the unrest took great pleasure in upending the status quo, destroying property, defying the white power structure, and, I would argue, offending the moral sensibilities and ethics of many across the city, including some members of the African American community. In so doing, they made themselves legible as supporters of an emergent, radical vision and ethos of Black liberation, one that shook the city to its very foundation. Motown music was central to both this local cultural struggle and to a nationwide cultural and political struggle to end racist oppression and give birth to a new, more inclusive social modality. It continues to be an invaluable repository of Black intellectual thought, labor, and history.

RCAH students had to learn Motown songs to understand this context and the importance of the music for Black community formation. I required them to work in small groups to memorize a verse and a chorus of their favorite song and to come up with some choreography for our in-class lip sync contest. The students split themselves into groups of four or five, selected their songs, and got to work rehearsing in their dorm rooms or in empty hallways and classrooms at night and over the weekend. A week later, they presented. As I watched and played DJ from behind the classroom computer tech cart, I realized that the students had approached the assignment in two ways. Some groups collectively adopted the persona of the lead vocalist, and all sang and moved as if they were one person. Others divided the responsibility, allowing one member to take the lead vocals while the others backed them up and executed more detailed choreography. Without the pressure to sing well (or at all), everyone focused on the music, lyrics, and choreography, making definitive choices as to when, where, and how to move to communicate the message of the song. Because their group grade could only improve their individual scores, there was little incentive for anyone to try to outshine the others. Instead, students bonded over the shared experience, and a healthy competition between the groups emerged, like what I imagine might have occurred at Motown when Aretha Franklin and Stevie Wonder crossed paths or when Junior Walker and the All-Stars encountered Martha and the Vandellas, the Temptations, or the Supremes at the Hitsville Recording Studio. Students boasted about and took real pride in their group's accomplishments and expressed genuine admiration for the

[7] This line of thinking was inspired by Stalling 180; Lewis.

creative choices of others. During our postperformance discussion, they collectively expressed greater appreciation for Motown's music and a deeper appreciation for the intellectual, artistic, and physical labor that went into crafting, rehearsing, and performing the shows. In the weeks that followed, I regularly saw them reference their own and other students' performances in class. Three student artists—one an African American young man and a poet from Detroit, one a young gay white male dancer-choreographer who grew up in a Detroit suburb, and one a young African American woman actor also from Detroit—occasionally restaged bits of choreography or broke into song to contribute to our class discussions. I recall their using short snippets of "Dancing in the Street," the Four Tops' "Reach Out," Aretha Franklin's "Respect," and "Ain't Too Proud to Beg" by the Temptations to subtly signify on my assigned readings, the archival materials, and the occasional sticky interaction between students in class as they struggled to work and learn together. Their ability to recall and repurpose the music to communicate their own ideas, well beyond the original parameters of the assignment, signaled to me that deep learning was taking place.

An exercise that I designed to introduce them to the popular music and expressive cultural practices of the era also taught them how previous generations of young adults their age not only heard but moved to, felt, and understood that music. Taking their own pleasure in the lyrics and the beats, they had a stronger sense of how and why Motown spoke to its broad fan base around the world. Further embedded within the Motown lip sync assignment was an invitation to engage a far more complex narrative about Detroit's past and the role of Black Detroiters in shaping both that past and the city's future. To get at that past from a different angle, I next assigned oral history interviews. These opportunities to meet and talk, one on one, with people who had lived through the rebellion brought the histories we had read to life, complicating some narratives, revealing tensions and silences in others, and making what could feel like distant history pulse and breathe again.

Oral Histories

No one forgets the shudder of a tank rolling down their street, the sight of a loaded rifle pointed in their face, or the bark of a National Guardsman as dusk approaches ordering you off your own front porch *or else*. Researching the history and impacts of the '67 rebellion I repeatedly met men and women whose childhoods were defined by the insurrection. Fifty years later they could remember exactly where they were when they learned the city was burning. They could describe in vivid detail the houses and businesses lost to fire and looting. They readily recalled the shock when the Michigan National Guard began to patrol the streets, weapons drawn, with orders to shoot to kill, and the fear they felt when their parents or other family members told them to duck for cover when the shooting started. In addition to the psychological effects of the violence, some had lost family members, and others still carried physical scars and shrapnel from clashes with Detroit police and Guardsmen.

I wanted my students to meet people who had lived through and recalled the social context of the struggle for Black liberation and civil rights that preceded the unrest. Located in East Lansing, I thought such interviews would be difficult to arrange. But it turns out that just about everybody who was alive in Michigan in 1967 has a rebellion story to share. Most of my students had a relative with a story to tell, and for those who did not, the campus was bursting with faculty and staff members willing to talk. With the oral histories, we hoped to circumvent some of the pitfalls of traditional Detroit historiography, which typically has overlooked the experiences of women, LGBTQ folks, immigrant communities, and many more. More than simply adding women's or other overlooked constituencies' histories to the existing archive, I hoped that the oral history project would shed new light on the causes of the rebellion, insights that might significantly expand our knowledge. I hoped that the experience of sitting down with a knowledgeable interlocutor would also reveal some of the limitations of other approaches, especially the narrow historical accounts that attributed the unrest solely to the fictive figure of the *angry militant Negro*.

Using Cynthia Hart and Lisa Samson's *The Oral History Workshop* as a guide, the class prepared our interview questions. They included:

- Do you have a favorite Motown song? What images come to you when you hear it?
- Riot, rebellion, uprising, or civil unrest? Which term do you prefer to use to describe the events of 1967, and why?
- How old were you when the riot/rebellion/uprising/unrest started on July 23, 1967?
- How did you learn about the events?

- How were the people around you—parents, friends, family, neighbors, coworkers, and others—affected?
- Was anyone you know arrested or killed?
- Did someone you know lose property, a home, or a business?
- What about women and girls? I rarely hear stories about their involvement, but police records show that at least nine hundred women and nearly one hundred girls were arrested.
- How did the women and girls in your family respond?
- How was the riot/rebellion/unrest discussed at home?
- How has Detroit changed over the years? How has it stayed the same?
- What has happened to the Twelfth Street (now Virginia Park) neighborhood since 1967?
- What are your hopes or dreams for the city?
- Have you ever engaged in any political organizing or attended a public protest?
- If you could immediately change three things about Detroit right now, what would they be?
- Is there anything else you think I should know?

I required everyone to ask the first four questions, but after that they were to listen and allow the conversation to flow naturally. Perhaps unsurprisingly, the fact that the students all knew at least one Motown song created an immediate bridge between them and their interlocutors.

Nearly fifty students conducted thirty- to forty-five-minute interviews in fall semester 2015 and spring 2017.[8] Listening to them share excerpts from the transcripts at the time, and again after having reviewed my teaching notes, it was clear that Michiganders on the whole were excited to tell these stories. Family friends, elders, and MSU faculty and staff were delighted that the students turned to them as experts on this topic. One "snowbird" grandmother living in Florida gathered together all the folks from Michigan at her retirement community so her grandson could conduct a long-distance group interview via speaker phone. Another white student learned that his uncle purposely drove into Detroit with several buddies to vandalize and loot businesses and was severely injured when Detroit police or National Guardsmen interrupted their fun with gunfire. The uncle survived, but was

---

[8] FERPA laws designed to protect students' intellectual work limit my ability to reproduce these interviews here.

forever scarred. At a family gathering in Detroit, an African American student was able to put together pieces of old family stories in a new way and realized in conversation with her great-aunts and -uncles that she was actually related to the riot's youngest victim, four-year-old Tanya Lynn Blanding, who was killed by National Guardsmen while she slept. The RCAH dean, Steve Esquith, vividly recalled the pervasive tension throughout the Midwest, which he saw represented in nearby Indianapolis by the deployment of troops on the city's perimeter. Another white staff member shared his deeply personal memories of his stepfather, a Michigan National Guardsman, who, as he prepared to deploy to Detroit, handed his wife a loaded shotgun with a sensitive trigger to defend the family, just in case. Nervous, she almost took off her own head putting the gun in a bedroom closet for safe keeping. RCAH professor Doug DeLind, a longtime East Lansing area resident, revealed that his family's local hardware store sold out of guns and ammunition almost as soon as the unrest began. One of the enduring memories of his childhood was seeing his father, uncles, and other armed white men sitting on the roofs of their houses night after night, their eyes scouring the horizon for the first glimpse of the rumored caravans of *angry militant Negroes* marching on their city.

I made multiple fieldwork research trips to Detroit to meet people with stories about 1967 and employed a student researcher, Elizabeth Sauter, to conduct additional interviews. Because religious institutions often anchor and sustain communities, we reached out to churches and synagogues that had been on Twelfth Street in the 1960s. Speaking with members of a historic Jewish synagogue that had been located just a few blocks from Twelfth Street, Sauter heard the heartfelt gratitude in the voices of senior members of the women's council as they recalled how an African American handyman, long employed by the congregation, and his teenage son stood outside their building and talked people out of vandalizing it. The all-Black congregation of Grace Episcopal Church, located a handful of blocks from the Economy Printing building and in shouting distance of Motown, opened their doors for multiple group interviews after church. I learned from Brenda Philpot and other parishioners that Grace had been a vital gathering place for displaced community members in need of food and water during the rebellion, and for those searching for a way to restore peace and improve living conditions. Other Grace congregants revealed to me as we broke bread after church services how their own mothers had put themselves on the line to protect their children, in some cases by trying to create a sense of normalcy by turning off the radio and allowing them to play with nearby friends. Many of these women braved the racist taunts and physical threats barked by Guardsmen to lead their children safely home from neighbors' houses as the disturbance escalated. They spoke in glowing terms about Black radio DJ Martha Jean "The Queen" Steinberg, who stayed on the air for forty-eight hours to keep people informed and off the streets. They opened my eyes to the myriad ways women sought to de-escalate the conflict, including by bringing sandwiches and glasses of water or lemonade to troops who had been deployed without adequate provisions.

Taken together, the interviews confirmed for me that the script of the *angry militant Negro* dismissed the emotional, psychological, and material impacts of interpersonal and systemic racism. By ascribing only criminal agency to Black people, it had erased the deep intellectual and political work of African Americans who for decades had fought to make Detroit a better place to live, and that many continued to do so in varying ways in the midst of the upheaval. I was particularly struck by how this narrative not only erased their agency but also collapsed the complexity of life in Detroit on both sides of the color line.

Sitting in my office one day after class, I decided something more had to be done with all this material. The community had entrusted us with their stories, and I believed we had a responsibility to do more than just report back. D. Soyini Madison writes that when interlocutors entrust researchers with their stories and signal their desire to shift the position of the researcher/ reporter to that of a witness, a new set of expectations and obligations can emerge. As witnesses, researchers are entrusted to not only investigate and report on what they learn but to use what they learn to contribute to the broader human struggle for human well-being and belonging (830). As witnesses to this history, we had to act.

Performing Research

In her chapter in this volume, Stacy Wolf teaches us that from Broadway to the grassroots, theater is a "deeply and distinctively collaborative, communal enterprise ... [that] brings people ... together ... across generations to experience a story." Building off the work of Tay, Pawelski, and Keith, she posits that theater can contribute to human flourishing by encouraging "personal growth" and "reflection" while cultivating in participants and audiences alike a greater sense of "purpose in life" and of "self-acceptance." Understanding theater as a pedagogical tool and a practice of communal political engagement, I led RCAH students through an intensive, semester-long creative process to devise a new play about the rebellion, one that encouraged actors and audiences alike to reflect upon the value of Black lives and to ask ourselves how we could encourage human flourishing for ourselves, in Detroit and throughout the state.

In the 2017 spring semester, nine students who enrolled in my new class, Arts Workshop: Detroit '67 Performance Project—Norrlyn-Michael Allen, Emily Blair, Johnathon Finch, Mackenzi Jankowics, Christopher Kaifesh, Shannon S. F. McGlone, Nina Nakkash, Syd Pollack, and Destiny Spencer—and I wove together oral histories, archival research, and music from the 1960s with new scenes, monologues, and poetry they wrote to portray segregated Detroit and Twelfth Street before the rebellion began. They came to class with varying degrees of performance experience, primarily from high school musical theater, music studies, or public speaking, and almost no experience improvising, writing for the stage, choreographing, or directing. It was a leap of faith for us all when we sat down that first day in early January on the floor of the RCAH theater and committed to making something. Throughout the semester, students crafted characters and scripted scenes by lifting sections from the historical documents. They also wrote poetry and choreographed movement pieces and staged pictures (tableaux) that recreated and responded to events documented in the archive. I found ways to weave this dazzling array together in a nonlinear, episodic narrative that retold the '67 rebellion in a format more akin to PTSD-induced memory flashbacks than a historical textbook. The nonlinear approach allowed us to move back and forth through time, a method that mirrored our research process. The end product, a staged reading with students carrying scripts in late April 2017, was a deeply moving, nonlinear, cyclical work evocative to me of the *theatrical jazz* aesthetic found in Afro-diasporic performance which relies upon repetition as a process of narrative layering, interrupted by strategic breaks, to manage social ruptures (Jones). I named the forty-five-minute performance piece we devised *After/Life* to evoke how Detroit has been ghosted by urbicidal politics and fixed in the past in the collective social imaginary, yet lives on.[9]

---

[9] The title *After/Life* is indebted to Saadiya Hartman's "afterlife" of slavery and Christina Sharpe's "wake" thinking, which both address how transatlantic slavery as a system of racial inequality established and continues to shape current conditions. Sharpe's notion of the wake also reminds us how

After/Life began with a vivid portrayal of the people and circumstances that fed into the party at Bill Scott's, including a monologue I wrote from the perspective of an African American service man reflecting on the war in Vietnam and the war at home for civil rights. This monologue set the larger context for the unrest. Norrlyn-Allen Michael, a young African American poet who grew up near Detroit, dressed in Vietnam-era fatigues and a scarred combat helmet to invite audiences to consider the national contexts against which the rebellion raged:

> Times are changing. . . . It's July, 1967, and we are fighting a double battle-ground. There's a war going on back home and one here in Vietnam. . . . We are 11% of the U.S. population, 22% of the body bags. Yea, we here on a b.s. tip. . . . What's the black man doing fighting the yellow man for the white man? Why should I fight for prejudice in America? . . . I was going to get my pay, and my degree, and then help my family. . . . I just want to go home.

Here audiences heard how many African Americans felt about the nation of their birth, at once willing to serve but conflicted and frustrated by the limited opportunities that home had to offer them due to white citizens' un-relenting refusal to end racial oppression. I heard undertones of Langston Hughes's iconic poem "Let America Be America Again" (1938) with its plea "What is America to me?" every time Michael intoned these words alone at center stage.

With Michael's final words still in the air, the other students joined him on stage to reenact a slice of that American life in 1960s, the party at Bill Scott's. They danced in styles evocative of the time and sang along to a selection of Motown hits. A monologue written by sophomore Shannon S. F. McGlone, a young white woman whose family (somewhat reluctantly) followed the path of white flight after 1967 to the Detroit suburb where she grew up, helped paint a picture of the restless undercurrent and unmet desires of people out on Twelfth Street on the eve of the rebellion.[10] Its clipped, elliptical phrases,

---

Afro-diasporic peoples have (re)invented and sustained themselves, finding ways to live, to make community, to love, work, honor the dead and the divine both despite and because of the constraints.

[10] I believe McGlone wrote this monologue in part in response to excerpts of casual conversations I had with people who partied on Twelfth Street in the 1960s, including Brenda Philpot, a parish-ioner I met at Grace Episcopal Church in Detroit. Philpot painted a picture of Twelfth Street at night that hummed with youthful exuberance and anticipation, qualities that were unremarked in other

delivered with ease by Destiny Spencer, a young African American woman and native Detroiter, set the scene:[11]

> We work all day. Go out at night. The pulse of midnight 12th Street as quick and bloody as our hearts. The Hennessy, the Crown Royale. The dark. Daring folks to take another sip. How free can we get before dawn? Before the pastor preaches like a cock's crow? But he doesn't stop after three cries, he keeps going, and we never doubt. We can't forget. We get reminded of our faith in the confessionals of our place on the streets. But now we bask in the inebriation of 3:00 AM, hot breath and shadow on our necks. We need the release, the music.

These words offered a sultry catalogue of people on the Strip after dark from the perspective of a speaker who is at once part of the scene yet set somewhat apart from it. This perspective was critical to our production, as Spencer would come to embody the street and the ghostly presence of several female characters who lost their lives in the night.

We spent several classes working on how to stage the first moments of the rebellion. Few people were actually there to witness it, yet for me this moment was the birthplace of the *angry militant Negro*. Scenes and monologues portraying the experiences of white Detroiters, in particular the police who took part in the raid, provided a necessary counterpoint. I located an oral history given by Anthony Fierimonte, a white former DPD beat cop, in the Detroit History Museum online archives that proved invaluable. Fierimonte loved working in Detroit's Black communities and remembered the night of the raid. His detailed account served as the "official narrative" of the rebellion, with some colorful flourishes:

FIERIMONTE: I gotta admit to you . . . working in the black community was twice as much fun as working in the white community and I'll tell you why. 'Cause as we made these raids and stuff, they would go along with it and say, "Hey, you busted us. This is it." And I did eventually go into the white community and do the same thing, and they always had a friend

---

sources. McGlone may have drawn upon aspects of Philpot's memories along with archival material to craft this speech.

[11] Many, many thanks to Kevin Quashie for insights gained in conversation about this monologue; personal email exchange, April 16, 2020.

who was a judge and a police commander or lieutenant. "You can't take me in! It's going to be the end of my life." What B.S. You know? It was much more fun in the 10th Precinct. . . . We wait 5 minutes, and I say, this is gonna be easy! But we couldn't break the door down. Now they have all those battering rams, but then we didn't. A fire truck happened to come by and says "You wanna borrow our ax?" and I says "No, you do it," and they were able to break the door down. So we went up these tall flight of stairs and we go into the room. We expected fifteen people, twenty people. There were eighty-five, eighty-five in a room that fit, tops, forty. And we went in and announced, "Police, everybody calm down, it's a raid, up against the wall, dah-dah-dah-dah dah." And they started throwing cue balls at us—there was a pool table. So I grabbed my police officers to pull them out of the opening into the hallway but the other blacks held onto the black police officers, saying—

PARTY-GOER: You're not taking anybody to jail, mutherfucker!

Slow motion fight begins.

BLACK OFFICER CHARLES HENRY: There was really a fight in there. . . . We hit the street. People started throwing things out the window. . . . They drew a crowd. Fierimonte called for a couple paddy wagons, but there was only 204 cops working that night. Can you believe that, 204 men on duty in a city of 1.6 million? Dispatch told us there wasn't enough personnel. You think?

The fight builds.

FIERIMONTE: Somebody broke the back window outta the cruiser, the Buick—a great lookin' car—and it got outta hand.

There really is a fight.

To stage the fight in ways that refuted the notion that people on the street were *angry militant Negroes*, meaning rash or irrational actors driven by passion over intellect, I directed students to reenact this scene as if they were the party-goers but in super-slow-motion. Working together, they all reached for imaginary bricks and bottles, couched down, picked them up, felt their size and their weight, rose up, took aim, and hurled them with all their might over the heads of the audience. The slowed-down action allowed spectators to really see and connect with the effort and with the expressions on their faces, which ranged from excitement to euphoria to deep concentration and rage. As they slowly crested the top arch of their throws, one of them broke character and stepped forward as a narrator to announce a flashback, and everyone else on stage froze in a tableau. From that image we staged short vignettes that showcased how racial, economic, and spatial discrimination limited opportunities for African Americans in the city. The scenes restaged public confrontations between police and low-income Black people working street economies, and between middle-class African Americans and white Detroiters over the use of city parks and other public space. The police murder of Cynthia Scott in July 1963, in particular, became a focal point.

St. Cynthia (as she was locally known) had a history of sex work when two DPD officers pulled her over as she walked with a male companion early one July morning in 1963, four years prior to the rebellion. Within minutes she was lying face down on the street, dead. Her death became a rallying cry for Rev. Albert Cleage, Rosa Parks, and other Black leaders. Drawing heavily on reporters Don Beck and Hal Cohen's *Detroit Free Press* article "Cynthia Scott: 9 Versions of How She Died" to devise the scene, I divided the nine witness interviews they printed into individual narrator parts, one for each student. In this way the labor of telling the story was evenly distributed among the cast. They stood shoulder to shoulder downstage and spoke directly to the audience as if they were telling a family member, a police interrogator, or a reporter what happened, depending on their character. We were still experimenting with how to play this scene when we presented the stage reading, so I served as a conductor, directing students when to talk and for how long. I have tried to re-create a sense of the performance:

NARRATOR: Cynthia Scott: 9 versions of how she died.

ST. CYNTHIA: Cynthia Scott. 24 years old. 6' tall. 180 lbs. $43 dollars in one hand and a man on the other.

WITNESS JOSEPH MAIORANO: A police ran in front of the car with his gun out.

OFFICER SPICHER: I saw a colored female and a colored man walking south on John R and Edmund. The colored female I recognized as a known prostitute.

MEDICAL EXAMINER: Miss Scott.

SPICHER: A known prostitute. Her left hand was full of money.

WITNESS FRANCES MAE JONES: I was drinking that night so I was up. I heard her say, "I don't care if you shoot me, I'm not getting into the car."

SPICHER: I told the colored female she was being arrested for investigation of larceny from a person, at which time—

WITNESS CHARLES MARSHALL: That officer tried to sell me on some ole b.s.

SPICHER: The colored man said he knew the girl, she was with him. He got belligerent.

CHARLES MARSHALL: I was with Cynthia the night she was killed.

WITNESS JOSEPH MAIORANO: I was driving down John R when I thought I heard firecrackers going off.

WITNESS DONALD P. JOHNSON: I was driving my cab and I saw everything.

WITNESS ROBERT LEO FARR: She tole him she wasn't gon get in because she hadn't did nothing.

JOHNSON: The short one, he came out from the car, and drawed his pistol on his way across the street.

FARR: The tall one, Spicher, takes his gun out and fired.

SPICHER/JONES: She started running.

JOHNSON: He leveled down and shot her. She started walking, got about 12–15 feet and—

JONES: Two, three times and she fell. Flat on her face.

SPICHER: She cut me. She still had the knife in her hand when she fell.

CHARLES MARSHALL: How could she cut you? You didn't even get close to her and she was all the time walking away. She was walking away.

MEDICAL EXAMINER: Two bullets hit her in the back and lodged in pericardial sac. The third passed through her stomach and out her back.

ST. CYNTHIA: One out the back—

CHARLES MARSHALL (*Repeating to overlap the next several lines*): She was walking away.

ST. CYNTHIA: Two in the heart.

MEDICAL EXAMINER: Miss Scott was legally drunk the night she died.

CHARLES MARSHALL: She was walking away.

SPICHER: She cut me, I had to shoot her. She cut me, I had to shoot her.

The rapid fire, nonlinear cacophony of clipped, declarative phrases restaged the competing accounts of Scott's death. Visually, the staging signaled that no one narrative was more important or more truthful than the others, but audiences caught the nuances and the moments of cohesion and of contraction between the official statements issued by the police and medical examiner and those by witnesses on the street. The repetition of phrases like "A known prostitute," "She was walking away," and "I had to shoot her" invited them to attend to the nuances with each layered repetition. On a campus grappling with national #BlackLivesMatter organizers' insistence that bad police conduct ought not be excused due to the alleged criminality of their victims, St. Cynthia's story demonstrated that the conflict had a much longer history.

A second monologue written by McGlone and delivered by Spencer artic-ulated Detroiters' frustration with the police and foreshadowed the coming upheaval. Standing in a human doorway formed by the other students to evoke a portal linking home to street, past to present, life and death:

> The police, they prowl like chimera. Venom in their teeth, claws in their fingertips, white wings on their backs, the law on their side. They show up, bend us like a switch, and expect us not to snap. Not for much longer. This one is gonna be a doozy. They said they didn't expect Newark either. The government claims to be surprised. No. They ain't seen nothing yet.

These narratives created a rich groundwork for subsequent scenes and monologues that detailed how Detroiters reacted to the unrest. Moving in and out of the rebellion tableaux created a sense of circularity that encompassed both the flow of everyday human experience and the breaks, the moments of social rupture large and small (Harrison; Jones; Rose). Subsequent scenes retold stories about pre-rebellion conflicts over space and animated by ra-cial and economic discrimination felt connected to a much larger narrative of struggle. These set the stage for our restaging of the five days of unrest through short vignettes that demonstrated the scope and scale of the chaos and showed how people reacted. We quickly moved from the Fox Theatre with Martha and the Vandellas figuring out how to tell hundreds of audience members they had to go home, to flashes of mothers and fathers searching for their kids, to oral histories of folks caught out with no transportation who had to dodge National Guardsmen and police to make their way home. The piece took more time retelling stories of the rebellion's three known female victims: Sheren George, Helen Hall, and Tanya Lynn Blanding.[12] Their un-necessary deaths (two at the hands of the National Guard) painted a picture of the chaos and communicated how people tried to manage the crisis but

---

[12] Sheren George and her husband gave two African American male friends a ride home before heading out of the city. They ran into a confrontation on the street, and someone lit up their car with gunfire. George was shot multiple times and died in a nearby hospital. Helen Hall was only in town on a business trip. When she opened the draperies of her hotel room to demonstrate to a frightened colleague that the National Guard was there to protect them, a guardsman mistook her for a sniper and shot her to death. Tanya Lynn Blanding's mother, June, had gathered their entire family in one small apartment just off Twelfth Street for safety. A National Guardsman misread the flicker of a

were overwhelmed by circumstances beyond their control. The event concluded with a chance for the students to reflect on their experiences in class.

Student Learning Outcomes

Students left class with a much deeper understanding of the history of Detroit and of the rebellion. Two years later, during a group video conference interview,[13] they vividly recalled that the use of slow-motion "showed the buildup" of tension that ignited the unrest. They remembered snippets of "Dancing in the Street" and other Motown songs and excerpts of specific oral histories they or their classmates had conducted, such as the story of the Florida grandmother. They recognized how their research and performance filled in gaps in the archive. Johnathon Finch, who spent hours poring over microfiche of Detroit historical newspapers, recalled, "They didn't provide a ton of coverage, the newspapers, not to the extent that the oral histories that we went through. . . . It was just really cool to see what we had dug up document-wise and map-wise, and then compare that to what people remembered."

Others reflected on what the shows taught them about each other. Christopher Kaifesh, a young gay white man and emerging dancer-choreographer, talked about how they learned to look to each other in class to lead at various times: "We kinda looked towards Destiny to lead and in the most positive way because she had some knowledge of Detroit because she's from there and she was just so open to educating us about what we didn't know and what we needed to know."

One of the biggest lessons students learned was how to step into the shoes of others with care, especially when playing a character whose race and background are different from theirs. Unbeknownst to me, the white students felt enormous unease when I assigned them African American historical characters to play. They felt the roles were far outside of their own experiences, and they did not want to offend. They played their parts, under my strict direction, without deploying "Black," "urban," or "southern" accents or movements that could easily have been read as mimicry, mockery, or, in the worst-case scenario, minstrelsy. To do so, they had to reflect upon and

---

cigarette lighter in their apartment for the flash of a sniper's rifle and shot up their entire building. Several sleeping family members were injured, and Blanding was killed.

[13] Group interview by me conducted via Zoom on April 25, 2020.

push back them against the scripts they had learned about how Black people act. They had to locate every character's backstory as a human being and play their motivations and their actions in the moment without enacting a racial script. While I realize allowing white actors to play roles scripted as Black characters is controversial, as a classroom exercise it offered an unanticipated lesson about how racist scripts limit our knowledge of ourselves and of other people. Of all the lessons gained in class, this one may be the most long-lasting.

Trajectories for Human Flourishing and the Arts

I intended to teach MSU undergrads a history of African Americans in Detroit so that they would be better able to identify, analyze, and interpret popular narratives about the '67 rebellion. As I dove into the archive and published histories, I realized that without an honest reckoning with the segregationist past, the harmful half-truths and false representations of Black Detroit continue to circulate, authorizing discriminatory treatment and violence from public entities and private citizens alike. The questions my students and I surfaced at MSU and the methods we engaged to answer them through archival work and oral histories went to the heart of students' own explorations about who they were and how they might live in our society. The bonds they formed in class prepared them to reach out over time and space to connect with previous generations of Michiganders, living and gone, and to tell their own stories of living in our state. As young people learning to live independently for the first time, they needed this kind of deep learning opportunity to orient themselves in the world. Shying away from the hard stories, the ones of rupture and violence and loss, only left them with an incomplete record of the past. Societies that find creative ways to story rupture and use the breaks to identify important lessons ensure the future survival and well-being of their communities and compelling examples of how others might live. For human beings to flourish, I believe we need that kind of knowledge and connectivity. Theater and performance studies classrooms can without a doubt serve such a vital, urgent purpose.

Works Cited

Achebe, Chinua. *Hopes and Impediments: Selected Essays, 1965–1987*. London, Heinemann, 1988, pp. 138–53.

Ambrose, Susan A., with Michael A. Bridges, Michele DiPietro, Marsha C. Lovett, Marie K. Norman, and Richard E. Mayer. *How Learning Works: Seven Research-Based Principles for Smart Teaching*. San Francisco, Jossey-Bass, 2010.

Beck, Don, and Hal Cohen. "Cynthia Scott: 9 Versions of How She Died." *Detroit Free Press*, July 21, 1963.

Bernstein, Robin. *Racial Innocence: Performing American Childhood from Slavery to Civil Rights*. New York, New York University Press, 2011.

Boyd, Herb. *Black Detroit: A History of Self-Determination*. New York, Amistad, 2017.

Bransford, John D., et al. *How People Learn: Brain, Mind, Experience, School*. Washington, DC, National Academy Press, 2000.

Darden, Joe T., and Richard W. Thomas. *Detroit: Race Riots, Racial Conflicts, and Efforts to Bridge the Racial Divide*. East Lansing, Michigan State University Press, 2013.

"Detroit '67." *Detroit Free Press*, accessed April 22, 2022. https://www.freep.com/pages/interactives/1967-detroit-riot/.

Fine, Sidney. *Violence in the Model City: The Cavanagh Administration, Race Relations, and the Detroit Riot of 1967*. Ann Arbor, University of Michigan Press, 2007.

Georgakas, Dan, and Marvin Surkin. *Detroit, I Do Mind Dying*. Cambridge, MA, South End Press, 1998.

Hamera, Judith. *Unfinished Business: Michael Jackson, Detroit, and the Figural Economy of American Deindustrialization*. New York, Oxford University Press, 2017.

Harrison, Paul Carter. *The Drama of Nommo*. New York, Grove Press, 1972.

Hart, Cynthia, and Lisa Samson. *The Oral History Workshop*. New York, Workman Publishing Company, 2009.

Hooker, Juliet. "Black Protest/White Grievance: The Problem of White Political Imaginations Not Shaped by Loss." *South Atlantic Quarterly*, July 2017, pp. 483–504.

Jones, Omi Osun Joni L. *Theatrical Jazz: Performance, Àse, and the Power of the Present Moment*. Columbus, Ohio State University Press, 2015.

Lachman, Sheldon J. *The Detroit Riot of July 1967: A Psychological, Social and Economic Profile of 500 Arrestees*. Detroit, MI, Behavior Research Institute, 1968.

Lahey, Edwin A. "Detroit's Disaster Traced to Leniency." *Detroit Free Press*, July 27, 1967.

Lewis, Daniel Levering. *When Harlem Was in Vogue*. New York, Penguin Books, 1997.

Madison, D. Soyini. "Co-Performative Witnessing." *Cultural Studies*, vol. 21, no. 6, 2007, pp. 826–31.

Maraniss, David. *Once in a Great City: A Detroit Story*. New York, Simon & Schuster, 2015.

McGraw, Bill. "William Walter Scott III: The Man Who Started the 1967 Riot." *Bridge Magazine/Detroit Free Press*, December 24, 2016. https://www.freep.com/story/news/local/michigan/detroit/2016/12/24/william-walter-scott-riot-detroit/95606816/

McGuire, Danielle L. "Murder at the Algiers Hotel." *Detroit 1967: Origins, Impacts, Legacies*, edited by Joel Stone. Detroit, MI, Wayne State University Press, 2017.

McKittrick, Katherine. "On Plantations, Prisons and a Black Sense of Place." *Soul and Cultural Geography*, vol. 12, no. 8, 2011, pp. 947–63.

Metzl, Jonathan M. *Dying of Whiteness: How the Politics of Racial Resentment Is Killing America's Heartland*. New York, Hachette, 2019.

Rose, Tricia. *Black Noise: Rap Music and Black Culture in Contemporary America*. Hanover, NH, Wesleyan University Press, 1994.

Smith, Suzanne. *Dancing in the Street: Motown and the Cultural Politics of Detroit*. Cambridge, MA, Harvard University Press, 1999.

Stalling, L. H. *Funk the Erotic: Transaesthetics and Black Sexual Cultures*. Urbana-Champaign, University of Illinois Press, 2015.

Sugrue, Thomas. *Origins of the Urban Crisis: Race and Inequality in Postwar Detroit*. Princeton, NJ, Princeton University Press, 2014.

Takayama, Kathy. *Three Principles for Deep Learning*. Providence, RI, Brown University Sheridan Center for Teaching and Learning, 2018. Online video.

Tay, Louis, James O. Pawelski, and Melissa G. Keith. "The Role of the Arts and Humanities in Human Flourishing: A Conceptual Model." *Journal of Positive Psychology*, vol. 13, 2018, pp. 215–25.

Thompson, Heather Ann. *Whose Detroit? Politics, Labor and Race in a Modern American City*. Ithaca, NY, Cornell University Press, 2001.

Wolcott, Victoria W. *Remaking Respectability: African American Women in Interwar Detroit*. Chapel Hill, University of North Carolina Press, 2001.

"Woman Standing in Doorway Is Slain by 2 Men." *Detroit Free Press*, July 2, 1967.

7

Changing States

The Well-Being of English-Language Theater in Québec

Erin Hurley

In his rallying article, "Bringing Together the Humanities and the Science of Well-Being to Advance Human Flourishing," James O. Pawelski defines the aims of the "eudaimonic turn" in the humanities as "an explicit acknowledgement that well-being is a central value of human experience" (208).[1] This turn builds on insights from positive psychology, which aims "to discover and promote the factors that allow individuals and communities to thrive" (Pawelski, "Defining" 342).[2] Such discovery and promotion is essential to the vitality of official-language minority communities (OLMCs) in Canada, whose flourishing is often compromised by insufficient access to public services in their mother tongue, diminished workforce opportunities, assimilation, and out-migration. As we shall see, OLMCs value cultural production, and specifically theater, for its ability to establish their active presence, to reflect on collective memory, and to foster group cohesion, which together can buttress community and inculcate a sense of belonging. In what follows, I focus on the theater of one such OLMC—English speakers in the majority French-speaking province of Québec—and investigate how the dramatic repertoire and the structure of the theater sector can illuminate which groups are flourishing, in what ways, and by what mechanisms.

The premise of this inquiry resonates with many of the other chapters in this volume, which similarly address theater as a structuring and binding element of community (see, for instance, Ferguson; Wolf; Young). Moreover,

[1] Research for this chapter was funded in part by the Social Sciences and Humanities Research Council of Canada. For research assistance, I extend my gratitude to Alison Bowie.

[2] More local examples of such a "turn" in theater and performance studies would include David Román's modeling of "critical generosity" as an ethical rubric through which to engage performance, Jill Dolan's theory of the "utopian performative" as a mode of feeling toward a better world, and Sara Warner's "acts of gaiety" as antidote to the emphasis on negative affect, notably shame, in queer theory of the 2000s.

Erin Hurley, *Changing States* In: *Theater and Human Flourishing*. Edited by: Harvey Young, Oxford University Press.
© Oxford University Press 2023. DOI: 10.1093/oso/9780197622261.003.0008

it adds another example of the minoritized theater culture of a minoritized group to a number of other chapters similarly intent on highlighting the work of theater in correcting hegemonic narratives (Biggs) or interrupting dominant assumptions (Howe). Different is the fact of this minority group's elite status in the first period of analysis, and its subsequent status loss. This factor motivates the resolutely historical focus of this essay, which aims to articulate the shape and tenor of flourishing (or aspirations to the same) on either side of a major shift in the conditions for thriving of English-language speakers (Anglophones) and their theater in Québec. A high-level analysis of repertoire and of sectoral organization reveals the outlines of distinct models of wellness for the sector on either side of 1970. The first era, stretching from the 1930s through the 1960s, encompasses the rise and fall of a pair of core theatrical institutions that embody the period's dominant-culture theater scene. The second (the 1970s) is the decade in which the features and wellness dynamics of the contemporary, minority-culture theater scene are established. Importantly, each period's dramatic output and sectoral organization reflect and form community imaginaries of "Anglophone identity" to which the very notion of being a minority-language community is increasingly salient.

On Being *Small* and Eudaimonic

It feels strange in a North American context to approach English-language theater as a minority-language literature and practice. And yet, as determined by Canada's Official Languages Act, that is precisely its status in Québec, the Canadian province whose official language is French and where the English-speaking population is and has always been a statistical minority.[3] For theater historian Yves Jubinville, English-language theater in Québec operates in a "*minority* dynamic" (329). Indeed, English-language theater is both the longest-lived minority-language theater tradition in Québec, dating from the garrison theatricals of eighteenth-century New France, as well as its most diverse, thanks to the cultural diversity of its practitioners and audiences.

The roots of Québec's anglophone populations can be traced to Scottish, English, and Irish settlers, to American United Empire Loyalists (some of whom brought enslaved persons) and Black Loyalists (African Americans

[3] Canada's official-language minorities are French-speaking persons outside Québec and English speakers inside Québec.

who joined the British during the American Revolution in exchange for their freedom). Since the advent of settler colonialism in Québec, which was part of New France from 1534 to 1760, many of Québec's eleven distinct Indigenous populations use English as their first or second language.[4] From the 1880s forward, immigrants from Eastern Europe, especially Ashkenazi Jews who adopted English as their New World language, from anglophone regions such as South Asia and the Caribbean, and from other Canadian provinces and territories augment the English-speaking population of the region.[5] Moreover, until 1977, the ranks of Québec's Anglophones were swelled by "allophone" immigrants (persons speaking neither French nor English) who adopted English over French as their public language. The economic advantage of speaking the language of business and capital, evidenced in the colonialist monopoly that anglophone (Canadian and American) capitalists had over Québec's economy through the mid-twentieth century, was a key attractor to acquiring and using the language of Shakespeare. Up until the Great Depression of the 1930s, Montreal was "the commercial, financial, industrial and transportation centre of the dominion and the buckle that joined the United Kingdom to the . . . Canadian West" (Stevenson 43). At the turn of the twentieth century, the anglophone, mainly Protestant elite of Montreal—industrialists and financiers who owned and operated the railways, shipping, and power companies—controlled half of the wealth of Canada. But systematic exclusion of non-Christians, non-Catholics, and non-French Canadians from the French-language (Catholic) school system also moved allophones and Jews into the anglophone sphere. Shunted into the English-language (predominantly Protestant) school system, they further contributed to the social reproduction of English-speaking Québec.[6] Even so, this

[4] Notably, while Indigenous languages are clearly minority languages in Canada, the act that recognizes English and French as the languages of Canada's "founding peoples" erases those of the original peoples of the land. See Denise Merkle and Gillian Lane-Mercier's introduction to *Minority Language, National Languages, and Official Language Policies* (Lane-Mercier, Merkle, and Koustas) for an overview of growing criticism of Canada's official language policy and its conceptual grounding in the notion of "two founding peoples." Jacques Cartier took possession of New France for King Francis I in 1534. Montreal fell to the British in 1760, one year after the "Conquest" of Québec City, both battles of the French and Indian War.

[5] English Québec's most dedicated demographer, sociologist Gary Caldwell, describes the demographic composition of "English Québec" as follows: "[H]alf of [it] harkens to a British cultural tradition, one-tenth to the Jewish tradition, and four-tenths to various European, Asiatic, and central Caribbean cultural traditions" (170).

[6] Before 1988, Québec's public education system was organized as follows: Protestant (English) and Catholic (French) school boards; three Indigenous school boards; and a Jewish day school system, developed in response to Jewish students' inadmissibility to Catholic schools and diminished rights in Protestant ones. Designated "honorary Protestants" by the Québec Education Act of 1903, Jewish

minority-language group reached its peak proportionality in 1851 at 25 percent of the total population and has steadily declined since. The most recent
census indicates that 13.7 percent of Québec's population use English as their
first official-language, 8.9 percent of whom are native speakers.[7]

And yet reduced demographic heft can focus the mind—and the state—
on the good. Scholars of and advocates for minority French-language culture in a predominantly English-speaking Canada have long been eloquent
on the tight connections between theater, minority-language expression,
and community efflorescence; those studying and promoting minority
English-language art in francophone Québec have increasingly adopted similar positions. For instance, Lucie Hotte and Luc Poirier aver that minority
French-language "poets, playwrights, and novelists [in Canada] . . . recentre
identity, accelerate consciousness-raising and, especially, weave the memory
of minorities" (11).[8] Reports from the service organization for English-
language theater in Québec similarly highlight theater as an "all-important
forum for self-identity and adaptation [to broader Québec society and for]
redressing common and stereotypic perceptions of both linguistic communities" (Ad Hoc 8, 11). These eudaimonic assertions chime with the premise
of support programs for official-language minorities under the Official
Languages Act (1969, amended in 1988): "to enable these communities to
thrive and to enjoy the same benefits as the rest of the population" (Canada,
"Understanding"). Cultural funding delivered through Canada's federal
Office of the Commissioner of Official Minority Languages testifies to the
belief that the arts are an important source and signifier of community vitality; indeed, "arts and culture" form one of six pillars by which the office
of Official Minority Languages measures such vitality.[9] That office's 2013
report "Official Minority Language Communities: Thriving from Coast to
Coast," highlights the importance of the arts to the "development of social
capital and the organizational capacity to respond to change," that is, to fortify group status and group resilience. More broadly, the very existence of

students were guaranteed access to public education in English but with diminished rights; the Act
barred Jews from holding school commissioner seats, for instance (see Fédération CJA; Rosenberg).

[7] Peak population number is drawn from Table 1.1 in Rudin (28); 2016 figures are taken from
Statistics Canada.

[8] "[P]oètes, dramaturges et romanciers sont en quelques sorte les forces vives des cultures en situation minoritaire. Ils recentrent l'identité, accélèrent les prises de conscience et surtout tissent la
mémoire des minorités." All translations mine unless otherwise noted.

[9] The others are education, community economic development, justice, health, and demographic
vitality (Canada, "Chapter 4").

public funding for the arts at federal, provincial, and municipal levels evinces a similar logic: the arts are a public good for their contributions to a people's growth through self-expression.[10]

While the anglophone population and its drama and theater have been a minority since settlement, they have not always been perceived and presented as *small*. In François Paré's influential formulation in *Literatures of Exiguity* (1993), *small* literatures are "minority" literatures in two senses: numerically, as contrasted with "majority," and in terms of value, as contrasted with "priority."[11] (Paré maintains the italics of *small* throughout his text as a bulwark against the invisibility into which such literatures often slip.) If Anglophones and their cultural expressions have always been numerically minoritarian, their value and priority until the mid-1970s was distinctly majoritarian. As the repertorial and structural analysis below demonstrates, English-language theater in Québec shifts in the 1970s from a colonial minority wellness model, to a wellness model that more fully embraces the dual-aspect *small* status of English-speaking peoples and their theater.

The Hub-and-Spoke Wellness Model, 1930–c. 1962

This initial period of analysis encompasses the rise and fall of the first two major, seasonal English-language theaters producing their own work and aspiring to a professional[12] level of production: the Montreal Repertory Theatre (1930–61) and the Brae Manor Playhouse (1935–56), the metropolitan and regional hubs, respectively, of English-language theater in Québec. Before Martha Allan founded the Montreal Repertory Theatre (MRT) in 1929, professional theater in English "was no more than an annex of the large New York

---

[10] Mireille McLaughlin's study of the Royal Commission on National Development in the Arts, Letters, and Sciences of 1949 demonstrates the federal government's increasingly interventionist stance with respect to culture "in looking to create a sentiment of national belonging through its support of scientific and artistic institutions" such as the Canada Council for the Arts, founded in 1957 (quoted in Robineau, 562).

[11] Paré identifies four types of *small* literatures: minority literatures ("produced by ethnic minorities within unitarian states" [9], e.g., Maoris, Macedonians, Cree), colonial literatures (e.g., Jamaican, Senegalese), island literatures (e.g., Newfoundland, the Maldives), and *small* nation literatures (e.g., Québec, Lithuania). The *small* literature (and cultural sector) of English-language theater in Québec bears features of each of these.

[12] Brae Manor functioned as a semiprofessional repertory summer company; it paid the main actors, most of whom were from Montreal, while supporting roles (as well as scene-building) were held by unpaid company apprentices. Montreal Repertory Theatre, though not fully professionalized until 1955, was the "most consistent provider of high-quality English theatre" (Booth vi).

theatre empire," in the words of theater historian Jean-Marc Larrue (Booth et al.);[13] English Québec was a colonial outpost whose professional theatrical fare bore little relation to the region in which it was performed, except that it was in the tongue of a culturally and economically dominant minority and issued from anglophone countries (England and the United States) to which many Anglo-Quebecers at the time could trace their ancestry.[14] That colonial relation leaves its imprint on midcentury anglophone theater in terms of its dramatic repertoire and its field organization. Here, the aesthetic wellness of the anglophone theater system rests on mimicry of more mature—or, in the case of the United States, more extroverted—theater cultures; its time-scale wellness rests on self-sufficiency. Both operate on a "hub-and-spoke" or metropolitan organizational model that centers certain locations, stories, and identities and disseminates these to more marginal areas.

Let us begin with the repertoire.

In one of the "spokes," the historically Anglophone-dense Eastern Townships of Québec (about two hours driving distance from Montréal, Québec's cultural capital), the summer seasons from 1935 to 1956 at Marjorie and Filmore Sadler's Brae Manor Playhouse follow a pattern. *Billboard* writes in 1948, "Typical offerings in the Brae Manor repertory are *Arsenic and Old Lace, Yes, My Darling Daughter*, and *The Rivals*" ("Eastern Canada's Haylofts" 3). In generic terms, that means a dark comedy, followed by a slightly sugges-tive romantic comedy, capped off by a classic comedy of manners, set, respec-tively, in Brooklyn, New York, New Canaan, Connecticut, and Bath, England. Through a reconstruction of summer seasons in the Townships, I have dem-onstrated elsewhere that many of the Sadlers' choices—which also included a regular rotation of thrillers like *Dial M for Murder* and melodramas such as *Gaslight* (both set in London)—formed the staple diet of Townships summer theater into the 1970s. "Successors such as the North Hatley Playhouse

---

[13] "[N]'était plus alors qu'une annexe du grand empire théâtrale new yorkais."

[14] Of course, even a dominant language-minority group is not entirely composed of economically advantaged people. If English speakers controlled much of the commercial sector, most English-speaking Irish Catholics, Blacks, and Jews, the majority of whom were laborers, did not reap the same benefits as their Protestant, white counterparts. See Rudin (81–87). William Floch and Joanne Pocock's analysis of the economic profile of Québec Anglophones from 1971 to 2001 draws the fol-lowing conclusions about the internal economic diversity of the population: (1) "Anglophones tend to be over-represented at both the upper and lower ends of the socio-economic spectrum"; (2) their occupational status "appears to be declining across generations relative to the Francophone counterparts in the province"; and (3) "there is an important regional dimension to socio-economic status, with greater vulnerabilities [among those] in the eastern and rural parts of the province" (150). As we'll see, greater evidence of minoritized anglophone identities appears in the drama and theater of the second period of my analysis.

(1956–59) and The Piggery (1965–) took up those authors as well, often performing the same plays ten, twenty, or even thirty years later" (Hurley 23). In addition, Joy Thomson's Canadian Art Theatre (1944–50) toured a similar grouping of shows around smaller Townships communities. And even beyond the Townships, in Québec City, the two-play winter seasons of the amateur theater company the Quebec Art Theatre (1949–63) likewise took a page from this catalogue. So we see that the repertoire and the pattern of programming are both widely disseminated and also fairly circumscribed. In its reproduction of foreign content and mimicry of standard seasonal programming, Brae Manor affirms the normative practices of summer theater programming and establishes a common ground. Theirs was a practice and image of internal group cohesion achieved by echoing an external model.

Where the Brae Manor Playhouse repertoire differed from its successors was in its showcasing of Euro-American modern drama by the likes of Lillian Hellman, George Bernard Shaw, Oscar Wilde, and Clifford Odets. In this, it consolidated its status as the summer theater pendant of Montreal's leading English-language theater: the MRT.

Consistent with the Little Theater movement of which it was a part, the MRT aspired more to artistic excellence than to commercial success and aimed to develop new theater audiences. Its more daring and eclectic repertoire, which included experimental productions of new plays by Montreal authors,[15] evinces such a commitment to artistry and audience development. However, the MRT's role in sectoral and community wellness appears most clearly in its organizational structure. In short, the MRT was the nucleus around which gravitated a network of theater personnel, services, properties, and expertise that provided much of the infrastructure for an effervescent, amateur English-language scene.

As with the reproduction and dissemination of dramatic repertoire across English Québec, the institutionalization of anglophone theater in the

---

[15] The repertoires of Brae Manor and the MRT overlapped to some degree, with the MRT selections including more adventuresome fare along with the more conventional offer; MRT was the first Montreal theater to stage Brecht, for instance (Booth 120), and plays by Elmer Rice, Eugene Ionesco, Eugene O'Neill, and Jean Giradoux were also featured regularly across the years of the company's activity, largely in its Studio Theatre. One of MRT's members remembers their repertoire thus: "The Studio Theatre served the higher artistic aims admirably and economically, while recent West End . . . hits gave pleasure to larger audiences." He goes on to mention well-received Shakespearean productions as well as those of "contemporary dramas" by J. B. Priestley and Sidney Howard and "European Classics such as Ibsen's *Hedda Gabler*, Gogol's *The Inspector General*, and, for those who spoke French, Obey's *Noé*" (Whittaker, *Setting* 61). In addition, the MRT developed and produced new plays by local authors such as Yvette Mercier-Gouin, Percy Jacobson, and the theater's founder, Martha Allan, which sets it apart again from the other major players of the midcentury.

province banks on another hub-and-spoke structure to fortify this minority-language cultural sector. For the MRT effectively contained a whole theater sector within itself. It ran mainstage, studio, and French-language wings, housed a lending library of plays and research materials, oversaw a school of theater (with classes in playwrighting, acting, voice, movement, and more), and for more than a decade owned its own downtown theater space, to which it granted other companies access. Its set of "services," if you will, reflects the sense of public duty attributed to the theater at the time, now widely accepted as among its eudaimonic *raisons d'être* (Booth 163). Supported by the anglophone elite of which Martha Allan was a part, the MRT was self-funded through ticket sales plus patronage for the lion's share of its existence.[16] One source attests, "Allan telephoned people she knew for whatever she needed: actors, costumes, props, a hall—and got it" (Westley 224). The MRT's most fulsome chronicler, Philip Booth, notes the "countless similar accommodations between friends which helped MRT along the way," such as borrowing from Birks jewelers the tea sets required for a given show (163). Moreover, because the MRT did not require exclusivity of its members, it served as the hub for the personnel of an emergent and professionalizing scene. For instance, while a company member, the theatrical polymath Herbert Whittaker (critic, designer, playwright) designed for the amateur companies of the Young Men's–Young Women's Hebrew Association Players and the Everyman Players, as well as such short-lived wartime ventures as the Lakeshore Summer Theatre and the Shakespeare Society of Montreal (see Whittaker, *Setting* 120–24). Programs from this era confirm that the Sadlers of Brae Manor trod the boards of the MRT between their summer seasons in the Townships, as did Basil Donn, longtime actor-manager of the amateur troupe at the Trinity United Church, while Roeberta Beatty staged productions at MRT and at Norma Springford's Mountain Playhouse, a professional summer theater in the city. In the structural and structuring relation of the MRT to the other urban as well as summer theaters, the hub-and-spoke model again appears; it connects professional and amateur theaters in urban and rural areas, points to a taste culture, and offers a certain stability over a period of approximately thirty years.

[16] Public funding for the arts became available to Montreal theater companies in 1956; in that year, the MRT was the only theater troupe in Québec to receive funding from the newly established Montreal Arts Council (Schryburt 95).

The dramatic repertoire and the shape of this scene of theatrical expression demonstrate, first, the hub-and-spoke organization of this field
of practice and, second, the valorization of sectoral autonomy. This sector
grounds itself in certain stabilizing, self-funded, and relatively long-lived
core institutions around which orbit regularly appearing but short-lived
challengers (such as the Script Theatre [1955–56] and the Montreal Studio
and Drama club [1957–58]) and a goodly number of amateur groups, some
of which achieve the kind of longevity valued by their more professionalized peers. For instance, the Trinity Players of Trinity United Church lasted
more than fifty years (1909–61). Although its repertoire was just as foreign
as that of the professional-quality theaters—if more conservative since the
plays were vetted by their rector and performed largely by parishioners—
and its personnel and training indebted to the MRT, the Players' investment
in community flourishing was enacted in different, more expressly philan-
thropic ways. For instance, the proceeds of all productions were returned
to the parish to support community service projects, as was also the case
for the amateur theatricals of the Junior League and the Weredale Players.
A similar relation between community expression, support, and flourishing
is forged by the Negro Theatre Guild of Montreal's Union United Church.
Active intermittently across about forty years, the Guild was "formed in 1941
by a group of young members from the community, whose creative impulse
craved expression. The theatre seemed both a happy and a natural medium,
providing scope for a variety of talents, yet demanding group cooperation"
(Breon 4). Evidence of both the variety of talent and the need of group cooperation can be found in its first production: Marc Connelly's parable play *The
Green Pastures*. Mounted at His Majesty's Theatre in 1942, it featured a cast
of over one hundred and a chorus of thirty-five, all drawn from the drama,
dance, and music clubs of the Union United Church.

Mimicry as key to aesthetic wellness and self-sufficiency as guarantor of
timescale wellness envisage English-language theater's belonging to a super-
vening "elsewhere," a cultural commonwealth that is metropolitan and international; at the same time, such affiliation represents a turn away from the
more immediate cultural landscape of Québec and its particular majority-
minority dynamics. I offer two brief examples. One, in a moment when
French-Canadians massively opposed conscription into national military
service, the profits from the wartime presentation of *The Green Pastures* sent
fifty thousand pints of milk to Great Britain as part of the war effort (" 'Green
Pastures' "). Two, in my review of the extant, original plays (or summaries

thereof) written in English by Québec authors between 1930 and 1970, only four have a French-Canadian character; even the bilingual Martha Allan whose MRT produces French-language plays with francophone actors and directors sets her original drama in the south of England.[17] In terms of play setting, of the 137 plays in English by Québec authors between 1930 and 1970, 15 (or 9 percent of the corpus) are set somewhere in Québec.

As we shall see, by the 1970s such a colonial investment is no longer tenable. The "minor" and largely absent French-Canadian characters of anglophone drama take center stage in Québec in the 1960s and 1970s, occupying their majority place in society (and the theater) and securing it with new governmental, educational, health, and social services structures. Accordingly, the English-speaking "being" to be kept "well"—in part through theatrical expression—occupies a diminished place in Québec society and assumes a new visage. In the drama produced in English and the shape of the English-language theater sector in the 1970s, the measures of aesthetic and timescale wellness flip. Now aesthetic wellness is measured in terms of self-sufficiency (i.e., the production of original drama) while the model of timescale wellness is mimicry of the local, francophone-majority theater's institutionalization.

Status Change

The 1970s are a crucial decade for Québec's English-language theater. Ushered in by the aesthetic schooling provided by the 1967 International and Universal Exposition and its World Festival of performing arts, which brought international luminaries to Montreal stages, the decade closes with the first referendum on Québec independence. The events of these years reorient the anglophone minority to their place in a more concrete topography and in a francophone-majority society.[18] As such, the "being" part of Anglophones' well-being shifts remarkably. Or, more accurately, the change in the status of Anglophones and their cultural production that had been underway since the midcentury is accelerated in the 1970s and, for the first

[17] The four plays with French-Canadian characters are Janet McPhee and Herbert Whittaker's melodrama, *Jupiter in Retreat* (1942); William Digby's 1960 comedy, *Equal to the Sum of the Squares*; M. Charles Cohen's historical drama, *The Member from Trois-Rivières* (1959); and *The Hiders* by L. Decoteau (alias of Lawrence Wilson) (1963). Allan's play is *Summer Solstice: A Drama in One Act* (1935).
[18] On the impression of Expo 67 on the theater community, see Rodgers, Needles, and Garber. The second referendum on sovereignty took place in 1995; both referenda were defeated.

time in the theater, are fully registered as such. In fact, the thing we call the "anglophone community"—that is, an entity organized around language instead of around faith or origin—emerges as such only in the 1960s and 1970s. Unsurprisingly, the awakening of an "anglophone identity" happens in a period when the anglophone business elite sees their autonomy eroded by the rise of the bureaucratic, secular, francophone state. In his watershed article on the changing consciousness of anglophone Quebecers, political scientist Michael Stein writes:

> The self-confident "majority-group" psychology of the Quebec anglophones had first begun to be shaken by some of the important changes which were taking place in Quebec. . . [:] encroachment on the hitherto autonomous operations of Anglo-Quebec local institutions and social services by government efforts at reorganizing and standardizing educational structures . . . government regulation of professional and charitable institutions . . . regrouping of municipalities, and the creation of regional and metropolitan governments. (111–12)

For instance, prior to the creation of the Ministry of Education in 1964, the Protestant School Board of Montreal effectively ran itself as one of an interrelated set of English institutions analogous to those of francophone or Jewish civil society. Thus, what had been conceived of as an autonomous system constituted by the networked, internal relationships of one language group's key institutions of social reproduction (health, education, culture, and social services) was brought forcefully into a new set of external relations with majority-population governance structures.

Legislation francizing the public sphere, in effect claiming as francophone the previously Anglo-run commercial arena and circumscribing the use of languages other than French, also shifts the identity coordinates of anglophone artists and audiences. "Beginning in the 1960s through the 1970s, successive provincial administrations introduced public policies aimed at making language the basis for community needs, measures which strengthened the salience of language as a badge of group identification for both Francophones and Anglophones in the province" (Jedwab and Maynard 285). These include the Official Language Act of 1974, which established French as the official language of Québec, and the Charter of the French Language in 1977, which made French the language of government and the law as well as that of work, instruction, communication, and commerce. It is widely agreed

that these language policies "resulted in English speakers transitioning from ·
their identification with Canada's English-speaking majority to becoming a
language minority within the predominantly Francophone province" (285).
The felt experience of being a minority is compounded by Anglophones'
out-migration and absolute demographic decline. Historian Ronald Rudin
estimates that "[r]oughly 95,000 of Quebec's English-speaking population
left the province" in the five years following the election of the sovereigntist
Parti Québécois in 1976 (31). Thus, the anglophone community gained an
identity more rooted in local circumstances at the same time that its status,
demographics, and institutional support were increasingly tenuous.

English-language theater—similarly constituted as a self-sufficient system
invested in its own social reproduction—shares in both the fate of this newly
self-conscious "anglophone community" and in its commitment to cultivating community vitality. In its drama and its interrelated institutional
structures, the theater of the 1970s helps to express and address this lived dynamic of minoritization, registering this change of state. They make apparent
this shift to the *small* (*pace* Paré), where the English-speaking population
and its theater experience being a minority both numerically, as contrasted
with "majority," *and* in terms of value, as contrasted with "priority."

Assuming the *Small* and Promoting Wellness:
1970s Drama and Theatrical Institutionalization

As Paré's critical oeuvre attests, the first move in either articulating the role of
small cultural practices vis-à-vis their populations or assessing the vitality of
the same is proof of life. Evidencing in the drama the fact of English-speaking
populations in Québec—that they *exist*—thus assumes greater importance.
Indeed, as we'll see below, representation of this "self" in original drama by
anglophone playwrights becomes a key marker of the field's aesthetic wellness; in support of such flourishing, the sector takes as its model that of the
local, francophone-majority theater, built as a network to assure timescale
wellness.

As English-language theater in Québec assumes its *small* status, it begins to
affirm a collective existence of "Anglophones" and, to borrow Paré's formulation about other *small* literatures, to "remind us that the practice of language
is tied to the power structure" (27). This is evident, first, in the emergence of a
more robust minority-language original drama, in terms of both volume and

local address. To date, I have sourced ninety-four original plays in English by forty-six Québec authors that were produced or published in the 1970s. This almost doubles the number of such plays (fifty-two) from 1960 to 1969; I have found evidence of only ten such plays between 1950 and 1959 and nine between 1940 and 1949. Of the plays from the decade at issue, seventeen (5.5 percent) are set in or make reference to Québec.

Perhaps unsurprisingly given the reorganization of Québec society, original plays by Québec-based authors of this decade often foreground themes of existential crisis and relational tension, and this across a diversity of anglophone subject-positions. Aviva Ravel (1928–), one of Montreal's most prolific playwrights, writes plays that reflect complicated relationships among family members, many of them set in Montreal's Jewish lifeworlds. For example, *Soft Voices* (1973) juxtaposes the different life choices of two women and their increasing acceptance of themselves, and *Black Dreams* (1974) interrogates the reality-bending properties of racial stereotypes. The tragedy in *Dispossessed* (1976) arises out of the main character's confrontation with a life she might have led, and its lyricism from the immigrant speech patterns forged out of Yiddish syntax and English words (see Reid, "Reflections").

Another group of plays articulates existential crisis through characters striving to find their true selves in a world composed of images. For instance, in Robert Wallace's 1974 drama *'67*, the university students who populate the play are all on identity quests: the main couple is unhappily caught in s/m roles that feel neither authentic to them nor accurate to their relationship; a secondary couple finds respite and renewed attachment in reality-altering drugs. Heterosexual relational tension is a feature in all of Marjorie Morris's realist dramas of this era, and in *Big X, Little Y* (1974) foundational feminist playwright Elinor Siminovitch uses nursery rhymes and children's games to demonstrate how women are taught to see very different realities from men. In a similar vein, Dan Daniels of the Montreal Living Theatre writes politically engaged plays which expressly examine power relations—gendered in *The Inmates* (1971) and classed in *Underground* (1970).

Critics agree that the smash hit of 1979, *Balconville* by David Fennario (1947–), "served as the point of rupture between English-Canadian drama and québécois drama in English" (Hulslander 31).[19] *Balconville* mobilizes a specifically Anglo-Montrealer composite lingua franca: Québec English

---

[19] "[L]a pièce qui a servi de point de rupture entre la dramaturgie canadienne-anglaise et celle de la dramaturgie québécoise de langue anglaise."

(evident in vocabulary, pronunciation, and syntax); code-switching between English and French; *le franglais,* a kind of patois French structured syntactically by English; and reliance on passive bilingualism (about 30 percent of the stage dialogue is in French and untranslated). As such, Fennario develops what Louis Patrick Leroux calls a "parole collective" (collective speech) (88) which, Gregory Reid argues, reterritorializes English in Québec ("Is There" 68–69). Definitively emergent out of local conditions of minoritization and working-class struggle, this contact language results from geographical cohabitation with Francophones and mutual awareness. But, as Fennario insists, it is also birthed of insufficient formal French-language education in English-language schools and of anger at economic injustice (Milliken 22).

At the heart of this upturn in English-language drama was the 1963 founding of the still active English-language play development center Playwrights' Workshop Montréal (PWM). For Paré, writers' groups such as PWM are key to legitimating (and thereby proving and valuing the existence of) *small* literatures; in connection with "the system of education; . . . publishers and booksellers; literary history and criticism," writers' groups are "designed to ensure that certain works and writers retain a permanent place in history" (19). The center's mission was precisely to "build capacity" in English-language drama by cultivating playwrights and work-shopping plays to ready them for production for what was at the time an almost entirely imaginary sector (see Curtis).

I qualify the sector as "imaginary" because the autonomous, metropole-focused, predominantly amateur and semiprofessional English-language theater sector of the midcentury was effectively extinct in the early 1960s. Both the professional-quality pillar institutions and those amateur companies assuring the social reproduction of the English theater scene had shuttered. The stalwart MRT performed its final season in 1961, after almost a decade of decline which began in 1952, when their theater, library, and set and costume stores were razed by fire, thereby eliminating many of the sectoral components—and the structuring framework—of anglophone theater. Two professional summer theaters closed in 1962: the North Hatley Playhouse in the Eastern Townships (1956–62) and Norma Springford's Mountain Playhouse on Montreal's Mont Royal (1950–61). In addition, the major roadhouse of English-language production, Her Majesty's Theatre (opened in 1898), was demolished in 1963. In 1965, the Montreal *Gazette* declared English-language theater "moribund."

At the same time, the province's French-language theater sector was pro-fessionalizing, institutionalizing, and becoming clearly majoritarian. Indeed, with respect to institutionalization—defined by Anne Robideau as "the processes by which an ensemble of mechanisms, places, and actors furnish a framework for action promoting the creation, production, diffusion, and transmission of the community's arts and culture"—the 1960s and 1970s are an accelerated phase of development (567).[20] In brief, the area counts a playwrights center (1965), professional associations (1964 and 1972), a diversified theatrical offer at a range of venues, and a new dramaturgy (the *nouveau théâtre québécois*) that separates itself from earlier, founding gener-ations' writing and performance styles. External validation—evidence of its "priority"—arrives in the form of press and scholarly attention: by 1980, with the publication of Jean Cléo Godin and Laurent Mailhot's *Théâtre québécois I* and *II*, Québec theater in French enters the university as a legitimate object of study with its own critical discourse. In terms of the sector's majoritar-ianism, theater scholar Gilbert David counts twenty-odd French-language arts council–funded companies in 1975, of which nine are "established" theaters with their own spaces and mounting regular seasons; an additional fifty smaller companies are eligible for but not in receipt of grants (22). In comparison, in the 1974–75 and 1975–76 seasons, ten English-language companies received arts council funding, of which five owned or rented the spaces in which they mounted their seasons; two of these were summer theaters. By the early 1980s the number of funded, francophone companies has risen to one hundred. Although "[t]he mortality-rate [of these compa-nies] was quite high," David continues, "one may detect a strong upward mo-bility, promoted by an appreciable injection of public funds," which meant that some previously small theaters become established theaters (30).[21] On the English side, the number rises by two, to twelve funded theaters, of which only half are still in operation in the 1985–86 theater season. All accounts of the French-language theater in Québec in the 1970s describe it as "efferves-cent" and "efflorescent." In this decade of expansion, diversification, and con-solidation, French-language theater in the province, like Francophones in the province, are creating and sustaining conditions in which to "survive and

---

[20] "[L]e processus par lequel un ensemble de mécanismes, de lieux et d'acteurs fournissent un cadre d'action favorisant la création, la production, la diffusion et la transmission des arts et de la cul-ture de la communauté."

[21] "Le taux de mortalité y a été très élevé, mais . . . on peut y détecter une forte mobilité ascendente, favorisée par l'injection appréciable de fonds publics: quelques compagnies ont été ainsi promues au rang de théâtres établis."

thrive as a collective entity in [a] given intergroup context" (Giles, Bourhis, and Taylor 308).

It is to this active, locally rooted, neighboring structure of mutually reinforcing institutions and its logic of promotion that English-language theater in Québec strives to be parallel, if still significantly smaller in its footprint. It undergoes a process of catching up such that by 1972 the groundwork of the English-language theater sector is (re)laid. Its bases are composed of elements similar to those which held together the arena before 1960, but are distributed more widely across the field instead of being concentrated in one sectoral actor; these are two (or sometimes three) major companies with annual seasons and of which (at least) one is a summer theater; a number of amateur troupes of various timescales that develop both talents and publics for the theater; a small group of itinerant semiprofessional or independent companies; and a theater school. To this enduring mix is added a mechanism for developing new plays (PWM), state funding for the arts at the municipal and federal levels, and an experimental scene. The web is strengthened when a "system of education" enters the field, as per Paré's schema of legitimization for *small* literatures. Graduates from the English section of the National Theatre School of Canada (founded in 1960) and from the professional theater programs at the English-language colleges of John Abbott and Dawson, founded in 1970, form a nucleus of willing participants in PWM's experiments in local drama. "Publishers and book sellers," another legitimating force, soon step in to assure the historical inscription of play texts emerging out of PWM and, as of 1980, from the English-language playwrighting section of the National Theatre School of Canada. The Playwrights Co-op (Toronto) starts distributing copyrighted typescripts of member-authors' plays in 1972, occasioning an uptick in traceable Anglo-Québécois dramatic output. The Vancouver and Toronto publishers of Canadian literature, Talonbooks and Coach House Press, respectively, open their lists to drama near the end of the decade. Notably, the milieu must wait until 1978 for a Québec-based *maison d'édition* to disseminate its drama; this is when the Italo-Québécois poet and novelist Antonio D'Alfonso founds Guernica Editions, which publishes plays by Anglo-Québécois playwrights from the 1980s forward, including Marianne Ackerman, Henry Beissel, Lorne Elliott, Mary Melfi, Stephen Orlov, and Miriam Packer.

In terms of produced drama, the key differentiator of the pre- and post-1960s theatrical repertoire is its greater variety and, even more salient and like the form institutionalization takes in this period, its distribution across the sector. It is not simply that in the 1970s Quebecers who understand English have a real choice of the genres and types of theater they may take in—ranging from agit-prop plays to site-specific performances, from Neil Simon's bourgeois comedies to Joe Orton's dark comedies, from Shakespeare's tragedies to adaptations of Elie Wiesel, from new Canadian drama to French-language Québec drama in translation. This more ample buffet is laid by the greater number of professional and semiprofessional theaters in operation in this decade, compared with the previous period, in which the MRT dominated. Their eclectic fare is in turn enabled by public arts funding which diminishes the necessity of patronage. What Sylvain Schryburt observes of the French-language stage in this period is equally true of the English stage: "[O]ne must wait for the stabilizing effect of state intervention to see the polarization of theatre companies on the basis of repertoire" (99); such repertorial differentiation combined with an experimental scene are markers of "a properly constituted theatre field" (127).[22]

To the distinctive repertoires at English Montreal's two major professional theaters—the Saidye Bronfman Centre for the Arts, founded in 1967, and the Centaur Theatre, founded in 1969—the Montreal public responds enthusiastically, filling their houses to the point where both are extending runs and adding seats. Of this phenomenon, Catherine Graham writes that

> as of 1974, the theatre of the Saidye Bronfman Centre, under the direction of Muriel Gold, has 2000 subscribers, presents more plays, and extends each of their runs. . . . At the Centaur Theatre, the situation is similar. In 1972–73, there are so many subscribers that all of its shows sell out even before tickets are made available to the general public. (409)[23]

Graham suggests that the response lies in the programming at the Saidye and the Centaur, which "express the willingness to take on their past and prejudices, to recognize the role of colonialism in local history and to imagine a better future built on a vision 'de chez nous' [from our home]" (412).[24]

---

[22] "[I]l faudra attendre les années 1960, et l'effet stabilisant de l'interventionnisme étatique, pour assister à une polarisation des compagnies sur la base du répertoire." "[L]e premier champ théâtral montréalais dûment constitué."

[23] "Dès 1974, le Théâtre du Saidye Bronfman Centre, sous la direction de Muriel Gold, a 2000 abonnés, présente plus de pièces et prolonge chacune des péridoes de représentation. . . . Au Centaur, la situation est semblable. En 1972–1973, il y a tant d'abonnés que ses représentations jouent toujours à guichets fermés avant même que la vente de billets ne soit ouverte au grand public."

[24] "[E]xprime la volonté d'assumer son passé et ses préjugés, de reconnaître le role du colonialism dans l'histoire local et d'imaginer un meilleur avenir bâti à partir d'une visions 'de chez nous.'"

A newspaper critic, however, attributes the Centaur's success to "almost always offer[ing] up a program which is carefully calculated to harmonize with local bourgeois moral parameters" (Bailey 18). Both agree that the Saidye's seasons and aesthetics were more adventurous than those of the Centaur, whose inaugural-season experiment in the environmental staging of a play written about a recent uprising at a Montreal university soon gave way to a staple diet of box-set realism and dialogue-driven plays.

Be that as it may, it is clear that the Centaur's founding artistic director, Maurice Podbrey, saw his theater as a way to cultivate and expand the tastes of the Montreal public, to whom he introduced contemporary British playwrights like Howard Brenton and John Osborne as well as Podbrey's compatriot Athol Fugard. In fact, the first several seasons feature "teach-ins" about the plays on the boards and, often, an accompanying booklet of information. In this example, then, a key actor in institutionalization not only secures a "home" for English-language theater in Montreal—one that is also rented out to smaller companies—but also promotes a framework for the uptake of its theatrical offer by developing an audience base. In a similar vein, at the Saidye, Marion André inaugurates talkbacks after productions for similar purposes and to make his theater more relevant to the audiences of this Jewish cultural institution. In her history of the Saidye, Muriel Gold, the second artistic director (1972–80), characterizes André's tenure as assuring professional theater practice and promoting productions that "reflect relevant social and political issues" (44) while including one play per season with Jewish content.

Restricting our overview of the sector to Montreal for now, these two major players, who benefit from operational grants and therefore from relative autonomy, are joined by smaller companies with punctual project funding; it is at this "intermediate" level that the functional heteronomies of the anglophone theater scene come to the fore and parallel those of the francophone scene. Experimental theaters such as the Living Theatre of Montreal, Teatron, the Montreal Theatre Lab (MTL), and the Painted Bird Ensemble occupy this stratum. In keeping with the spirit of the times, Alexander Hausvater of the MTL (1974–79) explored the ritual elements of drama and theater, expressionistic representational strategies, political themes, sexualized content, choral effects (physical and vocal), projections as indicators of alternative realities on stage, as well as the moments before and after the theatrical performance, in a series of productions pitting a man against the state or another englobing power structure. The Painted Bird Ensemble (1974–84), an interdisciplinary troupe of actors, dancers, musicians, and visual artists led by Michael Springate, presented original, devised works that experiment with nonlinear dramatic structures, as well as well-reviewed productions of challenging European drama by Beckett, Büchner, and Stoppard.

With the MTL and Painted Bird, the Revue Theatre, founded in 1967 by an African American dancer and choreographer named Arleigh Peterson along with dancer Cynthia Hendrickson and actor Ruth Thomas, is, in my view, key in the attribution of "sector status" to English-language theater. Peterson's modestly budgeted, diversely cast, and experimental productions forged a distinctive public profile for his theater. On its small stage, one could take in Peterson's own original revues, such as *Opnotiques 5: A Psychedelic Revue* (1967) and *Corybantus* (1972), a "revue rock," which alternated with "American-style musicals" (Henry 29) that capitalized on Peterson's choreographic talents. Also featured were plays from the Black diaspora, including work by David Edgecombe and Lonnie Elder, and creations of original Québec plays by Lorris Elliott, Aviva Ravel, Maxine Fleischman, and Charles Godlovitch, the last three of whom were founding members of PWM. In producing plays by Montreal authors fostered at PWM, Revue entered into an active, heteronomous web of relations among the English-language theater institutions. It further activated those links by supporting fellow small theaters. Revue, run on a shoestring budget and occasional project funding from the Montreal and Canada arts councils, nonetheless supported other, emergent Black theaters through coproductions with the Negro Theatre Arts Club (intermittently active from 1963 to c. 1971) and in hosting two seasons of the Black Theatre Workshop (BTW), which celebrated fifty years of production in 2021. In turn, Peterson relied on the training provided by the BTW's classes in movement, voice, and text analysis to turn out Black actors for his shows, which also included all-Black productions of *Waiting for Godot* and *Loot* (Whittaker, "New Festival" 29). Notably, this reciprocal relationship with Revue secured BTW's professional status, required in order to be eligible for funding from the arts councils, which has supported its longevity.

Conclusion

The wellness principles of this renewed anglophone theater sector differ strongly from those that came before. The repertoire of the midcentury period was forged in two colonial relations: a relation of affiliation to Great

Britain and the United States and a relation of dominance vis-à-vis the francophone majority. The former sought heteronomy; the latter enacted self-
sufficiency. In this period, the status of the English-language community
sustained a hub-and-spoke model of theatrical production and cultural influence more broadly. The centrality and dominance of the MRT was un-
contested; its reach extended to regional theaters and amateur companies,
thereby reproducing a colonial model of culture to which it was itself subject, typified by diffusion from a center and reproduction across a field. The
field's play selections and structural organization nonetheless made sensible
the sector's valorization of durability with respect to repertoire and social reproduction with respect to local talent and audiences. Such were the signs of
"health" for midcentury English-language theater in Québec.

By contrast, in the 1970s, the diminished status and reduced demography
of Québec Anglophones created new challenges to sectoral flourishing.
Indeed, they necessitated a new model by which the anglophone theater
sector might come into being and achieve value—one that was grafted onto
the professional, institutional conditions of work in the francophone theater
sphere and enabled by the state funding of the arts. The value of English-
language Québec theatre of this period lay in internal, repertorial distinctions
of the major houses from each other and from the similarly internally diverse
smaller companies, and its perennity in its mutually supporting institutional
structures. In this way, the theater of the 1970s helped to express and address
this new lived dynamic of minoritization in which Anglophones and their
theater culture were *small* both demographically and in terms of priority.
This shift makes visible the fact that English-language theater in Québec was
both a projection of dominant, English-language culture into Québec *and* an
assertion of an anglophone, multicultural minority.

In this example of communal flourishing can be gleaned some of the key
eudaimonic roles theater can play in the well-being of a group *as a group*.
Theater can act as a point of identification for a minority linguistic community, as is the case in the more recent period analyzed above, or as a
standard-bearer for the same, as in the earlier period; it may provide an expressive outlet and can summon institutions, both of which hold across the
decades. Perhaps most significant, theater allows for the elaboration of cultural scenes, networks of exchange and circulation that assemble people into
communities of language, affinity, taste, situation, and practice. If these are
truisms of theater's potentially *eudaimonic* effects, they are perhaps brought
especially clearly into focus in the example of community flourishing of

minority-language or -culture performance where linguistic or even existential precarity motivates express attention to community well-being.

Works Cited

Ad Hoc Anglo-Québécois Theatre Committee and Alliance Quebec. "English Language Theatre in Quebec." Unpublished report, 1987.

Allan, Martha. *Summer Solstice: A Drama in One Act*. Toronto, Samuel French (Canada), 1935.

Bailey, Bruce. "Theatre in La Belle Province." *Canadian Forum*, September 1976, pp. 18–19.

Booth, Philip. "The Montreal Repertory Theatre: 1930–1961. A History and Handlist of Productions." MA thesis, McGill University, 1989.

Booth, Philip, Kimberly Diggins, Jean-Marc Larrue, Isabelle Roy, Peter Urqhart, and David Whitely. "Anglophone Theatre in Quebec from 1879 to 2000." Unpublished typescript, commissioned by the Quebec Drama Federation, 1998.

Bourhis, Richard Y., ed. *Decline and Prospects of the English-Speaking Communities of Quebec*. Canadian Heritage and the Canadian Institute for Research on Linguistic Minorities, 2012.

Breon, Robin. "The Growth and Development of Black Theatre in Canada: A Starting Point." *African-Canadian Theatre*, edited by Maureen Moynagh. Playwrights Canada Press, 2005, pp. 1–9.

Caldwell, Gary. "English Quebec: Demographic and Cultural Reproduction." *International Journal of the Sociology of Language*, nos. 105–106, 1994, pp. 153–79.

Caldwell, Gary, and Éric Waddell, eds. *The English of Québec: From Majority to Minority Status*. Québec, Institut québécois de recherche sur la culture, 1982.

Canada, Office of the Commissioner of Official Languages. "Chapter 4: Official Language Minority Communities: Triving [*sic*] in the Public Space from Coast to Coast to Coast." October 3, 2013. https://www.clo-ocol.gc.ca/html/ar_ra_2008_09_p9_e.php. Accessed May 18, 2020.

Canada, Office of the Commissioner of Official Languages. "Understanding your Language Rights." September 13, 2018. https://www.clo-ocol.gc.ca/en/language_rights/act. Accessed May 18, 2020.

Cohen, M. Charles. "The Member from Trois-Rivières: A One-Act Play." *National Bicentenary of Canadian Jewry, 1759–1959*. Canadian Jewish Congress, National Bicentenary Committee, 1959, 17 leaves.

Curtis, Ron. "A History of Playwrights' Workshop Montreal: 1963–1988." MA thesis, McGill University, 1991.

Daniels, Dan. *The Inmates*. Montreal, Alternative Probes Presentations, 1971.

Daniels, Dan. "Underground." Unpublished typescript, 1970.

David, Gilbert. "Une institution théâtrale à géométrie variable." *Le théâtre québécois, 1975–1995*, edited by Dominique Lafon. Québec, Fidès, 2001, pp. 13–36.

Decoteau, L. (alias of Laurence Wilson). *The Hiders*. Westmount, QC, no publisher, 1963.

Digby, William. "Equal to the Sum of the Squares: A Comedy." Unpublished typescript, 1960.

Dolan, Jill. *Utopia in Performance: Finding Hope at the Theater*. Ann Arbor, University of Michigan Press, 2005.

"Eastern Canada's Haylofts Pulling Best in Years." *Billboard*, August 7, 1948, pp. 3 and 43.

Fédération CJA. "The Association of Jewish Day Schools." 2016. www.federationcja.org/100/agencies/ajds/. Accessed May 18, 2020.

Fennario, David. *Balconville*. Vancouver, Talonbooks, 1980.

Floch, William, and Joanne Pocock, "The Socio-Economic Status of English-Speaking Quebec: Those Who Left and Those Who Stayed." *Decline and Prospects of the English-Speaking Communities of Quebec*, edited by Richard Y. Bourhis. Canadian Heritage and the Canadian Institute for Research on Linguistic Minorities, 2012, pp. 129–73.

Giles, H., R. Y. Bourhis, and D. M. Taylor. "Towards a Theory of Language in Ethnic Group Relations." *Language, Ethnicity and Intergroup Relations*, edited by Howard Giles. London, Academic Press, 1977, pp. 307–48.

"'Green Pastures' sur la scène." *Le Devoir*, April 28, 1942, p. 4.

Godin, Jean Cléo, and Laurent Mailhot. *Théâtre québécois I: Introduction à dix dramaturges contemporains*. Montréal, Hurtubise HMH, 1970.

Godin, Jean Cléo, and Laurent Mailhot. *Théâtre québécois II: Nouveaux auteurs, autres spectacles*. Montréal, Hurtubise HMH, 1980.

Gold, Muriel. *A Gift for Their Mother: The Saidye Bronfman Centre: A History*. Westmount, QC, MIRI, 2007.

Graham, Catherine. "Le théâtre anglophone au Québec." *Le théâtre québécois, 1975–1995*, edited by Dominique Lafon. Québec, Fidès, 2001, pp. 307–24.

Hall, Amelia. *Life before Stratford: The Memoirs of Amelia Hall*. Toronto and Oxford, Dundurn Press, 1989.

Henry, Jeff. "Black Theatre in Montreal and Toronto in the Sixties and Seventies: The Struggle for Recognition," *Canadian Theatre Review*, vol. 118, 2004, pp. 29–33.

Hotte, Lucie, and Guy Poirier. "Introduction." *Habiter la distance: Études en marge de* La distance habitée, edited by Lucie Hotte and Guy Poirier. Sudbury, ON, Éditions Prise de parole, 2009, pp. 7–14.

Hulslander, Keith. "Le *nouveau* nouveau théâtre québécois: L'émergence d'une identité québécoise dans la dramaturgie anglomontréalaise." *La problématique de l'identité dans la littérature francophone du Canada et d'ailleurs*, edited by Lucie Hotte. Ottawa, Le Nordir, 1994, pp. 29–38.

Hurley, Erin. "Townships Theatres: Identities and Circuits 1935–1982." *Journal of Eastern Townships Studies/Revue d'études des Cantons-de-l'Est*, vol. 46, spring 2016, pp. 15–35.

Jedwab, Jack, and Hugh Maynard. "Politics of Community: The Evolving Challenge of Representing English-Speaking Quebecers." *Decline and Prospects of the English-Speaking Communities of Quebec*, edited by Richard Y. Bourhis. Canadian Heritage and the Canadian Institute for Research on Linguistic Minorities, 2012, pp. 277–312.

Jubinville, Yves. "Appel d'air: Regards obliques sur l'institution théâtrale au Québec." *Théâtres québécois et canadiens-français au XXe siècle: trajectoires et territoires*, edited by Hélène Beauchamp and Gilbert David. Québec, Presses de l'Université du Québec, 2003, pp. 325–39.

Lane-Mercier, Gillian, Denise Merkle, and Jane M. Koustas, eds. *Minority Languages, National Languages, and Official Language Policies*. Montreal and Kingston, McGill-Queen's University Press, 2018.

McLaughlin, Mireille. "Par la brèche de la culture: Le Canada français et le virage culturel de l'état canadien." *International Journal of Canadian Studies/Revue international d'études canadiennes,* vol. 45-46, 2012, pp. 141–61.

McPhee, Janet, and Herbert Whittaker. "Jupiter in Retreat: A Melodrama." Unpublished typescript, 1942.

Milliken, Paul. "Portrait of the Artist as a Working-Class Hero: An Interview with David Fennario." *Performing Arts in Canada,* vol. 17, no. 2, summer 1980, pp. 22–25.

Morris, Marjorie. *Seven One-Act Plays.* Richmond, BC, M. Morris, 1995.

Paré, François. *Literatures of Exiguity.* 1993. Translated by Lin Burman. Waterloo, Wilfrid Laurier University Press, 2001.

Pawelski, James O. "Bringing Together the Humanities and the Science of Well-Being to Advance Human Flourishing." *Well-Being and Higher Education: A Strategy for Change and the Realization of Education's Greater Purpose,* edited by Don Harward. Washington, DC, Bringing Theory into Practice, 2016, pp. 207–16.

Pawelski, James O. "Defining the 'Positive' in Positive Psychology: Part I. A Descriptive Analysis." *The Journal of Positive Psychology,* vol. 11, no. 4, 2016, pp. 339–56.

Ravel, Aviva. "Black Dreams." *Contemporary Canadian Drama,* edited by Joseph Shaver. Ottawa, Borealis Press, 1974, pp. 168–204.

Ravel, Aviva. *Dispossessed.* Toronto, Playwrights Co-op, 1976.

Ravel, Aviva. *The Twisted Loaf and Soft Voices.* Toronto, Simon and Pierre, 1973.

Reid, Gregory. "Is There an Anglo-Quebecois Literature?" *Essays on Canadian Writing,* vol. 84, Fall 2009, pp. 58–86.

Reid, Gregory. "Reflections on the Plays of Aviva Ravel and the Anglo-Québécois Theatre." Conference of the Association for Canadian Theatre Research, May 1998, University of Ottawa. Conference Presentation.

Robineau, Anne. "La scène musicale anglo-québécoise." *Recherches sociographiques,* vol. 55, no. 3, 2014, pp. 559–81.

Rodgers, Guy, Jane Needles, and Rachel Garber. "The Artistic and Cultural Vitality of English-Speaking Quebec." *Decline and Prospects of the English-Speaking Communities of Quebec,* edited by Richard Y. Bourhis. Ottawa, Canadian Heritage, 2012, pp. 245–76.

Román, David. *Acts of Intervention: Performance, Gay Culture, and AIDS.* Bloomington, Indiana University Press, 1998.

Rosenberg, Louis. *Jewish Children in the Protestant Schools of Greater Montreal in the Period from 1878–1962.* Montreal, Canadian Jewish Congress, 1962.

Rudin, Ronald. *Forgotten Quebecers: A History of English-Speaking Quebec, 1759–1980.* Québec, Institut québécois de recherche sur la culture, 1985.

Schryburt, Sylvain. *De l'acteur vedette au théâtre de festival: Histoire des pratiques scéniques montréalaises, 1940–1980.* Montréal, Presses de l'Université de Montréal, 2011.

Siminovitch, Elinor. *Big X, Little Y.* Toronto, Playwrights Co-op, 1975.

Statistics Canada. "Census in Brief: English, French and Official Language Minorities in Canada." August 31, 2017. www12.statcan.gc.ca/census-recensement/2016/as-sa/98-200-x/2016011/98-200-x2016011-eng.cfm. Accessed May 18, 2020.

Statistique Canada. "Tableau 5-10-0003-01: Population selon la langue maternelle et la géographie, 1951 à 2016." May 18, 2020. doi.org/10.25318/1510000301-fra. Accessed May 20, 2020.

Stein, Michael. "Changing Anglo-Quebecer Self-Consciousness." *The English of Québec: From Majority to Minority Status,* edited by Gary Caldwell and Éric Waddell. Québec, Institut québécois de recherche sur la culture, 1982, pp. 107–26.

Stevenson, Garth. *Community Beseiged: The Anglophone Minority and the Politics of Quebec*. Montreal, McGill-Queen's University Press, 1999.

Wallace, Robert. *'67*. Toronto, Playwrights Co-Op, 1974.

Warner, Sara. *Acts of Gaiety: LGBT Performance and the Politics of Pleasure*. Ann Arbor, University of Michigan Press, 2013.

Westley, Margaret. *Remembrance of Grandeur: The Anglo-Protestant Elite of Montreal, 1900–1950*. Montreal, Libre Expression, 1990.

Whittaker, Herbert. "New Festival." *The Globe and Mail [Toronto]*, December 16, 1976, p. 15.

Whittaker, Herbert. *Setting the Stage: Montreal Theatre, 1920–1949*. Edited and introduced by Jonathan Rittenhouse. Montreal and Kingston: McGill-Queen's University Press, 1999.

8

Refusing to Flourish

Jennifer Moon and Anat Shinar Perform Self-Help

Gwyneth Shanks

Jennifer Moon, a Los Angeles–based conceptual artist, begins her/their manifesto-esque pamphlet, *Definition of Abundance*:[1]

> The two steadfast, basic principles . . . are transferable and pertinent to absolutely anything imaginable today. They are filters, so to speak, through which everything will be applied—or perhaps, more accurately, a way to remove the filters—in order to live a revolutionary life inspiring continuous adventure, discovery, and expansion for all on this earth and beyond! And when I say, "always," I mean pertaining to any manner of actions that can be deemed revolutionary. (3–4)

Moon's first principle is to "operate from a place of abundance," and the second involves choosing the "most expansive route" as a means of staying in the present moment (4–5). Their multimodal and long-term project, *The Revolution*, of which *Definition of Abundance* is a key element, reimagines the contours of self-help literature, personal improvement, indeed, human flourishing by funneling such ideas through the format of the political manifesto. Moon's revolution extends beyond their artistic output and becomes a way of being in the world counter to the heteronormative and hegemonic dictates of capitalism, colonialism, and patriarchy.[2] This essay explores how Moon and dance artist Anat Shinar challenge notions of human flourishing visible in self-help literature, revealing the unacknowledged structures of racial, gendered, and national exclusions that determine what it means to flourish.

---

[1] As Moon prefers both she/her/hers and they/their pronouns, I will use they/their moving forward.

[2] Moon began to work with the concept of the revolution in graduate school in the late 1990s at the Art Center College of Design.

Gwyneth Shanks, *Refusing to Flourish* In: *Theater and Human Flourishing*. Edited by: Harvey Young, Oxford University Press. © Oxford University Press 2023. DOI: 10.1093/oso/9780197622261.003.0009

As a framework for understanding *being*, human flourishing has proved to be lasting, as it places personal fulfillment in service of living a complete life at the center of ethical thought. The Greek term *eudaimonia*, often translated as "human flourishing," is, in Western moral or ethical philosophic traditions, a means of understanding how we can achieve a more complete or full state of being. From the Greek words *eu* (good) and *daimon* (soul), eudaimonia was most extensively discussed by Aristotle; he contended that through hard work, the cultivation of certain virtues, and excelling at specific or chosen roles—physician or scribe, for example—one could flourish. Aristotle discussed the cultivation of friendship, pleasure, and honor, as well as the accumulation of wealth as means of imagining a cohesive and most gratifying life. In short, the term came to articulate one of the ultimate goals of Aristotelian thought, and indeed the broader fields of moral philosophy. How does one become a better person, or more precisely, how does one most fully achieve one's particular potential as a human? Human flourishing is now often discussed within academia under the umbrella of positive psychology, which "equates well-being with living well or actualizing one's potentials" (Schueller 2661).[3] Within the framework of this anthology, focused on theater and performance studies' interdisciplinary contributions to human flourishing, I found myself wondering: For whom is flourishing *not* an option? For whom—socially, economically, politically—have the articulations of flourishing rehearsed above been foreclosed and why? Within this line of questioning, I wondered how artists might offer ways of revealing not simply the structural or systemic pessimisms of such foreclosures, but also the potential for a radical refusal of flourishing.

While positive psychology continues to explore the contours of what human flourishing might mean, these ideas find their most pervasive popular expression in self-help literature and the broader self-help industry. Moon's and Shinar's art practices focus on or variously take inspiration from self-help. Moon's *The Revolution*, for instance, draws upon Michel Foucault, Michael Hardt, TED Talks speakers, and life coaches and aims to dethrone

---

[3] While Stephen Schueller's arguments regarding positive psychology prove a useful starting point for the elaboration of my analysis of Moon's and Shinar's work, his understanding of the field is but one of many. For example, describing human flourishing, Alan S. Waterman asserts that happiness is not prescriptive but subjective, with a focus on the "character and characteristics of a life lived well" and the centrality of self-realization "to a life well lived." Other scholars in the field emphasize communal or collective understandings of human flourishing, rejecting the individual as the sole locus of flourishing. I am indebted to James O. Pawelski for his careful and generous feedback on the points of interdisciplinary overlap between positive psychology and performance studies.

capitalism (Ballegaard). Moon evangelizes these ideas through platforms as diverse as a radio show, museum exhibitions, and free pamphlets. Here I focus on their *Phoenix Rising Saga*, which is part of their larger revolutionary project; it was created in three parts and displayed at the Los Angeles gallery Commonwealth & Council (parts 1 and 3), the Transmission Gallery in Glasgow (part 1), and the Hammer Museum (part 2) in Los Angeles. Shinar, a conceptual choreographer based in Minneapolis, likewise examines the self-help industry in her most recent piece, *Here's How (Refuted)*, which premiered in 2018 at Red Eye Theater in Minneapolis. The dance work, featuring Shinar, Kara Motta, and Kristin Van Loon, aligns the language of self-help books with exhaustive and durational dance phrases, using performers' bodies—sweaty, panting, and stumbling—as vehicles for revealing the (gendered) capitalist compulsion for continual self-improvement that undergirds the self-help industry. Moon and Shinar mine the vague, utopic language of self-improvement to radical ends, challenging narratives of individualism and self-advancement. Their performances reveal the ideological and biopolitical imperatives ghosting self-help by rejecting the pervasive tenets of self-actualization and improvement. By translating the "self" discussed within self-help into and onto their bodies, Moon and Shinar reveal how the logics of self-help aim to control the subject as a means of regulating the broader social body. Instead, Moon and Shinar perform refusal, interrogating the capitalist and self-negating logics that undergird the American self-help industry.

Their work illustrates how self-help and human flourishing are deeply embedded in the ideological imperatives of neoliberal capitalism, liberal democracy, and nationalism. Contemporary self-help literature, for example, draws together several distinct moments in American history, coalescing a series of concerns around national narratives of self-making, racial and gendered uplift movements, and large-scale shifts in the U.S. economy. The term "self-help" traces its origins to Samuel Smiles's widely read and hugely popular 1859 book *Self-Help*, published the same year as Charles Darwin's *On the Origin of Species*. As literary scholar Barbara Leckie reminds us, this is a useful coincidence as, "with their divergent foci on *self* and *species*, respectively," the two texts collectively shed light on the emergence of modern thought, and Smiles's text is key to understanding popular understandings of selfhood (305). Smiles advocated, for instance, the now familiar formulation "Heaven helps those who help themselves" and championed the self-determined and industrious individual who could lift himself out of

Figure 8.1 Performer Kristin Van Loon in Anat Shinar's *Here's How (Refuted)*, May 31–June 3, 2018. Red Eye Theater, Minneapolis, Minnesota. Photograph by Bill Cameron.

his squalid beginnings into knowledge and productivity (1). Similarly, self-help traces its roots, albeit in fictional form, to the latter half of the nineteenth century and the pervasive narrative of hard work epitomized by the serial novels of Horatio Alger. Alger did much to popularize the mythos of American individualism, hard work, and class uplift as the twentieth century dawned and the country's reliance upon an ever-industrializing workforce increased. Indeed, the majority of the serial novels for which Alger is known were published in the magazine *Student and Schoolmate*, which was aimed at young boys and teenagers, thus underscoring the pedagogical and didactic tone of these early fictional self-help narratives.

While Alger popularized the narrative tropes and characterizations that have become ubiquitous in the literary history of a distinctly American version of self-help, Frederick Douglass likewise espoused the tenets and virtues of the self-made man. In a lecture from 1894, Douglass wrote:

Self-made men are the men who, under peculiar difficulties and without the ordinary helps of favoring circumstances, have attained knowledge, usefulness, power and position and have learned from themselves the best uses to which life can be put in this world, and in the exercises of these uses to build up worthy character. They are the men who owe little or nothing to birth, relationship, or friendly surroundings; to wealth inherited or to early approved means of education; who are what they are, without the aid of any favoring conditions by which other men usually rise in the world and achieve great results. (104)

Douglass positioned himself as the archetypal self-made American man, counter to the roughly concurrent fictionalized rags-to-riches heroes popularized in Alger's and others' works. This lecture was to become one of his most popular; indeed, it is thought he delivered it some fifty times beginning in 1859. In it, he defined the American self-made man as one who has attained certain markers of success and knowledge by depending solely upon himself. (One of the most studied and remarked upon elements of Douglass's biography during his life and posthumously remains his pursuit of literacy, a not unproblematic revalidation of certain epistemologies distinctly linked to "prequalifications for liberal democratic citizenship" [Alfaro 237].)

As gender studies scholar and political theorist Ange-Marie Hancock Alfaro writes, "Much of Douglass's antislavery rhetoric has been characterized as quintessentially 'American' in its rugged individualism, particularly regarding his conscientious presentation of himself as a self-made man in league with America's love affair with self-determination" (238). Likewise, African America historian and scholar Wilson J. Moses argues that in "appropriating the Euro-American myth of the self-made man," Douglass located the political struggle and cause of emancipation within the rhetorical and literary canon of an emerging American imaginary (177). This positioning, in other words, is an inherently political and performative act, as it places the figure of a formerly enslaved individual within the framework of the capitalist nation-state and, thus, as one who has access to that most potent of American mythos.[4]

My aim in evoking Douglass's speech and certain of its afterlives is to point to the triangulation of economic advancement, subject formations as parsed through race and gender, and nationalism within American conceptions of the self and self-actualization. If Douglass's rhetorical appropriations aimed to figure Blackness squarely within the national imaginary and the nation's

[4] In part belying the rhetoric of his address, throughout his life Douglass discussed his reliance upon other people, most particularly women (his grandmother, two wives, a daughter, and countless abolitionist women who supported his career) for his trajectory.

preoccupation with the self-made man, the reception of his claims to self-determination did not undo the myth, but merely expanded it. Narratives of self-actualization, which formed alongside whiteness and masculinity and aimed to preserve and fulfill one's citizenship obligations laid the foundation for the modern self-help industry that emerged in the early 1970s.

From 1972 to 2000, "the number·of self-help books more than doubled, increasing from 1.1 percent to 2.4 percent of the total number of books in print" (McGee 11–12). The self-help industry's growth from the 1970s onward parallels the shifted economic and social landscape of the United States, in which employment had become increasingly precarious and unstable. By the early 1970s, the nation had entered a period of prolonged stagflation (Bailey and Farber 2). Only a few months after Gerald Ford took office in 1974 the poetically named "misery index" (which aimed to determine how the average citizen was doing by combining unemployment data with inflation) reached a high of 19.9 percent (4). The affective toll the rapidly shifting economic sector had upon individuals helps explain in part the rise of self-help. Likewise, the partial legislative success of the civil rights and feminist movements stoked white, identitarian fears of social and financial displacement for portions of the nation—that is, white men—for whom the promise of the American dream was designed. Self-help programs intervened in these social shifts by offering not a structural diagnosis but an individual antidote designed to ameliorate personal anxiety. Perpetual self-improvement offered one solution to combat the anxiety of economic and identity-based insecurity, and tidily sidestepped systemic class and economic inequity or deep-seated racism and sexism. Identity and economic security thus became the foundational tenets of the modern self-help industry.

Since the 1970s, self-help literature has expanded into a full-scale industry, worth nearly $2.5 billion by the early 2000s (McGee 11). By 2016 the industry was worth almost $10 billion, and in 2022 it is projected to be worth $13 billion (Sinclair). One of the latest rhetorical shifts in the movement is the metaphor of one's life as a work of art. The result of this idea is that one's intimate life and space are subject to "ongoing and tireless production [and becomes] a design studio for reinventing one's most marketable self" (McGee 22). It is an assertion not unconnected to one made by art historian Miwon Kwon. She writes that in the early twenty-first century, "an artist's characteristic mode of operation . . . [circulates] as a new art commodity," replacing the art object and forcing the artist to function as a kind of brand ambassador for her work (47). Across both these models, the individual becomes a brand, situating herself and her labor—artistic or otherwise—within advanced capitalism, thoroughly obscuring the boundaries between labor and nonlabor. Mainstream self-help literature and programs largely fail to address the fact that the desire for such narratives is inextricably tied to the steady decline of standard employment contracts and the rise of precarious labor.

In light of this history, Moon's art seems to blur the boundary among their body, biography, and art as a means of intervening in such self-branding logics. *The Revolution* draws equally upon the format of the political manifesto and self-help literature. Its content is loosely Marxist and anticapitalist, grounded in notions of self and collective love, and espouses the two basic principles with which I opened this essay. Moon's revolution probes the pleasurable dialectic between "solitary pursuit and collective longing," imagining the radical potential of an all-encompassing notion of love (Holte 9). While *The Revolution* begins with individual love, it quickly expands to imagine a vast collective of love-filled individuals whose abundance transforms the very makeup of the planet. Moon becomes, in their work, a kind of anti-self-made artist; their project is riddled with confessions of their own anxiety, self-reflexive humor, and a magical mysticism that pushes ideas of self far beyond any sort of new-age spirituality and into the realm of cosplay-fueled fantasy. This play between the collective longing of the revolution and the individualistic drive toward ever-greater self-love and -actualization maps onto the narratives espoused by the self-help industry.

While *The Revolution* includes performances—for example, Moon has a radio show titled *Adventures Within*; gives talks modeled after inspirational speakers, many of which are posted on YouTube; and leads team-building workshops—here I focus on how they complicate the rhetorical structures common to self-help literature through both visual and textual invocations of the body. For example, accompanying *The Revolution* are staged and theatrical photographs of the artist either posing as various historical revolutionary leaders or galloping through the cosmos astride a sleek stallion. Such texts include assignments they create for followers of their self-improvement program or booklets they produce that detail the tenets of the revolution, imagined as instructions for living. These assignments, I argue, are akin to performance scores: one must put pen to paper and complete the assignment, an activity that implicates one's body in the act of writing and creates a relay between textual inscription, body, and self.

Between 2008 and 2009, Moon was incarcerated at Valley State Prison, previously Valley State Prison for Women, in Chowchilla, California, on robbery charges. While there, they began a series of pieces, exhibited, upon their release, as *Phoenix Rising, Part 1: This Is Where I Learned of Love*. One of these works, *Assignment #1*, was part of a larger piece they undertook in prison: *Pseudo-Life Coaching Prison Project*. Moon was involved in, as they term it, "the tobacco trade," and developed this life coaching project as a way to incentivize their fellow prisoners' smoking habits. In exchange for a cigarette, Moon's fellow prisoners had to "make a list of things people cannot say, think, or feel about you." Moon's own list included lines like "I'm a capitalist," "I'm a fascist," "I look like Yoko Ono (or some other famous asian [*sic*] woman)," "I'm smart," and "I'm not a good friend" ("Assignment #1" 24–25). Their list strategically vacillates between the geopolitical, the racialized and stereotypical that eroticize Asian women or frame Asian Americans as model minorities, and intimate insecurities specific to Moon. Moon's list frames the "self" as inherently relationally dependent upon the responses and opinions of others. "Self" also moves seamlessly from the introspective idea that Moon might be a bad friend to the structural rhetoric of the political economy, jumping between interiority and social structure. Their list aligns distinctly different ideological framings of the self as a means to expand the parameters of self-improvement narratives. Such an expansion of the term points to the limits of self-help as a project invested in the individual, revealing the extent to which the genre is predicated upon the maintenance of larger social forces, like capitalism, racism, and sexism, which such literature often aims to obscure.

Moon's notion of revolution, however, is most fully articulated in their published manifesto. The blue-bound booklet was printed for their exhibition in the Hammer Museum's 2014 *Made in L.A.* biennial.[5] For the exhibition, the booklets were placed on a low bench positioned beneath a large-scale photograph of Moon and their dog Mr. Snuggles imitating the iconic photo of Black Panthers cofounder Huey P. Newton. The original photograph, attributed to Blair Stapp, was used in a 1967 poster designed by Eldridge Cleaver. In the image, which takes up the majority of the 34 5/8 × 23 3/8-inch poster, Newton sits in a rattan peacock chair, dressed in a black leather jacket and beret. In one hand he holds a rifle and in the other a spear; on the floor beneath his feet is a rug printed with zebra stripes, and two leaf-shaped Zulu-style shields lean against the wall behind him. At the bottom of

---

[5] The manifesto is currently in its fourth edition and was reprinted by Onomatopee most recently. The booklet is also available online as a free pdf.

Figure 8.2 Installation view of Jennifer Moon, *Made in L.A.*, June 15–September 7, 2014. Hammer Museum, Los Angeles. Photograph by Brian Forrest.

the poster is the line "The racist dog policemen must withdraw immediately from our communities, cease their wanton murder and brutality and torture of black people, or face the wrath of the armed people." While art historians have argued that the image, iconic of Newton and the Panthers, is reminiscent of European traditions of portraiture, "Christ in majesty, or Napoleon enthroned," it also visually challenges nineteenth- and early twentieth-century genres of colonial portraiture, in which objects like Zulu shields and zebra-printed rugs would have functioned as markers of conquest (Morgan 129). In Newton's portrait these objects are not indexes of European colonialism but are instead repurposed as symbols of Black Power. The photograph stages a usurpation of colonial rule and, by extension, frames the policed and hypersurveilled U.S. streets *as* colonial spaces and as sites from which to issue an armed resistance and a revolutionary overthrow of such oppressive and violent forces.

Moon's restaging of the photo, titled *There Is Nothing Left but Freedom, Detail of You Can Kill My Body, but You Can't Kill My Soul* (2013), aligns these various vectors and histories of revolutionary thought and action with their revolution. Beneath Moon's feet is a rainbow rug, and to either side of them is a typewriter and a recorder connected to the microphone they hold in their hand. While the rainbow rug seems, in juxtaposition to Moon's serious countenance, a campy index of the modern LGBTQIAP+ movement and the typewriter and recorder are Moon's chosen "weapons" of the revolution, I am interested in the cross-racial and gender-queer performance activated between Newton's and Moon's images. Moon evokes their own subject formation (queer, Korean American) in the photograph. These various articulations of difference render legible a set of identitarian solidarities that transhistorically link Newton's and Moon's distinct revolutionary projects, somewhat promiscuously drawing together the aesthetic strategies of a queer artist of color and the iconic image of a Black revolutionary.

While the photo is in dialogue with Moon's broader oeuvre of work that makes explicit reference to their sexuality, their subtle reframing of the 1967 photo likewise queers it: the rainbow rug and their Pomeranian, Mr. Snuggles, in his own revolutionary beret add a camp charge not present in the original. The piece, however, is both uneasy and *not* uneasy in its cross-racial quoting of the iconic image. If Moon's photograph works to align the artist with the cofounder of the Black Panthers, it also, paradoxically, circumvents certain delimiting formations of difference, from which whiteness and heterosexuality always already manage to escape. The photo is at once a performance of transhistorical revolutionary solidarity *and* a disavowal of the need to place Moon and *The Revolution* within such histories. The artist, in the first footnote to their manifesto, writes:

> Everything, including myself (my physical body as well as how I feel and regard myself, which informs how I perceive and interact with the world), is constantly shifting from moment to moment, or from situation to situation. . . . Hence, it is more accurate, as well as less painful, to understand that my identity is formless and who I am can simply be described as beingness or awareness and/or consciousness. (*Definition* 2)

The artist's extended, opening footnote intervenes in delimiting discourses of identity politics, reframing any readerly attempts to categorize them through an appropriation of the amorphous and apolitical rhetoric of new-age spirituality. In it they ruminate on how one might imagine a self not predicated on fixed categories like woman, mother, American, or artist but rather based in formlessness. Analyzing *There Is Nothing Left but Freedom, Detail of You Can Kill My Body, but You Can't Kill My Soul* through this footnote, then, produces a different articulation of the artist's politicized allegiance to the iconic image. The photograph provides a liminal and performative (if stilled) space in which Moon's replication of Newton's pose complicates an easy understanding of their identity.

In part, Moon supports this turn to formlessness through the philosophies of life coaches and self-help gurus like Michael Blomsterberg, Byron Katie, and Eckhart Tolle. Blomsterberg's book *It Begins with Me* depends upon "self-discovery," "delving inward," and "gentle support," phrases meant to lead the reader toward "recognizing who . . . [they] truly are." His rhetorical focus on personal truth imagines his reader as free of identity categories. Rather, the assertion of the need to find—against one's parents, friends, or community—a personal truth becomes his program's starting point for profound transformation. Such rhetoric, however, tacitly disavows large-scale social, economic, or political shifts that impact how an individual is able to access or frame her own "truth." Beyond denying systemic or structural forces that might curtail individual agency, "the idea that one can make oneself, invent oneself, is . . . a profoundly alienating [idea]" (McGee 8). As scholars like Micki McGee and Jeffery Decker have noted, this privileging of the individual—and not identity or identification—fits within the discourse of self-help literature and, more broadly, the mythos of the self-made man. It is, after all, only in imagining oneself as free from identity constructs that one can access—or at least imagine—a future in which self-fulfillment and success are possible.

Moon's opening footnote continues, "A straightforward and thorough book on identity and identification is Eckhart Tolle's *A New Earth*. If you are not inclined to mainstream spiritual reading and/or you lean more towards critical theory and art, check out Deleuze and Guattari's *Anti-Oedipus*" (*Definition* 2). While Moon acknowledges the vast differences in style and audience between these authors, they nevertheless argue that "both address the same issue of ego-loss and disentangling oneself of beliefs to enable a greater freedom from the repression of self by self" (2). I take Moon's evocation of these authors as, at the very least, playful and, at most, an ironic critique made possible by aligning Deleuze and Guattari's theory of the affective and social "madness" born of capitalism—deeply informed by the student uprisings of 1968—with a book that manages to advocate for anticonsumption without critiquing the capitalist structures that undergird the industry within which Tolle's brand circulates. In other words, the political differences between Deleuze and Guattari's work and the late-capitalist turn toward self-actualization that underwrites the commercial success of the self-help industry are tacitly revealed in Moon's syntactical alignment.

This collision of ideological positions mirrors the tension that scholars like McGee note are increasingly visible in the growing conservative ethos of much contemporary self-help literature. "The idea," McGee writes, "of self-invention has long infused American culture with a sense of endless possibility" (11), yet, as American studies scholar Jeffery Decker writes, this sense of endless possibility is not "timeless nor transcendent but historical and contested" (xiv). Who has access to self-invention has radically shifted since the mid-twentieth century as women and communities of color increasingly gained visibility and modicums of authority within the workforce. In response to such cultural and economic changes, "there seems to be an ongoing effort" on the part of self-help authors to reinforce traditional values in the face of "their own internal contradictions" (McGee 17). In other words, by espousing ideas of self-actualization such programs leave open a space for anyone to gain success, even though the notions upheld in self-help literature are premised on American advancement, itself predicated upon whiteness and masculinity. If Blomsterberg's or Tolle's work is marked by a conservative ethos of self-sufficiency, a disavowal of systemic marginalization, or even relationality, Moon leverages these authors' rhetoric of transformation in service of a philosophy that embraces not the individual but the collective.

Moon defies prescribed narratives of labor, articulating through their use of the descriptor "revolution" the links among self, labor, time, and (personal) economic success so often conflated in self-help literature. Self-help programs are often aimed at training one how to master time—think of Stephen Covey's *The 7 Habits of Highly Effective People* or Sheryl Sandberg's book *Lean In*. The idea that self-fulfillment is achievable only if one could use time better is a capitulation to the prevailing capitalist assumptions about how one should be spending one's time. Marx's labor-time is reimagined in modern self-help literature for our post-Fordist moment. No longer is the laborer "an incarnation of time," their worth calculated in relation to how long it takes to produce a certain number of commodities (Marx 58–59; Lukás 89–90). Rather, as the commodity becomes immaterial, the laborer has been transformed into the nebulous and formless version of the "self" described in self-improvement literature. It is a self which defies categorization and is, instead, able to endlessly transform, readily adaptable to our ever shifting, unstable economic landscape. If this framing of the self seems not discon-nected from midcentury thought focused on "becoming"—and this link seems of particular interest to Moon—espoused by thinkers like Deleuze and Guattari, in conventional self-help the ideological imperatives of immaterial labor and intangibility are firmly yoked to late capitalism. Moon's framing of their self-help-cum-conceptual-art program as a revolution asks us to imagine, instead, an implosion of our allegiances to clock-time or immate-rial labor.

Moon's art practice reveals the pleasurable and painful contradictions between the self and the collective, love and the revolution within narratives of self-help. Moon challenges prevailing ideas within self-improvement literature that focus on the individual in ways that become incommensurate with collective action and, instead, reproduce the status quo. The rhetorical figure in the Alger myth is no longer the eager newsboy who works his way up the corporate ladder; instead, in Moon's *Revolution*, the self-made man has become a revolutionary who wears their queer desires on their sleeve.

* * *

Contemporary choreographer Anat Shinar's *Here's How (Refuted)* opens with a stage space empty of performers. Instead, placed upstage are three freestanding clothing racks, a chair or stool accompanying each. Clothing hangs neatly from hangers—blazers, spandex exercise wear, a glamorous cocktail dress—and shoes are arranged in rows beneath the hangers. The mise-en-scène lingers for long moments as the audience is left to contem-plate the multiple connotations of clothing racks: an actor's dressing room, costumes waiting to be tried on; a closet; a shop; or some merging of the three. Beyond these associations, the racks also seem to reference the po-tential for clothing to shift one's presentation of self and, indeed, one's *sense* of self: think the common advice, "Dress for the job you want, not the job you have."

After several minutes, Shinar herself enters, dressed in what appear to be her rehearsal clothes: loose shorts and an oversize red sweatshirt. As she walks and stands downstage center, a spotlight illuminates her and canned applause plays loudly. Shinar begins to speak; her words are punctuated by carefully choreographed hand gestures. Precise and oddly held, her gestures are meant to reference the thoroughly rehearsed yet pseudo-natural, or ca-sual, mannerism of TED Talks or inspirational speakers. Shinar's speech begins:

Figure 8.3 Anat Shinar performs in *Here's How (Refuted)*, May 31–June 3, 2018. Red Eye Theater, Minneapolis, Minnesota. Photograph by Bill Cameron.

I want to start by offering that you change.
I want to ask you, do a little audit.
How many of you are smaller?
Sometimes we hold on, like this.
Sometimes we spread out.
I see you.
I want you to pay attention.
I'm hoping that you learn.[6]

[6] All text from *Here's How (Refuted)* was shared with the author by Shinar.

Her speech draws upon a formula familiar to TED Talks or inspirational self-help speakers. The pronouns—"I," "you"—are pronounced, drawing the listener (or audience) in and performatively indicating how much the speaker cares for *you*. On the line "How many of you are smaller?" Shinar raises her own hand, a gesture that seems to invite the audience to engage, to not feel uncomfortable or embarrassed. When she says "I see you," she points at the audience directly. The clarity of her spoken and embodied references, however, is fractured as her speech is made up of a series of distorted phrases. Nouns are almost completely removed from her lines, the subject of each sentence obscured, rendered bizarre and parodic. Shinar, however, remains posed and earnest in her delivery.

After delivering her final line, she turns and walks to stage right, the lights falling dark as she moves. Kristin Van Loon enters and replaces Shinar at center stage. Van Loon, like Shinar, is dressed for rehearsal, wearing baggy gray sweatpants and a sweatshirt. Placing herself precisely, Van Loon brings her hands together in a prayer-like posture before looking out at the audience; on her first line, "I want to start by offering that you change," she opens her hands, palms up, in a gesture of welcome. Van Loon repeats the same set of lines Shinar just performed with the same accompanying gestures. Concluding, Van Loon turns and walks to stage left, as Kara Motta replaces her at center stage. Motta wears slippers and an oversize sleep shirt. She begins again the set of lines already uttered by Shinar and Van Loon, but continues:

We're really fascinated with other people.
Think about, think about, think about interactions.
What is yours to me?
What's mine to you?
We have spent a lot of time looking at effects.
We make sweeping judgments and inferences and those predict meaning
    like who we ask.

As Motta introduces this new text, Shinar and Van Loon turn and walk upstage to two of the clothing racks and begin to slowly undress and re-dress. Van Loon, who next replaces Motta, makes the simplest of costume shifts, putting on a pair of flip-flops and hiking up one leg of her sweatpants. Coming to center stage, she repeats and continues the text Motta just uttered.

This text, and indeed the majority of the scripted lines the three performers repeat and pass back and forth among themselves throughout the piece, come from Dr. Amy Cuddy's 2012 TED Talk, "Your Body Language May Shape Who You Are." Other, barely discernable citations are from Barbara Ehrenreich's 2009 critique of American self-help, *Bright-sided: How the Relentless Promotion of Positive Thinking Has Undermined America,* and Gary Bishop's 2016 book, *Unfu*k Yourself: Get out of Your Head and into Your Life.*[7] Cuddy's talk—which remains one of the most popular in the conference's history and reportedly netted the social psychologist a $1 million advance on a book deal—makes up the vast majority of the dance's script (Morris). The subject of her talk, and subsequent book, was "power poses," and the emotional effects and hormonal changes adopting such poses had upon a person. During her twenty-minute talk, Cuddy explained that aping splayed, open, or otherwise expansive postures for as little as two minutes could positively change one's testosterone and cortisol levels, associated with, respectively, dominance and stress. She claimed that by adopting these power poses test subjects' level of testosterone went up anywhere from 10 to 20 percent, while their cortisol decreased between 15 and 25 percent. Heightened testosterone and lowered cortisol have been linked to alpha figures, as Cuddy says in her talk. Thus, her suggested two-minute power poses increase feelings of confidence and, most important, positively impact one's chances for success.

She begins her talk by saying, "So, I want to start by offering you a free no-tech life hack, and all it requires of you is this: that you change your posture for two minutes.... I want to ask you to right now do a little audit of your body and what you're doing with your body." As a reminder, *Here's How (Refuted)* begins, "I want to start by offering that you change. I want to ask you, do a little audit." By removing key words and collapsing distinct thoughts, Shinar rendered the text nonsensical, Cuddy's specific meaning lost in semantic contractions. While enough of Cuddy's original sentiment remains that a viewer understands the milieu from which *Here's How (Refuted)*'s text originated or to which it pays homage, this absurdist and collectively performed sendup of self-help talks reveals the individualist logic ghosting such rhetoric. This lack of coherence makes grammatically legible, the dance piece reveals, the groundlessness of such programs. Cuddy, of course, is a particularly pointed figure to choose to make this argument; the research on which her TED Talk was based has been largely—and rather publicly and

---

[7] Anat Shinar, interview by author, May 14, 2019.

dramatically—debunked by a number of different peer-reviewed scientific studies (Morris).

Cuddy's talk is also a useful foil in relation to dance and choreographed movement; what, after all, are power poses but choreography by another name? Toward the beginning of her talk, she sets up the importance of body language as a means of introducing her research on power poses:

> We're really fascinated with body language, and we're particularly inter-ested in other people's body language.... So obviously when we think about nonverbal behavior, or body language—but we call [it] nonverbal as so-cial scientists—it's language, so we think about communication. When we think about communication, we think about interactions. So what is your body language communicating to me? What's mine communicating to you?

This text is maintained in the dance performance, although transformed into the fragmented lines quoted earlier, and spoken at various points by all three performers. When Shinar, Motta, and Van Loon each utter "What is yours to me? What's mine to you?," the key words "language" and "communi-cating" have been removed, and the emphasis of the dance's text becomes its pronouns. "Yours," "me," "mine," "you": the repetition of such terms divorced from parts of speech that might render their use logical serves to under-score the transactional and, indeed, completely impersonal nature of much contemporary self-help programs. By uttering what becomes, however ab-surd, a series of platitudes common to self-help while replacing each other, the three dancers literally enact the shifting role of the individual within such programs. The utility of this type of narrative depends upon a clear and specific evocation of the individual. Yet that evocation is in service of a program—here TED Talks—aimed at tens of thousands of subjects: the self becomes a vehicle of collective seduction and, ultimately, regulation.

This notion of regulation becomes clear not only in relation to Cuddy's discussion of achieving success but also in her explanation of the scientific experiments that initially supported her findings. She describes how test participants were first asked to adopt certain poses—either power poses or small, meek poses—and then spit into a vial. The spit was tested to determine whether participants' hormonal levels had changed after adopting high- or low-power poses. The alignment of scientific (or pseudo-scientific) research with self-help programs is not new. Beginning in the 1920s, for example, the French psychologist Émile Coué penned one popular alignment of the two fields, his book *Self Mastery through Conscious Autosuggestion*. In it, he advocated for self-improvement through the use of what he termed "optimistic autosuggestion"; he encouraged people to repeat mantras like "Every day, in every way, I'm getting better and better" (10). Coué's findings, initially grounded in the emerging field of psychoanalysis, are visible in Cuddy's evocation of power poses, the nonverbal equivalent of his mantras, and, similar to Coué, she too aimed to bolster the claims of her idea through scientific research.

In *Here's How (Refuted)*, Cuddy's explanation of her experiment is transformed into the lines "Spit into a vial for two minutes. You need to do this. They don't look. We want them to be feeling. How do you feel? It's an opportunity to gamble. Take another saliva sample. That's it." The specter of regulation, which, of course, undergirds the self-help industry and is successfully marketed as both a desired and ever-shifting target, is viscerally and corporeally evoked in these lines. The seemingly banal regulation of the self—adopt a power pose or tell yourself a positive mantra—is transfigured into the prescriptive and controlled environment of the scientific lab. Cuddy's explanation is transformed, in the spoken text, into a command— "Spit into the vial for two minutes"—and the sense of autonomy her power poses seemingly offer is ghosted by far more coercive and violent histories of bodily scientific experiments, which nevertheless were framed as in service to a broader regulatory good. While such experiments are by no means equivalent to those Cuddy and her collaborators carried out, nor does *Here's How (Refuted)* overtly evoke such histories, the transformation of Cuddy's original text reveals the slippage between such modes of bodily and social regulation. The aim, I would argue, in self-help is to obscure the regulatory practices that simultaneously position the autonomous and determined individual helping herself as always already acting in service to a larger body politic.

Like Cuddy's original TED Talk, Shinar, Motta, and Van Loon's text lasts for approximately twenty minutes. As their lines progress, the three continue to change their clothes, moving back and forth from the clothing racks upstage to center stage. With each costume change, the three become progressively more dressed up: replacing rehearsal wear with casual jeans and T-shirts, upgrading to wrap dresses and pumps, and, in the final iteration, donning black trousers, button-up blouses, and blazers. Dress for the job you want (and seemingly the job of contemporary dancer occupies the bottom rung of this sartorial hierarchy). Their costuming changes, totally visible to

Figure 8.4 *Here's How (Refuted)*, May 31–June 3, 2018. Red Eye Theater, Minneapolis, Minnesota. Photograph by Bill Cameron.

the audience, track the development of Cuddy's talk, and indeed so many self-help seminars that draw listeners on a journey toward self-actualization. The dancers' slim-cut trousers and blazers are sartorial markings of success that reify corporate culture and, more unconsciously, structures of whiteness and masculinity.

Cuddy's talk ends as she reveals the personal impact her research and the notion of power poses has had. She begins by explaining how, as a young woman in graduate school, she felt unworthy of being at the elite, private institution: like an imposter. Her advisor told her, "Fake it until you make it." Jumping forward to her present-day experiences as a professor in the classroom, Cuddy describes one young woman who, never participating in class and so in danger of failing, comes to Cuddy's office. Cuddy gives the same advice to the young woman: "Fake it until you make it." Predictably, in the next class the young woman offers an amazing comment, impressing Cuddy and her peers. Visibly tearing up as she concludes her story, Cuddy pauses for long seconds in her delivery to gather herself, then offers a revision of her advisor's tip: "Fake it until you become it." At the conclusion of her talk a few minutes later, the audience leaps to its feet in applause in the recorded footage.

In *Here's How (Refuted)*, there is no cathartic release for performers or audience. The pathos of Cuddy's final story is replaced with a few lines, again the pronouns punctuated, this time "I" and "she." While the text's scrambling of this story follows the same operation in use throughout the dance performance, it quickly turns. What would have been the conclusion to Cuddy's story and her final plea to the audience to practice power poses becomes instead, as Van Loon speaks, a series of fragmented, halting, mostly two-word lines:

> She comes back.
> So, I want to say.
> So, that's what you want to do. Don't leave.
> So they
> So when
> So again
> So what
> So if
> So I'm
> So you
> So women
> So this
> So business
> So I
> So my
> So we
> So. Give it away.

Motta and then Shinar continue, "So we were/So that's what/So for five/So this really/So this is/So this is/So when I/I want to start. So I said/So I'm taken/So I ended/So that's what/So at the/So I was/So she had/So I want/So this is. No. Don't do that." This final section refuses the logic of the pathos-driven, personal story, refuses to allow the logic of biography and uplift, so key to self-help rhetoric, to persist. Instead, Cuddy's evocation of imposter syndrome and the charge "Fake it until you become it" dissolve into the repetition of the single word "so." The entirely nonsensical directives of the original talk become a series of exhausting aural conjunctions: therefore, therefore, therefore. The remainder of Cuddy's content stripped from these final lines produces a series of a single linking word that has no before and no after. The relational and economic imperative of Cuddy's work and self-help—Do this, so you can achieve this—is left unmoored.

Upon concluding her lines, Shinar walks upstage to her clothing rack, joining Motta and Van Loon, who are already seated at their respective racks. The pounding beats of K. Flay's 2017 song "Giver" begin to play. As the song continues, the three change into spandex, loose gym shorts, tennis shoes, and kneepads. Standing up, they each stretch, loosening hamstrings and calves, swinging arms and dropping into deep lunges. All the while "Giver" keeps playing, and then repeats. Seemingly unconcerned with their pace, the three slowly transition to unison movement, the precise, small hand gestures of the opening section replaced with increasingly intricate and virtuosic movement phrases. The moves, first performed in unison and with great fluidity, are based on the high- and low-power poses Cuddy showed during her presentation.

This initial unison breaks down after one rotation through the movement phrase, and the three continue to repeat the sequence individually. "Giver" plays on a loop. Slowly, the initial precision and energy of each dancer slightly crumbles. The high kicks are not quite so high; the speed of the floor work slows incrementally. The black Marley floor is soon splashed with sweat. Perspiration runs down each dancer's face; Motta's hair, initially pulled back in a tight ponytail, flies around her face and neck. The dancers' gasps and pants are faintly audible beneath the loud song, offering a live syncopated beat to the recording. The section continues, long past the point of exhaustion for all three dancers. Finally, one by one, each woman retreats to the chair positioned by their clothing rack. Sitting slumped, they pull down their sweat-soaked kneepads and gulp water. As the final loop of the song plays, the three sit, panting and staring out at the audience.

Here's How (Refuted) aligns the language and gestures of self-help with exhaustive and durational dance phrases, privileging the embodied choreographies—however banal—that accompany self-help lectures, speeches, and programs. To work on the self, the dance piece argues, is never divorced from working on the body. The dance's second half, though, clarifies its pointed critique of self-help. By choreographing performers' bodies to the point of sweat, gasps, stumbles, and beyond, Shinar uses the (imagined) flexible and virtuosic body of the dancer as an embodied metaphor for the neoliberal compulsion for continual and constant self-improvement upon which the industry thrives.

Figure 8.5 Kara Motta rests at the end of *Here's How (Refuted)*, May 31–June 3, 2018. Red Eye Theater, Minneapolis, Minnesota. Photograph by Aaron Luetzen.

While I have discussed some of the assumptions that support certain understandings of human flourishing as it becomes popularly legible in the self-help industry, theater and performance studies need not, of course, function only as combative cross-disciplinary foils to positive psychology. As Erin Hurley writes in her contribution to this volume, "the arts are a public good in part for their contributions to a people's growth through self-expression." Nevertheless, a key and important contribution theater and performance studies scholarship can offer positive psychology and human flourishing is an attention to unchecked notions of power and authority. In her essay, Kelly Howe writes that Theater of the Oppressed "interrupts . . . hegemonic assumption[s]" and Stephani Etheridge Woodson calls for "an orientation toward justice" in artistic and scholarly practice. It is precisely performances' capacity to interrupt certain hegemonic assumptions that propels my own writing here.

My analysis of Moon's and Shinar's work is not aimed at debunking the self-help industry, which is undoubtedly useful and generative to many. Rather, I argue that their projects reveal the nationalistic, political, financial, and neoliberal structures that undergird the industry, and which it works to obscure through a rhetorical invocation of individual success, well-being, and flourishing. Such critiques of self-help are not new or novel, of course. What Moon and Shinar offer, however—indeed what performance and performative artistic projects offer—is a critique that centers the body, embodiment, and labor. The two challenge the racialized and gendered assumptions that ghost the self-made man, a figure whose ideological grounding in notions of self-sufficiency is an important precursor to contemporary self-help literature. They do this not by foregrounding their particular subjectivities as a means to define the "self" but by refusing, and indeed exhausting, such categories. This centering of the body offers a methodology for revealing how the self-help industry delimits the extent to which bodies and our labor, subjectivity, and marginalization are continually displaced by the specter of the autonomous individual to whom future success is waiting.

Gender studies scholar Brenda Weber writes in *Makeover TV: Selfhood, Citizenship, and Celebrity* that the specific tactics espoused for improving one's self combat shifting notions of identity as a means of "bringing coherence, solidity, and empowerment to the fractured and schizophrenic [nation-]state" (14). In the shows Weber explores (*The Biggest Loser, Queer Eye for the Straight Guy, What Not to Wear*), the self, the body, and the nation are conflated such that the regulatory mechanisms of self-improvement—some psychic or affective shift—become legible *on* and *through* the specific body of a contestant yet gesture toward larger national apparatuses of control. While Moon and Shinar perform a similar self/body slippage in their work, their bodies and selves do *not* emerge more cohesive. Rather, in their performative failures and gestures of refusal, the two challenge cultural narratives imbricated within conceptions of citizenship, labor, and Americanness. Their work proposes porous, exhaustive, and collective forms of the self/body and, in so doing, reveals the regulatory and hegemonic logics that undergird the image of a cohesive and gratifying life deployed in self-help literature.

Their artistic practices make legible the ideological and biopolitical imperatives undergirding the self-help industry precisely through performance. Their materialized and performative translations of self-help literature into and onto their bodies allow both to reveal the ways self-help seeks to regulate individuals' bodies as a means of controlling the social body. Their work illustrates how self-help is thoroughly embedded in the ideological imperatives of neoliberal capitalism, liberal democracy, and nationalism. It is imperative to dwell alongside artistic propositions like those of Moon and Shinar, which encourage an examination of these tensions through what I have termed a refusal. Such refusals profoundly engage the body—incarcerated, porous, desirous, sweaty, gasping, and panting—in service of disrupting a body politic. Their refusals are performed gestures at once radical and revolutionary.

Works Cited

Alfaro, Ange-Marie Hancock. "Black Masculinity Achieves Nothing without Restorative Care: An Intersectional Rearticulation of Frederick Douglass." *A Political Companion to Frederick Douglass*, edited by Neil Roberts. Lexington, University Press of Kentucky, 2018, pp. 236–51.

Aristotle. *Nicomachean Ethics*. Translated by Christopher Rowe. Oxford, Oxford University Press, 2002.

Bailey, Beth, and David Farber, eds. *America in the 1970s*. Lawrence, University Press of Kansas, 2004.

Ballegaard, Caroline. "DISmiss | Jennifer Moon." *Dis Magazine*, January 14, 2016. dismagazine.com/blog/79890/dismiss-jennifer-moon/. Accessed January 16, 2020.

Benjamin, Walter. *Illuminations*. Translated by Hannah Arendt. New York, Schocken Books, 1968.

Blomsterberg, Michael. *It Begins with Me: Navigating Your Journey to Personal Freedom*. Los Angeles, MLR, 2015.

Coué, Émile. *Self Mastery through Conscious Autosuggestion*. American Library Service, 1922.

Cuddy, Amy. "Your Body Language May Shape Who You Are." TEDGlobal, June 2012. ted.com/talks/amy_cuddy_your_body_language_shapes_who_you_are/transcript?language=en. Accessed April 14, 2019.

Decker, Jeffrey. *Made in America: Self-Styled Success from Horatio Alger to Oprah Winfrey*. Minneapolis, University of Minnesota Press, 1997.

Douglass, Frederick. "Self-Made Men." *Great Speeches by Frederick Douglass*, edited by James Daley. Dover, 2013, pp. 102–22.

Holte, Michael Ned. "Microclimates." *Made in L.A. 2014 Reader*, edited by Connie Butler and Michael Ned Holte. Munich, DelMonico Books, 2014, pp. 4–15.

Kwon, Miwon. *One Place after Another: Site Specific Art and Locational Identity*. Cambridge, MA, MIT Press, 2004.

Leckie, Barbara. "Sequence and Fragment, History and Thesis: Samuel Smiles's Self-Help, Social Change, and Climate Change." *Nineteenth-Century Contexts*, vol. 38 no. 5, 2016, pp. 305–17.

Lee, Josephine. *Japan of Pure Invention: Gilbert and Sullivan's* The Mikado. Minneapolis, University of Minnesota Press, 2010.

Lukás, George. *History and Class Consciousness: Studies in Marxist Dialectics*. Cambridge, MA, MIT Press, 1971.

Marx, Karl. *The Poverty of Philosophy*. Moscow, Foreign Languages Publishing House, n.d.

McGee, Micki. *Self-Help, Inc.: Makeover Culture in American Life*. Oxford University Press, 2005.

Moon, Jennifer. "Assignment #1." *Made in L.A. 2014 Reader*, edited by Connie Butler and Michael Ned Holte. Munich, Delmonico Books, 2014, pp. 24–25.

Moon, Jennifer. *Definition of Abundance: Principle 1 of The Revolution*. 3rd edition. Los Angeles, Hammer Museum, 2014.

Morgan, Jo-Ann. "Huey P. Newton Enthroned—Iconic Image of Black Power." *The Journal of American Culture,* vol. 37 no. 2, 2014, pp. 129–48.

Morris, David. "'Power Poses' Researcher Dana Carney Now Says Effects Are 'Undeniably' False." *Fortune,* October 2, 2016. fortune.com/2016/10/02/power-poses-research-false/. Accessed April 12, 2019.

Moses, Wilson J. "Where Honor Is Due: Frederick Douglass as Representative Black Man." *Prospects,* vol. 17, 1992, pp. 177–89.

Schueller, Stephen M. "Understanding Our Best: Eudaimonia's Growing Influence in Psychology." *Quality of Life Research: An International Journal of Quality of Life Aspects of Treatment, Care & Rehabilitation*, vol. 22, 2013, pp. 2661–62.

Sinclair, Marshall. "Why the Self-Help Industry Is Dominating the U.S." *Medium,* February 24, 2019. medium.com/s/story/no-please-help-yourself-981058f3b7cf. Accessed March 15, 2019.

Smiles, Samuel. *Self-Help*. New York, Forgotten Books, 2012.

Waterman, Alan S., ed. *The Best within Us: Positive Psychology Perspectives on Eudaimonia*. American Psychological Association, 2013.

Weber, Brenda. *Makeover TV: Selfhood, Citizenship, and Celebrity*. Durham, NC, Duke University Press, 2009.

9

On Laughter and the Bonds of Community

Harvey Young

When you walk into a coffee shop or even an elevator, it is immediately evident that technology has managed to render people less present and decreasingly attentive to those who surround them. Glowing smartphones attract the eye and hold it captive. Although technology can virtually collapse geographic distance and ease communication with folks on the other side of the globe, it also can make it possible to neither engage nor notice the people who stand nearby or sit within an arm's reach. The distance that can exist between physically proximate individuals in everyday scenarios makes those occasions at which attendees are urged to temporarily separate themselves from their pocket devices and consciously share space with others—in the theater, the classical music recital hall, and even the cinema—more special.

The community-galvanizing potential of the arts, especially live performing arts, is well documented. For millennia, theater has brought people together. Although societal divisions could persist as a result of restricted seating areas set by decree or custom, live performance facilitated the witnessing and co-participation in the sharing of an experience. Attendees assembled to partake in the telling of a story and, in so doing, to have the spectrum of their own emotions triggered by the narrative presented. Part of the concern or alleged danger of theater rested in its engaging quality and potential capacity to spur groupthink, a collective politics, which might not be aligned with the extant political structure or desired social mores. Live community entertainments, as Plato observed, can "satisfy and delight" but also can unsettle the existing order (*Republic* 606a).

This chapter centers on one signal of satisfaction and delight of live performance: laughter. While laughter can be prompted by nervousness or anxiety, the emphasis here is on joyful laughter or laughs that make you feel good. There are extant studies that seek to quantify the health benefits of laughter. For example, Dexter Louie, Karolina Brook, and Elizabeth Frates offer an overview of the benefits of spontaneous or "genuine" laughter—noting that

Harvey Young, *On Laughter and the Bonds of Community* In: *Theater and Human Flourishing*. Edited by: Harvey Young, Oxford University Press. © Oxford University Press 2023. DOI: 10.1093/oso/9780197622261.003.0010 laughter has been shown to reduce stress, decrease anxiety, and increase pain tolerance—before proposing that physicians might consider giving their patients "laughter prescriptions." Addressing potential skeptics, they write, "While more research must be done, it is also important to acknowledge there is not much to lose in laughing. With no downsides, side-effects, or risks, perhaps it is time to consider laughter seriously" (267). The aim here is not to echo others on the positive attributes of laughter but rather to explore its complexity, including moments in which a good laugh was deemed bad (or inappropriate) for the theater.

Moved by the Spirit

Playwright Dominique Morisseau, a former John D. and Catherine T. MacArthur "Genius" fellow, is one of the most produced playwrights in our contemporary era. According to *American Theatre*, she was the third most produced American playwright at U.S. regional theaters in the 2018–19 season and the fifth most produced playwright in the 2019–20 season (Tran, "Top Ten" [2018]; Tran, "Top Ten" [2019]). Her first play was produced on Broadway in 2022. Only Lucas Hnath and Lauren Gunderson among playwrights both living and dead (excluding William Shakespeare) had more productions. Morisseau's "Detroit Cycle," consisting of the plays *Paradise Blue*, *Detroit '67*, and *Skeleton Crew*, is the most compelling theatrical treatment of the industrial rise and postindustrial decline of the "Motor City." Like August Wilson before her, Morisseau tells the history of a particular Black cultural community in a manner that resonates with similar experiences across the nation. Although the spotlight shifts from (Wilson's) Pittsburgh to (Morisseau's) Great Lakes Midwest, the emphasis on Black experiences remains. Reflecting on the effect of Wilson's plays on residents of his native Hill District, Morisseau said, in a 2015 *New York Times* profile, "They have to feel so documented, so like they matter" (Soloski). She added, "They have to feel so important. And I wanted to do that for Detroit."

Beyond opening the stage to stories about the land of Motown, Morisseau has led a campaign to diversify the makeup or composition of her theater audiences and also the manner in which they respond to her produced writings. She often encourages the theaters that produce her plays to tuck a leaflet, a directive from her to their patrons, in the program. The insert titled "Playwright's Rules of Engagement" reads:

You are allowed to laugh audibly.

You are allowed to have audible moments of reaction and response.

My work requires a few "um hmmms" and "uhn uhnnns" should you need to use them. Just maybe in moderation. Only when you really need to vocalize.

This can be church for some of us, and testifying is allowed.

This is also live theater and the actors need you to engage with them, not distract them or thwart their performance.

Please be an audience member that joins with others and allows a bit of breathing room. Exhale together. Laugh together. Say "amen" should you need to.

This is a community. Let's go.

These "rules" serve as prompts for engagement. They exist not necessarily because audiences need a reminder to respond audibly but because they have been conditioned to sit quietly and passively. Seeking to expand the possibilities of meaningful audience participation, Morisseau aims to inspire a greater level of activity among those who attend performances of her plays. She calls upon spectators to assert their presence and voice their reactions. She wants them to know that it is okay to laugh.

An African American playwright, Morisseau shared her belief that theaters need to grant their audiences permission to express their honest reactions in an *American Theatre* article titled "Why I Almost Slapped a Fellow Theatre Patron, and What That Says about Our Theatres." In that essay, she recounts experiences in the theater in which "white privilege" sought to police and silence her. Recalling an incident at an off-Broadway theater and the interventions of an older white patron whom Morisseau calls "Jane," she writes, "In the middle of the play's opening, as my friend and I laughed and enjoyed ourselves, Jane leaned in toward me and whispered, 'Can you stop and keep it down?'" Morisseau replied, "I will laugh whenever I think things are funny, so get used to it. You're not going to tell me how I should respond to art." The playwright tells her reader, "Jane tried to chastise me further, but I simply put my hand up and said, 'No more.'" This incident reminds her of others in the theater: "That time at a prestigious theatre festival when black women were responding exactly how I want them to respond to my play—loudly and expressively and 'ummm hmm'-ing—and an older white patron approached them at intermission and said: 'Can you enjoy the play a little quieter, please?'" In calling out white privilege and the harassment of Black audience members, Morisseau notes that such policing behavior runs contrary to efforts to diversify theater audiences. "It further marginalizes audiences of color and tells them they are not fully welcome in the theatre, except by permission of the white audience." As a corrective, she insists, "We need to say that, just like in church, you are welcome to come as you are in the theatre. Hoot and holler or sit quietly in reverence. Worship and engage however you do."

Morisseau is not alone in calling out the efforts to control the reactions of audiences, especially nonwhite attendees. Shortly after the publication of her article, people inspired by her story and her request that they share their experiences on social media began to post their own encounters (and label them with the hashtag #ppit, privilege problems in theater). Diep Tran, a former senior editor at *American Theatre* who may be most recognized for her annual lists of the most produced plays by regional theaters or her popular podcast *Three on the Aisle*, observed, "Reading the #ppit feed. Some eye-opening stories about theater elitism? Is it racism? Ageism? Whatever it is, it's harmful." Along these lines, actor, playwright, and *Hamilton* creator Lin-Manuel Miranda revealed the ongoing persistence of overly zealous spectators who attempt to curb the behavior of fellow attendees. Recalling an exchange during the intermission of a 2018 production of *My Fair Lady* with a person he identifies as "Condescending Theatergoer," Miranda re-creates their conversation in play structure.

CONDESCENDING THEATERGOER: Well, I didn't know this show had so many laughs—you were certainly enjoying yourself. (*Passive-aggressive shaming me for laughing—at the jokes*)
ME: Yup! It's a great show!

The conversation eventually ends after "CT," recognizing the Emmy-, Grammy-, and Tony Award–winner, apologizes "for just being an ass." Miranda concludes, "The lesson here, if there is any: there is ALWAYS the type of Theatergoer that defines themselves by excluding others. You could WRITE musicals, and they'll still try to make you feel like you don't belong. Don't you dare let 'em. You love theater? You belong. Welcome." More recently, theater critic Lily Janiak, referring to efforts to police sincere audience responses, observed, "American theater has a chronic inflammatory condition that gets triggered by perceived faux pas in audience etiquette." She concludes, "We want people to come to shows. We don't want to scare them away with infighting about rarefied norms. We should focus on welcoming new audiences, not controlling them."

Within live performance venues, there is an often-expressed set of behavioral expectations intended to show respect to the artists and allow attendees an equal opportunity to engage the work. Morisseau's "rules" include a cautionary note: "[A]ctors need you to engage with them, not distract them or thwart their performance." The conditions can be quite strict, such as when pianist Alfred Brendel warned his audience, "Either you stop coughing or I stop playing" (Clark). Venues regularly reveal their own expectations for audience engagement, recommended (and often required) etiquette for participating as a spectator in the theater. Some of these conditions are commonsensical. Silence your cell phone. Refrain from eating crunchy food (or eating any food). Unwrap candies before the show starts. Others appear obvious but require interpretation to determine whether they have been transgressed. For example, one prominent seller of Broadway theater tickets cautions:

> Your enthusiasm for the show is wonderful, but should be tempered out of consideration for both the audience and the performers. Nobody needs to hear people shrieking, whooping, screaming, and hollering after every song. It is a Broadway show, not a rock concert, not an arena or a sports stadium. If you are so moved to react to the show, then a gentle clap after the song is appropriate, but whooping is not. Save your whooping for the final curtain call, where you can whoop as much as you would like. Woop, woop! (NY Tix).

The same source encourages audiences not to sing along: "Your fellow Broadway fans paid the big bucks to hear the professionals flex their vocal muscles, not you. Save your sweet singing for post-show karaoke." Is singing along when moved by the moment inappropriate? David Lister, writing for the *The Independent*, offers, "There are breaches of etiquette that one simply can't foresee and scarcely knows how to react to." Remembering a production of *Jerusalem* in which a young actress sang the title song, Lister writes, "When I saw the production, an elderly gent in the audience was involuntarily singing along, visibly startling the actress. Perhaps it was a reflex action by the elderly gent, his subconscious transported back over the decades to school assemblies." Did the old man violate theater etiquette? More generally, should we prohibit an honest reaction emerging from a felt need to engage or respond through laughter or song?

As jarring as active audience participation can be, passive spectatorship can be equally challenging for critics. Angela Helm, a contributing editor at *The Root*, shares her dismay at the initial behavior of the Broadway audience at *Tina: The Tina Turner Musical*:

> It's always amazed me that some people can watch a concert or musical with no visible emotional response. I always say that it's cultural—that in the African (American, Caribbean, Latinx, etc.) tradition we "talk back," "chat back," "shout back," "sing back"—and though I know different communities have different cultural norms, it is nonetheless jarring to see how *some* white people (especially the older, out-of-town Broadway folk) can hear music, sweet music—pop music even—and remain transfixed in their seats as if weighted by a centrifugal force. Nan a head nod, toe-tap, or handclap.

Frustrated by the "folks who sat like zombies in their seats," Helm praises the production and its ability to activate even the most passive observer: "[B]y the musical's end, everybody was up on their feet for a rousing concert performance." Embedded in both Helm's and Morisseau's observations on the experience of live theater is a racial critique, an assertion of racially inflected cultural differences that complicate efforts for an inclusive theater experience. This racialized difference blurs with and overlays expectations of theater audiences. An exploration of the racial politics of Broadway and the West End (and major regional theater) is deserving of a separate study.

There is not a uniform way to experience a live performance. Spectators who sit side by side and watch the same production can have—and always have had—different reactions to what they have witnessed. Although Vsevolod Meyerhold and his assistant director Vasily Fyodorov observed that audiences react in a similar manner, which allows for their response (a laugh or a gasp) to be tracked and, across productions, predictably anticipated, there are always outliers—for example, the man singing *Jerusalem* or the laughter of Morisseau—that remind us that an audience is comprised of freethinking individuals with the agency to respond and react in a host of ways (cited in Posner 89). Although an audience, a group of attendees, may share a common experience, their perspectives can vary. Is it reasonable to expect that individuals will (or can) suppress their honest, felt, embodied reactions to a performance? Is catharsis, an expressive emotional release, acceptable only when it is a collective (and not an individual) act?

Laughter Flourishes

Laughter is pleasurable. Robert Provine in his study on this physiological and psychological act notes, "Think of the last time you sat in an audience, laughing and letting waves of laughter wash over you. A pleasant experience—one of life's best" (6). To laugh is to experience humanity. "Although we cannot know for sure that other animals do not laugh like us," Mordechai Gordon observes in *Humor, Laughter and Human Flourishing*, "it is a pretty safe bet to say that humans are the only beings that are *aware* of themselves laughing, much like they are the only ones who know that they suffer" (93). Despite the fact that several scientific studies have concluded that other species possess the capacity to consciously laugh (and contemplate suffering), Gordon's celebration of our collective sense of self through a giggle, chuckle, or guffaw is commendable (Langley). Nevertheless, the experiences of Morisseau and Miranda remind us that laughter can simultaneously bring joy and offend.

It is not surprising that Plato, who was highly critical of theater and performance, would be similarly dismissive of the operations of humor, comedy, and, indeed, laughter within an imagined society governed by reason. For the ancient philosopher, laughter possessed the power to destabilize the existing social order, and therefore the objects of (and prompts for) laughter required restrictions: "[S]uch representations [should] be left to slaves or hired aliens" (*Laws* 816e). In *Laws*, Plato insists that comedy "receive no serious consideration whatsoever." He adds, "No composer of comedy, iambic or lyric verse shall be permitted to hold any citizen up to laughter, by word or gesture, with passion or otherwise." Laughter, which certainly was assumed to be irreverent, was neither to be condoned nor embraced. Aristotle was comparatively more sympathetic toward the role that performance could play within society. However, he continued to align humor with base behavior. He says that "a jest is a form of abuse" (*Ethics*) and contends that comedy "makes men . . . worse than they are" (*Poetics*). In short, an environment filled with laughter immerses one in corruption. Such spaces are to be avoided.

Of course, humor persisted despite the skepticism of a host of philosophers, especially Hobbes, who consistently identified the negative elements of comedy and laughter. Its dismissal was attributed to its tendency to negatively target people. Laughter can be directed at a person; it can be an expression of mocking that belittles. Certainly, this perspective accounts for the warnings that comedy could be destabilizing (subverting the authority of established individuals by making them objects of ridicule) or produce pleasure through its engagements with populations lacking in social capital: slaves and foreigners. From a contemporary perspective, it is not difficult to appreciate the anxiety that comedy can bring. For decades, late-night talk show hosts have used their monologues to find humor—to generate laughs—at the expense of established figures. The laughter inspired by satirical jokes has helped to make individuals, such as national leaders, who would have been the subjects of myth-making in an earlier historical period appear undeniably human and, perhaps, ordinary.

The effort to curb social laughter anchored itself in a desire to preserve an existing hierarchical structure and prevent its toppling through allegedly mean-spirited public discourse. However, this classical perspective overlooks its community-forming potential and power. In *The Morality of Laughter*, F. H. Buckley writes:

> Superiority theories are incomplete, for they do not account for the sociable side of laughter. If relations of dominance were all there was to it, then why are jokes so often associated with feelings of solidarity and community? The answer is that laughter means something very different for the listener who laughs along with the joke than it does for the butt. (5)

We laugh not at a person but rather *with* other members of our society. Buckley adds, "By laughing the listener accepts a tie of solidarity—a *lien derire*—with the wit" (5). Laughter, as psychologist Giovannantonio Forabosco (among numerous others) has observed, is a "social phenomenon" (cited in Sabato). It can foment a bond among audience members as well as positively enhance the experience of theater-going, providing assistance and potentially propelling a comedic narrative. Each honest laugh is an audible expression of appreciation for the mind of a master dramatist and the skill of a performer. Indeed, there is a sense of belonging, of being united as part of a shared perspective on the world, that emerges with those chuckles. Beyond merely bridging spectator, creator (or playwright), and actor, these expressions of enjoyment also signal communitas and people's comfort in sharing their sense of delight with others. More commonly, the laugh is not a solitary voice of protest but a collective expression that reinforces a sense of being together and present for one another.

The ability of laughter to serve as a structuring element of community is readily apparent. It is common knowledge that the pleasures of spectatorship are bolstered when a performance is witnessed alongside others who are either physically or virtually present. As psychologist Bill Kelley observed in a 2011 interview, "We're much more likely to laugh at something funny in the presence of other people" (Nierenberg). Sophie Scott, a neuroscientist, remarks:

> We can catch laughter in a contagious way—laughing just because others are laughing—and we are much more likely to catch a laugh from someone we know than someone we don't. And research has even shown that in romantic relationships, couples who deal with stressful situations with positive emotions like laughter get over the stress, but are also happier in their relationships and stay together for longer.

Scott reveals the biological operation behind the joy generated from being with others:

> We usually encounter positive emotions, such as laughter or cheering, in group situations, whether watching a comedy program with family or a football game with friends. . . . This response in the brain, automatically priming us to smile or laugh, provides a way of mirroring the behavior of others, something which helps us interact socially. It could play an important role in building strong bonds between individuals in a group. (quoted in Schlossberg)

It is the group dynamic and the amplification of emotional response within such settings that often accounts for the uniqueness of live performance within a contemporary moment in which most forms of entertainment (including theater) are recorded and mediated. Indeed, it is the sense of copresence that theater allows that has enabled investigators to conclude that attendance increases a person's ability "to recognize and appreciate what other people think and feel" (Greene et al.; "Major Benefits"). This is one of the expressed benefits of attending live performance and sitting with fellow audience members who are reacting in real time. Provine is correct when he observes, "Laughter can serve as a bond to bring people together or as a weapon to humiliate and ostracize its victims" (2).

The Gift of Togetherness

For every study on the positive effects of theater-going, such as its ability to cultivate empathy and encourage the recognition of emotion, there seem to be anecdotal accounts, such as those shared by Morisseau, that draw attention to less celebratory aspects of group viewing. The challenge in considering the value of theater, which can manage to delight and offend spectators in equal measure, is to acknowledge the particular experiences of the people who form the collective, the audience. Furthermore, it is important to recognize the interconnectedness of responses. Whereas a moment in a production may spur delight in individual spectators and prompt laughter, those voiced expressions of pleasure can either prove infectious, encouraging more robust laughs in an audience, or trigger discontent (or even anger) in another person.

In considering laughter, Buckley warns that "[e]mpirical tests have no place" because "claims can neither be proven nor disproven." He writes, "Though 90 percent of the subjects of a psychological study might laugh, I may still say, 'That's not funny!'" (6). When the object of study expands from an incident of laughter at a particular joke to an evening of theater, which is replete with innumerable scenarios to which an audience may respond in a variety of ways, such spaces and responses can be and have been analyzed. In recent years, researchers have explored audiences and the similarity of their reactions by measuring levels of carbon dioxide in the air to account for shared bodily reactions across entertainment genres (e.g., comedy or thriller) and by evaluating empathetic engagement when presented with stories across a variety of media (e.g., stage, novel, or cinematic screen) (Williams et al.). Even within the diversity of audiences, there is commonality.

In contrast to Buckley, a cadre of positive psychologists have embraced the possibility of empirical studies within the arts related to human flourishing and well-being. "Despite the powerful rhetoric on both sides of this debate," Louis Tay, James O. Pawelski, and Melissa G. Keith write that surprisingly little scientific work has been done to investigate empirically whether or not the arts and humanities have a significant impact on individual and collective well-being, particularly beyond merely economic outcomes. They "propose four mechanisms through which the modes of engagement and the activities of involvement with the arts and humanities may lead to positive effects: immersion, embeddedness, socialisation, and reflectiveness" (217). More recently, Stuti Thapa and colleagues have proposed a revision to the former conceptual model: replacing "embeddedness" with "acquisition" and adding "expressiveness" as a fifth mechanism. Although all are worthy of extended engagement, socialization most aligns with the exploration into communitas that animates this chapter.

It is through the arts that children are socialized. Initially, it begins with "stories, songs, movies, and art." Tay, Pawelski, and Keith contend:

> As [youth] advance through their years of schooling, they are introduced more formally to literature, music, history, the visual and performing arts, philosophy, and other similar cultural pursuits. Adults continue to partici-pate in the arts and humanities, appreciating them for their intrinsic value and the personal enrichment they bring, as well as for the social bonds they create among members of a community. (215)

As I have written elsewhere, such engagements, which can be "explicit" or "implicit or environmental," can inspire an awareness and appreciation of the operation of race, as an assumed identity with a relatable subjectivity, within a community (Young). It is an engagement with arts and culture that makes apparent the operations of society and sutures the individual within it. It can introduce new perspectives and, as Tay, Pawelski, and Keith assert, "can bring about more cultural sensitivity in individuals" (218).

As an element of socialization, present and prospective attendees learn how to be actively participating audience members in addition to (arguably) passively receiving the story told by the performer. It is common practice for family or "all ages" theaters to offer instruction on how to behave in the theater and, at the same time, to outline and therefore frame expectations of audience members. The website of the Kennedy Center in Washington, D.C., offers "Advice for First Time Theater Goers." In addition to making available pre-performance research, such as "study guides and other educational ma-terial," the theater is prescriptive in terms of what to do and, equally impor-tant, what not to do during a performance:

> **Don't snore!** Or talk, text, eat, or drink. In short, model good theater be-havior. Remind your kids that if they can hear the actors, the actors can hear them.
>
> **Do clap!** Loudly (but in the right places). For musicals, it's fine to clap after songs. For dramas, though, reserve clapping for intermission breaks and the final curtain.

In effect, the lesson is to attend to others. Appreciate the gift of being together and be mindful of how our presence can impact others. To attend a performance is to be immersed in community and continually engaged in a multi-directional flow of influences.

Audience members who are seated near each other, such as Miranda and the Condescending Theatergoer, can have an outsize influence on each other's enjoyment. A single laugh can be amplified and passed on (*pace* Sophie Scott), heightening a person's sense of engagement and connection with a staged moment. A single laugh also can seem amplified as the result of being an outlier and can lessen another's sense of absorption within a dramatic narrative. To attend the theater is to be a coparticipant in the performance. The attendee is a key part of the *live* experience—for both good and bad. In fact, a "warm audience," a pleasantly and actively engaged group of spectators, is cultivated in most scenarios. "Cold audiences," disinterested, emotionless, quiet attendees, are dreaded by performers. In television and film, great efforts are undertaken to avoid (or convert) having a cold live audience. My lasting memories of attending tapings of television game and talk shows center on the audience warm-up, being taught not only how to cheer and laugh but also how long to cheer and laugh when prompted by the audience wrangler. Although sometimes coerced, mandated crowd participation—akin to joining "the wave" in a sports arena—elevates the experience and makes it collectively enjoyable. That said, I always was aware that desired behavior was actively modeled and, in fact, required. There were moments when we were tasked with applauding or laughing longer and, perhaps, more enthusiastically than felt natural. I also understood that an ill-timed vocalization, a laugh or cheer at the wrong moment, would not be appreciated by producers. It is here that the discipline of theater separates itself from the televisual and cinematic arts involving live audiences. Theater does not prescribe audience response in the same manner as these other media, which literally teach the live audience how to respond.

It is also on this point that disciplinary differences between theater and psychology emerge. In "Psychology of Laughter," Willibald Ruch writes that "psychology is not only interested in describing, explaining and predicting behavior but also controlling it" (69). It is possible to teach a person how to laugh spontaneously and naturally but also deliberately in a manner consistent with preferred virtues. In a 2016 interview, Ruch offered, "We can conclude that while laughing and entertaining others with humor is beneficial for our mood, it is the humor which is built on virtues and character strengths that strengthens interpersonal relationships and it contributes the most to our wellbeing." At first glance, the effort to "control" laughter may seem extreme. However, it occurs frequently. It is not uncommon for parents to instruct their kids not to laugh when witnessing something unfortunate happening to another person, such as seeing a pedestrian trip and fall on the sidewalk. *Stop laughing. Be nice.* To place limits on laughter can be an expression of empathy or a sign of respect for another. To not laugh can be a step taken toward one's own flourishing as well as a show of support for another's well-being.

This perspective resonates with the intent of Morisseau's "rules." She invites her audiences to consider when the voicing of their honest reactions can be helpful to the experience of theater-going and the desire of the actors for an engaged audience. She also hints that those expressions should be scalable, perhaps muted or even held back if you deem that their articulation could "distract [actors] or thwart their performance." These suggestions metaphorically put rails on laughter to limit its potential to undermine the experience of performance and—more likely than not—to improve it. Morisseau offers guidance to her audiences because she wants them to laugh and, hopefully, to laugh freely and honestly. She actually encourages spectators to be less controlled and less inhibited. Although playwrights, directors, and their production teams certainly script moments that they hope will generate predictable laughs, the laugh itself is rarely coerced. In the theater (unlike in television), a live audience is the unknown variable which makes the theatrical experience feel unique.

Increasingly, professional theater companies are attempting to be less restrictive, especially as they aim to attract younger or more diverse audiences. Rather than leaving the work of inclusion to playwrights such as Morisseau who insist upon a warm welcome for attendees, select theaters make a concerted effort to offer a wide embrace. The Guthrie Theatre, a Tony Award–winning regional theater in Minneapolis, signals its commitment to inclusion on its website. In their "First Timer's Guide," the following answer appears in response to the question *What should I wear?*: "Come as you are and be yourself—there is no dress code at the Guthrie." The theater further advises:

> Laugh. Be moved. Read the program from cover to cover. Cheer and give a standing ovation if you feel so inclined. Chat with the folks around you. Theater is a beautiful, meaningful way to bring people together. It's why we do what we do at the Guthrie, and we can't wait for you to join us.

What the Guthrie's management and Morisseau seek are opportunities for audience members to be themselves in the theater. A person who sincerely, genuinely finds an exchange of dialogue funny should have the freedom to laugh without being reprimanded by a fellow attendee or the theater establishment itself. A hard-working person who simply wants to see a show should not feel othered by an expectation to wear expensive (or uncomfortable) formal wear.

At its best, theater helps to forge bonds of community. There are numerous examples throughout this book, from the sense of connection created by the lip sync exercise in Lisa Biggs's class at Michigan State, to the uplift in the community theater introduced by Stacy Wolf and the formation of a safe, shared space in which deeply personal stories can be relayed, as occurs in the civilian-military activities at the heart of Laura Lodewyck's analysis of *Telling* performances. Theater encourages people to gather to share in the hearing and, indeed, the audiencing of a story. It invites attendees to participate in its presentation as actively engaged witnesses. The resulting communitas is what gives the art form its majesty: a profound feeling of interpersonal connection with others in the same place and in real time together. Laughter is a key part of this communal feeling. The function of laughter within such settings helps us appreciate the potential and challenges for human flourishing. We understand that a laugh often feels good. Its cathartic release offers a window into our emotions and feelings. Many people have felt the thrill of laughing with others after hearing a joke and, in that moment, developed a profound sense of belonging. Some have experienced being the lone laugher and the awkward silence (and side glances) of others, becoming aware of oneself as being apart and oddly alone in the company of others. The reactions of fellow attendees in these moments of honest expression best reveal the inclusiveness (or lack thereof) of a community. Those seconds after a laugh grant a glimpse at the potential and possibility for flourishing.

In conclusion, it is helpful to consider how best to participate in theater in order to realize and appreciate the benefits of laughter. I offer the following neither as rules nor as guidelines but simply as suggestions to maximize flourishing possibilities.

First, it is useful to remember that the magic of theater is anchored in its live nature. Something might happen today that did not occur yesterday and probably will not take place tomorrow. It is conceivable that an understudy might perform tonight. It is possible that the sound of heavy rainfall thumping on the roof could serve as a bonus sound effect throughout the event. It just might happen that someone will laugh loudly or chuckle audibly at a moment that strikes you as being inappropriate. Imagine these and numerous other possible occurrences as a component of the unique experience that you are witnessing. Each time something seemingly disruptive occurs, try to recall that that disruption is what separates theater from more controlled entertainment forms.

Second, embrace the fact that people enjoy and find delight in different aspects of the same theatrical experience. Ruch writes, "Everyday observation tells that there are enduring interindividual differences in humor behavior and experience. Some people tend habitually to appreciate, initiate, or laugh at humor more often, or more intensively, than others do" (35). Rather than labeling another person's response (when it differs from your own) as wrong, accept that it probably is right for them. Be generous about those differences.

Third, allow yourself to ride the wave of laughter alongside others. Laughter is infectious. Try to imagine how the other person might be experiencing the same performance in an attempt to gain access to a similar flow of joy.

Finally, as Morisseau advised, "Be an audience member that joins with others and allows a bit of breathing room. Exhale together."

Works Cited

Aristotle. *Nicomachean Ethics*. Translated by W. D. Ross. Classics Archive, n.d. http://classics.mit.edu/Aristotle/nicomachaen.html.

Aristotle. *Poetics*. Translated by S. H. Butcher. Classics Archive, n.d. http://classics.mit.edu/Aristotle/poetics.html.

Buckley, F. H. *The Morality of Laughter*. Ann Arbor, University of Michigan Press, 2003.

Clark, Nick. "Cacophony of Sound?" *The Independent*, January 29, 2013. https://www.independent.co.uk/arts-entertainment/classical/news/cacophony-of-sound-people-cough-on-purpose-during-classical-concerts-research-finds-8471735.html.

Gordon, Mordechai. *Human, Laughter and Human Flourishing*. New York, Springer, 2014.

Greene, Jay P., Collin Hitt, Anne Kraybill, and Cari A. Bogulski. "Learning from Live Theater." *Education Next*, Winter 2015. https://www.educationnext.org/learning-live-theater/.

Guthrie Theatre. "First Timer's Guide." n.d. https://www.guthrietheater.org/plan-your-visit/first-timers-guide/.

Helm, Angela. "*Tina: The Tina Turner Musical* Will Surprise You with Its Depth and Move You with Its Songs." *The Root*, November 26, 2019. https://www.theroot.com/tina-the-tina-turner-musical-will-surprise-you-with-it-1840046546.

Janiak, Lily. "The Dog Whistle of Phones in Theater, or Why Audience Behavior Is Always the Wrong Conversation." *San Francisco Chronicle*, October 1, 2019. https://datebook.

sfchronicle.com/theater/the-dog-whistle-of-phones-in-theater-or-why-audience-behavior-is-always-the-wrong-conversation.

Kennedy Center. "Advice for First Time Theater Goers." https://www.kennedy-center.org/education/resources-for-educators/classroom-resources/articles-and-how-tos/articles/collections/syya/advice-for-first-time-theater-goers/.

Langley, Liz. "Do Animals Laugh?" *National Geographic*, June 13, 2015. https://www.nationalgeographic.com/animals/article/150613-animals-laughter-apes-evolution-science.

Lister, David. "Audience Etiquette: The Dos and Don'ts of Theatre, Concert and Cinema Viewing." *The Independent*, May 17, 2018. https://www.independent.co.uk/arts-entertainment/theatre-dance/features/audience-etiquette-theatre-concerts-cinema-english-national-opera-coliseum-a8353901.html.

Louie, Dexter, Karolina Brook, and Elizabeth Frates. "The Laughter Prescription: A Tool for Lifestyle Medicine." *American Journal of Lifestyle Medicine*, vol. 10, no. 4, 2016, pp. 262–67.

"Major Benefits for Students Who Attend Live Theater, Study Finds." *Science Daily*, October 16, 2014. https://www.sciencedaily.com/releases/2014/10/141016165953.htm.

Miranda, Lin-Manuel. "Condescending Theatergoer." Twitter, July 9, 2018. https://twitter.com/lin_manuel/status/1016334178785398784?lang=en.

Morisseau, Dominique. "Playwright's Rules of Engagement." Actors Theatre of Louisville, n.d. https://actorstheatre.org/2017/11/13/playwrights-rules-engagement/.

Morisseau, Dominique. "Why I Almost Slapped a Fellow Theatre Patron, and What That Says about Our Theatres." *American Theatre*, December 9, 2015. https://www.americantheatre.org/2015/12/09/why-i-almost-slapped-a-fellow-theatre-patron-and-what-that-says-about-our-theatres/.

Nierenberg, Cari. "We May Hate Laugh Tracks—but They Work, Studies Show." NBC News, September 23, 2011. https://www.nbcnews.com/healthmain/we-may-hate-laugh-tracks-they-work-studies-show-1C6436923.

NY Tix. "Broadway Show Theatre Etiquette." September 10, 2018. https://www.nytix.com/articles/broadway-show-theatre-etiquette.

Ohlin, Birgit. "The Psychology of Humor: Interviewing Professor Dr. Willibald Ruch." Birgit Ohlin Coaching & Development, December 6, 2016. https://www.birgitohlin.com/single-post/2016-12-06-the-psychology-of-humor-interviewing-prof-dr-willibald-ruch.

Plato. *Laws*. Translated by Benjamin Jowett. Classics Archive, n.d. http://classics.mit.edu/Plato/laws.html.

Plato. *Republic*. Translated by Benjamin Jowett. Classics Archive, n.d. http://classics.mit.edu/Plato/republic.html.

Posner, Dassia. *The Director's Prism*. Evanston, IL, Northwestern University Press, 2006.

Provine, Robert. *Laughter: A Scientific Investigation*. New York, Penguin, 2001.

Ruch, Willibald. "Psychology of Humor." *The Primer of Humor Research*, edited by V. Raskin. Berlin, Mouton de Gruyter, 2008, pp. 17–100.

Sabato, Giovanni. "What's So Funny? The Science of Why We Laugh." *Scientific American*, June 26, 2019.

Schlossberg, Mallory. "Seth Rogen Is Right: Here's Why Comedy Is Funnier in Movie Theaters." *Business Insider*, January 9, 2015. https://www.businessinsider.com/watch-comedies-in-movie-theaters-2015-1.

Scott, Sophie. "Laughter Is a Completely Social Phenomenon." *Science Focus,* BBC, January 17, 2020. https://www.sciencefocus.com/the-human-body/laughter-is-a-completely-social-phenomenon-we-are-30-times-more-likely-to-laugh-if-there-is-someone-else-with-us/.

Soloski, Alexis. "Playwright Dominique Morisseau Can't Forget the Motor City." *New York Times,* December 30, 2015. https://www.nytimes.com/2016/01/03/theater/playwright-dominique-morisseau-cant-forget-the-motor-city.html.

Tay, Louis, James O. Pawelski, and Melissa G. Keith. "The Role of the Arts and Humanities in Human Flourishing: A Conceptual Model." *Journal of Positive Psychology,* January 16, 2017, pp. 215–25.

Thapa, S., H. Vaziri, Y. Shim, L. Tay, and J. O. Pawelski, J. O. "Development and Validation of Arts and Humanities Mechanism Scale." Unpublished manuscript, 2021.

Tran, Diep. "Reading the #ppit Feed." Twitter, December 11, 2015. https://twitter.com/diepthought/status/675351430476120064.

Tran, Diep. "Top Ten 10* Most Produced Plays of 2018–2019 Season." *American Theatre,* September 20, 2018. https://www.americantheatre.org/2018/09/20/the-top-10-most-produced-plays-of-the-2018-19-season/.

Tran, Diep. "Top Ten 10* Most Produced Plays of 2019–2020 Season." *American Theatre,* September 18, 2019. https://www.americantheatre.org/2019/09/18/the-top-10-most-produced-plays-of-the-2019-20-season/.

Williams, Jonathan, et al. "Cinema Audiences Reproducibly Vary the Chemical Composition of Air during Films, by Broadcasting Scene Specific Emissions of Breath." *Nature,* May 10, 2016. https://www.nature.com/articles/srep25464#auth-1.

Young, Harvey. *Theatre and Race.* London, Palgrave, 2014.

10

Touching Theater

Practice, Criticism, and Aesthetics of Touch in the Flourishing Theatrical Moment

Marcia Ferguson

Performing touch, in life and on stage, does not merely relay already-formed thoughts, it is in itself, a form of alternative thinking.
—Naomi Rokotnitz, "Between Faulty Intellects and Failing Bodies,"
2013

How does touch factor in flourishing theatrical practice and reception, in all its experiential and aesthetic fullness? Optimal theatrical experiences, on the part of both performer and spectator, profoundly connect us, make us feel, and accentuate our common humanity. This experience is characteristic of a desirable state of human flourishing. The goal of this essay is to explore the role of touch in what I am calling *theatrical flourishing*, that is, optimal involvement in a theatrical moment. Through a brief (and necessarily incomplete) examination of the status of touch in contemporary theater practice, I will argue that touch is a radically overlooked, often pathologized element of theatricality, and by looking at rehearsal anecdotes and observations about the efficacy of touch in my own practice as an actor and director and drawing on instances of touch in dramaturgy, criticism, and theory, I will claim that touch, as a conceptual category and physical activity, plays a crucial role in *theatrical flourishing*.

Researchers Louis Tay, James Pawelski, and Melissa Keith introduce useful vocabulary in their discussion of human flourishing. They propose "mechanisms through which the modes of engagement and activities of involvement with the arts and humanities may lead to positive effects" (217). Three of the mechanisms they identify are immersion, socialization, and

Marcia Ferguson, *Touching Theater* In: *Theater and Human Flourishing*. Edited by: Harvey Young, Oxford University Press.
© Oxford University Press 2023. DOI: 10.1093/oso/9780197622261.003.0011

reflectiveness. These terms allow me to describe the narrower functions and characteristics of theatrical flourishing. The flourishing theatrical moment involves *immersion* in story, atmosphere, theme, or image; *socialization* in the sharing of space and experience with others in real time; and *reflectiveness* on the event itself, when, through reviews, more formal written criticism, or just plain conversation, spectators and theater artists process, comment upon, and make sense of what they have communally created and/or experienced. Setting aside for now the many, admittedly arguable assertions I just made (some theater eschews story altogether; some performances address audiences of one; some theater actively seeks to alienate—rather than immerse—spectators from theatrical illusion, etc.), I nonetheless maintain that humans flourish and experience well-being when they are engaged by high-quality, effective theater, regardless of genre, style, or emotional impact. The skillful, aesthetic use of touch, in both practice and dramaturgy, is key to achieving this state.

Flourishing encompasses all genres, and all emotional responses to theater. It is important to point out that not all cases of theatrical flourishing necessarily result in human flourishing in a general way. Any effective theatrical technique, including touch, may be used to animate negative ideologies, repressive hegemonies, or misinformation. Indeed, while this essay focuses mainly on its positive contributions to theatrical flourishing, it must be acknowledged at the outset that touch as an element of contemporary theatrical practice is a two-edged sword.

In theater practice and in pedagogy in general, touch is a hot topic. At the university where I teach, for example, touch has been discussed as a site of potential danger, in its capacity to trigger, dominate, (re)traumatize, microaggress, contaminate, inappropriately or inadvertently sexualize, or otherwise adversely affect students, practitioners, and audiences. Such discussions have penetrated backstage as well as in the classroom. My colleagues have made new rules for themselves around opening-night student hugs, replacing them with high-fives, elbow bumps, or handshakes. Perhaps I'm showing my age, but gone are the days when one could reliably count on a "theater person" to engulf one in gratuitous hugs or to "kiss-kiss" one at the drop of a hat. On every level, from broad-ranging, institutional policymaking to intimate one-on-one interactions, casual touch is being replaced with respectful distance, even in rehearsal rooms, where such off-the-cuff physical bonding was once as common as coffee.

More than ever, discussions of power, inclusion, and agency in the culture at large are paralleled by the struggle to awaken individuals and institutions within the field of theater to the importance of being conscious—and conscientious—when rehearsing and improvising theatrical touch. Just as fight choreography evolved in the wake of too many people being hurt in staged combat, evolving positions and documents in contemporary theater practice reflect the necessary growth of an ethic of care around touch, suggesting the dangers of underestimating its power.[1] For example, the development of the *intimacy choreographer* reflects this evolution and demonstrates that it is no longer assumed that all directors are always adequate to the "touch-needs" of any given script, particularly scenes involving intimacy and sexuality (Campanella). In fact, the growth, specific area of expertise, and global reach of the need for such a theater professional can be seen in the founding of the larger organization Intimacy Directors International, whose website defines intimacy directors as "highly skilled collaborators trained in movement pedagogy, acting theory, directing, body language, consent, sexual harassment, Title IX, mental health first aid" and notes that intimacy directors (or choreographers) take responsibility "for the emotional safety of actors and anyone else in the rehearsal hall while they are present" (1). Increased societal tolerance of staged sexual content also fuels this need for oversight, further mandating the sensitive management and regulation by trained intimacy professionals of the development, rehearsal, and performance of sexually charged work.[2]

The goals and qualifications for intimacy choreographers and intimacy directors are thoughtful and broad-ranging, but they are still not enough. In an impressive testament to the enduring agency, ongoing dangers surrounding, and persistent relevance of performative touch, contemporary theater practitioners are taking collective action to address and contain the potential damage of unregulated, improper, and coercive instances of touch on an institutional level. Depending on how widely it is adopted in the future, the development of this kind of sensitive protocol augurs well for the expansion of safety around performative touch. For instance, *The Chicago Theater Standards*, a free, downloadable document created by a group of concerned theater artists from the greater Chicago theater community, proposes

[1] My thanks to theater scholar John Fletcher for this observation, and to the many other scholars for their sensitive readings of an earlier draft of this essay during my participation in a meeting of the Humanities and Human Flourishing Project in November 2018.
[2] For an overview of this phenomenon, see Collins-Hughes.

standards for the safety and security of all theater artists. According to the introductory paragraph, it was "born of artists and administrators at all levels of our community working together toward a cultural paradigm shift away from turning a blind eye to sexual harassment" (1). Addressing myriad instances of unwanted touch in theater practice, ranging from the audition situation to costume fittings, privacy backstage, and staged moments of touch in actual performance, this thoughtful document offers useful protocols to prevent and address broad-ranging negative iterations of theatrical touch in practice. It has been widely adopted and adapted in the laudable efforts of theaters and institutions across the United States and elsewhere to address and regulate performative touch, especially vis-à-vis the vulnerabilities of performers and the power dynamics of rehearsal and performance generally.

Perhaps this kind of attention to the outright dangers of inappropriate/ unlawful touch accounts for the relative lack of attention touch receives as an active aesthetic element in the flourishing theatrical moment, especially from writers about theater practice, where it would be most expected. Touch is also, of course, the cornerstone of myriad approaches to human development, a critical component in theories of attachment, affect, psychotherapy, somatics, dance therapy, movement therapy, contact improvisation, and drama therapy. Yet, despite the intrinsic role touch plays in all such therapeutic theories and approaches, it is paid relatively little attention in writings about theater per se. I began this investigation of the role of touch in the flourishing theatrical moment by simply looking for discussions about and serious considerations of its efficacy in realizing emotional states in performers and audiences.[3] I found little that specifically engages touch in and of itself; most writing about theater technique emphasizes embodiment or movement rather than shades and variations of tactile contact and their impact. In seeking out writing about theater practice where touch is discussed as a practical aesthetic element on the flourishing theatrical moment, I find little meaningful engagement with touch in these terms. With some notable exceptions (Welton), and despite the current popularity of writing about adjacent theoretical and critical positions on the body in performance, touch is an all too frequently invisible element in discussions of embodiment, movement, affect, gesture, haptics, or other features of felt, performative physicality.

---

[3] For more in this volume on the relationship between physical presence, tragic emotion, human flourishing, and theater, see Lodewyck.

For instance, in a contemporary publication regarding the relationships and practices that comprise theatrical physicality, *Physical Dramaturgy: Perspectives from the Field* (Bowditch et al.), the subject of touch does not even appear in the index. And while Eve Sedgewick's promisingly titled and influential *Touching/Feeling: Affect, Pedagogy, Performativity* importantly uses touch as a metaphor for fascinating conceptual categories and larger social movements, ranging from gender to politics to imaginative possibility, touch here serves mainly a linguistic function and is not granted its own agency as a doing, a practice, or a device for realizing art in practical terms. Similarly, while neurocognitive studies grows a theatrical branch across questions yoking perception and theatrical practice to proprioception and brain function, and theories of affect and embodiment are sites of key critical writings about theater and reception, the specific subject of touch in and of itself, as opposed to the body generally, is largely absent from formative conversations about how physicality and feeling affect actors, spectators, and meaning.[4]

It seems that, somewhere along the line, touch became the performative baby that got thrown out with the critical bathwater. Yet if we are to plumb the depths of power around performative touch, assign it a true value, and understand its agency and characteristics in creating emotional and intellectual impact on an audience, I suggest that it is just as important to theorize touch, to name it and use it in our practice, as it is to develop protocols to prevent its potential to harm. Just as we must collectively wake up to the reality of its misuse, we must cultivate a tandem awareness of its contributions to the well-being and flourishing of both spectator and practitioner.

Indeed, while it does not center on touch specifically, some critical work has already blazed a trail in this regard. I will now turn to scholarship that directly addresses the connections between active theater practice, body, mind, and text in ways that I believe open potential fruitful pathways for the intersecting study of touch. Although touch is not at present its focus, this kind of scholarship nonetheless models a way forward for continuing research that could and *should* eventually include touch practice in critical and performative contexts. In a related chapter in this volume, for example, Harvey Young explores laughter in the theater as both a visceral and a cultural

---

[4] Ironically, there is a more thorough engagement with touch as practice and as key to spectatorial experience in contemporary studies of cinema and literature. See Marks; Barker. Berlant facilitates a turn in literary theory toward an interest in feeling and its relationship to flourishing, a platform that also inspires my interests here.

phenomenon. Theatrical experience in this analysis is both tangibly organic (like my investigation of touch) but also deeply connected to social context.

Rhonda Blair's *The Actor, Image, and Action: Acting and Cognitive Neuroscience* straddles scientific (neurocognitive) and performative disciplines to cogently address specific strategies of acting and conditions of performance affecting both audience and actor in ways that echo my present emphasis on touch. The book is an example of performance research that combines a focus on acting and active performance practice with a scientific awareness and theoretical cultivation of neurocognition and the body/mind. While I distinguish my much narrower focus in this essay from Blair's broadly generative study of mind and performance, I still see profound parallels and take inspiration, in my own use of studies of positive psychology, from its interdisciplinary reach.[5]

Bess Rowen's article "Undigested Reading: Rethinking Stage Directions through Affect" examines the intertwining of performative feeling, physicality, and writerly intent in active theater practice. I see a clear connection here with the study of touch in her emphasis, which privileges the artistic agency of bodily sensation in the realization of the script. Rowen looks at what she calls "affective stage directions," that is, connotative, rather than denotative, stage directions that do not direct actors to assume specific emotions or to occupy particular spatial positions onstage, but instead summon active participation by actors and directors into the creation of the staged moment. She argues that these more abstract stage directions appeal to the feelings of individuals realizing characters by inviting the imaginative, physical, psychological, and emotional engagement of whatever individual actor and director happens to be staging the text, in any particular time or place. As opposed to more traditional, strictly denotative stage directions, then, affective stage directions facilitate the script's ability to change and adapt across production teams, individual artists, cultures, and time periods. As Rowen writes, "Affective stage directions require actors, directors, and designers to think through their own embodied experiences in order to make meaning out of these moments of the script, allowing for production teams to make these parts of the plays relevant to a particular moment and location" (308–9).

---

[5] For a cogent overview of the pitfalls and ultimate benefits of interdisciplinary research on performance and cognition, see Tribble and Sutton. Welton contains an account of a devising process centering on the touch of bare feet on various surfaces.

For instance, Rowen examines Sarah Ruhl's stage directions in her 2009 play, *In the Next Room (or The Vibrator Play)* that guide the performance of a Victorian female character's first orgasm. In what follows, I combine a focus on touch with the implications, as I see them, of the gist of Rowen's critique. In her words, affective stage directions such as Ruhl's "are written to be shared by the actor's body and the character's body, who are sharing the same 'skin-envelope' for the duration of the play" (311). In her emphasis on the primacy of the actor/character's "skin-envelope," I would argue that the attendant subject of touch is of key importance, especially with regard to the stage directions around the moment of sexual ecstasy. The affective stage directions here demand a close consideration of touch: how the character is touched by the vibrator, how that touch is in turn an extension of the male character penetrating her, whether the character has knowledge of self-touch or masturbation, and so on. These and other questions of touch are, I argue, as necessary to the production team responsible for bringing the character to staged life as are questions of motivation, costume, design, or blocking. Rowen's approach models the simultaneous specificity and range I advocate in my claim for the importance of examining theatrical touch as at once a specific practice in the living performative moment, a critical category, and an enduring cultural and artistic manifestation of human flourishing across cultures.

As important and suggestive as this critical analysis is, it does not finally answer the question that fuels my inquiry here: How does touch, in and of itself, contribute to a staged representation that has meaning for both maker and spectator and embed them in a flourishing theatrical moment? As we have seen, the vocabulary of positive psychology facilitates a fruitful analysis of flourishing performance. Martin Seligman and Mihaly Csikszentmihalyi's "Positive Psychology: An Introduction" thrillingly proposes to liberate the practice of psychology from what had become its default relationship to pathology. The authors propose to focus instead on psychology's capacity to "help document . . . how peoples' lives can be most worth living" (13). They acknowledge the efficacy of psychology for the treatment of mental illness (as well as the undeniable economics of that treatment, a boon to both individual psychologists and larger entities with expertise in the field) but also argue persuasively for another, more positive, "liberated" use for their discipline: to cultivate well-being. Their critical position puts me forcibly in mind of the precariousness of theatrical touch. As we have seen, performative touch can be dangerous and potentially pathologized and is in need of expert oversight. (And again, there is an economy to the proliferation of this new kind of theater professional, whose well-deserved salary will nonetheless impact the bottom line in any production budget.) Yet largely relegating touch to this "preventative" perspective is aesthetically costly and potentially impacts our ability to create and cultivate theatrical well-being and flourishing. Like Seligman and Csikszentmihalyi, I therefore propose, for the purposes of this essay, to liberate the subject of touch not only from a relative baseline inattention paid it in performative terms but also from its negative associations, which have historically complicated the fuller understanding of its role, usage, and function in theatrical flourishing. To borrow and adapt Seligman and Csikszentmihalyi's phrasing, this approach to the study of touch in theater can help document how theatre can be most worth experiencing (5).

Indeed, making theater that is worth the spectator's time is a baseline value that animates every moment and activity of my directing practice. I see touch as a key expression of that value. I now realize that I have never adequately thought through the role of touch as a separate practice and entity, one with its own distinct brand of theatrical potency, even when it so often and so clearly solved many of my directorial problems. The following anecdotes, drawn from rehearsals of various projects, serve as examples of my own use of touch in theatrical practice. They demonstrate its profound agency and flexibility as an artistic tool, a key device in the collaborative project at the heart of all rehearsals: that is, to realize, to the best of our collective abilities, flourishing theatrical moments.

From a rehearsal of a Lady Gregory and W. B. Yeats's *Cathleen ni Houlihan*, **for a production in a sixty-seat black box theater:** The moment containing the climax of a play is making no emotional sense. A mother is consoling the woman who was to marry her son as he is walking out the door, never to be seen again. He is magically lured to join the suicidal but spiritually irresistible fight for Ireland by the eponymous mystical character (and the embodiment of the spirit of Ireland), Cathleen ni Houlihan. But there is little connection between the actresses playing the mother and the beloved, and the moment looks and feels wooden. I ask the actress playing the mother to pull back from her embrace of the other actress slowly, make direct eye contact, and tenderly brush her cheek with her hand. The touch brings tears to both actors' eyes and smart in my own. The moment now makes sense, their abandonment is authentic, the emotion flows, and the climax is achieved. We can move on to other scenes needing attention.

From a rehearsal of Aeschylus's *The Eumenides*, for a site-specific production in an archaeology museum: The actor playing Orestes is chased from one gallery to the next and lands at the feet of a priceless relic from ancient Egypt, a seated heroic statue of Ramses II. The immense sculpture serves as our stand-in for an image of the goddess Athena. The movement from gallery to gallery enacts the scenic movement of the play from Delphi (the Temple of Apollo) to Athens (Ares Hill and the Aeropagus). Orestes cowers, believing himself hidden in the Temple of Athena, but he is discovered. The Furies chant, "Here he is! The smell of human blood/Smiles to greet me. He has twined his hands/round the image of the goddess immortal." But the actor cannot in fact "twine" his hands around it, because it is a precious antiquity, and we, the company, are invited guests in the museum, performing around and among vulnerable, venerable objects that are specifically protected *against* being touched by actors and spectators. We work in various ways to subvert this "don't touch" atmosphere, which is quite natural in a museum of antiquities but which works against the atmosphere of proximity (of actor to spectator, spectator to myth, past to present) that we are trying to create. We interrupt the "don't touch" atmosphere with movement (the audience travels along with the actors from gallery to gallery, at times moving among them, at times tracing their steps; actors touch audience members at various points, handing them ballots, sitting next to them, playing instruments alongside them) and design (Clytemnestra sports a forty-foot umbilical cord that trails over the feet of the audience; Athena's oversized sleeves float and sweep across their heads; the furies stamp along with a drum that vibrates up spectators' bodies through the floor).

From a rehearsal of Beckett's *Rough for Theatre I*, for a production in a 110-seat black box theater: We struggle with a climactic moment toward the end of the play, when A, a blind beggar playing a violin, discovers that B, in a wheelchair, has only one leg. A gropes his way to B, falls to the ground, and rests his head on B's one knee, saying, "I could stay like that forever, with my head on an old man's knees." B subsequently "pushes him roughly away." The push looks and feels fake, and it becomes frustratingly clear that without a shove that feels authentic, a key moment of existential angst is lost. The more we, director and cast, discuss the moment, the less we seem able to achieve its tone and potential; we are talking it to death. The actors decide to stop speaking, and I lead them in an improvisation inspired by a Viewpoints technique. Wordlessly, they move slowly, taking time to receive one another's touch and adjusting to it before continuing. Each actor reacts to the physical contact in different ways, creating mini-beats between the movements. They work the head-on-knee, push-to-the-ground movement in slow motion, garnishing it with wordless mutual emotional reactions, then repeat the exchange in regular time. It gradually takes on the intensity and authenticity we have been seeking, their physical exchange finally freighted with the very "Beckettian" tonality we had been trying too hard to achieve by talking about it. Now the challenge is to weave the language of the dialogue back into the moment, without losing the ground we gained solely through touching.

These diverse instances from my practice as a theater director have one thing in common: all serve to illustrate the primacy of touch in realizing and creating a flourishing theatrical moment, both for makers and for spectators. At once "real" and ineffable, touch is an exquisitely deft tool that underscores beauty, complicates (and clarifies) feelings in viewing and practice, and contributes solutions to myriad textual and physical problems in the process of theater making. By meditating on these instances from my own practice, it became clear that further study of touch as a *working aesthetic* will be useful to both critics and makers in their tasks to identify, analyze, and implement theatrical flourishing.

Theater provides us with an incredible variety of kinds, levels, and conditions of touch, real and imaginary. As an actor (like most actors), for instance, I have at various points been faux-strangled, -slapped, -stabbed, and -kissed. As a director, I have guided the creation of those kinds of theatrical moments. Relying on guidance from the text, actors' insights and inspirations, critical commentaries, production histories, movement specialists, trusted outsiders, and mostly my own intuition, I have participated in the development and performance of staged physical contact, from intimate to violent, from the ground up.

Directing *The Eumenides* in an archaeology museum, a venue which naturally had clear boundaries for the interaction between the ancient artifacts on view, with the museum visitors–turned–audience members in the space, for instance, made me thoughtful about our assumptions around touch and theater. I was made more aware of how performance situations that prohibit or limit touch create specific performance pressures that have profound viewing implications for spectators and performers, and I became more cognizant in general of how touch operates on multiple levels at once (text, audience, performer, and space). While I respect the broad array of practical knowledge, research on embodiment, and plain intuition that has led me and several collaborators over the years to our own achievements in illustrative physicality, mainly through improvisation, experiments, research, and staged choreographies of contact, my new awareness of touch as an aesthetic modality in and of itself feels overdue. Where was the handbook, I wondered, on the specific use of touch in theatrical composition, creation of character, cultivation of atmosphere, or implementation of rhythm in production? How can we as theater artists *communicate* more specifically and flexibly with one another, and with the audience, about this key element in the creation of the positive/flourishing theatrical experience?

At base, in its aesthetic function, touch can broadly be described as container, vehicle, and metaphor for flourishing theatrical experience. A tender caress, for instance, stands in for a loving relationship; a vicious punch denotes anger and hatred. The exact nature of touch between actors onstage contains and relays all the vital relational information the audience needs in one economic visual and physical illustration. I need to reiterate at this point that I use the term "flourishing" here to refer to a degree of efficacy in a production's ability to immerse the spectator in the qualities of its story, atmosphere, or rhythm, as opposed to any specific positive or negative emotion. The function of effective theatrical touch can be seen as positive simply in its capacity to manifest all *possible* emotional states. The successful stagings of antagonism, fear, hostility, or tragic emotion, for instance, are prime examples of what I mean by positive theatrical experience. It is the business of theater to invite audiences to experience their own humanity, and in so doing, to flourish.

A further refinement is in order here about the relationship between *human* flourishing and what I am calling *theatrical* flourishing. As Aristotle points out in Book 6 of *The Poetics*, tragedy is "an imitation of a worthy or illustrious and perfect action, possessing magnitude" (quoted in Clark 9). In response to Plato's general distrust of imitation and images, Aristotle sees in mimesis an intrinsic part of human activity, a redemptive and organic component of human imagination and learning. The imitative theatricalization of human action in drama provides a secondary, vicarious experience of an original action, for both viewer and performer. The dual nature of all such theatricalized experiences necessitates *awareness* of the relationship between the image and that which it imitates. It is the enjoyment and realization of this awareness, this mental dialogue between the source action and its image in the viewer and the player, that finally characterizes the fullness of a specifically theatrical flourishing. The vicarious dramatic experience, and its attendant consciousness, not only entertains; it prompts thought about what it means to be human, to have experiences, and, on a broader plane, to have a consciousness capable of discerning the difference between an action and its image. Human flourishing is the larger category, apprehending and containing every variety of human fulfillment. Theatrical flourishing is narrower; it is not itself human fulfillment but a special kind of experience that helps us prioritize among and differentiate all the ways humans can flourish.

Theater practitioners use every tool at their disposal in the realization of that flourishing experience. Note that the sampling of "positive" touch I provided from my own theatrical practice includes not only a tender caress of sympathy between two women united by mutual loss but also the beating of Orestes by the Furies and the violence of existential dread in a Beckett play. Theater's enactment of the full spectrum of emotion provides a significant and distinguished activity of human value, and the role of touch within that activity is vital.

Some of the larger questions underlying my inquiry that currently exceed my reach in this chapter include the following: What distinguishes touch as a communicative language, as an element in the staging of (vicarious) human experience, and how does it effectively reference and/or represent shared social values onstage? What exactly does touch contribute to the effective creation and reception of theatrical art? How can one describe touch as an aesthetic element of the total live performance—what does it *do*? When used badly or without awareness, does it impede the positive theatrical experience or prevent theater's capacity for promoting flourishing in certain specific ways?

The earlier anecdotes from rehearsals serve as examples of the kind of research that might begin to answer these questions. By analyzing instances from process, performance, and audience reaction, and regarding this material as data in an ongoing project to document the materiality and usefulness of touch as an aesthetic tool of rehearsal and performance research, we can begin to envision the creation of a "grammar" or a glossary of touch—which will in turn facilitate communication between theater artists (and hence audiences) about best practices for its use in creating specific kinds of moments, emotions, atmospheres, and rhythms. That is, we can draw conclusions, create categories, and begin to refine vocabulary, based on collective observations, experiments, and other evidence pertaining to how touch functions to derail, or perfect, specific kinds of flourishing performative moments.

Theatrical touch can also be fruitfully considered in terms of the separate and contingent conditions of performance: *actor, audience, and space.* Careful examination of touch in relation to each of these key components of the performance situation is another way to gather information/data that can be used toward the creation of the grammar (or glossary) of touch that I envision here and that I claim is worth developing. The creation of a taxonomy of touch will move us toward a fuller understanding of the function and contribution of touch to the aesthetics of theater and the attendant flourishing of spectator and practitioner. In the following, I suggest that, even before a script is introduced to organize and interpret them, these basic components of performance already contain crucial information about the function of touch in performance.

Actors: Theatrical touch is grounded in the physicality of actors on stage. Here we can immediately begin to make distinctions between kinds of touch, to distinguish how touch brings about different registers of emotion. Simply put, by touching each other, or by preventing each other (or otherwise being prevented) from touching, through touching props and set pieces, touching themselves, touching elements of the onstage world, touching audiences, and so on, actors demonstrate on several levels how touch realizes different meanings through contact with the living body and nonliving object entities. By tracing such instances of touch, it is possible to determine and categorize the relative value of different kinds of theatrical touch in illustrating or bringing to life aesthetic effects. Like visual or aural design cues, the ways actors touch (each other, themselves, props and set, etc.) on stage create systems that distribute and communicate nonlinguistic meaning to an audience. The goal of proposing such detailed attention to these systems is to explore exactly *how* this particular communication system is activated, and after introducing a script alongside the simple presence of potential touch in the living bodies of actors, we can further trace its value in realizing story, image, atmosphere, rhythm, and emotion that specifically results in the well-being or flourishing of actors and characters on stage and of spectators off-stage. (This work also entails, perhaps, the development of a more specific definition of flourishing and well-being in their theatrical senses, foundational work which remains beyond the purview of this essay.) Existing research, such as that on phenomenology,[6] embodiment, and haptics, supports but does not

---

[6] See States, in which he famously cites the perspiration on the actor's face, which is not the character's perspiration, as the classic example of the duality residing in the performing body. The actor's body performs/touches itself, even as the actor performs the character; actor and character

replace the work of simply assigning performance values to differing kinds of theatrical touch among actors onstage.

Audience: Touch is also central to the project of actuating empathy in audiences. Aristotelian separation between audience and actors has historically served as the critical battleground for discussions of spectatorial space. In the royal entries of the Renaissance, Artaud's (mis)understanding of proximity between actors and audience in Balinese theater (Gillit 1), Brecht's innovations for effectively alienating audiences from theatrical illusion for ideological or artistic purposes, touch that bridges space between performers and watchers or, on the contrary, posits the impossibility of such touch to bridge that gulf remains a significant site for the creation and reception of theatrical meaning. To what extent does touch and the potential to touch or the prohibition from touching create a grammar of its own in terms of audience? In the production of Aeschylus's *The Eumenides* that took place in an archaeology museum, the audience was simultaneously prohibited from touching precious objects, touched by floating and trailing costumes, and in close proximity with actors who occasionally touched them while handing them objects. Teasing out the many levels of touch at work in the audience for this one production serves as a model for how to isolate and identify all the specific effects of touch in any production, moving us toward a larger goal of creating a useful vocabulary of touch for practice, dramaturgy, training, and theory. Even taking into account the multiplicity of receptions among audiences, the individual experience within the group experience, their involvement is key to identifying how touch works as a performative aesthetic. Data drawn from such identification, across multiple productions, methodologies, and performance locations, would yield important information, and the resulting distinctions in kinds of audience response would enable sophisticated discourse about touch in performance. Current research on empathy, liveness, phenomenology, mimesis, vicarious emotion, and the haptic experience would aid in this phase of the work.

Space: I have already discussed some of the material pressures concerning touch that condition the audience's and performers' experience in museums or galleries. Such "alternative" viewing spaces have specific regulations for touch and the potential for touch, which impact the viewing and performing

---

touch one another in the performing moment (my emphasis). The potential for touch also exists between the living bodies of spectator and actor, giving live performance its danger and its special frisson of phenomenological liveness.

experience in specific ways. Tracing out and identifying those myriad effects of touch will bring the subject of aesthetic touch into conversation with questions about the relationship of a flourishing viewing or making experience with institutional and regulatory structures, and with the role of culture, history, and artifacts in performance. This discussion importantly focuses on institutional atmospheres and on the role of objects, touchable and untouchable, in the performative moment.

It is worth noting here that social boundaries and expectations around personal space always challenge or complicate the possibility of touch within the audience, regardless of the nature of the theatrical venue. Traditional venues, especially a proscenium stage situation, set up recognizable physical limitations on touch between actors and audience, thereby organizing the performance situation. This is not to say that the space between them is unbridgeable; the possibility always exists, such as for those seated in the closest rows, of being inadvertently spat upon by working actors, of having objects thrown into/onto audience (as happens in performances of Blue Man Group), or having actors unexpectedly walk into, on, or among the very seats of the audience (*Slava's Snow Show* and Roberto Benigni's Oscar acceptance performance are examples). The *hanamichi* platform of Kabuki theater, which runs directly into audience space, facilitates dramatic exits and entrances and other elements of the dramatic action, and indeed deposits actors directly into the midst of the audience space as a matter of protocol. The risks of such contact may in some cases heighten the excitement or raise the tension of the performance condition for audiences. This kind of research could branch out into discussions of the function of touch in various performance traditions, such as "audience participation" techniques, immersive theater, ritual, and environmental theater practices and situations, to name a few. Other institutional or regulatory conditions of performance space overlap here, such as ticketing, technologies at work in the onstage and offstage spaces, and transportation to and from venues, and as such these are also fruitful areas of further research on touch.

The previous examples demonstrate ways the aesthetics of touch can inform future studies of theatrical flourishing through the creation of a taxonomy of touch, which would be useful to both makers and writers of and/or about theater. As noted earlier, my original observations about the need to invest in the study of touch grew largely out of my own directing practice. But in resources as diverse as stage directions, letters, production histories, and dramatic criticism, I find further confirmation of my perception of touch as containing that ineffable essence of the performative moment beyond language, where perhaps the fullest expression of (theatrical) meaning paradoxically resides. Even away from the tactility and presence of actors' bodies, that is, touch is alive in the words of authors, audiences, and critics as they strive to convey, interpret, and create the essence of drama.

By *immersing* the spectator in moments of desire to inhabit the experiences of the other (the characters), by *socializing* them in their shared realization of that mutual experience, and by creating, through design, atmosphere, and especially rhythm, the space and time for an audience to *reflect* on the ideas and emotions born of their spectatorial experience, a director facilitates an experience of true *theatrical flourishing*. This optimal involvement in a theatrical moment is a felt connection and an affective bond that invites real emotional flow between and among actors and audience across character, story, atmosphere, mood, and image. Theatrical touch will always have the potential to cut both ways, its potency available to a theater that promotes either a human flourishing or a human languishing, depending on who (or what) is shaping it. A more nuanced understanding of the relationship of theatrical touch to human flourishing leads to a new sensitivity to the power of touch as a key directorial responsibility and opportunity.

Works Cited

Auster, Paul, ed. *Samuel Beckett: Poems, Short Fiction, Criticism.* Vol. 4. New York, Grove Press, 2006.

Barker, Jennifer. *The Tactile Eye: Touch and the Cinematic Experience.* Berkeley, University of California Press, 2009.

Berlant, Lauren. *Cruel Optimism.* Durham, Duke University Press, 2011.

Blair, Rhonda. *The Actor, Image, and Action: Acting and Cognitive Neuroscience.* London, Routledge, 2008.

Bowditch, Rachel, et al., eds. *Physical Dramaturgy: Perspectives from the Field.* London, Routledge, 2018.

Campanella, Tonia. "Intimate Encounters: Staging Intimacy and Sensuality." MFA thesis, Virginia Commonwealth University, 2006. https://scholarscompass.vcu.edu/cgi/view content.cgi?article=2070&context=etd.

Chicago Theater Standards. #NotInOurHouse. https://theatreartsguild.org

Collins-Hughes, Laura. "Need to Fake an Orgasm? There's an 'Intimacy Choreographer' for That." *New York Times,* June 15, 2017. https://www.nytimes.com/2017/06/15/thea ter/need-to-fake-an-orgasm-theres-an-intimacy-choreographer-for-that.html.

Clark, Barrett. *European Theories of the Drama.* New York, Crown, 1918.

Gillit, Cobina. "A Legacy of Theatricality: Antonin Artaud's Encounter with Balinese Gamelan." Smithsonian, n.d. https://asia.si.edu

Global Shakespeares, Video and Performance Archive. Hanamichi (Kabuki Stage Design), n.d. https://globalshakespeares.mit.edu/glossary/hanamichi/.

Intimacy Directors International. "Intimacy for Stage and Screen," 2022. Intimacyforstageandscreen.com.

Intimacy Directors International. "The Pillars: Rehearsal and Performance Practice," 2016. https://docs.wixstatic.com/ugd/924101_2e8c624bcf394166bc0443c1f35ef e1d.pdf.

Marks, Laura. *The Skin of the Film: Intercultural Cinema, Embodiment, and the Senses.* Durham, NC, Duke University Press, 2000.

Plato. *Republic.* Penguin Classics, 2012.

Rokotnitz, Naomi. "Between Faulty Intellects and Failing Bodies: An Economy of Reciprocity in Wit and 33 Variations." *Affective Performance and Cognitive Science: Body, Brain and Being,* edited by Nicola Shaughnessy. London, Bloomsbury, 2013, pp. 117–130.

Rowen, Bess. "Undigested Reading: Rethinking Stage Directions through Affect." *Theatre Journal,* vol. 70, no. 3, 2018, pp. 307–26.

Ruhl, Sarah. *In the Next Room (or The Vibrator Play).* Theatre Communications Group, 2010.

Sedgwick, Eve Kosofsky. *Touching/Feeling: Affect, Pedagogy, Performativity.* Durham, Duke University Press, 2003.

Seligman, Martin, and Mihaly Csikszentmihalyi. "Positive Psychology: An Introduction." *American Psychologist,* vol. 55, no. 1, January 2000, pp. 5–14.

States, Bert. *Great Reckonings in Little Rooms.* Berkeley, University of California Press, 1987.

Tay, Louis, James O. Pawelski, and Melissa G. Keith. "The Role of the Arts and Humanities in Human Flourishing: A Conceptual Model." *The Journal of Positive Psychology,* vol. 13, no. 3, January 16, 2017. doi:10.1080/17439760.2017.1279207.

Tribble, Evelyn B., and John Sutton. "Introduction: Interdisciplinarity and Cognitive Approaches to Performance." *Affective Performance and Cognitive Science: Body, Brain and Being,* edited by Nicola Shaughnessy. London, Bloomsbury, 2013, pp. 27–37.

Welton, Martin. "Footage: Surface Feelings." *Affective Performance and Cognitive Science: Body, Brain and Being,* edited by Nicola Shaughnessy. Bloomsbury, 2013, pp. 159–69.

11

Theater, Performance, and Community Cultural Development for Human Thriving

Stephani Etheridge Woodson

I am the daughter of an itinerant, evangelical minister (think tent revivals) and a child protective services social worker. As a theater artist and an academic, I don't save lives or souls, but my upbringing has provided me deep, lived experience in human-centric values and an expectation that my work should make the world a better place. Always. In this essay I explore that challenge by mapping three lessons I learned as an artist and a theater scholar rooting the building of an ambitious community engagement program at Arizona State University (ASU) developed around a frame focused on human thriving and public health. I take seriously the challenges in Jill Dolan's epilogue to *Performance Utopias* when she asks:

- "How can we take the space opened in performance and imagination and actively encourage utopian performatives?"
- "What strategies of artistic and critical production might enable the proliferation of utopian performatives, without commodifying them and emptying them of their necessarily spiritual, idiosyncratic is-ness?" (169)

For me too, the follow-up question has been: How do I take artistic utopian ideals into daily practice and strategically organize to make the world a better place? or How do we manifest our imaginations toward human flourishing?

ASU is a unique institution that President Michael Crow labels "A New Era Public Enterprise Model" or the New American University. This transformational process has had the effect of blurring traditional disciplinary boundaries and promoting experiments in educational and research innovation

Stephani Etheridge Woodson, *Theater, Performance, and Community Cultural Development for Human Thriving*
In: *Theater and Human Flourishing*. Edited by: Harvey Young, Oxford University Press. © Oxford University Press 2023.
DOI: 10.1093/oso/9780197622261.003.0012

while also further weaving neoliberal understandings of capital, markets, and technocratic approaches to both human identity and community engagement into the deep structures of the university. If you can imagine it, then ASU will allow you to build it. In general, however, they will not support the work until after you "prove" your concepts. This is an institution that throws spaghetti at the wall to see what sticks.

ASU's scale is also unique. Enrollment has more than doubled since academic year 2000–2001 and currently is well over 100,000 students. In academic year 2018–19, ASU awarded degrees to 19,340 undergraduate and 8,145 graduate students. Like ASU itself, my home college, the Herberger Institute for Design and the Arts, is the largest comprehensive arts and design school in the United States, with almost 6,000 students, 260 full-time faculty, and around half a million square feet of dedicated space. As our dean, Steven Tepper, points out, the Herberger Institute represents more artists and designers than the entire city of St. Louis can claim. In October 2016, Dean Tepper appointed me to build a community-engaged arts and design program to involve all Herberger Institute students across our more than 125 degree programs and at all levels, freshmen to doctoral students; this became the Design and Arts Corps (DAC). My task is to provide each of these students with at least one deep experience in community-engaged arts or design, appropriate mentorship, and competency-based curriculum. At the time of this writing, DAC has codeveloped online curricula with both community partners and the Herberger Institute schools (Music; Art; Design; Film, Dance, and Theatre; Arts, Media, and Engineering) and hosted hundreds of students in projects ranging from design work in hospitals to companies specializing in commercial interior design. We have developed a track record of success but are still years away from being fully scaled.

I have been a community-engaged artist and scholar for the whole of my career and since 2008 have worked at the intersection of arts practices and health. First at a program in the Hematology and Oncology Unit at Phoenix Children's Hospital and then in 2010–11 with Cultural Engagements in Nutrition, Arts and Science, a research and arts collaborative that explores theater making, cooking, and healthy eating as preventative mechanisms and health promotion in populations at high risk for obesity and diabetes. In each, I depend on the World Health Organization's 1948 conceptualization of health as "a state of complete physical, mental and social well-being and not merely the absence of disease or infirmity" (https://www.who.int/about/gov ernance/constitution). So you can see how concerns with human well-being form the warp to the weft of my diverse practices in art, engagement, and scholarship. When appointed DAC director, I doubled down on my concern for human flourishing, focusing on how ASU, the Herberger Institute, and DAC can manifest utopic spaces in which all people thrive rather than just survive. Further, I am interested in how love, creativity, and joy manifest as resilient practices and also frames contributing to communitas. In a system built on change with multiple projects, research frames, and creative initiatives winging around like a herd of over-tired toddlers hopped up on birthday cake, how do I contribute positively to collective well-being practices in a high-speed change environment? In this essay I divide the three central lessons drawn from theater and a theater scholarship structuring my approach to answering this question: (1) narrative and collaborative creativity, (2) asset spaces of ensembles, and (3) performance theory and representational ethics.

Narrative and Collaborative Creativity

I tell this story from my perspective, but I also need to foreground that, like author Chimamanda Ngozi Adichie, I believe in the danger of a single story. Further, as adrienne maree brown points out:

> We have lived through a good half century of individualistic linear organizing (led by charismatic individuals or budget-building institutions), which intends to reform or revolutionize society, but falls back into modeling the oppressive tendencies against which we claim to be pushing. Some of those tendencies are seeking to assert one right way or one right strategy. Many align with the capitalistic belief that constant growth and critical mass is the only way to create change, even if they don't use that language. (8)

This is not a story of a super-special institution, nor one about a super-special individual. Do I have unique knowledges? Of course, but I have built them slowly, over time in relationships and through the specific gifts that theater and performance have taught me. I am my community. When I was tasked with building DAC from the ground up, I relied on my making skills and the thoughtful practices honed in performance analysis, understanding the dramaturgies of lived experience and the collaborative, embodied knowledges built in studio practices, applied theater, and social-profit leadership and management. Much like any performance, then, I approached designing DAC through thematic frames and art as inquiry processes. DAC's guiding questions—or my directorial concept, if you will—included:

- What would a large-scale socially engaged arts and design program look like when the arts and design are *already understood* as essential components of a healthy society?
- Where can the arts and design intervene to build assets in the complex interactions between individual psychosocial and environmental, educational, cultural, and political systems?
- How can DAC form and function model justice and democratic lived experience and allow for multiple ways of knowing and being human?
- How can DAC promote well-being—not only in communities but also for student artists and designers, university faculty, and staff?

Drawing deeply on my previous work in applied theater and well-being, DAC is organized around a model of human thriving understood broadly. I have also been heavily influenced by philosophical and ethical frames that recognize both universities (and education more broadly; e.g., Dewey) and arts/design practices as democratically situated. Here I am interested not in democracy as a political system but rather as lived experience and sets of performance practices that not only contribute to identity formation but also help diverse peoples live together equitably (Boyte; Saltmarsh and Hartley). I have experienced the delightful flow state formed in studio practices and collaboratives teams that clicked. Theater can build deep skills necessary to facilitate making processes that harvest creativity, negotiate conflict productively, and center human experiences and embodiment positively. Like many, I have also experienced rehearsal processes that harmed, practiced patriarchal control, and produced narratives centering whiteness as "universal." (I recommend Scott Magelssen's chapter in this volume for a much deeper discussion of these concerns.) In unpacking my experiences and learning how to teach performance and facilitation skills to my students, I lean into democracy as applicative, able to be rehearsed, and necessary to living ethically in a pluralistic society. I therefore understand applied arts and design as a democracy maker-space in which we strategize on utopics through intentional collaborative practices modeled on participatory democracy.

Democracy, then, functions as a fundamental organizing principle for DAC. We work *with* people, not *for* them. This means paying attention to democratic *depth* (the how and the quality of people's participation), democratic *breadth* (the number of people affected by decisions who participate in the decision-making processes), and democratic *range* (the kinds of decisions in which people participate and decide). Marilyn Wise and Peter Sainsbury point to the deep connection between democratic practices and the social determinants of public health that connect to persistent inequalities in health outcomes. Using a research review, they hypothesize that democracy contributes to health through two mechanisms: processes and products (181). Like Community-Campus Partnerships for Health, Imagining America, and other such organizations, or public land-grant universities more broadly, I understand one of our primary responsibilities in DAC as contributing to democratically situated well-being while centering processes, products, and participatory publics across institutional and disciplinary boundaries. Peter Huang and Jeremy Blumenthal point to research that connects higher levels of subjective well-being with higher levels of participation in procedural contexts: "[F]rom trial juries to political institutions, individuals' subjective well-being from an institution in which they participate correlates with that institution's formal arrangement, and with those individuals' opportunities to participate in that institution" (590). I understand democracy as a guiding principle *and a process* contributing not just to the education of our students or the proper functioning of our nation, but also to overall individual satisfaction and the conditions supporting human thriving.

So how does this show up? For me, thinking through democratic depth, breadth, and range—the how and the quality of people's participation, the number of people affected by decisions who participate in the decision-making processes, and the kinds of decisions in which people participate and decide—meant that the development of the DAC must model our best ideas of how to work collaboratively toward the betterment of shared human thriving. This meant that I needed to both facilitate collaborative design and build processes and learning frames that promote collaborative settings over time. In the first seven months of DAC development, for example, we surveyed stakeholders inside and outside of the university system. We interviewed students, faculty and staff, and administration as well as arts and design community leaders and industry professionals. We spoke to national-level arts, design, and cultural organizing leadership and had the opportunity to present some of our ideas at a conference for municipal arts and culture directors. We also spoke to local activists, elementary school children, their teachers and principals, neighborhood organizers, civic representatives, and elected officials. In each meeting (some individual and some collective) we asked DAC's guiding questions and mapped people's responses using a socio-ecological frame borrowed from public health and prevention initiatives to build our theory of change, a value-added model. Socio-ecological models recognize that individuals are situated in systems (from the micro to the macro) that promote or prohibit development, health, and wellness. For months and months, I walked around with a large roll of butcher paper and markers as we collectively mapped potential indicators of successful positive change necessary for human thriving. We "mapped our utopics," in other words.

Visual artist John Borstel facilitated a critical response process that helped clarify and distill our framework with stakeholders. We used design thinking protocols along with community organizing principles, and applied theater techniques to gather and refine DAC's mission, vision, and values along with collaboratively building the value proposition/theory of change though democratic principles (see Figure 11.1). I paid attention to practicing radical welcome within decision-making as well as the quality of the participatory experiences and the structural importance of the decisions being made. From a theatrical perspective, this work can be understood as our production map, our casting, and our rehearsal processes. Rather than starting with

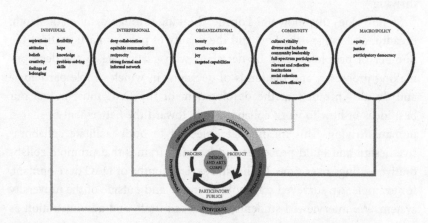

Figure 11.1 Theory of change for Design and Arts Corps, Arizona State University.

what we needed to teach students, I started with our central questions/concept and iterated between external and internal collaborators to model democratic depth, breadth, and range.

The Asset Spaces of Ensembles

We know from both lived experiences and research that our connections to one another matter for human health and that our many communities feed our happiness differently. Around the U.S. West, there is a subculture of people who actively prepare for apocalyptic emergencies. In some cases, their lifestyle is driven by religious fundamentalism, and in others by a deep desire to take absolute control of their destinies. Called "Preppers," they organize intentional living communities with a balance of skills necessary for how the community understands human thriving entirely separate from formal municipal, state, and federal frames. In fact, intentional living communities can be found across the United States, driven by diverse politics and value systems. These formal and informal arrangements harvest relationships and individual skill sets to provide for one another. I once had a Latter-day Saint student tell me that no one paid for their child's piano lessons in his community; instead they bartered services to one another. Anyone that paid, he said, was "doing Mormon wrong." Another student was appointed by her bishop to serve as director for women's and children's emergency services for her faith community. She was a first responder for cases of abuse, trauma, and emergencies and the point person to organize teams of community members necessary for ongoing supports. Her position did not replace city and county responses but supplemented them. In my own neighborhood, we have had a weekly potluck for the past twenty years. Unorganized and lowkey, sometimes we have only meat dishes, sometimes only salad. The pattern of coming together across food allows us to build deep connections and care.

In the five proxy categories of the Gallup Well-Being Index, human networks appear twice, as "social relationships" and "relation to community." Communities are not problems to be solved, nor should every community look and act the same. In each of the examples above, communities have organized themselves in responsibility frames accessed and nurtured by members. This is second principle of the DAC connected to concerns with human thriving, or what Saul Alinsky refers to as "native leadership" and John McKnight and Peter Block identify as "abundant community."

Both of these ideas acknowledge communities as networks of interdependent relationships and understand that lasting positive change is driven from the bottom up rather than the top down. Importantly, these ideas resist understandings of university-community partnerships as service or technocratic problem-solving to frames of reciprocity and mutual benefit.

So how does this show up? Like positive psychology itself, DAC focuses on assets rather than pathologies. Our frame is not scarcity, but abundance. As Martin Seligman and Mihaly Csikszentmihalyi write in their introduction to the positive psychology issue of *American Psychologist*:

> The field of positive psychology at the subjective level is about valued subjective experiences: well-being, contentment, and satisfaction (in the past); hope and optimism (for the future); and flow and happiness (in the present). At the individual level, it is about positive individual traits: the capacity for love and vocation, courage, interpersonal skill, aesthetic sensibility, perseverance, forgiveness, originality, future mindedness, spirituality, high talent, and wisdom. At the group level, it is about the civic virtues and the institutions that move individuals toward better citizenship: responsibility, nurturance, altruism, civility, moderation, tolerance, and work ethic. (5)

My personal creative practice focuses primarily on working with children and youth in a state in which whites are not, and have not been, dominant in the under-eighteen population since 2010 (Annie E. Casey Foundation). Children and youth more frequently than not are defined by what they lack rather than what they are. I have always had a deep suspicion about "needs"-based rhetoric that postulates identity structures for a whole class of people, as these are often built on racist, patriarchal, and homophobic frames, (e.g., "at-risk" and "moral panic" narratives). I have been super-sensitized in both my artistic and my scholarly work to ideologies limiting human creative and agentic strengths. Thus, I have intentionally organized my work for years on asset-development practices. Understanding humans and communities through abundance frameworks changes how conversations happen. This parallels theatrical making. Stacy Wolf's chapter in this book, "Community Musical Theater as a Human Flourishing Project," lyrically explores this process. Her work, like that of many in this volume (see especially Laura A. Lodewyck and Erin Hurley), explores formal and informal performance's intrinsic eudaimonic value. While we might wish for enormous production budgets and racks of robotic lights, we map our assets and leverage them to *build something together* that did not exist previously. The DAC emphasizes strengths—not needs—and leveraging those strengths to build further capabilities as identified by community through native leadership. DAC is thus rooted in an asset model of community development that recognizes communities as centers of thriving and social connectivity, not as deficit locations common to more technocratic and hierarchical community-university engagement strategies. A focus on community leadership within partnerships, too, can work to dismantle colonial practices that are "both prescriptive and assimilative" in the worst modes of structural oppression (Jojola 47).

Our asset-based frame means that our community partners define themselves by who they *are*, not what they are "missing." Rather than a psychological approach to assets here, though, I use an economic model to more thoroughly address our constructivist tactics and my own materialist leanings. What assets does the community want to leverage in order to grow assets in another area? I pull particularly from sociologist Pierre Bourdieu (*Distinction*; *The Field*; Bourdieu and Passeron) and his theory of capital transference. In order to ground DAC asset-based community cultural development protocols and products, I use a multiple capital system I adapted from the Community Capitals Framework developed by the National Rural Funders Collaborative as "an analytical tool to determine the effectiveness of [their] investments in addressing structural conditions of rural poverty" (Emery and Flora 20). While the Community Capitals Framework used seven overlapping domains, I expand that to nine and added Tara J. Yosso's and David G. Garcia's critical race work on *resistant* capital built in marginalized communities of color and through theatrical practice.

- *Built capital* includes community infrastructure and built environments, both those owned individually and those built collectively (roads, water, sewer).
- *Civic capital* refers to those places and institutions that bring people together in the same place and time (libraries, festivals, protests).
- *Cultural capital* includes language, skills, patterns of dress, and value systems. Cultural capital can be particularly complex as individuals belong to multiple, overlapping cultures with diverse values and beliefs. Cohen-Cruz explains, "Cultural capital constitutes a set of resources: the

particular music, performance, poetry, folk wisdom, customs, food and dress that are frequently sources of collective strength and pride and a way to bring people together" (126).

- *Creative capital* includes aesthetic structures and creative abilities, adaptive reuse, creative expression, and capacity for creative problem-solving along with divergent thinking patterns.
- *Environmental capital* includes a community's natural resources; these resources can be geographical or ecological.
- *Financial capital* means money and credit markets; it can be both formal and informal.
- *Human capital* includes people's singular and collective capacities and formal and informal education and implicit and explicit knowledge systems. Morse points to a larger understanding of human capital investment that includes "secondary investments that enhance [people's] ability to participate better in society" (24). Much of the resistant capital built by marginalized communities functions as a form of human or social capital.
- *Political capital* includes access to and influence over decision-makers and policy crafters.
- *Social capital* is comprised of specific and collective social networks. Sociologists divide social capital into two particular forms: bridging and bonding. *Bonding social capital* strengthens ties within social networks. *Bridging social capital* functions as baggy networks connecting one social network with another. My colleague Maria Rosario Jackson refers to people functioning in this way as a community's "gas" and "glue" (quoted in Etheridge Woodson).

In my experience, an asset approach refocuses our collaborative understandings of skills, knowledge, and ensemble. I find it particularly relevant in education settings that train us to understand one another in relationship or competition to a symbolic "normal/traditional" learner or academic. Not quite 50 percent of the Herberger Institute student population are students of color and the first generation in their family to attend college. Many have been taught by the K–12 system and our state's embrace of standardized testing to focus on their deficits, not their strengths. Mapping community abundance—as defined by the community—is a key part of DAC's emphasis on human thriving. Not incidentally, this capital system positions the arts and design as significant mechanisms harvesting capital in one domain to invest in another determined by a community to increase the material and cultural preconditions for the community's well-being.

Performance Theory and Representational Ethics

I am a huge reader. I suspect most academics are. Since my teens, I have been haunted by a short story by Ursula K. Le Guin titled "The Ones That Walk Away from Omelas" that reverberates for me particularly when I think about my ideal place or imagine utopias for human thriving. This story describes an ideal city, "bright-towered by the sea," in which artists are revered, children are nurtured, and the people are joyful and happy. Le Guin describes Omelas as a place that has solved the existential crises of our own existence:

> The trouble is that we have a bad habit, encouraged by pedants and sophisticates, of considering happiness as something rather stupid. Only pain is intellectual, only evil interesting. This is the treason of the artist: a refusal to admit the banality of evil and the terrible boredom of pain. If you can't lick 'em, join 'em. If it hurts, repeat it.

In Omelas during the summer festival, happiness reigns supreme, guilt does not operate, and the darker pleasures of conquest, violence, and evil have been overcome. But Omelas has a secret. In a small, dark closet sits a child: "It could be a boy or a girl. It looks about six, but actually is nearly ten. It is feeble-minded. Perhaps it was born defective, or perhaps it has become imbecile through fear, malnutrition, and neglect."

The child lives in this locked closet, alone and afraid, with the looming brooms and old, musty mops as lone companions and fed gruel and dank water. "[B]ut the child, who has not always lived in the tool room, and can remember sunlight and its mother's voice, sometimes speaks. 'I will be good,' it says. 'Please let me out. I will be good!'" The child lives in its own filth and suffers festering sores and malnutrition, fear and despair.

> They all know it is there, all the people of Omelas. . . . [T]hey all understand that their happiness, the beauty of their city, the tenderness of their friendships, the health of their children, the wisdom of their scholars, the skill of their makers, even the abundance of their harvest and the kindly weathers of their skies, depend wholly on this child's abominable misery.

The child serves as a psychopomp for all the anger, unhappiness, and despair in the city. Its short, brutal life makes the thriving of thousands possible. This is the social contract of Omelas:

> If the child were brought up into the sunlight out of that vile place, if it were cleaned and fed and comforted, that would be a good thing, indeed; but if it were done, in that day and hour all the prosperity and beauty and delight of Omelas would wither and be destroyed. Those are the terms.

And so thousands of people live in that city of bright towers and shining sea, a city of happiness and joy and achievement bought at the expense of one child, a sacrifice for the greater good.

But there are those who reject this social contract:

> They leave Omelas, they walk ahead into the darkness, and they do not come back. The place they go towards is a place even less imaginable to most of us than the city of happiness. I cannot describe it at all. It is possible that it does not exist. But they seem to know where they are going, the ones who walk away from Omelas.

Who are we willing to sacrifice for our own thriving? The themes in Le Guin's story have been pondered and explored multiple times in theater and performance events and from multiple perspectives. What does it mean to work for a better world? Whose Utopia? What does it mean to walk away from Omelas? And how is that different from walking toward something else, something that cannot be described yet? The seductive frame of Le Guin's story is that she draws such a vivid picture of a place where I want to live. I want artists and scholars to be revered. I want people to be free to pursue their own understanding of happiness and to work collaboratively for human happiness. But I do not believe collective thriving has to come at the expense of even one person. That is a myth we tell ourselves in order to claim moral superiority when the systems we do have so very clearly harm whole swaths of people. Another visionary science fiction writer, Octavia Butler, wrote, "Belief/Initiates and guides action/—Or it does nothing." I believe that we are enough, and we have the skills and creative adaptabilities to craft radically welcoming spaces. I believe U.S. America was founded on white supremacy structures that still organize many of our social, cultural, and political systems. And I believe that just societies are necessary preconditions for human thriving. As Emma Lazarus famously said, "Until we are all free, we are none of us free."

So an orientation toward justice grounds several key principles of DAC: a focus on equity and inclusion, equitable collaboration, and contextual specificity leading to reciprocity. Again, we are focused not just on the outputs of artistic community engagements but also on the outcomes, understood as measurable change mapped by our value-added model. From a public health perspective, equity functions as a measure of justice. We know beyond a shadow of a doubt the ways that health disparities reflect social, ethnic, and economic marginalization in the United States. In an essay titled "Health Disparities and Health Equity: The Issue Is Justice," Braveman et al. lay out a comprehensive definition of health disparity:

> Health disparities are health differences that adversely affect socially disadvantaged groups. Health disparities are systematic, plausibly avoidable health differences according to race/ethnicity, skin color, religion, or nationality; socioeconomic resources or position (reflected by, e.g., income, wealth, education, or occupation); gender, sexual orientation, gender identity; age, geography, disability, illness, political or other affiliation; or other characteristics associated with discrimination or marginalization. (S150)

Key here is the term "plausibly avoidable," which strongly tracks with Ruth Wilson Gilmore's definition of racism as "the state-sanctioned or extralegal production and exploitation of group-differentiated vulnerability to premature death" (37). These authors recognize and connect systemic discrimination to the social determinants of health and well-being.

Ann Taket, author of *Health Equity, Social Justice, and Human Rights*, connects human rights and public health more deeply:

> First, human rights violations can directly affect health: for example, torture, slavery, violence against women and children and harmful traditional practices. Secondly, the promotion of human rights, in particular those connected to the social determinants of health, for example rights to education, to food and nutrition, shelter and employment, lead to reduced vulnerability to ill health and promote health. Thirdly, health development can involve promotion or violation of human rights depending on how it affects rights such as the right to participation, freedom from discrimination, right to information and right to privacy. There is a reciprocal impact of health

and human rights. The promotion, protection, restriction or violations of human rights have direct and indirect impacts on health and wellbeing, in the short, medium and long term. (75)

In other words, a human thriving approach to engaged arts and design also demands a concomitant commitment to human rights and justice. The World Health Organization asserts that "the enjoyment of the highest attainable standard of health is one of the fundamental rights of every human being without distinction of race, religion, political belief, economic or social condition" (http://www.who.int/about/mission/en/). Here, a tool I use is the philosophical framework of Amartya Sen and Martha Nussbaum known as the Capabilities Approach. This theory bridges economics, moral philosophy, and politics, linking freedom and well-being in both macro and micro systems. Sen points out that the freedom to achieve well-being depends on what people can be and do—their capabilities—and therefore development (including arts and design-based community cultural development) should promote freedom along multiple axes (11). By positioning people's ability to make choices in support of their own well-being a moral command, Sen argues that utilitarian economic theories common in unfettered capitalistic structures are unjust.

Look, the arts and design have been used throughout time to control, to subjugate, and to promote illiberal philosophies. Creative placemaking, for example, is rightfully criticized for promoting white-oriented municipal frames at the expense of community, as well as making key contributions to gentrification. One of DAC's community thought partners is the pastor at a local African American church in downtown Phoenix. He told me the story of when Phoenix first hosted the Rock and Roll Marathon and promoted the event through economic development and cultural development frames. The marathon route was carefully planned to take advantage of the relatively flat Phoenix landscape and to create as few disruptions as possible for local businesses. But Arizona's three largest African American churches—concentrated in one neighborhood—found out about the event only from postcards alerting residents to street closures. These three churches have literally thousands of parishioners collectively, yet Phoenix planned to shut down access to these houses of worship on a Sunday. Nussbaum points out, "The purpose of . . . development, like the purpose of a good domestic national policy, is to enable people to live full creative lives, developing their potential and fashioning a meaningful existence commensurate with their equal human dignity" (185). Phoenix leaders did not show up with principled practices that honored all the ways residents make meaning and build cultural and faith-based connections. Sen developed the Capabilities Approach as an answer to traditional welfare economics philosophies and made the right to be free primary. The Capabilities Approach thus serves as another tool to ground DAC's justice-centric mandate to maximize human freedom to live full and happy lives.

This orientation is not an easy sell, however. In fact, a justice-centered approach to human rights conflicts with more traditional and romantic academic and artistic foci on creative exceptionalism and individualism. In 1963, President John F. Kennedy gave a speech at Amherst College in which he highlighted this traditional narrative of arts and design, two years before he would go on to found the National Endowment for the Arts:

> The artist, however faithful to his personal vision of reality, becomes the last champion of the individual mind and sensibility against an intrusive society and an officious state. The great artist is thus a solitary figure. He has, as Frost said, a lover's quarrel with the world. In pursuing his perceptions of reality, he must often sail against the currents of his time. This is not a popular role. (National Endowment)

The artist (and that artist is always male) stands as a romantic figure boldly facing down the currents of history and contemporary society in search of something more real, more transcendent than people's day-to-day experiences. Here the journey of that individual genius stands in as metonym for Western understandings of human identity and, perhaps, U.S. American exceptionalism itself. This romantic ideal functions oppositionally to how theater historian Tobin Nellhaus defines people: "[W]e are only partly individuals: we are born into preexisting *social* conditions that possess some array of resources, susceptibilities, and options (given by class, gender, race, geography, etc.), and with ties to some range of people. We are born immersed in history" (261). Both academics and artists are trained by tenure systems and the industries of art, performance, and design to constantly brand themselves through narratives of how special we are. In the case of academics, we often have to literally map how our work matters more than another's work. Nellhaus's insight cross-references not just constructivist principles but also contemporary sociologies of the body and the embodied practices of theater and performance. As Chris Schilling notes in *The Body and Social Theory*, human bodies are biologically and socially constructed, and humans are, in effect, in a continual cycle of being and becoming. This means that our health and wellness practices are always in flux in complex cycles in which some people have differentiated access to assets that promote well-being while others experience micro and macro traumas as sacrifices in Omelas. Who counts as public? Good for whom? Whose Utopia? An Indigenous colleague tells me that we can't even begin to think comprehensively about contemporary contexts until we have considered the seven generations before us and the histories and reasoning of the ancestors, and seven generations into the future. What will our actions become? Or perhaps, as another DAC thought partner asked, "How are you becoming good elders?" I believe that only diverse and well-functioning collectives can address the complexities of time and place and power. Our way forward is together. The romantic idealization of the artist as singular genius works against commitments to a just and equitable future. DAC understands justice as a moving target and that a pledge to equitable human thriving demands decentering the university and how arts and design are understood and, in many cases, taught.

In order to capture the complexity of how we center justice and human rights, DAC has several principles:

- Inclusion and Collaboration: We take responsibility for one another. DAC projects focus on just and inclusive collaborations that reject racism, inequitable hierarchies, and white supremacy.
- Reciprocity: DAC features a multidirectional flow of knowledge and creative problem-solving. And we understand ASU as a part, not the center, of a creative knowledge ecosystem focused on human thriving.
- Relational, Contextual, and Localized: We blur the distinctions between creative producers and creative consumers/clients to focus on co-creation. And our work results in the co-creation of knowledge/actions that measurably contribute to positive change.

The principals and thematics discussed in this chapter capture the DAC orientation to human thriving. DAC's mission is to partner with communities to place designers, artists, scholars, and educators in public life and prepare ASU students to use their creative capacities to advance culture, strengthen democracy, and imaginatively address today's most pressing challenges. We center communities, designers, and artists working together to make the world a better place. To date this has looked very different depending on the community partner and the involved students. Music students have built pop-up cultural parks in parking lots; theater artists have worked with city governments to build narrative frames for tourism; mask-making installations in a library tackled racism; film students worked bedside in the children's hospital using digital storytelling; hip hop dancers partnered with a furniture store to increase employee volunteerism during off-hours; and fiber artists worked in palliative settings with elders. In other words, the projects are specific and feature unique outputs (dances, installations, murals, blankets), but the *outcomes* focus on increasing human thriving. DAC is a large-scale institutional program devoted to transformational partnerships centering arts and design as collective investments in human thriving. Part of my focus on thriving too is my attempt not to just talk the talk, but to walk the walk. Maria Avila, building from Mark Rudd's 2013 speech at Drew University, distinguishes between *activism* and *organizing*, declaring that "activism is mainly about self-expression, and organizing is about movement building" (88). I am reminded here too of Alinsky's exhortation to build communities. And I have taken a community-building approach inside ASU and the Herberger Institute to build the DAC, taking as given our location in a particular place and time and our many allies who are equally committed to building cultures and institutions of human thriving and wellness. Like Avila, I believe that "to create the culture change in higher education that is essential for reciprocal, transformational, co-created campus-community engagement . . . faculty must enact their individual civic agency and turn this into collective, collaborative civic agency with other faculty colleagues, with their students, and with those with whom they partner in external communities" (85). I share this chapter in the spirit of becoming and possibility. On any given day I vibrate between excitement for potentials and dismay over challenges. And I fail in ways both small and large. What I do know, however, is that I learned to vision, to collaborate, and to imagine, enact, and evaluate in the theater. And I fully understand the arts and design as a public good that can contribute to human thriving in ways both mundane and profound.

Works Cited

Alinsky, Saul D. *Reveille for Radicals*. New York, Vintage Books, 1989.

Annie E. Casey Foundation. "Child Population by Race in Arizona." Kids Count Data Center, 2010–18. https://datacenter.kidscount.org/data/tables/103-child-population-by-race#detailed/2/4/false/37,871,870,573,869,36,868,867,133/68,69,67,12,70,66,71,72/423,424. Accessed July 21, 2021.

Arendt, Hannah, et al. *The Human Condition*. Chicago, University of Chicago Press, 1958.

Avila, Maria, et al. *Transformative Civic Engagement through Community Organizing*. Sterling, VA, Stylus, 2018

Braveman, Paula A., et al. "Health Disparities and Health Equity: The Issue is Justice." *American Journal of Public Health*, vol. 101, no. 1, 2011, pp. 149–55.

Brown, Adrienne M. *Emergent Strategies: Shaping Change, Changing Worlds*. Chico, CA, AK Press, 2017.

Bourdieu, Pierre. *Distinction: A Social Critique of the Judgment of Taste*. Cambridge, MA, Harvard University Press, 1984.

Bourdieu, Pierre. *The Field of Cultural Production: Essays on Art and Literature*. Edited and introduced by Randal Johnson. New York, Columbia University Press, 1993.

Bourdieu, Pierre, and Jean Claude Passeron. *Reproduction in Education, Society and Culture*. London, Sage, 1977.

Boyte, Harry C. *Everyday Politics: Reconnecting Citizens and Public Life*. Philadelphia, University of Pennsylvania Press, 2004.

Butler, Octavia E. *Parable of the Sower*. New York, Four Walls Eight Windows, 1993.

By the People: Designing a Better America. Curated by Cynthia E. Smith for Cooper Hewitt. Smithsonian Design Museum, October 25, 2016.

Cohen-Cruz, J. *Engaging Performance: Theatre as Call and Response*. New York, Routledge, 2010.

Dewey, John. *Democracy and Education: An Introduction to the Philosophy of Education*. New York, Macmillan, 1916.

Dolan, Jill. *Utopia in Performance: Finding Hope in the Theatre*. Ann Arbor, University of Michigan Press, 2008.

Emery, Mary, and Cornelia Flora. "Spiraling Up: Mapping Community Transformation with Community Capitals Framework." *Journal of the Community Development Society*, vol. 37, no. 1, 2006, pp. 19–35.

Etheridge Woodson, Stephani. *Theatre for Youth Third-Space, Performance, Democracy and Community Cultural Development*. Bristol, UK, Intellect Press, 2015.

Gallup Global Well-Being. https://news.gallup.com/poll/126965/gallup-global-wellbeing.aspx.

Huang, Peter H., and Jeremy A. Blumenthal. "Positive Institutions, Law and Policy." *The Oxford Handbook of Positive Psychology*, edited by C. R. Snyder and Shane J. Lopez. Oxford, Oxford University Press, 2009, pp. 589–97.

Jojola, Theodore. "The People Are Beautiful Already: Indigenous Design and Planning." *By the People: Designing a Better America*, edited by Cynthia E. Smith. New York, Cooper Hewitt, 2016, pp. 45–53.

Karimi, Milad, et al. "The Capability Approach: A Critical Review of Its Application in Health Economics." *Value Health*, vol. 19, no. 6, 2016, pp. 795–99.

Le Guin, Ursula K. "The Ones Who Walk Away from Omelas." 1973. Anarchist Library. https://libcom.org/files/ursula-k-le-guin-the-ones-who-walk-away-from-omelas.pdf. Accessed January 6, 2019.

McKnight, John, and Peter Block. *The Abundant Community: Awakening the Power of Families and Neighborhoods*. Oakland, CA, Berrett-Koehler, 2012.

Morse, Suzanne W. *Smart Communities: How Citizens and Local Leaders Can Use Strategic Thinking to Build a Brighter Future*. San Francisco, Jossey-Bass, 2004.

National Endowment for the Arts. "President John F. Kennedy: Remarks at Amherst College." October 26, 1963. https://www.arts.gov/about/kennedy-transcript.

Nellhaus, Tobin. "Big History." *Theatre, Performance, and Change,* edited by Stephani Etheridge Woodson and Tamara Underiner. New York, Palgrave Macmillan, 2018, pp. 261–69.

Nussbaum, Martha. *Creating Capabilities: The Human Development Approach.* Cambridge, MA, Belknap-Harvard University Press, 2011.

Nussbaum, Martha. *Women and Human Development.* Cambridge, Cambridge University Press, 2000.

Raw, Anthony, et al. "A Hole in the Heart: Confronting the Drive for Evidence-Based Impact Research in Arts and Health." *Arts Health,* vol. 4, no. 2, 2012, pp. 97–108. doi:10.1080/17533015.2011.619991.

Saltmarsh, John, and Matthew Hartley. *To Serve a Larger Purpose: Engagement for Democracy and the Transformation of Higher Education.* Philadelphia, Temple University Press, 2012.

Sampson, Robert J., et al. "Assessing 'Neighborhood Effects': Social Processes and New Directions in Research." *Annual Review of Sociology,* vol. 28, 2002, pp. 443–78. doi:10.1146/annurev.soc.28.110601.141114.

Schilling, Chris. *The Body and Social Theory.* Thousand Oaks, CA, Sage, 1993.

Seligman, Martin E. P., and Mihaly Csikszentmihalyi. "Positive Psychology, an Introduction." *Flow and the Foundations of Positive Psychology,* vol. 55, no. 1, 2000, pp. 5–14. doi:10.1007/978-94-017-9088-8_18.

Sen, Amartya. *Development as Freedom.* New York, Anchor Books, 1999.

Sen, Amartya. "What Do We Want from a Theory of Justice?" *The Journal of Philosophy,* vol. 103, no. 5, 2006, pp. 215–38.

Taket, Ann. *Health Equity, Social Justice, and Human Rights.* New York, Routledge, 2012.

Tay, L., et al. "The Role of the Arts and Humanities in Human Flourishing: A Conceptual Model." *The Journal of Positive Psychology,* vol. 13, no. 3, 2018, pp. 215–25. doi:10.1080/17439760.2017.1279207.

Wilson Gilmore, Ruth. *Prisons, Surplus, Crisis, and Opposition in Globalizing California.* Berkeley, University of California Press, 2006.

Wise, Marilyn, and Peter Sainsbury. "Democracy: The Forgotten Determinant of Mental Health." *Health Promotion Journal of Australia,* vol. 18, no. 3, 2007, pp. 177–83. www.ncbi.nlm.nih.gov/pubmed/18201159.

World Health Organization. "Constitution." https://www.who.int/about/governance/constitution

Yosso, Tara J., and David G. Garcia. "'This Is No Slum!' A Critical Race Theory Analysis of Community Cultural Wealth in Culture Clash's *Chavez Ravine.*" *Aztlán: A Journal of Chicano Studies,* vol. 32, no. 1, 2007, pp. 145–79. eric.ed.gov/?id=EJ760979.

12

Theatrical Flourishing

A Roundtable Discussion

In November 2018, the contributors to this edited collection gathered at the Shawnee Inn and Golf Resort in Shawnee on Delaware, Pennsylvania, to discuss theater and human flourishing. Early drafts of chapters were discussed, ideas shared, and the intersection of the arts and psychology considered. Joining the conversation were James Pawelski, professor of practice in the Positive Psychology Center at the University of Pennsylvania and convenor of the Humanities and Human Flourishing project; Thalia Goldstein, associate professor of psychology at George Mason University; and Laura Taylor, managing coordinator of education in the Positive Psychology Center at the University of Pennsylvania. This is an edited version of the final roundtable conversation.

HARVEY YOUNG: So here we are, at the end of two amazing days talking about human flourishing. We've covered a lot of topics: process and product, theater and performance, community, different ideas and assumptions of well-being. James Pawelski shared with us a metaphor: his passion for "broccoli." James, as a reminder "broccoli" is—

JAMES PAWELSKI: Fractal flourishing. It's flourishing at all levels. Broccoli has a similar shape, whether you are looking at the entire stalk or just one piece of it. Although different people flourish in different ways, our ideal should be one of human flourishing at all levels: for individuals, communities, and society as a whole.

H. YOUNG: Fantastic! I love that. So [*to everyone*] . . . what stands out to you in the papers we've read and the conversations we've engaged? What will shape your thinking?

JOHN FLETCHER: I love what Stacy Wolf said about community theater so often falling into its purpose: to perpetuate itself. Which reminds me of the dangers of doing something again and again, and the ways that doing the same thing can become addictive. It's giving us just enough to block out the subjunctive wondering "what if it were different?" Then, finding

Theatrical Flourishing: A Roundtable Discussion In: *Theater and Human Flourishing*. Edited by: Harvey Young, Oxford University Press. © Oxford University Press 2023. DOI: 10.1093/oso/9780197622261.003.0013

that flourishing involves the very difficult task of finding that break and trying something else. Do plays that don't take place in the world. [*laughter from the group*] That's not just a joke. That's an expression of what theater can do. It can give us an idea that doesn't take place in this world. That can give us an idea of something other than this world.

GWYNETH SHANKS: Stacy [Wolf]'s and John [Fletcher]'s papers in particular prompted me to think about questions of labor and pleasure as existing in—I don't know if it's a spectrum or a constellation or a Venn diagram in which they are constantly rotating and switching places and overlapping with each other, and how our assumptions about what flourishing means or failures to flourish mean are also imbricated within how we might frame something as work or as wage labor (or as valued). And I'm thinking about your schematic, Stephani [Etheridge Woodson], and the ethical imperative of [John's Braver] Angels: an urgency or necessity of listening as a kind of labor.

STACY WOLF: Many of the papers touched on virtuosity, either directly or indirectly. I think for anyone who's writing about a professional production, virtuosity or the desire for virtuosity goes under the surface. And it pushes me so much to think about what I'm writing about because one of the things that's very challenging for me about my project—and I felt the challenge from all of you—was to talk about the problems of the theater that I'm writing about.

I can make a contribution because I have established a connection with so many people there. They will talk to me. They have a lot of really interesting things to say about obstacles to human flourishing. But I would have to hide their identities. Which could easily happen with their consent, of course.

I think that virtuosity is something these theaters are always striving for because everyone wants to perform well and do well, but seldom are the performances good or virtuosic. That continues to be my challenge as someone trained as a theater scholar and critic: to say "That doesn't matter, that's not what this is about." In so many of our conversations here [discussions about] virtuosity really pushed my buttons—in a good way—because I really care about virtuosity, and so do some of the people I write about. Every paper made me rethink something that I thought I understood. I wrote down "virtuosity," "labor," "community," "vitality," "intergeneration." That was my first pass at things that really shifted my thinking.

SCOTT MAGELSSEN: I pulled out a quote from Laura Lodewyck's paper: "The fullness of human experience includes both joyful and grievous events, and theater as an art takes them both seriously. . . . Part of the contradiction of theater, as with other forms of artistic expression, is the bittersweet evocation of emotion from content that is not strictly 'enjoyable' content. That is, great moments of self-realization and deep connection occur when experiencing extremely negative stories." In my paper, I came out pretty hard with regard to the holding up of the negative experience and the collective gnashing of teeth as something that could be read as coercive. I framed it in the beginning as "What if?" It wasn't necessarily in the beginning that I was trying to convince you all, but over the course of the paper I started getting more up on a high horse about it, especially when it comes to the treatment of our most vulnerable people. Laura's paper pushed me to pull back a little bit . . . to recognize the communal experience and individual experience. There is a flourishing to be found in—I think James put it as "both the darkness and the light." It would be weird to disregard one or the other. I don't know who said it in relation to John's paper, but "sometimes a problem is as good as a vacation." I can't remember if that was a good thing or a bad thing.

S. WOLF: It was good because it gets you into flow.

S. MAGELSSEN: That's right. Sometimes when things are rough just dealing with the everyday, a really great crisis can make you feel really good because it gives you that break—

J. FLETCHER: It can distract.

S. MAGELSSEN: Yes, you can use it as an excuse to lift yourself out of being present to the things that you need to be present for. So, yes, complicated, but that resonated with me.

ERIN HURLEY: The notion of crisis that came up in Laura's paper and John's and Scott's in different ways also resonated with me, in thinking about a theater whose self-identity at least since the eighties has been one of perpetual crisis. In perpetual need of saving or great heroics on the part of the theater workers to make it . . . so that it can fulfill a teleological logic, so that it can just keep going. Thank you for shifting my frame around what the purposes and outcomes of that might be.

Two other things. First, Harvey's paper. I like the idea of "the structuring elements" of theatrical flourishing and theatrical experience. Laughter was the one that you [Harvey] lighted on. Also, "structuring elements of perceived community" was the phrase I wrote down that I'm now attributing to you. Again, because community is about perception, and it is organized in certain ways according to certain structures. And then to Marcia [Ferguson]'s paper about touch being another organizing principle or structuring element. The definition that you [Marcia] offered today in your comments, in your preamble, summed up much of what we've been doing. We defined theatrical flourishing as "communitas, plus ownership of the space and the story, plus no policing in the course of receiving and/or creating live virtuosity."

MARCIA FERGUSON: I will be thinking a lot about, and no doubt quoting, Stephani's phrasing of "the weaponization of individuality." That's a really evocative frame to think about. And alongside that, as a result of several people's papers and the discussion of them, I feel like the entire conversation has pushed me to have even more precise discussion in my essay for talking about how human flourishing has to always be recursive in its thinking about the tension between individual and collective.

I am reminded, that, as many theorists have talked about (on the one hand), there is no such thing as the self, and (on the other hand) the talk about [the self] is not a historical accident. We turn back to that at a moment when a lot of people who were not historically marked as selves or even as individuals and often were marked as property or as otherwise not-selves. All of these tensions. I want to be careful about talking about the weaponization of individualism, the individual, and holding space for why people would need the autonomy of declaring self. And also caring for self.

LAURA LODEWYCK: Your [Marcia's] paper and Stephani's reminded me to attend to scope in my paper. I think about how this project that I write about has the political woven into it and how I need to tend more carefully to these larger systems and the theatrical projects placed within it. I want to carefully reconsider the particular claims that I choose, and what I want to highlight about theater and these projects given these larger systems.

M. FERGUSON: I feel much more attuned to the fact of cultures operating in almost everyone's papers, and the culture of community theater as a certain kind of culture versus an MFA program's culture, which is loaded politically in different ways that affect the individual. We have to be careful about culture. We have to be alive to it. I really appreciated the discussion of the different cultural codifications we attach, and all the different experiences of individuals and different kinds of individuals who come into contact with a culture—touch, aesthetic touch, touching classrooms.

So helpful. It also brings me to Kelly [Howe]'s paper on the Theater of the Oppressed, and "always fight as if the game is not over." That connects with Jennifer Moon's precept [in Gwyn's paper] to always move from a place of abundance. Taking control, taking power—not asking permission. Taking power in the face of a fight. Those are two things that are really going to stay with me. Among many, actually.

H. YOUNG: I wouldn't say that the primary reason you buy a ticket and go to the theater is for healing or personal transformation. You go for entertainment, enjoyment, passion for culture. What emerged out of our conversations was that—again and again and again—there's a transformative aspect to theater. In Kelly's paper, it is being able to name oppression. Or in Lisa [Biggs]'s paper, looking at how performance enables a community to address a history. Or in John's paper, you can find common ground. You're still going to be "red" or "blue," but there is a sense of a shared understanding that allows for thinking beyond stereotypes. Again and again, there is this sense that healing emerges through theater. Self-transformation can occur. Within Erin's paper, the existence of anglophone communities itself becomes a space for and a place for self-realization as a person who is a minority, who also might be an immigrant.

What do we mean when we bring the phrase "human flourishing" into theater? What is "human flourishing" in a theater context?

M. FERGUSON: Deep engagement. You engage so deeply that you are transformed on some level. That has to happen for the flourishing to happen. That engagement can be across politics, across story. It can be a device, it can be a design. You can be engaged as a spectator. The kind of work that Gwyn was talking about is deeply engaging and deeply disturbing. But I think you would come out a bit changed.

This notion of transformation that Harvey's talking about: *time* is a really important factor, whether it's a history in the making, a history that is previously undocumented or unexamined in the past. Duration, time, that seems almost a necessary part for the transformation to take place.

J. FLETCHER: When (and at what time scale) and at what scope does flourishing happen? We've all had stories of a single encounter, person-to-person, where "Oh my gosh that transformation occurred," something that seems to touch near flourishing. And then there are other times when you can't rely on just that one thing. It must be within [a larger plan]; in a long-term way, there is flourishing that, if not a straight causation, this play helped to crystallize.

S. WOLF: Stephani's twenty-year plan.

KELLY HOWE: I've been thinking all day about Lisa's paper relative to "witness," the notion of "witnessing." And the multiple different connotations of witness. There's so much to be said about it. Theater is very well set up (in the context of human flourishing) to acknowledge—I'm always hesitant to say "inherent"—humanity, how humanity needs witnessing especially in the context of trauma, and provides it in a sustained and focused way.

G. SHANKS: Several papers ask us to displace the human as the subject of analysis or as the subject of flourishing. Erin, your paper: thinking about the nation, French-speaking Canada and anglophone theater as a kind of placeholder for the human in human flourishing. Lisa, your paper: this broader sense of imbrication between the sort of personal oral history and to the scope of city and to the structure of decades-long, centuries-long processes, and what it means for Detroit to flourish.

S. MAGELSSEN: Is it possible to say that to flourish is an inherently performative thing, in the oldest sense of flourishing? It's the showiness of a plant with flowers. If you're writing, in penmanship, flourishing is where you put that extra fanciness on it to show feeling, or a flourish of trumpets to show a particularly important time. Or to flourish a gun, an ostentatious show of force. You're feeling pretty powerful, you're feeling pretty good.

But also, I wonder if the idea of flourishing—if that's the root that we as human beings choose to follow—is a performative idea of *showing* that we're doing, well, like flowers. (I don't know botany). Flowers are not permanent on a plant. They're seasonal. They wax and wane with the seasons or the conditions, or they're ready to bear fruit or to invite the bees, the pollinators. I wonder if we can be okay with not measuring the success of flourishing with a kind of "we're always flourishing at the same level [approach]." What's special about a plant flourishing is that it's a different state than the normal plain old green. But you can tell the plant is doing okay by how well it looks when it's just plain old green too. The flourishing is something extra-special.

E. HURLEY: That's interesting, that metaphor, Scott. If you're flourishing, and flourishing is ostentation or display, then you're de facto standing out from the background, right? Whose background? Who is in the foreground in that? I think it's clear in that [flower] metaphor which is which, but it focuses our glances more on the individuation line.

S. WOLF: But what about when all the flowers bloom at once?

E. HURLEY: Right. So these are the different lenses, right?

S. MAGELSSEN: And if the flourishing is part of the backdrop of leaves that are also part of the community, it's all part of the same plant.

H. YOUNG: What does it mean to take a philosophical concept, and then to apply it to the arts? And to see it in practice?

J. PAWELSKI: It means to have a whole lot of fun. [*laughter*] I think it's really rich to see how these ideas can be played out in these different ways, based on the particular context that we bring to it, the particular thoughts, our work. To my mind, that itself is part of what flourishing is. I'd like to think of flourishing both in terms of that moment of flowering, as nothing to be apologetic for. In fact, plants can't survive if they don't have those from time to time. But also to think of flourishing more generally as "I used to get very depressed in the fall because the leaves would die. And then I started to think 'but you know the trees aren't dying,' so I changed my focus and I realized that the leaves changing are a part of the overall long-term flourishing of the tree, to do well." Was it Albert Camus who said "autumn is a second spring, where every leaf is a flower"? So there are different ways of thinking about things.

Heidegger said that we don't spend enough time asking the question of being. What we need to do as scholars and as human beings is to spend more time thinking about the question of well-being. What does it mean? What might it mean? How can we identify it happening? How can we think of it subjunctively? All of that, to my mind, is a flowering and a real flourishing together.

H. YOUNG: We're in this moment where the disciplines are coming together. We have psychology and theater. Hanging out, riding in golf carts. I want to acknowledge an expert in the room: Thalia Goldstein, who has a background as a theater artist and deep expertise in psychology, specifically looking at these ideas around well-being within the arts. Thalia, where are these points of intersection that you see within your own work? Are there areas that haven't been addressed that conversations like this are touching upon?

THALIA GOLDSTEIN: First I wanted to say that I have a really deep appreciation for both how this group of scholars were put together and the contributions of everybody in this room. It is a delicate line to walk: to use but not misuse psychological thought. It's very easy to hang your hat on a single psychological construct and sort of run off while holding it and leave actual psychology behind entirely. Often, research in psychology has moved on significantly while scholars who are not in psychology hammer a single point to death. I saw none of that over the course of the past few days, which is unusual in any room I've ever been in.

The point [that stands] out for me is theater as holding, containing, being a safe space to try out different questions having to do with well-being and flourishing. Holding ideas of democracy and democratic ideals of collaboration; ideas of emotion and what it means to be emotional, *who* is allowed to be emotional, who is allowed to express anger, feel anger, engage anger; who is allowed to be in relationship with each other; from who is allowed to touch and in what ways are they allowed to touch, all the way through "What does a power structure look like?" and "Who's allowed to hold power over another person?" And I think that what's special about this safe space and this contained space is this question of what you leave in it and what you bring with you. But also that rehearsal, and the joy of theater, is play. And play is one of the primary ways in which we all learn. Trial and error, testing things out. Having no consequences in the immediate moment is how we're able to change our understanding of the world.

One big thing I wrote—in all capitals on four different pieces of paper— is this idea that people often ask, "What is theater for? What is the purpose? Why do we do it? Why does it continue to survive?" "I keep cutting the funding, and yet you guys keep coming back!" Why do we keep doing that? "You should have gone away by this point!" And then of course the counterpoint to that has been "Well, this is art for art's sake. The reason we do art is because art is important, and we do theater because theater is important, period." It's a self-contained reason: "I don't have to give you any other reason other than that theater is important."

What's been articulated in several ways, pretty much through every paper, is that there are three levels to it. [First level:] There is art, theater, as a way of knowing in and of itself. There are structures to theater. There are traditions within the theater. There is a psychology of fiction, there is a psychology of separation, there is a psychology of containment and safety that exists sort of *in* the theater. [Second level:] Then, there is the *use* of those traditions and the *use* of those ideas in order to explore concepts: well-being, memory, social justice, oppression, equality, touch, flourishing, self-care. What you do is you apply the *structure* of the artistic experience to the *function* of this sort of other element, this sort of other psychology. And then there's the third level, which is: now you've done that. You've explored it in this way. What do you get to take with you (as you try to live a flourishing life, where you're not always inhaling the drug of theater)? When you're not always drinking from the cup of theater? It's in the transference that you have to pay particular attention. And it's in the transference from "art for art's sake" to "art for social justice's sake," to take one of the examples, to "social justice out in the real world." It's in that transference that I think a lot of the careful work is happening and has been happening.

The last point I wanted to talk about, which we touched on a little bit in the last session, is this idea of the body. Psychology doesn't know what to do with the body. We all admit we have bodies. We all admit that our bodies are important, and it's hard to have a sense of flourishing and well-being when the body is sick. When the body isn't functioning, it's almost impossible for the mind to function sort of automatically. You have to do work there. If the body isn't functioning, you have to do work to make the mind function. And if the body is functioning, you still have to do work to make the mind function. What is the unique role of theater in using body and mind as instruments simultaneously? In having opinions about what the body is and is not allowed to express? As a way to practice the variety of ways the body can exist in relationship to other people, in relationship to other objects? In the allowance for all bodies to be part of it, which is work still to be done? And the role of the body in emotion, emotional expression, emotional understanding, and in reading emotions in other people? There was a question yesterday: What is the difference between the sublime and joyful? From a psychological perspective, it is about the arousal of the body. Sublime has sort of a low arousal state. It's very, very positively valenced, but it's not very physiologically aroused, whereas joy has the same amount of positive valence but a higher sense of awakeness, a much higher sense of positive arousal. So if sublime and joy are sort of affective states of flourishing, we can think about the fact that theater allows the body to exist in multiple states, in a safe contained way that we can then do the careful work of bringing it back out into the real world.

Thank you all for letting me come into this space and hang out. It's been a transformative experience for me. I appreciate that.

H. YOUNG: Final thoughts? What are you leaving thinking?

STEPHANI ETHERIDGE WOODSON: I'm so blessed that y'all are so cool.

LAURA TAYLOR: I'm thinking how much it matters to be having this kind of interdisciplinary discussion. And to be in a place of building collaboratively, and how much that matters.

S. WOLF: I'm thinking about how elegantly the two of you [Harvey and James] have facilitated this time. You have managed to move us from one thing to the next, seamlessly. It seemed so organic, like "of course now we're going to talk about this." And I'm sure you have your schedules written out in front of you. It's been very impressive facilitating, which is not easy to do.

S. ETHERIDGE WOODSON: Marcia said something that I wrote down. I would like your permission to quote it, if I might? "Theater comes down to concrete choices and virtuosity." And that was one of those aha moments, when I think back to my own ability to convince people that you could move across scale and still make concrete choices and be virtuosic. Thank you.

J. FLETCHER: Laura said something that has stuck with me and is going to change the way I teach: being wrong and being right feel the same. The feeling comes in the revelation. Or maybe that's anagnorisis, that recognition, rethinking.

LISA BIGGS: I was struck by how very hopeful we are. I don't know if it's because of the theater that we do, which doesn't seem to be the kind that seeks to grind people up and waste them as quickly as possible, and then get younger, fresher, more naïve, more vulnerable models to replace [folks] when the wrinkles appear and the weight changes and the ankle's broken and the hair going gray can no longer be denied. I know, as a person who worked—tried to work—in the other [commercial theater] world, that that other world so overwhelms so much of the business, so much of the talk about the discipline of art-making as a theater practitioner and performance person. I feel very fortunate to be in a room of very hopeful people, but I feel sad when I think about the business and the kind of training that I got, and the kind of training I witnessed other people get alongside me, which set them up to be—set all of us up to be—in the most precarious, dangerous theater settings. I'm glad about the Chicago call to arms now [to address harassment and abuse], but I feel like there's a very huge gap between the hopeful aspirations that have been articulated in this room—that we have witnessed and been part of—and the business. Not to be a downer, but—

L. TAYLOR: There is an urgent call. It can be answered in a number of ways. You have to go through difficult moments to build and develop resilience skills. But you don't have to traumatize [people to help them] develop resiliency. You can help them develop those skills so that they can be more effective within a business, and help them learn to change that structure.

Index

For the benefit of digital users, indexed terms that span two pages (e.g., 52–53) may, on occasion, appear on only one of those pages.

Figures are indicated by *f* following the page number